Comics in French

Polygons: Cultural Diversities and Intersections
General Editor: **Lieve Spaas**, *Emeritus Professor, Faculty of Arts and Social Sciences, Kingston University, UK*

Volume 1
Reynard the Fox: Social Engagement and Cultural Metamorphoses in the Beast Epic from the Middle Ages to the Present
Edited by Kenneth Varty

Volume 2
Echoes of Narcissus
Edited by Lieve Spaas in association with Trista Selous

Volume 3
Human Nature and the French Revolution: From the Enlightenment to the Napoleonic Code
Xavier Martin
Translated from the French by Patrick Corcoran

Volume 4
Secret Spaces, Forbidden Places: Rethinking Culture
Edited by Fran Lloyd and Catherine O'Brien

Volume 5
Relative Points of View: Linguistic Representations of Culture
Edited by Magda Stroińska

Volume 6
Expanding Suburbia: Reviewing Suburban Narratives
Edited by Roger Webster

Volume 7
Cultures of Exile: Images of Displacement
Edited by Wendy Everett and Peter Wagstaff

Volume 8
More than a Music Box: Radio Cultures and Communities in a Multi-Media World
Edited by Andrew Crisell

Volume 9
A 'Belle Epoque'? Women in French Society and Culture 1890–1914
Edited by Diana Holmes and Carrie Tarr

Volume 10
Claims to Memory: Beyond Slavery and Emancipation in the French Caribbean
Catherine Reinhardt

Volume 11
The Meanings of Magic: From the Bible to Buffalo Bill
Edited by Amy Wygant

Volume 12
Stardom in Postwar France
Edited by John Gaffney and Diana Holmes

Volume 13
London Eyes: Reflections in Text and Image
Edited by Gail Cunningham and Stephen Barber

Volume 14
Comics in French: The European Bande Dessinée in Context
Laurence Grove

COMICS IN FRENCH

The European Bande Dessinée in Context

Laurence Grove

Berghahn Books
New York • Oxford

First published in 2010 by

Berghahn Books

www.berghahnbooks.com

Library of Congress Cataloging-in-Publication Data

Grove, Laurence.
Comics in French : the bande dessinée in context / Laurence Grove. -- 1st ed.
p. cm. -- (Polygons : cultural diversities and intersections ; v. 14)
Includes bibliographical references and index.
ISBN 978-1-84545-588-0 (alk. paper)
1. Comic books, strips, etc.--France--History and criticism. 2. Comic books, strips, etc.--Belgium--History and criticism. I. Title. II. Title: Bande dessinée in context.
PN6745.G76 2010
741.5'6944--dc22

2010004346

British Library Cataloguing in Publication Data

A catalogue record for this book is available from the British Library

Printed in the United States on acid-free paper

ISBN: 978-1-84545-588-0 (hardback)

Contents

PART III: THE CULTURAL PHENOMENON

List of Figures

* Figures are not to scale. Figures 1, 4–9, 11, 13–15, 20, 23, 27–31, 34-36 and 38 are in colour in the original. All efforts have been made to contact copyright holders (as indicated on the individual captions).

Foreword

Whereas in English-speaking countries comics are for kids or adults who should know better, in France and Belgium the form is recognised as the Ninth Art and follows in the path of poetry, architecture, painting and sculpture. The bande dessinée, 'BD', has its own national institutions, regularly obtains front-page coverage and has received the accolades of statesmen from de Gaulle onwards. Historically, the bande dessinée can be seen as the culminating point of a tradition of text/image interaction that appears throughout France's literary and sociological development, from medieval illuminated manuscripts and Renaissance emblem books to modern cinematography. *Comics in French: The European Bande Dessinée in Context* is a book that will encourage you to consider (with and without 3D glasses) priceless manuscripts, a Franco-American rodent, Nazi propaganda, museum-piece urinals, intellectual gay porn (optional) and a prehistoric warrior who's really Zinedine Zidane.

It might have been more honest, but less snappy, for me to title this book *European Comics in French*, although that might have suggested a work primarily on translations and their reception. What I am trying to say is that this book is about the context and history of original bandes dessinées and, as the full subtitle implies, is unashamedly Euro-centric, concentrating on the French and Belgian traditions, and not excluding *Titeuf* and Rodolphe Töpffer, who are Swiss. I would like to underline that my choice is by no means a value judgement, but one based on the desire for unity and concision in a work whose subject matter is vast, but little explored in English. I will of course refer to French-language comics of non-European origin, but rather than do them an injustice I have preferred to say that they would make an excellent subject for another book that is yet to be written.

With the exception of commonly accepted book titles, all translations are my own, and are aimed at helping the non-French (or occasionally non-Latin) speaking reader to understand the literal meaning of the texts in question. In order to avoid clutter I have provided translations of book, article, exhibition, painting and journal titles only when they are first mentioned (but also in the bibliography), and only for cases where the meaning is less than obvious (e.g., I do not translate *Mythologies* or *Journal de Mickey*). Similarly, in cases where speed of reading is paramount I limit provision of full bibliographic details to the bibliography alone.

Throughout this book I use the term *bande dessinée* in the original, taking for granted that the reader knows it to be the French-language comic strip. A broader discussion of what its exact definition might be forms an important section of Chapter 2.

This book would not have been possible without the generous support I have received from the University of Glasgow and from the Arts and Humanities Research Council. I would also like to express my gratitude to staff and students in French at the University of Glasgow, in particular to Noël Peacock, Alison Adams and Stephen Rawles.

As series editor Lieve Spaas provided the initial impetus for this book, and has continually been an invaluable source of aid and advice. Similarly, Ann Miller has been tirelessly generous with her time and erudition, providing input that has improved this work beyond recognition. From the BD world I would also specifically like to thank Roger Sabin, Paul Gravett and Mark McKinney for their help and encouragement.

Once again I am indebted to David Weston and his team at Glasgow University Library, who, as I have said before, put the Special into Special Collections.

Above all I would like to thank Jane, Harry – who has shown me the real pleasure of reading bandes dessinées – my dad and my mum, who often asked when this book would be out and who would have enjoyed it more than anyone.

Chapter 1

Introduction: French Strippers Viewed from Afar

> Rappelons tout d'abord qu'il n'existe pas de discipline académique consacrée aux littératures dessinées. Un chercheur ne peut donc par définition se prévaloir de sa qualité d'universitaire pour asseoir sa compétence dans des matières qui ne correspondent à aucun champ disciplinaire ni à aucun programme de recherche.
>
> Let us remember first of all that there is no such thing as an academic discipline dedicated to the literature of graphic art. By definition therefore it is impossible for researchers to take advantage of university status so as to assert their competence in a subject area that does not correspond to any field of study or programme of research.
>
> Harry Morgan and Manuel Hirtz, *Le Petit Critique illustré*: *Guide des ouvrages consacrés à la bande dessinée* [The Illustrated Pocket Critic: A Guide to Secondary Studies on the Bande Dessinée] (Montrouge: PLG, 2005), p. 7.

I recently opened my University of Glasgow Honours option on the bande dessinée (also known by its initials as 'BD') with the distribution of a single page taken from *Le Téméraire* [The Bold] (Fig. 1). The idea was that students would give an unprepared reaction, one which would then allow us to reflect on how to 'read' a bande dessinée, indeed how to define a bande dessinée, how to situate it historically, socially and in cultural terms, and what, if anything, a French or Belgian comic strip could teach us about life in general. The aims of that half-hour discussion are now the broader aims of this book.

Initial surprise turned to inquisitive deliberation as students soon realised that even without knowing the strip in question, *Vers les mondes inconnus* [Towards Unknown Worlds], the angles from which we viewed characters, the physiognomy and the layout of the space accorded to them allowed us to tell who were the 'goodies' and who were the 'baddies' (try it yourself, dear reader). Further information

Figure 1. 'Goul roi des Marais'. *Le Téméraire*, No. 12 (1 July 1943). Back cover.

could be gleaned from the use of colours, or the way in which text – in narrative or speech format – imparted key information. The cinematographic qualities of the strip, and in particular its apparent mimicking of Fritz Lang's *Metropolis* of 1927, allowed us to reflect upon the nature of the BD as a mixed media text/image form, and on wider questions of the specificity of visual culture in general.

Students had trouble putting a date to the strip (I had removed it from the handouts), with guesses pointing to the 1930s art deco style, or to the contemporary modernity of the science fiction intrigue. When the date was revealed students were able to spot the anti-Semitic and even anti-communist nature of the strip,[1] although it was agreed that the propaganda was unquestionably subtle and for that reason effective. One student even pointed to the fact that Gaudron, the 'Gérant' or Managing Editor, was clearly a French rather than a German name, thereby raising the tricky question of wartime collaboration.[2] The obvious influence of American strips such as *Flash Gordon* raised the pertinent question of France's cultural independence or, rather, its constant and ongoing transatlantic dialogue.

The fact that the discussion had to be cut short by time restraints underlined how heavily packed a bande dessinée can be, this despite initial reactions being hesitant, even along the lines of, 'it's only a kids' comic strip'. Because it was 'only a kids' comic' it was felt that the possible findings were all the more interesting, as this represented an unlikely source of cultural richness, an everyday tap into France's history and society, into methods of expression and towards understanding the visual world that is increasingly our own. The overriding conclusion was that bandes dessinées were definitely worth a second look, a conclusion that hopefully will also be reached by the reader who finishes this book.

One further question raised was that of the extent to which the strip was primarily 'foreign'. Would a group of French students have had the same reaction as a group consisting largely of Scottish students? To what extent did the students from other countries (Greece, Northern Ireland, England, USA) have a different take on the handout? On an immediate level we were aware that certain linguistic and, moreover, cultural references could be grasped less readily: the fact that Goul's despicable kingdom, the 'Marais', brings to mind the Jewish district of Paris was less than obvious to Scottish students.[3] Perhaps more importantly, for students not having grown up with the bande dessinée as an everyday mass cultural phenomenon, the mechanics of the strip did not come as second nature, and the tradition of BD journals with leading 'to be continued'-style features may have seemed less everyday.

On the other hand, English-language readers are perhaps more likely to grasp the debt to American culture and to seize upon the specificity of the adaptation to a French context. It seemed to me that Scottish students were more willing, in this instance at least, to engage with aspects in the strip relating to critical theory (the role of women, the colonialist implications) than their French counterparts might have been, and the element of cultural distancing meant that tricky issues such as that of wartime collaboration could be assessed with a different level of objectivity. For the same reasons that our discussion was far different from one that could conceivably have taken place at the École Européenne Supérieure de L'Image (L'EESI) at Angoulême,[4] so this book, one of the first general studies in English on the French-language comic strip, does not do the same thing as the numerous works on the bande dessinée that are available in French.

There are several publications in English that will be relevant to the student of the bande dessinée. Randell W. Scott's *European Comics in English Translation: A Descriptive Sourcebook* (2002) gives bibliographic details and summarises the plot of bandes dessinées available in English, as well as giving notes on authors and translators and a brief but valuable list of secondary sources. *The World Encyclopedia of Comics*, edited by Maurice Horn,[5] is one of a general number of works based upon alphabetical entries that include French-related information. As a specific monograph, Roger Sabin's *Comics, Comix & Graphic Novels: A History of Comic Art* (2002 [first published 1996]) provides a colourful and thought-provoking overview of comics in their cultural context, and includes a clear précis of the French situation in the ninth chapter, 'International Influences' (pp. 217–35). Paul Gravett's *Graphic Novels: Stories to Change Your Life* (2005) gives a thematically linked descriptive selection of comic 'greats' that includes and contextualises works in the French language, and his website (www.paulgravett.com) continues to update such work. On the mechanics of the comic strip and related text/image theory, Scott McCloud's *Understanding Comics* and its subsequent volumes *Reinventing Comics* and *Making Comics* are essential reading.[6] The success the translations have had in France bear witness to the works' general import and relevance to the French tradition as well as to that of the USA.

Various early articles specifically on the bande dessinée have appeared in English-language press publications, such as a 1955 analysis of reactions in France to horror comics in the *Guardian*, a 1960 piece on *Tintin* in *Newsweek*, 1968 articles in *Playboy* and *Penthouse* on *Barbarella*, one in 1975 in the *New York Times* on *Peanuts* in France, and a 1978 overview of the work of Claire Bretécher that appeared in *Ms.*[7] The *Astérix* phenomenon in particular has been the subject of much press ink, going as far as a front-cover feature in *Time* in July 1991. Inevitably such works have tended to be descriptive, presenting an unknown exotic commodity to a foreign audience and in general lacking the space (or sometimes desire) for original insight or analysis.

By contrast, Russel B. Nye's 1980 article on *Astérix* in the *Journal of Popular Culture* does provide an early description of a series now taken for granted,[8] but it also contextualises the phenomenon in terms of the history of the comic strip, narrative strategies, the possible political content of *Astérix*, and its national specificity. Ten years later and on the other side of the Atlantic, a further landmark article in English was Hugh Starkey's 'Is the BD "à bout de souffle"?', a sixteen-page piece in the second issue of *French Cultural Studies* (number 1.2,

1990, pp. 95–110). Starkey was a pioneer in that, starting from the 1960s and moving forwards, he assessed the bande dessinée as a French cultural phenomenon in the way others had considered French literature or cinema, pointing to defining moments, analysing the specifics of the French form, and looking towards future trends. Often in a similar vein, the glossy Seattle-based *Comics Journal* has provided various snippets, starting in the late 1970s and still continuing, on the French and Belgian scene from Hergé to Enki Bilal and David B.[9]

Just as Paul Gravett's online musings (see above) and the *Comics Journal* are specific fora that have on occasion delved into the not-unrelated world of BD, so the *International Journal of Comic Art* (*IJOCA*), founded by John Lent from his base in Pennsylvania in 1999, has provided a number of articles on the French tradition, many of which I will draw upon in the pages of this current book. Early contributions included Pascal Lefèvre on the representation of the senses with specific reference to the francophone authors (issue 1.1, 1999), Elizabeth McQuillan on the development of the journal *Pilote* (2.1, 2000), Thierry Groensteen on Gustave Doré (2.2, 2000), Pierre Horn on the depiction of America in *Les Pieds Nickelés* [The Leadfoot Gang], *Zig et Puce* and *Tintin* (3.1, 2001) and Nhu-Hoa Nguyen on Claire Bretécher (3.2, 2001). As the *IJOCA* has become more established there has been an increase in the number of French-related articles, with subjects including Hergé and Franquin, Plantu, Jacques Lacan and superheroes, Chantal Montellier, Jacques Tardi, Lewis Trondheim, Edmond Baudoin and *Le Téméraire's* Vica.[10] Nonetheless the *IJOCA* remains true to its roots with the vast majority of its pages dedicated to the tradition of the USA.

In North America 1999 saw the launch of the *IJOCA*; in Europe it was the year of the first International Bande Dessinée Conference in Glasgow, the event that would lead to the creation of the International Bande Dessinée Society or IBDS.[11] Although a largely academic-based organisation of limited resources, the IBDS is important in that it represents the concretisation of the study of the BD as a discipline within English-language scholarship, a tangible sign of the will to place the bande dessinée on a par with French cinema or literature in general. The society's efforts led to the publication of *The Francophone Bande Dessinée*,[12] the first work on the BD predominantly in English, whose various chapters explore the history of the form and its relationship with other disciplines such as architecture or sociology, whilst analysing the artistry of cutting-edge authors including Moebius, André Juillard, Baru and Enki Bilal.[13]

The early years of the IBDS also saw its members produce three doctoral dissertations in English on the bande dessinée. Elizabeth McQuillan's 'The Reception and Creation of Post-1960 Franco-Belgian BD' (University of Glasgow, 2001) outlines the key steps to the form's consecration in France and Belgium, whilst drawing upon case studies of Christian Binet, Claire Bretécher and Benoît Peeters and François Schuiten. Wendy Michallat's '*Pilote* Magazine and the Evolution of French Bande Dessinée between 1959 and 1974' (University of Nottingham, 2002) places bande dessinée in its broader social context, looking at factors such as market pressures in a study that uses a BD publication, *Pilote*, as the key to an understanding of postwar French culture. Ann Miller's 'Contemporary *Bande Dessinée*: Contexts, Critical Approaches and Case Studies' (University of Newcastle, 2003) again introduces the reader to the defining moments and creations of BD history, but via the angle of applied critical theory, demonstrating the suitability of certain BDs to the most rigorous examination. Her key case study authors are Marc-Antoine Mathieu, André Juillard, Jean Teulé, Cosey and Chantal Montellier.

An updated and expanded version of Michallat's thesis is to be published by the New York-based Edwin Mellen Press, and in 2007 Intellect of Bristol released Ann Miller's *Reading Bande Dessinée: Critical Approaches to French-Language Comic Strip*, much of which is based on the work for her doctoral dissertation. In addition, Matthew Screech's *Masters of the Ninth Art: Bandes Dessinées and Franco-Belgian Identity* (Liverpool University Press, 2005) has provided a bio-bibliographic analysis of the form's development through seven main chapters, each based on one or more key creators: Hergé, André Franquin, René Goscinny and Albert Uderzo, Moebius, Jacques Tardi, Marcel Gotlib, Claire Bretécher, Régis Franc, Alejandro Jodorowsky and François Bourgeon. In contrast to Miller's application of critical theory, Screech comes closer to the traditional *l'homme et l'oeuvre* approach, and as such provides an accessible introduction to readers with virtually no knowledge of the French and Belgian traditions of comics. So as not to reinvent the wheel, this current book has tended not to concentrate on authors already covered by Screech's and Miller's case studies.[14]

The twenty-first century has also seen a growth in English-language bande dessinée scholarship outwith Europe. The International Comics Arts Forum has held annual conferences in Washington since 1997, often with panels delving into aspects of the French tradition.[15] More specifically, Mark McKinney, the main instigator behind the founding of the American Bande Dessinée Society in 2004, continues to work extensively on imperialism, colonialism and immigrant ethnicities in bande dessinée and has a corresponding monograph forthcoming. Bart Beaty, working from Calgary, examines in *Unpopular Culture* the rise of experimental comic artwork in Europe in the last fifteen years, paying particular attention to the work of L'Association, the French alternative publishing venture.[16] Working from Australia, Murray Pratt explored the expression of gay identity and related issues through the BD, and has provided a chapter in *The Francophone Bande Dessinée*,[17] as well as an article on Fabrice Neaud for *Belphégor*.[18] *Belphégor* is a Canadian-based e-journal on popular culture (www.dal.ca/~etc/belphegor) that has dedicated two special issues, volume 4.1 of November 2004 and volume 5.1 of December 2005, to the bande dessinée, the first with the overall guiding theme of autobiography.

The gradual expansion of scholarship in English specifically on French-language comics can be gauged by the 2009 IBDS London conference, at which at least sixteen countries were represented. Although this current overview is not entirely complete (further references will be found throughout the pages of this book), it is an indication of the main thrust of English-language scholarship pertaining to the bande dessinée. Nonetheless, in comparison with other fields such as film studies or period-based literary analysis, BD studies are, as might be expected, relatively new and limited. Comparison can also be made with the industry in French, which, as the chapter on the consecration of the Ninth Art will show, not only dates back to the 1920s but is furthermore the object of top-selling news-stand publications and regular TV and radio spots. As stated in the Foreword, in France the bande dessinée is commonly known as the Ninth Art, following on from the likes of poetry, sculpture, music and film,[19] and receives the attention of politicians, from Charles de Gaulle's famous statement that *Tintin* was his main rival, to Jack Lang's 1982 *Quinze mesures pour la bande dessinée*.[20]

Of course it is natural that the BD in France should receive more attention from critics in France, but the scale of the discrepancy is disproportionate. A further anomaly is that despite the mainstream attention the form receives and despite its institutionalisation through organisations such as the Centre National de la Bande Dessinée et de l'Image [The National Centre for the Bande Dessinée and for the Image] or CNBDI at Angoulême (again, see Chapter 9), it is virtually a taboo subject in French universities, as Harry Morgan makes clear in his *Petit Critique illustré*, a quote from which opens this Introduction. In Anglo-Saxon countries, by contrast, analysis of the BD is almost exclusively via academics,[21] the form receives funding from university bodies and research councils (even if only tentatively), and several institutions offer undergraduate courses on the bande dessinée.[22]

The result is that the ensuing analyses reflect very different perspectives. French publications can aim at a wider money-spinning audience and often have no need even to broach the subject of whether or not a comic strip is an art form. With an almost captive adulating audience it is not uncommon for mainstream works in French to be excessively admiring of even the wobbliest pillar of the Ninth Art's temple. English-language publications, including this one, are, perhaps even unknowingly, based upon the critical givens of academic discourse, bearing marks of the cynicism that comes with the deconstruction of minutiae. These are of course generalisations, but there is no doubt that different systems produce different viewpoints, and so, as one of the first books on the bande dessinée in English, and the first with a specifically historical perspective, this current publication will tell us about the curious BD phenomenon, but it will also tell us about us.

Starting with the assumption that the English-language reader will be approaching the BD as a foreign phenomenon, the first major section of this book, 'What is a Bande Dessinée?', will present and debate the tools of the trade for the reader of comics in French, and the basic notions and knowledge needed for understanding the form. The initial chapter on definitions and component parts will present terms that will often have direct equivalents in the world of English-language comics, but will draw upon very specific French-language examples. In the second chapter, on the formal specificity of the BD, comics in French will be considered in terms of their essential functioning, the text/image interaction that makes them what they are, and how this can be contextualised with respect to other forms of French expression such as the *Nouveau Roman* or New Wave cinema.

Armed with an initial knowledge of the technical and formal qualities of the bande dessinée, the reader will then be presented with a broader overview of what the Ninth Art has to offer. Several approaches could have been possible, for example a dictionary-style selection by author's name, or a geographically based survey that might have given particular prominence to bandes dessinées from Belgium and Switzerland, as well as differentiating centralised and regional French production. As more than one approach would have resulted in overlap, I opted singularly for 'The Chronological Approach' (as I have called Part II), the one that allowed me to engage with what has been the most biting question amongst French critics of recent years, the suggestion that the true inventor of the bande dessinée, indeed the comic strip as a whole, was the early nineteenth-century Swiss schoolteacher of French expression, Rodolphe Töpffer.[23]

By deflecting attention away from Töpffer I have aimed to provide a broader view of the BD's development and current form, one that takes roots in a rich text/image tradition dating back to the Middle Ages. It should be underlined, however, that this wider angle is a far cry from certain misplaced attempts falsely to ennoble the BD via the bestowing of a tenuous direct lineage. In many ways one of the central points of this current book is its concern not just with the bande dessinée in its narrow definitions, but with the notion of French-related text/image culture in general. The early aspects of this culture are explored in the first historical chapter, whereas the second, the one dedicated to Töpffer's era, the early nineteenth century and its immediate aftermath, chooses to look away from 'great men' and towards the defining waves of text/image culture, namely the new interest in photography, the rise of the illustrated journal, and, finally, the moving image.

My chapter on the twentieth century allows me to present the traditionally discussed eras of the bande dessinée's development (and at least to broach the question of Belgian BD production) whilst suggesting defining areas, such as the influence of Disney or of Nazi collaboration, that are, understandably, generally underplayed in French accounts of the BD's history. Finally, a chapter on contemporary BD examines some of the currently influential and interesting creations, but again from a comparatively detached critical stance, whilst nonetheless providing an overview of many of the names that a dictionary listing could have featured. Overall the choice of an idiosyncratic historical overview is the backbone to my presentation of the bande dessinée, and is as such the defining element of this book.

Once the reader knows what a BD is and how it works, and has a more precise idea of the creations the form (including its close relations) has produced throughout time and indeed continues to produce, it will be appropriate to ask the outsider's broader question: how can the bande dessinée help us better to understand French-language culture, or indeed world culture, as a whole? Part III, 'The Cultural Phenomenon', opens by looking at the implications of the BD's status as popular art, in terms of both visual aesthetics and applied critical theory, whilst not forgetting the more pragmatic view of the BD as big business. To comprehend the BD's place as a pillar of French culture also requires an overview of the path to consecration into a form whose status is far beyond that of parallel creations in the Anglo-Saxon world.

Finally, with these areas explored (and they can only be explored; there are no definitive answers) the final chapter will consider how knowledge of the bande dessinée might be applied to further our understanding of sexism in France, the colonial Other, the popularity of Disneyland Paris, as well as a plethora of other issues. Broader case studies will provide examples of the BD in its relationship with popular icons of global culture (specifically James Bond) and, on an internal level, methods of textual and visual construction. Further suggestions will point to studies already available and areas that could be explored, with the broad aim of leaving the reader with the lasting impression that we know nothing about how our curious French-speaking allies live their lives until we have read and digested their comic books.

I should close my Introduction with a few words of explanation regarding its opening subtitle. The subtitle is of course a mediocre pun on the term 'comic strip' (indeed it was once jokingly suggested that the IBDS could have been called 'Strippers'); however, it is also intended to bring to mind aspects of Roland Barthes's text on the striptease, one of his *Mythologies*.[24]

This collection of musings on phenomena of everyday culture, from advertising to political discourse, first published in book form in

1957,[25] is a key document in terms of contextualising the bande dessinée, as we shall see in our chapter on BD and Pop Art. In the section entitled 'Strip-tease',[26] Barthes explains how this increasingly popular phenomenon depends not only on the pleasure of what is to be viewed, but, moreover, on how it is presented, on the décor within which we view it, and, increasingly, on the element of exoticism brought about by costumes evoking foreign lands. It is not just what we are seeing, but how we see it. Furthermore, the striptease may be a national art form – Barthes concludes that 'en France le strip-tease est nationalisé' ['in France the striptease is a national asset'] – but others might well find it less acceptable.

The French-language comic strip, although arguably less sexy, is also a national asset that may seem prurient to onlookers. The aim of this book is to unveil its attraction, whilst bearing in mind that it is the décor of an Anglo-Saxon vantage point that inevitably defines what we are seeing.

Notes

1. For example the Star of David on the evil Vénine's hat, the red that dominates his clothing, and his very name, a reminder of Lenin. *Le Téméraire* will be discussed further in Chapter 6.
2. I will return to this subject in the case studies discussed in Chapter 10.
3. 'Goul roi des Marais' literally means 'Goul king of the Marshes'. The Jewish district of Paris is thus called as it is in an area that was originally marshland.
4. L'EESI gives its English title as the European School of Visual Arts.
5. (Philadelphia: Chelsea House, 1999). First edition 1976.
6. *Understanding Comics: The Invisible Art* (Northampton, MA: Tundra, 1993; with frequent reprints and re-editions); *Reinventing Comics: How Imagination and Technology Are Revolutionizing an Art Form* (New York: Paradox, 2000); *Making Comics: Storytelling Secrets of Comics, Manga and Graphic Novels* (New York: Harper, 2006). The French translations are *L'Art invisible: Comprendre la bande dessinée*, trans. Dominique Petitfaux (Paris: Vertige Graphic, 1999) and *Réinventer la bande dessinée*, trans. Jean-Paul Jennequin (Paris: Vertige Graphic, 2002).
7. For full bibliographic details of these and other such pieces, see John A. Lent, *Comic Art of Europe: An International Comprehensive Bibliography* (Westport, CT: Greenwood, 1994).
8. Russel B. Nye, 'Death of a Gaulois: René Goscinny and Astérix,' *Journal of Popular Culture* 14.2 (1980), 181–95.
9. If the names cited in this Introduction are not familiar to the reader, they will become so as he or she continues through the pages that follow. In particular, Chapter 7 on contemporary BD presents many of the cutting-edge authors of today.
10. Many of these *IJOCA* articles are discussed later in this book with references given in full, and all are included in the extensive listing available at the journal's website (www.ijoca.com).
11. The early development of the IBDS will be discussed in Chapter 9 on the consecration of the Ninth Art. The society's website can also be consulted (www.arts.gla.ac.uk/ibds).

12. Charles Forsdick, Laurence Grove and Libbie [Elizabeth] McQuillan, eds, *The Francophone Bande Dessinée* (Amsterdam: Rodopi, 2005).
13. The specifics of individual chapters will receive attention and full referencing throughout the pages of this present work.
14. The main exception will be my own case study of the work of André Juillard and of Marc-Antoine Mathieu that forms part of the chapter on cultural studies and beyond. Here, however, one of the case study's concerns will be to pinpoint differences in the analytical approaches used by French and English scholars.
15. The Forum's website (www.internationalcomicsartsforum.org) provides a listing of all programmes.
16. Bart Beaty, *Unpopular Culture: Transforming the European Comic Book in the 1990s* (Toronto: Univeristy of Toronto Press, 2007). The work of L'Association will be discussed further in Chapter 7 on contemporary BD.
17. 'The Dance of the Visible and the Invisible: AIDS and the Bande Dessinée,' on pp. 189–200.
18. Ann Miller and Murray Pratt, 'Transgressive Bodies in the Work of Julie Doucet, Fabrice Neaud and Jean-Christophe Menu: Towards a Theory of the "AutobioBD"', *Belphégor* 4.1 (2004), no pagination.
19. The full list is architecture, sculpture, painting, music, dance, poetry, cinema, television and bande dessinée.
20. Charles De Gaulle is reported to have told André Malraux: 'Au fond, vous savez, mon seul rival international, c'est Tintin!' ['All things considered, you know, my only international rival is Tintin']. Lang's *Quinze mesures,* a series of government innovations aimed at promoting the bande dessinée, will be discussed briefly in Chapter 6 on the twentieth century.
21. Paul Gravett, some of whose output has been cited above, provides a prolific exception to this rule. Gravett works as a journalist and independent scholar with no university affiliation.
22. The Universities of Glasgow, Leicester and Sheffield, Manchester Metropolitan University, Wheaton College Massachusetts, Duke University and the University of Calgary are just a few examples.
23. Again, if this name is not a known one such should no longer be the case after perusal of the chapters to come.
24. The general notion of comics as striptease is explored by Jeffrey Miller (with reference to Barthes), who points to the excitement created by the expectations of narrative build-up as akin to that of the de-layering of clothing. See Jeffrey A. Miller, 'Comics Narrative as Striptease,' *International Journal of Comic Art* 4.1 (2002), 143–50.
25. (Paris: Pierre Vives).
26. Pages 165–68 of the 1957 edition; pp. 147–50 of the 1970 (Paris: Seuil) edition.

PART I

WHAT IS A BANDE DESSINÉE?

Chapter 2

Definitions and Component Parts: How a BD Works

'Bande Dessinée' or 'Bande + Dessinée'?

How a BD works depends on what a BD is and, ironically, although the former can be clearly demonstrated, the latter is open to debate. In such defining moments one normally heads for the dictionary, but in this case *Le Petit Robert* adds a further, or rather an initial, layer of confusion through the question of historical etymology. The *Nouveau Petit Robert* tells us that the term 'bande dessinée' dates from 1929,[1] presumably when it appeared in the contracts that Paul Winckler issued for the *Journal de Mickey*. But was that *bande dessinée*, the cultural entity, or merely a reference to a strip – *bande* – that had been drawn – *dessinée*? The latter seems more likely given that as late as 1969, forty years after the supposed invention of the term, 'bande dessinée' did not yet feature as an entry in Robert's dictionary.

Now that the BD undoubtedly is a cultural entity scholars have turned their hand to pinpointing the first examples of its named usage, as in the valuable history of the term 'bande dessinée' that Jean-Claude Glasser summarises in a 'Note' for the 'Rubrique Courrier' [Readers' Letters] of *Cahiers de la Bande Dessinée* 80 (March 1988). We find that Elisabeth Gerin, in *Tout sur la presse enfantine* [Everything About Publications for Children],[2] analyses the relationship between the form's constituent parts (image, text, speech bubbles ...) as early as 1958. In 1961 a serialised strip in *Pilote* signed Remo Forlani gave us *Le Roman vrai des bandes dessinées* [The True Story of Bandes Dessinées]. In short, vague postwar terminology that included such formulations as 'histoires en images' [stories in pictures], 'histoires dessinées' [drawn stories] or 'histoires imagées' [image-based stories] drifted upon 'bande dessinée' sometime towards the end of the 1950s. By the mid-1960s the term was in current usage and by the 1970s it was official.[3]

Although this does not get us any nearer to knowing what a bande dessinée is, it does remind us that the invention of the term 'bande dessinée' is not the same as the invention of the thing itself, or as any student of Saussurian linguistics would tell us, it is not because a thing does not have a name that it does not exist. Luckily for us, otherwise *Tintin*, *Spirou* and even *Astérix* would all be excluded from this present study. But if we allow for creations that existed before the term 'bande dessinée' did, it is not enough to go back to 1929 and the first appearance of Tintin. *Tintin* followed in the footsteps of *Le Sapeur Camembert* [Fireman Camembert], who followed on from nineteenth-century caricatures, which continued the tradition of eighteenth-century narrative engravings… One can go back as far as the Bayeux Tapestry and beyond, and indeed we will, but it all really depends on how we define things …

So, What Is a BD?

A bande dessinée is a French-language mixture of images and written text that together form a narrative.

Images

Although the images are generally drawn or painted, that is not exclusively the case: photographs have been incorporated sporadically from the time of the earliest journals onwards and by the time of *Pilote* were reasonably unsurprising, as in the vision of the future, a photo of a 1970s housing block, that we are given in *Le Devin* [Asterix and the Soothsayer]. More recently, the works of Jean Teulé (*Gens de France* [Folk from France], *Gens d'ailleurs* [Folk from Elsewhere]), Peeters and Schuiten (*L'Écho des Cités* [The Journal of the Cities]) and Guibert, Lefèvre and Lemercier (*Le Photographe* [The Photographer]) have created the narrative sequence through the intermingling of drawing and photography.[4] Nonetheless works whose only images are photographic are classed as *romans photo*, a term that like 'graphic novel' lays increased emphasis on the narrative element. The question of the medium of the image is likely to become even more blurred – perhaps literally – as web-based BDs incorporate computer animation into text-based pages.

Written text

It is the notion of written text that distinguishes the bande dessinée from other visual narratives such as the *dessin animé* (cartoons), or, quite simply, the motion picture. Here the text/image interaction is via spoken text, with written elements subservient to the main image (e.g., beginning and end credits) or subsumed by the image (e.g., shots of newspapers or badges).

Mixture of images and written text

The interaction of text and image – the forming together of a completed whole – differentiates the images of the bande dessinée from those of other pictorial works such as illustrated books, whilst upholding the importance of the text. Here I take issue with one of the main French analyses of recent years, Thierry Groensteen's *Système de la bande dessinée* (1999).[5] Referring to Rodolphe Töpffer's 1837 preface to his *M. Jabot* of 1833 (more on that later ...), Groensteen states:

Figure 2. 'Pigalle'. Didier Daeninckx and Jacques Tardi. *Le Der des ders.* Tournai: Casterman, 1997, p. 44.

> Töpffer voyait dans le texte et l'image deux composants à égalité de la bande dessinée, qu'il définissait à partir de son caractère mixte. Ce point de vue, qui était encore soutenable à son époque, ne l'est plus aujourd'hui. En effet, ceux qui reconnaissent au verbal un statut égal, dans l'economie de la bande dessinée, à celui de l'image, partent du principe que l'écrit est le véhicule privilégié du récit en général. Or la multiplicité des espèces narratives a rendu ce postulat caduc.
>
> Considérer que la bande dessinée est *essentiellement* le lieu d'une confrontation entre le verbal et l'iconique est, selon moi, une contre-vérité théorique, qui débouche sur une impasse. (10)
>
> [Töpffer saw the text and the image as two equally important components of the bande dessinée, which he defined in terms of its mixed nature. That viewpoint was still acceptable in his time, but such is no longer the case. Indeed those who accord as much weighting to the verbal elements in the bande dessinée's make-up as to the image are working from the principle that the written medium is in general the preferred vehicle for narrative. In reality the fact that the different types of narratives have multiplied means that such a notion is no longer valid.
>
> To consider that the bande dessinée is *essentially* a place where the verbal and the image [*iconique*] confront each other is, in my view, a theoretical falsehood that leads nowhere.]

The tradition that *mixes* text with image goes back well beyond Töpffer,[6] and there always has been, and still is, a difference between a textual narrative that includes images, and an image-based narrative that draws upon written text as an intrinsic element. Even in cases such as Jacques Tardi's version of Louis-Ferdinand Céline's *Voyage au bout de la nuit* [Journey to the End of the Night], the removal of the images would not diminish our understanding of the storyline. But in the case of bande dessinée adaptations of literary works, as in Tardi's 1997 version of Didier Deninckx's *Le Der des ders* [The Last of the Last] (Fig. 2), the story is presented through the images.[7]

Text

Groensteen, quite rightly, is at pains to point out that although it is difficult to imagine a BD without images, BDs without texts, whilst not common, are entirely feasible: Caran d'Ache, at the end of the nineteenth century, produced numerous image-only strips and had presented an ambitious project to *Le Figaro* for a series of text-free 'romans dessinés' [drawn novels]; Sempé, Reiser and Lewis Trondheim have all produced humorous narratives devoid of speech; Moebius's silent *Arzach* (1975–76) pushes experimental sci-fi BD to the limits.[8] Nonetheless, to exclude or even make optional the textual element in the definition of a BD is misleading. 'Silent' BDs working in the current tradition gain much of their power from the contradiction of expectations. The text remains an important element by its very exclusion, as attention focuses on the way that the images are adapted to overcome the practical difficulties arising from such elimination. That does not make the text the 'véhicule privilégié du récit en général', but just a primary element in a certain tradition of récit, of which the current BD is an example.

Narrative

Similarly, one of the tendencies of the modern BD has been the move away from conventional narrative. The work of Moebius has spearheaded this tendency: in creations such as *Le Garage hermétique* [The Hermetic Garage] or *Arzach* artistry and imagination take over from logical progression as characters transform into others, time reverses and different worlds merge together. Moebius literally loses the plot and the reader seeking a coherent storyline will be sorely disappointed. But here again the narrative sequence is central precisely due to its absence, in the same way that the novels of Alain Robbe-Grillet might be anti-novels or new novels, but they are novels all the same (more on this subject in the next chapter).

French language

'French language' is a defining element of the bande dessinée not on account of the specifics of its grammatical structures or vocabulary, but as a container for the cultural system it carries. The importance of an image-based culture in France's history, from the presence of Leonardo in the French court to the spread of surrealism, forms the backcloth to the continuation of such a tradition through the Ninth Art. 'French language' operates as an equivalent of 'francophone', a reminder that Belgian, Swiss or Québecois strands of the culture are also to be found, even if there is no unifying geographic term such as 'North American' or 'British'. It is the mentality behind the language that matters, not the language itself: even in one of its fifty-eight translations, *Les Bijoux de la Castafiore* or *The Castafiore Emerald* is still a bande dessinée.

Even though this definition is deliberately wide, it will not be difficult to find, amongst the vast output of the current BD industry, works that stray from or even contradict it. The example cited above is that of Groensteen's definition, one that classes the BD as a specifically visual form. Other definitions, such as those of Benoît Peeters, Henri Filippini, Yves Frémion or Harry Morgan, will lay emphasis elsewhere. Peeters underlines the role of the relationship between the different parts (specifically the individual frame and the page as a whole), as his title, *Case, planche, récit: Comment lire une bande dessinée* [Frame, Plate, Narrative: How to Read a Bande Dessinée] would suggest. Filippini (et al.) makes the use of speech bubbles a defining quality. Frémion sees the narrative that is implied in the gap between images as being the distinguishing feature of the BD. For Morgan the literary qualities provide the essence of a form he views as 'littérature dessinée' [drawn literature].[9]

To a certain extent these differences, and the intensity of the debate that has produced them, reflect the fact that the BD is now an accepted art form, like cinema or photography, and perhaps unlike comics, even when these are known as graphic novels. The different definitions reflect the critics' different areas of emphasis, and these can be

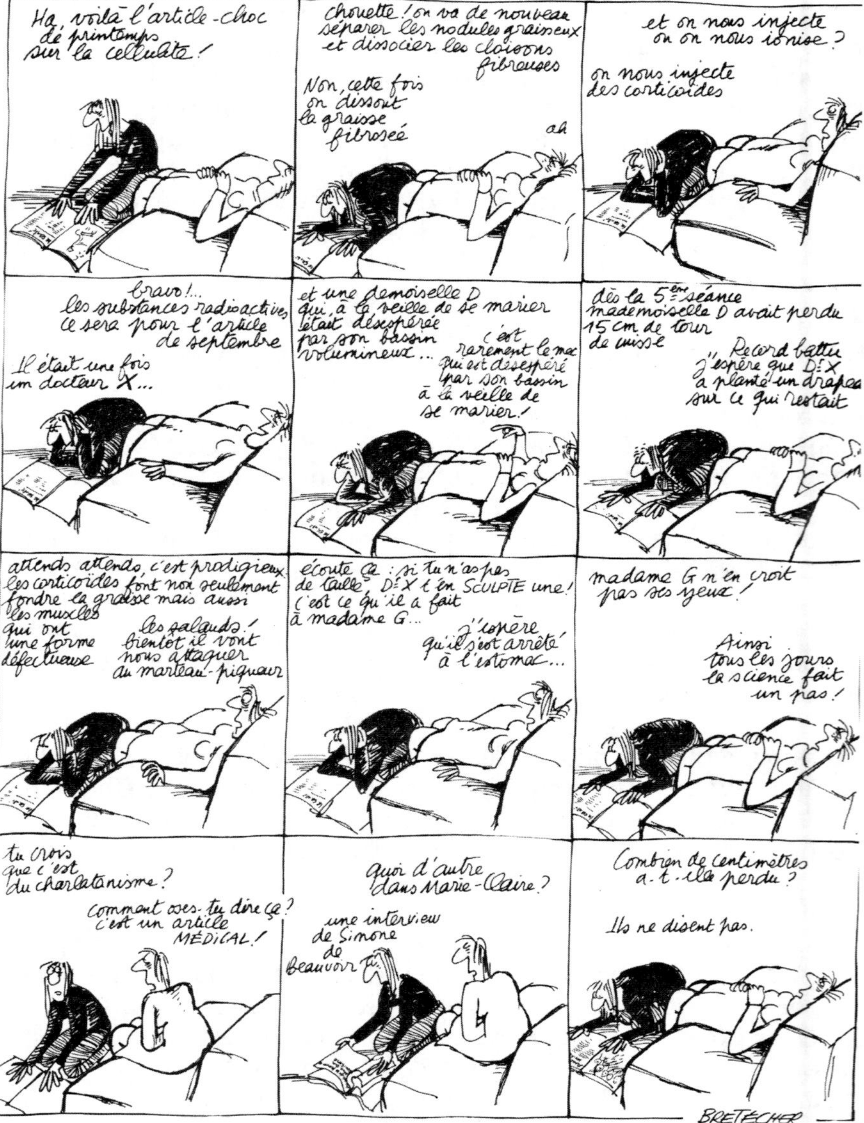

Figure 3. 'Les Vampires'. Claire Bretécher. *Les Frustrés 2*. Paris: Claire Bretécher, 1977, p. 45.

historical, semiotic, sociological, literary, art-historical and so on. It is also possible that the label of bande dessinée can be misleading when applied to certain works that nonetheless fit our definition. The Bayeux Tapestry fits our definition (or nearly – the text is in Latin rather than French) but one would hesitate in putting Harold and William in the same category as Spirou or the Smurfs. The Bayeux Tapestry has something more than our definition: it is precisely a tapestry, but it is also a historical artefact, and it is this something more that becomes its defining point. Assessing an artistic creation in the context of a thriving culture to which it belongs and in a context of innovative isolation are very different exercises, and part of what makes a BD what it is is the way it interacts – or does not – with the BD's tradition.

As well as existing within the context of a historical tradition, a bande dessinée also gains specificity from the way in which its defining elements interact.[10] We have already seen that much depends on whether it is text or image that dominates: whereas a text-based BD such as Claire Bretécher's *Les Frustrés* [Frustrated] (Fig. 3) can thrive upon intellectual word-based humour and use the lack of image dynamics to suggest inaction on the part of the protagonists, a BD that goes to the opposite extreme and excludes words, as in Moebius's *Arzach*, creates an atmosphere of action devoid of defined reflection.

It is not just the balance between text and image that decides the make-up of each individual bande dessinée. The type and size of text used, the space given to the image and the angle from which it is drawn, the use (or not) of colours, the overall page shape and indeed even the blank spaces can be manipulated according to each creator's aims. Finally we are getting there: how does a BD work?

Definition of Terms

Not quite there yet. Before exploring the ways the parts of a BD interact it is useful to define our terms, although the hardest term to define, *bande dessinée*, has already been discussed. To see how the theory I am about to outline works in practice, one can refer to the 'making of' versions that are increasingly produced to accompany the most popular albums. Perhaps the best example of this is Albert Uderzo's *Astérix et Latraviata: L'Album des crayonnés* [Astérix and the Actress: The Album of the Preparatory Work] (2001) whereby the reader can follow the numerous stages of production from preparatory sketches to digital scanning and printing, via lettering, inking and colouring.

The following is a general glossary.[11]

Overall production

Scénario/découpage/storyboard

The *scénario* is a rough written outline of a BD's plot, of which the *découpage* is a more detailed version. The *storyboard* is a visual sketch giving the plot's outline.

- The use of such terms bears witness to the lengthy step-by step process that is part of the creation of a modern BD. They also provide a point of contact and exchange between different members of a BD team. These can be no more than the scriptwriter (*scénariste*) and the artist (*dessinateur*), as in René Goscinny and Albert Uderzo's collaboration for the creation of most of the *Astérix* series, or a studio system employing several people each with specific tasks, as was the case with later Studios Hergé productions. An artist working on his or her own may go through the process of *scénario* and *découpage* and/or *storyboard*, or may rely on idiosyncratic methods.
- A bande dessinée produced by a team or a studio will inevitably have a different outlook from an individual independent production. In general, a studio-produced work will have a greater budget, a more polished product as a result, but often middle-of-the-road content aimed at a mainstream audience. An independent work may lack technical sophistication, but boast greater audacity. The debate is similar to that applied to cinema productions, and indeed the *scénario, découpage* and *storyboard* stages of studio production for the two are basically the same, but whereas truly independent BD production requiring little more than paper and ink is possible, the same is not true of even the most spartan filmmaker.

Album/journal

A bande dessinée can either be published as part of a continuing publication – *journal* – or in book – *album* – form. In general, but not exclusively, *album* publication gives a far greater number of pages to an individual BD.

- The format of a work's publication defines how we read a bande dessinée, and a work that appears in a journal will inevitably be more fragmented than a complete album, although certain *journaux* of the 1980s, such as *[À Suivre]* [To Be Continued], would regularly publish extensive BDs.
- The distinction between serialised publication, which is generally the case for works that appear in *journaux*, and the greater credibility implied in immediate full-length production, suggests comparison between the BD and the nineteenth-century novel, for which the distinction was also pertinent.

- The general switch from journal to album publication is an intrinsic part of the BD's development and as such will be discussed in our history chapters.

One-shot/série

A *one-shot* is a bande dessinée whose characters and setting are unique to that particular BD. A bande dessinée that is part of a *série* features familiar characters and/or settings and in some cases its plot may continue through to another album.

- The growth of the modern bande dessinée through the journal system (more on this in our history chapters) and the corresponding use of *à suivre* strips means the tradition has its roots in the *série*. However, the more recent tendency towards narrative disintegration (see above) has been accompanied by a proliferation of *one-shots*, or even albums, such as Frank Margerin's *Bananes métalliques* [Metallic Bananas], consisting of a number of *one-shot* shorter BDs. Nonetheless, sales figures seem to indicate that 'tried and tested' classics, inevitably therefore *séries* such as *Tintin* and *Astérix*, remain most popular.
- A further recent development has been a hybrid of the two formats, a number of autonomous *one-shot* albums, each with their own creators, characters and settings, that come together under an umbrella grouping. Dupuis's *Décalogue* series, for example, consists of ten *one-shots*, each of which is based on the breaking of one of the Ten Commandments. Works that are published under the auspices of L'Association or l'OuBaPo (more on these later) are individual creations, but they conform to the group's iconoclastic codes (cf. the Dogma school in cinema).
- The distinction between *one-shot* and *série* affects our reception of a bande dessinée in a way that separates it from visual media with the same distinction – essentially television and cinema – but unites it with the novel. The physical presence of a bande dessinée means that even a first-time reader knows when he or she is approaching the end of an album. If the album is part of a *série*, such as that of *Astérix*, we know that the dénouement – the traditional banquet – is but a few pages away. Suspense is not therefore as to whether the end is near, as is the case for a film, but rather how the approaching finale is to be achieved.

The individual page

Planche

A single page of a bande dessinée, generally consisting of several *bandes*.

- Nowadays the prevalent format is such that each *planche* is of A4 size, with generally forty-eight, sixty-two, or other multiples of sixteen *planches* to an album. Alternatives are of course possible, as in the giant B3 format of Peeters and Schuiten's *L'Archiviste* that

Figure 4. 'The Circus'. René Goscinny and Albert Uderzo. *Astérix gladiateur*. Paris: Dargaud, 1977, p. 38.

in itself gives the impression of the giant tomes surrounding the central character, the eponymous archivist, or, for purely economic reasons, the reduced size of the many popular BDs that the Livre de Poche series have re-edited.

- The intrinsic nature of the *planche* gives the BD an element of suspense that moving pictures cannot have: we have physically to turn the page in order to find out what happens next. Artists will often therefore design the page so as to create a key moment in the bottom-right of the *planche*. To a certain extent this harks back to

Figure 5. 'HIV Positive'. Derib. *Jo*. Paris: Fondation pour la Vie, 1991, p. 52.

the postwar era when weekly publications dominated the BD market and strips would appear as single *planches*. It was important to leave the story on a moment of suspense so as to encourage readers to purchase the sequel.

- Within a single *planche* artists can create visual effects that override the left-to-right and top-to-bottom sequential movement naturally associated with Western text. A large central *case*, for example, can draw the attention to a central key scene (see Fig. 4

Figure 6. 'Philémon: Simbabbad de Batbad'. *Pilote*, No. 571 (October 1970), p. 36.

or Fig. 5), or repeatedly emphasised visual elements, such as an outsize character, can send our eyes zooming around the page (see Fig. 6). The amalgamation of two facing *planches* might create an effect of magnitude. If an artist sets up a *planche* so that it does not read from top-left to bottom-right, the effect can be to disorientate the reader by undermining the expected order of events.

Bande

A single row of images, the equivalent of a 'strip' in English.

- The traditional *bande* of the inter- and postwar period would consist of three *cases* of equal sizes, and there would be four *bandes* to a *planche*. Alternatively, a single *bande* might be published on its own: translated imports that appeared in journals such as *Le Journal de Mickey* or *Robinson*, but also strips, such as *bandes* taken from the adventures of Tintin, that would be syndicated to newspapers.
- The modern BD increasingly strays from this traditional '3 x 4' system. A *bande* consisting of a single elongated *case* can provide a scene-setting panorama (as in Fig. 4), or one packed with thinner *cases* gives the impression of rapid movement, as in the darting eyes of a worried character. Increasing or decreasing the number of *bandes* per *planche* can achieve similar effects, and adjacent *bandes* can be interrupted to allow for a larger 'double-layer' *case* or *cases*. When the '3 x 4' system is maintained it can create a nostalgic effect by reference to the previous tradition, or it can evoke an atmosphere of static stability, even monotony, as in Claire Bretécher's *Frustrés* (Fig. 3).

Encrage/bleu/colorisation

Encrage is the initial inking-in stage in the creation of a BD. The *bleu* is the technical term for the initial print taken from inked version. This will then be the base for the *colorisation* or the adding of colour.

- The adding of colour is the last stage of the creation of a BD after lettering and inking. Traditionally colour was added through the four-colour printing process (*quadrichromie*) that involved the combining of three transparencies – one blue, one red and one yellow – onto the monochrome outline. More recently the initial print or *bleu* (from its blue tint) is coloured, and a transparency of the inked outline is then superimposed, thereby giving the drawing its full force. Nowadays it is normal for artists to rely upon digital composition, using computers for direct colouring.
- The use of colours can be the most immediately striking aspect of a *planche*, as in the psychedelic blues, yellows and greens used by artists such as Philippe Druillet or Fred in the 1970s, often to create

an atmosphere of confusion or carefree anti-conformism. The prolonged and unusual use of an individual colour, as in the blue tinges Enki Bilal applies to his erotic *Femme piège* [The Woman Trap], can create a sensual leitmotif that evokes far more than images or words can portray. Conversely, many of Jacques Tardi's works (e.g., *Le Der des ders*, see Fig. 2) are conspicuous in their lack of colour. Here the starkness of the black and white strokes evokes the starkness of post-First World War conditions, as well as an effect of implied reminiscence by association with black and white films and photography.

- Individual colours create traditional associations with emotions or physical states: red is anger, green envy, blue cold, and so on. Such stock usage is generally for comic purposes, and is exemplified throughout the *Astérix* series, but politically associated colours can (see chapter 1), turn the BD to propaganda: in Licquois's *Vers les mondes inconnus*, the star strip of the pro-Nazi *Téméraire*, the villains are clearly identifiable by their red tinges and the ensuing association with communism.

More specifically

Case

The individual image, generally within a border or *cadrage*.

- The traditional shape of the *case* is either square or rectangular, and divergence from this creates specific effects: a circular *case* can emphasise a character's face, a T-shaped *case* can reflect the wings of an aeroplane, a zigzag *case* can suggest a lightning strike ... Re-use of unusually shaped *cases* on a single *planche* can underline parallels or create contrasts in a way that is more immediate than a linear textual reading.
- Variations in the size of the *cases* can alter the pace of the narrative or give emphasis to a key moment. Smaller *cases* means there are more to a *planche*, more developments, and thus the impression of faster action. If these correspond to textual narrative, then a larger *case* provides the equivalent of description, often for scene setting, as the reader pauses to consider background detail (Fig. 7). The use of a larger *case* can underscore the loss of time-based progression in favour of 'eternals', such as the banquet at the end of each *Astérix* album, or the everlasting village adoration Tintin has left behind in *Tintin au Congo* [Tintin in the Congo].
- The use – or not – of the space available within a *case* determines the effect created. A *case* crowded with detail, perhaps with elements bursting beyond the *cadrage*, portrays urgency or disorder (cf. Fig. 5). A *case* with few details and a high percentage of blank space can suggest a pause in the action or a period of reflection (Fig. 8).

Figure 7. 'Hadrian's Wall'. Jean Van Hamme and Ted Benoit, based on the characters by Edgar-Pierre Jacobs. *L'Affaire Francis Blake*. Brussels: Éditions Blake et Mortimer, 2005, p. 46. First edition 1996.

Cadre/cadrage/filet

The boundary around a *case*.

- Although it is normal for each *case* to be separated from the next by a border of straight lines, this does not have to be the case. A series of *cases* without *cadres* might suggest an informal running

Figure 8. 'Fraternal Bonds'. Manu Larcenet. *Le Combat ordinaire: Tome 1*. Paris: Dargaud, 2003, p. 10.

together of the narrative, and when none of the *cases* have *cadres* the boundaries of the page become those of the *planche*. It is also possible for *cases* to spill over onto one another, or for elements within individual *cases* to transgress the *cadrages*, as in Figure 6. Such effects can be used to undermine traditional expectations, and/or to create a self-referential bande dessinée.

- In terms of the way in which the BD achieves its creation of meaning and the ambiguities therewith associated (in other words, in terms of enunciation theories), the gaps or *gouttières, caniveaux* or even *blancs intericoniques* between the *cadrages* have an important role to play. The images of a bande dessinée are in themselves static and it is only the relationship between them that creates the illusion of movement or progression in time. Much of what happens in a bande dessinée happens therefore 'in the *blancs*'. If the artist creates a series of *cases* depicting closely linked events, the construction of the *blancs* in the reader's imagination will have a lesser role. The less the apparent link between *cases* the greater the ambiguity of the *blancs*, as in works such as Moebius's *Garage hermétique*. Artists can also vary the physical size of the gap between *cadres*, using a larger *blanc* to suggest, for example, a greater elapse of time between *cases*.

Phylactère/bulle/ballon

The enclosures used for the representation of direct dialogue, what we call 'speech bubbles' in English.

- *Phylactère* is the term traditionally used to describe the casing that surrounds groups of Egyptian hieroglyphics. Its usage in the context of the bande dessinée, first coined, so it seems, by Jean de Trignon in his *Histoire de la littérature enfantine de Ma Mère l'Oye au Roi Babar* [History of Children's Literature from Mother Goose to Babar] of 1950,[12] now elevates the notion of *bulles* and, by implication, the BD genre in general. Although such usage may appear to be no more than pretentious self-inflation, the appropriation of a term with historical antecedents does remind us of the important tradition of early text/image narratives or 'proto-BDs' (more on this in the first history chapter). 'Speech bubbles' can be traced back to Roman inscriptions, illuminated manuscripts, early printed books (see Fig. 9), gravestones and satirical prints, to name but a few.
- The fact that the term *phylactère* should have become common in the late 1960s is indicative of the general institutionalisation and intellectualisation that the BD underwent at that time.
- In modern bande dessinée usage it is the *bulles* that provide the equivalent of a soundtrack. The shape of the *bulles* corresponds to the sound effect required: a 'normal' bubble for normal speech, a zigzag for a crackling effect, such as a radio transmission, a broken-line *bulle* for whispered speech, or a series of bubbles leading to the main one for thought (see Fig. 4), an effect that cinema can only achieve with difficulty.

Figure 9 'Temptation'. *Biblia pauperum*. [Netherlands]: n.p., [mid fifteenth century]. Page 10. Glasgow University Library Hunter Ds. 2. 4.

Lettrage/récitatif

The lettering used within *bulles* to report speech, or, outwith the *bulles*, to provide purely textual narrative. In this latter case, the textual block containing the *lettrage* of the narrator's voice is known as the *récitatif*.

- Like the shape of the *bulles*, the lettering within them can be used to represent speech patterns or sound effects: bold lettering for shouting (see Fig. 4), flowery script for soft persuasion, miniscule type for barely audible words. The additions of pictograms, generally for comic effect (again, the *Astérix* series is a clear example), can enhance such usage, with hammers to represent anger, skulls and asterisks for profanities, or foreign scripts, such as Gothic or Greek, for foreign-language speech.
- Often a series will adapt its own distinctive *lettrage*, almost a visual accent or leitmotif. Of these Hergé's *Tintin* is the best example, but Tardi, Bretécher and Uderzo (Figs. 2–4) are just three of the more recent artists to adopt a 'trade mark' script.
- The use of the *récitatif* provides the bande dessinée with a narrator's voice and in so doing introduces many of the ambiguities of textual narrative discourse, ambiguities which may be confirmed or contradicted by our visual approach to the images. Whose viewpoint is the reader being given? Is it that of the characters or that of someone else? What is the difference between the narrator and the creator? Is the narrator reliable?

- Such lettered panels might be no more than a few words – 'Deux jours plus tard' [Two days later], 'Pendant ce temps là' [Meanwhile], 'Enfin' [Finally] – or they might occupy an entire *case* (or more) and significantly advance the narrative. The dynamics of an individual BD will depend upon the relationship between the texts and the images in terms of the distribution of narrative and descriptive roles.

In addition, a number of terms from the worlds of literary and cinematographic analysis (more on the question of BD/literature/cinema overlap in the next chapter) can usefully be applied to our reading of the BD. Here are just some of the more common ones.

From literary criticism

Onomatopée

Words or phrases whose sound is their meaning. The 'pop', 'bang', 'whizz' onomatopoeia that were an integral part of 'Golden Age' superhero action scenes have become a leitmotif for the comic/BD form as a whole.

Style indirect libre

A narrative style [Indirect Free Style], generally associated with that of Gustave Flaubert, whereby the subjective opinions of the characters or narrator are presented in third-person pseudo-objective form.

Voix de l'auteur/voix du narrateur

It is often important to distinguish between the words, or, in BD, thoughts, of the characters, and those of the narrator. In general, those of the characters are expressed by the *bulles*, and those of the narrator by the *récitatif*, although any divergence from these norms (e.g., having the character as narrator) can unsettle the reader or, alternatively, create an effect of shared *confidence*. The author or authorial voice should also be distinguished from the narrator, although in autobiographical works, such as those of Fabrice Neaud (Fig. 10), this distinction becomes blurred.

Intertextuality

Referencing, be it visual or textual, to the wider world of cultural expression. This can create a complex, and often ambiguous, layering of meaning, as in the implicit debt to Franz Kafka that Marc-Antoine Mathieu fosters in his Julius Corentin Acquefacques series (more on this in Chapter 10), or quite simply a nod-of-the-hat for comic effect, as in the *Astérix* references to modern-day celebrities or monuments of canonical literature (see Fig 4).

Figure 10. 'Open Homosexuality'. Fabrice Neaud. *Journal 4: Août 1995–juillet 1996: Les Riches heures*. Angoulême: Ego Comme X, 2002, p. 111.

From cinema

Plan général/panorama

A wide-angle shot that is used for scene setting.

Plan moyen

A full-length shot, generally used to situate characters within the general décor (see Fig. 7).

Plan américain

A shot from the knees upwards often used for dialogues involving several characters, or allowing the viewer to progress from the *plan général* to the specifics of a *gros plan*.

Plan rapproché

A view of the head and upper body, generally to concentrate on dialogue between characters (see Fig. 7).

Gros plan

A close-up. Generally used to home in on an object or a character's face at a key moment, allowing the plot to remain static (see Fig. 5).

Plongée

A high-angled shot, one that looks down upon the subjects viewed. This puts them in a position of inferiority.

Contre-plongée

A low-angled shot, the opposite effect of a *plongée*. See for example the portrayal of Caesar in Figure 4, or the Scotsman in Figure 7.

Travelling

A series of shots showing progression within the same background scene. Progression in time is thereby matched by spatial progression.

This glossary is by no means exhaustive, and a glance at any dictionary of literature or cinema, or indeed at many of the general French works on the bande dessinée cited in the bibliography, will provide further terms and examples of their usages. Nonetheless the terms given here are those that form the skeleton of BD criticism and in themselves they go a long way to telling us how a BD works.

Is that all that needs to be said then? Not quite. Most of the terms outlined here have a direct English equivalent, or in some cases are taken from English, so one might ask to what extent the discussion really centres on the bande dessinée rather than on the graphic novels of any other cultural tradition. The answer will lie not so much in the terms themselves, but their application. To see how a bande dessinée works, to make the abstractions a little bit more concrete, let us apply the above terminology to a mainstay of the BD, a *planche* taken from *Astérix gladiateur* [Astérix the Gladiator].

Astérix gladiateur: How a BD Works

The *planche* (Fig. 4) is that of page 38 of *Astérix gladiateur*, the fourth in the *série*. The album first appeared in 1964 (Neuilly-sur-Seine: Dargaud), with the story having initially run from March 1962 in the journal *Pilote*. Our *planche* provided the back cover to issue 158 of 1 November 1962. As the work is clearly part of a *série*, we adjust our expectations accordingly: we ask not who are the heroes and what shall be the final outcome, but how they will arrive there. The *Astérix* series can be further divided into two types of adventures, 'home' and 'away'. As this is an 'away' adventure – Astérix and Obélix are in Rome having enlisted as gladiators in order to save the captured bard Assurancetourix – our interest lies in the portrayal of the place visited and the anachronisms thereby associated, and the way in which the Gauls will overcome the local obstacles they encounter.

This *planche* sets the scene for the gladiatorial show in which Astérix and Obélix will take part. Whilst forming part of a clearly pre-scripted story, it also stands as a separate entity from the preceding *planches* – a gaol scene – and those that follow: the chariot race and arrival of the lions. As such it bears witness to the original format of journal publication, whereby one *planche* would appear each week on the back cover of *Pilote*, and would, to a certain extent, have to be self-contained.

The first *case* covers the whole *bande* and thus provides a scene-setting *plan général*. Most of the *case* is divided horizontally, with the top two-thirds providing the stability and immensity of the coliseum architecture – identified by the text in the top left – and the bottom third the movement and diversity of the crowd. This is emphasised by a wide range of colours and a number of incidental details, essentially the cries of the stadium traders whose words – 'chauchiches chèches arvernes', for example – provide textual humour by anachronistic reference to modern stadium events, in this case the sale of snacks.

This *case*, like the central square *case* below it, is to be savoured for both its visual and textual details, which can be viewed and re-viewed, read and re-read, and as such it provides a hybrid moment of reflection that has no direct equivalent in literature or cinema. One such detail, the soap-powder seller, is given prominence both visually and textually. Textually, his *bulle* is larger and thus louder than that of the other tradesman, a fact reinforced by the use of bold *lettrage*.

Visually his wagon spans all of the *case*'s horizontal sections and is further brought to our attention by its bright purple colouring. It is the colour that forms the basis of the anachronistic joke, namely soap products that normally associate purity with the colour white here use purple as their standard by reference to the toga of Roman nobility. The joke is a reference to modern advertising techniques, and reminds us of Roland Barthes's 'Saponides et détergents' [Soaps and Detergents], the eighth chapter of *Mythologies*, published seven years earlier in 1957 (more on *Mythologies* in Chapter 8 of this book).

The central square case provides the next layer of scene setting, now inside the stadium. Whereas the elongated first *case* portrayed the movement from right to left as the spectators entered the building, the square case, in contrast, implies stability: all are now seated. Time has elapsed between the moment when the crowds flock in and the full house awaits the arrival of Caesar, and in terms of space the scene has shifted from outside to within the stadium. This movement in time and space is represented by the *blancs intericoniques* and here, as in the *Astérix* series in general, there is little ambiguity sewn into such events between the *cases*.

The shape of the *case* also frames the central podium, with the magnitude of the former reflecting that of the latter. The use of heavy *lettrage* ('Vive César' [Long live Caesar], 'César avec nous' [Caesar's one of us]) and the absence of surrounding *bulles* portray the effect of the crowd's vociferous enthusiasm. Textual humour is provided by the clichéd inscription 'Panem et Circenses' [Bread and Circuses], with the incidental details, such as the minuscule sweeper accomplishing his pointless task, as the source of visual amusement. The flashes of bright colour in the podium's red and purple awnings draw our attention to Caesar, whom they envelop, and who will be the subject of the next *cases*.

The third and fourth *cases* of the *planche* break with tradition in that they are to be read from top to bottom rather than from the traditional left to right. As such the downward reading matches the downward motion of Caesar's hand. The two *cases* provide virtually the same background décor, with the shift in Caesar's stance being the main element of change. Although there is no *travelling* as such since the 'camera viewpoint' remains static, these *cases*, by their closeness to each other, can be compared to two frames of a motion picture. In both *cases* the viewing angle is that of a *contre plongée*, thereby giving appropriate authority to Caesar.

Frames four and five of this *planche* give an interesting example of crossover between omniscient narrator and characters in a way that interacts text and image. The *récitatif* at the top left of the third *case* informs the reader that 'Tout le monde applaudit le dictateur' [Everyone applauds the dictator], an observation that is supported by the *onamatopée* ('Clap! Clap!') but blatantly contradicted by the image of Brutus slumped in his chair. Caesar's remark in the following *case* – 'Tu quoque fili' [You too, my son] – is therefore a follow-up to the narrator's statement. This in turn is reappropriated by the narrator in the form of the translation, one that plays upon the intertextuality of the quotation. This intertextuality is made explicit by the *récitatif* of the following *case*, by which time the image has reacted accordingly with Brutus now applauding fanatically. The humour functions therefore through the layering of enunciation and the interaction between textual narrator, image-based progression and external cultural reference.

The final *bande* of the *planche* is closest to that of the traditional 4x3 set-up, a 'return to normality' that underlines the divergences of the previous *cases*. It also signals the switch from scene setting to narrative as the games begin.

The bottom-left *case* gives an example of the *bulle* being used for thought rather than speech, as indicated by the smaller bubbles. The foray into the character's mind provides information normally associated with an omniscient narration and authorial intervention rather than the third-person viewpoint to which image-based forms are generally tied. The use of red colouring for Brutus's face creates a light-hearted visual metaphor for embarrassment.

The final frames show a shift from a *plan moyen*, showing the characters full-length in their social surroundings, to a *plan rapproché*, allowing us to concentrate on the specifics of the conversation. The *plan rapproché* takes the emphasis away from the external scene – the arena – to the internal dilemma that will be presented by their speech: the show had better be good or Caius Obtus will be part of it! This *case* does not present key concepts or authorial (via the characters) philosophy as would often be the case with the *gros plan*, but it does allow for a moment of verbal as opposed to visual humour, whilst also forming and underlining the tough characterisation of Caesar, one of the work's central figures. The panning out in the next *case* prepares us for wider scenes and the action they will portray, but the end-marker of the *planche* is textual: 'Que les jeux commencent' [Let the games begin].

This is undoubtedly a mainstream bande dessinée, one enjoyed by millions who for the most part would not stop to consider the techniques by which Goscinny and Uderzo achieve their effects. Nonetheless this brief examination of a seemingly ordinary *planche* shows how the authors play upon a variety in *case* size and shape, colours for emphasis, usage of different 'camera angles', and an interplay between text and image and intertext. Even the casual reader will recognise the technical sophistication of this BD, but the artistry is subtle, and it is only with an awareness of the workings of the genre that we are able to pinpoint precisely why and how the authors direct the reader.

One could still contend that the tools of this analysis are not specifically French and that the same sort of close reading could equally well be applied to *Asterix the Gladiator*, or indeed to a transatlantic superhero light years from 50 BC. A glance at Scott McCloud's *Understanding Comics* might support this view:[13] McCloud provides, in comic book form, an overview of the techniques used for the creation and reception of the medium, drawing upon examples from world traditions – although largely American – as he goes.

As stated in my Introduction, McCloud's work, and other general studies that refer to the world tradition of comics, will of course be useful to the student of the BD, a fact attested by the success of the French translation.[14] But what matters here is that although the definitions need not be specifically francophone, the traditions to which we apply them are, and the importance they then assume is in proportion to these traditions. Just as a French reader might not catch McCloud's reference to Marshall McLuhan's *Understanding Media*, for an English-language reader, perhaps less familiar with Barthes's *Mythologies*, the interplay between colour and language in the opening *case* of our Astérix *planche* does not reach its full effect.

The technicalities of the bande dessinée reach full pertinence in the light of the text and image traditions that form the backcloth, and it is this backcloth that is specifically French. The development of the bande dessinée in the 1960s to 1980s to a self-aware form trampling its own limitations matched the challenges that the *Nouveau Roman* had offered to traditional prose writing. Similarly, the use of the image in the latter half of twentieth-century France was unavoidably conditioned by the influence of *Nouvelle Vague* cinema. Fuller consideration of these influences will lead us towards answering our initial question: what is a BD?

Notes

1. The edition consulted is that of 1994 (Paris: Robert).
2. (Paris: Centre de Recherches de la Bonne Presse, 1958).
3. For a fuller discussion of the early stages of BD criticism and of the BD's path towards becoming a known term recognised in dictionary usage, see my 'BD Theory before the Term "BD" Existed', in *The Francophone Bande Dessinée*, ed. Charles Forsdick, Laurence Grove and Libbie [Elizabeth] McQuillan (Amsterdam: Rodopi: 2005), pp. 39–49. The subject will also be discussed in Chapter 9 on the consecration of the Ninth Art.
4. Peeters and Schuiten in particular will be discussed further in Chapter 7 on contemporary BD.
5. The importance of this work, originally published in Paris by the Presses Universitaires de France, can be seen in the fact that it is one of the few theoretical works on bande dessinée to have been translated into English. The University Press of Mississippi, based in Jackson, published Bart Beaty's translation, under the title of *The System of Comics*, in 2007.
6. On this question see my *Text/Image Mosaics in French Culture: Emblems and Comic Strips* (Aldershot: Ashgate, 2005).
7. See the 'Novel Novel?' section of the next chapter for further mention and analysis of these works.

8. For discussion of these and numerous other examples (although most are not taken from the French tradition), see Thierry Groensteen's two-part 'Histoire de la bande dessinée muette' [History of Silent Bande Dessinée] in *9e Art 2* (January 1997), 60–75 and 3 (January 1998), 92–105.
9. These definitions are to be found in the following works: Benoît Peeters, *Case, planche, récit: Comment lire une bande dessinée* (Tournai: Casterman, 1991; updated versions in 1998 and 2002); Henri Filippini, Jacques Glénat, Numa Sadoul and Yves Varende, *Histoire de la bande dessinée en France et en Belgique des origines à nos jours* [The History of the Bande Dessinée in France and in Belgium from its Beginnings to Today] (Grenoble: Glénat, 1979); Yves Frémion, *Le Guide de la bédé francophone* [Guide to French-language BD] (Paris: Syros, 1990); Harry Morgan, *Principes des littératures dessinées* [Principles of Drawn Literatures] (Angoulême: Éditions de l'An 2, 2003). The following works may also be consulted for definition of 'bande dessinée' (in general not too far from my own): Annie Baron-Carvais, *La Bande dessinée* (Paris: Presses Universitaires de France [Que Sais-je?], 1985; numerous re-editions); Claude Moliterni, Philippe Mellot and Laurent Turpin, *L'ABCdaire de la bande dessinée* [The ABC of Bande Dessinée] (Paris: Flammarion, 2002); Benoît Mouchart, *La Bande dessinée* (Paris: Le Cavalier Bleu [Idées Reçues], 2003); Jean-Louis Tilleuil, Catherine Vanbraband and Pierre Marlet, *Lectures de la bande dessinée: Théorie, méthode, applications, bibliographie* [Bande Dessinée Readings: Theory, Method, Applications, Bibliography] (Louvain-la Neuve: Academia, 1991).
10. On this specific point see once again Peeters, *Case, planche, récit.*
11. Jan Baetens and Pascal Lefèvre in *Pour une lecture moderne de la bande dessinée* [For a Modern Reading of the Bande Dessinée] (Brussels: CBBD, 1993) provide a glossary of terms before exploring the functions of component parts (e.g., text/image interaction, composition, colour, *mise en page*, the book format ...) by drawing upon specific case studies. The work stands as a model for analysing the way in which the constituent elements of the BD come together to create its overall effect.
12. (Paris: Hachette).
13. Scott McCloud, *Understanding Comics: The Invisible Art* (Northampton, MA: Tundra, 1993).
14. Scott McCloud, *L'Art invisible: Comprendre la bande dessinée*, trans. Dominique Petitfaux (Paris: Vertige Graphic, 1999).

CHAPTER 3

FORMAL SPECIFICITY: NOVEL NOVEL OR *NOUVELLE NOUVELLE VAGUE*?

Novel Novel?

To most people a bande dessinée album is first and foremost a book and it is this that defines the tradition to which it belongs: as printed narrative literature the BD is closest to the novel. Historically, further affinities are to be found in that both the BD and the novel grew from forms that were considered to be low-class or second-rate literature, both saw an important period of development in the nineteenth century (although the novel's came a little earlier) often through journal serialisation, and, as stated above, both saw a period in the latter half of the twentieth century during which the basic precepts of the forms were questioned.

Perhaps above all, during the period that led up to the so-called 'Golden Age' of the bande dessinée, the interwar years during which illustrated publications boomed and American superheroes flew into France, many of the works associated with the growth of the BD used a system of consecutive images each with an explanatory prose text beneath the case rather than bulles within the picture. One such example is Caumery and Pinchon's *Bécassine* series (see Fig. 11),[1] the tales of the hapless Breton maid and her comical misunderstandings that appeared from 1905.

At first glance one might suggest that this is no more than an illustrated story, with the prose narrative sufficiently self-contained to render the pictures superfluous. In reality this was not the case, since what assured Bécassine's booming success as compared with the dozens of other prose adventures circulating in children's publications at the time was precisely the coexistence of the visual element, Bécassine's dot-and-line face and the numerous expressions it could nonetheless convey. Bécassine became the first BD character with spin-off products such as dolls, tea sets, games and clothing, a development that resulted from the mark her image (more than her text) had made on France's youth.

As noted above, the closeness between bande dessinée and illustrated novel is still an issue today. The final years of the twentieth century saw a number of traditional prose works transformed into

Figure 11. 'Bécassine mobilisée'. *La Semaine de Suzette.* Year 14 no. 3 (21 February 1918), p. 31.

bande dessinée, from the Gargantuan tales of François Rabelais, to the mysteries of Agatha Christie, and Marcel Proust's A *La Recherche du temps perdu* [In Search of Lost Time]. Slightly different is the question of the illustrated novel, a phenomenon that can be traced as far back as the novel itself. But novels illustrated in distinctive BD style, by recognised BD artists, have provided at least an element of ambiguous overlap between the two genres. One such example is Jacques Tardi's version of Louis-Ferdinand Céline's *Voyage au bout de la nuit* (1988), in which each double page contains between one and four of Tardi's distinctive *croquis*, often taking up the majority, if not all, of the spread. Tardi saw the vivacity of Céline's style as akin to that of a comic strip, and in many ways he recreates the *histoires en images* that dominated the BD tradition at the time Céline was writing.

The launch in 1978 of Casterman's *[À Suivre]*, a journal dedicated to giving more extensive space to BDs than had been the case in previous productions, took a further step towards classifying the bande dessinée as 'traditional' literature. On a purely presentational level chapter divisions were used, thereby giving the BD the physical set-up of the novel. In the publication's first editorial (number 1, February 1978), Jean-Paul Mougin made his aim clear: 'Avec toute sa densité Romanesque, *[À Suivre]* sera l'irruption sauvage de la bande dessinée dans la littérature' [With all its novel-like density, *[À Suivre]* will be the bande dessinée's raw breakthrough into literature].

Just as the bande dessinée has been moving closer to the literary qualities associated with the novel, so an increasingly common phenomenon has been that of novels with elements of graphic art. In Alexandre Jardin's *Le Petit Sauvage* [The Little Savage] (1992), an example of a high-profile popular work and Prix Fémina winner, changes in typographic layout, colouring, and even the inclusion of a bande dessinée sequence have distorted the commonly accepted boundaries of the novel form.

There are therefore both historical and contemporary reasons for viewing the bande dessinée in terms of its relationship to the (non-graphic) novel. But it is also important to keep a firm awareness of the specificity of each form. This is best demonstrated through a precise but representative example, Didier Daeninckx's *Le Der des ders* (1984), a detective thriller set in the period immediately following the First World War. Thirteen years later Daeninckx worked with Jacques Tardi to produce a bande dessinée of the same name (1997).[2]

In *Le Der des ders* what initially appears to be an adultery case turns out to be a political cover-up linked to the slaughter of Russian mutineers in 1917. Although the narrative development is clearly an essential element of the novel, as with the bulk of Daeninckx's work the real interest lies elsewhere. The book includes location-specific descriptions and a patchwork of *fait divers* that build up to form a lively portrait of Paris of the time whilst, in this case, continually evoking the horrors of the previous years. The informality of the first-person *récit*, with its colloquialisms and wordplays, adds the human element that takes the work away from historical description.

Tardi's bande dessinée keeps the central narrative thread whilst leaving pride of place to the distinctive style of his artwork. In a 1996 interview for *Presque tout Tardi* [Almost All of Tardi], a retrospective of his work by Alain Foulet and Olivier Maltret, the artist (he points indeed to his initial vocation as artist) explains that by adapting novels, the pre-existence of the narrative allows him to 'garder [s]es forces pour la mise en scène' [keep his strength for the production] (1996: 100). Indeed in *Le Der des ders* the direct quotes from Daeninckx's work are often those that supply or advance the plot. In such cases, as in page 44 (Fig. 2, Chapter 2), the visual aspect can become secondary, often no more than a close-up of the characters, with the text taking up the majority of certain *cases*. The impression one receives is of the artist expediting the plot before returning to the 'real business' of visual creation.

Some of the key elements of Daeninckx's text are lost with Tardi making no attempt to recreate them. Wordplay, such as a reference to prostitutes who 'se crevaient le cul pour payer le loyer' [bust their arses to pay the rent] (36) or to clients 'tombées dans mes filets' [fallen into my net] on boulevard Poissonnière [literally, 'Fish-seller's Boulevard'], (47) is not reproduced. Similarly, Daeninckx's introduction of *faits divers* that add to the portrait of the time is not always duplicated: one discussion centres on anti-German linguistic changes – 'Eau de Louvain' for 'Eau de Cologne', 'berger d'Alsace' for 'berger allemand' [German sheepdog] etc. – that had been introduced (123–24). Other in-jokes with the modern reader are similarly textually based: a discussion of the unfeasibility of the new concept of one-way streets (102–3) or the irony of the statement, after a car chase, that 'Roissy-en-France n'avait jamais dû connaître une telle circulation' [Roissy-en-France must never have known so much traffic] (112) given the town's aeronautic destiny.

On the other hand, Tardi uses the visual so as to add an extra dimension to the work as a whole. This might be on the level of an image-based pun, such as on page 9 where a poster behind the main character proposes 'Daeninckx dans son repertoire réaliste' [Daeninckx in his true-to-life repertoire] with a portrait of the novelist in the style of Aristide Bruant. More strikingly, it is by juxtaposition of images that Tardi conveys the horrors of the First World War, the main theme of the work. On page 15 of the album we are presented with the scene in which the detective shies away from a Montmartre orgy when haunted by memories of the trenches. Tardi conveys the association by use of parallel *cases*, each elongated with an insert of the character, whereby the respective mounds of flesh evoke the comparison.

Perhaps Tardi's work is most successful in the way the background detail of certain *cases* create the time-and-place atmosphere that is really the book's *raison d'être*. Examples include the Pigalle scene at the bottom of page 44 (see Fig. 2, Chapter 2) or the evocation of the bygone Ceinture railway in the Belleville district of Paris (page 53). In the case of the central *case*, the view is that of Willy Ronis's photograph as published in his *Belleville-Ménilmontant* (1989). For the collection's 1999 re-edition, the photos have been 'completed' with a text by Daeninckx.

There is no doubt that the narrative provides the framework to both versions of *Le Der des ders*, but in Tardi's BD this is surpassed by a series of visual 'asides' or atmospheric *tableaux* whose global impression leave the lasting effect on the reader. In the 1996 interview cited above, Tardi sums up this process when he refers to the use of a pre-existing narrative so that he can concentrate on 'un travail d'horlogerie au niveau de l'utilisation de l'image dans son efficacité' [work that on the level of the most efficient use of the image is as finely tuned as a watch] (100).

The case of *Le Der des ders* is a good example of the way in which a modern bande dessinée version of a previous novel gains its particular effect by using text to underpin the visual and non-narrative, but it is not atypical. Adaptations, such as those cited above, are most successful when they evoke through image and play upon flexibility of *mises en page*, as is also the case in the famous *madeleine* scene of Stéphane Heuet's adaptation of Marcel Proust's *À La Recherche du temps perdu: Combray* [Remembrance of Things Past: Combray] (1998), whereby the memories emanating from the cup of tea stream across the double page. The modern bande dessinée often appears at its strongest when it privileges global images over step-by-step narration. The fact that an individual *planche* of a BD can be static rather than just part of a linear progression permits time for reflection and allows the form to evoke in a way that other adaptations, such as those of the cinema, cannot do.

Many of the tendencies hinted at here – moves towards evocative ambiguity rather than diegetic statement, playful experimentation, construction of meaning by the reader as much as by the author – also underpinned the *Nouveau Roman* movement. Although it is difficult to provide umbrella coverage for a group that never saw itself as such, one can summarise by noting that from the 1950s to the 1970s Alain Robbe-Grillet, Claude Simon and Michel Butor (and others) each adapted different approaches to producing novels that questioned the generally accepted givens of the form. To take the example of Robbe-Grillet's *Le Voyeur* (1955), the work provides no single 'correct' interpretation, with the reader's subjective viewpoint becoming the only key to meaning. Much of our understanding of events – Mathias's act of violence and subsequent attempts to avoid detection – depends on how we view the authorial gap, represented quite literally by a blank page, that occurs at the time of the crime, between parts one and two.

Overlap between the bande dessinée and the *Nouveau Roman* is not necessarily coincidental. Many of the critics who have been involved in the questioning of the status of literature have also shown an interest in comics, although this might be presented as a light-hearted hobby. Umberto Eco is a point in case, when he justifies his intellectual interest in popular culture:

> Ce fut incontestablement un bel acte de libération de n'avoir plus honte de ses preferences et d'affirmer: 'Las Vegas, les *comics*, le jazz me plaisent parce qu'ils me plaisent.'[3]
>
> [It was without doubt a wonderfully liberating act no longer to be ashamed of one's personal preferences and to proclaim: 'I like Las Vegas, comics and jazz because I like them.']

The history of the bande dessinée's twentieth-century development and institutionalisation (a subject that will receive considerable attention later in this book) can be linked to the growth of BD (auto)criticism in the same way, albeit considerably later, that the *Nouveau Roman* and its commentators developed in the tradition of Lewis Carroll, James Joyce and André Gide. It was not just critical discourse following a path away from stability of narrative, but also the direction taken by many of the artists leading the BD forward.

Perhaps the best example in this respect is the work of Moebius, the pen name used by Jean Giraud for his science fiction and futuristic styles, as opposed to the more conventional westerns signed 'Gir'.[4] The *Garage hermétique* series that ran in *Métal Hurlant* [Heavy Metal] from 1976 is typical of the explosive disjunction to which the artist refers in his autobiography, *Moebius Giraud: Histoire de mon double* [Moebius Giraud: The Story of my Two Sides] (1999): 'Mon travail est d'être libre intérieurement, comme une sorte de bombe thermonucléaire en fusion permanente' [My work is to be free internally, like a sort of thermonuclear bomb in permanent fusion.] (158).

The series tells of Major Grubert's construction of his own universe on Fleur, a distant asteroid. Characters he encounters include Jerry Cornelius, a science-fiction creation of Michael Moorlock transposed to the world of Moebius; Barnier, an engineer who will eventually switch gender, and the Bakalites, a race of all-resistant superhumans, as the name implies. The basis of Moebius's style owes much to Hergé's *ligne claire*,[5] an influence he acknowledges in the autobiography, although variations in case size, flamboyant scenery and costumes and the piling on of (seemingly) incidental detail from worlds as different as sci-fi, the western or the Paris métro, take us well beyond Tintin's adventures.

One of the most immediately noticeable features of the *Garage hermétique* series is its lack of linear progression. Moebius himself points to this in his introduction to the 2000 re-edition published by Les Humanoïdes Associés (Paris) in album form:

> 'Le Garage' a commencé comme ça. Dans mon esprit, les deux premières pages n'étaient qu'une plaisanterie graphique, une blague, une mystification qui ne pouvait, ne devait mener à rien, qui n'appelait aucune suite. [...] J'ai dû travailler comme un forcené pendant deux jours, mais n'ayant pas conservé de photocopies des premières pages, j'en ai dessiné deux autres dont la cohérence n'était pas garantie. Toute l'histoire a été plus ou moins réalisé dans cette espèce de panique décousue ... [...] Le 'Garage hermétique' n'est pas une oeuvre fermée. (4–5)
>
> [*The Garage* started like that. In my mind the first two pages were no more than a graphic pleasantry, a joke, a mystification that could not, that should not, have led to anything, that could be taken no further. [...] I had to work like a slave for two days, but as I had not kept any photocopies of the first pages, I drew two more without any guarantee of coherence. The whole story was more or less created in that sort of unbridled panic... [...] *The Hermetic Garage* is not a closed work.]

Within individual *planches* movement can be from left to right, bottom to top or vice versa. Indeed often it is for the reader to interpret (and reinterpret) as he or she sees fit. Such ambiguity is continued on the level of the series as a whole: as we zoom between the different worlds and times, characters come and go, incidental details later play major roles and the introductory plot précis brings in previously unmentioned twists.

As with the novels of Robbe-Grillet, it is to some extent possible, retrospectively, to decipher the work's plot, but it is hard to imagine the narrative sequence being of primary concern to the public of the 1970s serial. The reader who requires a satisfying build-up leading to a denouement in which all loose ends are tied together will be disappointed. The satisfaction of the *Garage hermétique* comes rather from its ambiguity and incoherence despite the fact that its component elements are often recognisable. It is appropriate that the notion of a Moebius strip, a twisted paper that represents the disintegration of conventional sequential movement, should be applied both to Jean Giraud and Alain Robbe-Grillet, as underlined by Alain Goulet in *Le Parcours moebien de l'écriture*: *Le Voyeur* [Writing's Moebian Path: The Voyeur] (Paris: Lettres Modernes, 1982).

Breakdown in conventional narrative marks the work of many leading BD authors of the same period. Of these we have already cited Fred, the pen name of Fred Othon Aristidès, in reference to the 'cat' *planches* from Philémon's *Simbabbad de Batbad* series (Fig. 6, Chapter 2). Although it is composed of individual *cases*, these are superseded by the effect generated by the page as a whole. An initial narrative sequence would take the reader from the top left and the initial appearance of Philemon to his descent on the bottom right towards the cat's mouth; nonetheless at all stages the suspense of a traditional linear reading is undermined by the global reading – the cat in its

Etienne Lécroart, Strips-Acrostiches (lecture de gauche à droite et de haut en bas), 1996. © OuBaPo.

Figure 12. 'Strips-Acrostiches'. Étienne Lécroart. *OuPus 1*. Paris: L'Association, 1997, p. 8.

entirety – that Fred provides. The overall effect is one of narrative ambiguity but visual delight.

A further overlap between the worlds of conventional (or indeed distinctly non-conventional) literature and that of the bande dessinée now exists via the Ouvroir de Bande Dessinée Potentielle [The Workshop for Potential Bande Dessinée], or OuBaPo. Like its model, OuLiPo or Ouvroir de Littérature Potentielle [The Workshop for Potential Literature], whose exponents include Raymond Queneau, Georges Perec and Jacques Roubaud, OuBaPo imposes constraints so as to push the potential of the form to the limits. In Etienne Lécroart's *Strips-Acrostiches*, for example (Fig. 12), the constraint is to create an arrangement of sixteen cases that can be read in eight different ways, in this case ranging from 'existentialisme' to 'blague' [joke] or 'science fiction'. At the time of the major Angoulême OuBaPo exhibition in 2005, four volumes of the group's work had been published, entitled *OuPus 1* to *OuPus 4*.[6]

Whilst accepting that the vast majority of current BDs, like the vast majority of novels, are 'traditional' in format, it seems fitting to conclude our discussion of the overlap between BD and novel with the OuLiPo or *Nouveau Roman*, and not just because it allows for a final note of ambiguity. It was the textual element of the early bande dessinée that underpinned the central narrative requirement, one that has nonetheless faded as the prerequisites of a now established form are increasingly questioned.[7] The BD can stand as a *nouveau Nouveau Roman* in that in its current form it is pushing literary boundaries further, beyond even the one base element, the text, whilst mirroring, by its own historical progress, the experimental developments that the novel has crossed in its postwar development.[8]

Nouvelle Nouvelle Vague?

Given that the bande dessinée is a hybrid narrative form consisting of text and image, a comparison with the novel, the text-based narrative genre, should be countered (or supplemented) by a comparison with the image-based narrative genre of the twentieth century, the cinema. In many ways this latter comparison may seem more appropriate: the bande dessinée takes its title of Ninth Art by reference not to literature but to cinema, the Seventh Art; much of the founding BD criticism played upon the visual aspects of the genre, as in the 1967 exhibition *Bande dessinée et figuration narrative* [Bande dessinée and Narrative Figuration] or the *Cahiers de la Bande Dessinée*, which appeared from 1969 to 1989 and whose title drew upon that of the *Cahiers du Cinéma*; taken literally, a film is no more than a series of celluloid cases which when played at speed create the illusion of movement.

A starting point for the BD/cinema comparison is the use of so-called 'camera angles', points of view within the individual *cases* that achieve the same technical effects as those sought by filmmakers. In the *Astérix* extract studied above we saw how the drawing of César from a low angle allowed Uderzo to give the character dominance befitting his status (Fig. 4, Chapter 2). This use of *contre-plongée* can be compared to the opening sequences of François Truffaut's 1959 *Les Quatre-cents coups*,[9] in which the foreboding teacher is portrayed as such via the low-angle shots, while the camera bears down upon the unfortunate schoolboy Antoine Doinel about to receive his punishment. 'Narrative-eye' camerawork or *plan subjectif* can also transfer to bande dessinée. One of the early scenes of Jean-Luc Godard's *À Bout de souffle* [Breathless] (1960) has the main protagonist Michel (played by Jean-Paul Belmondo) jumping into his car and driving off, with the camera then showing the open road ahead as if we were seeing events from Michel's viewpoint. A similar effect, but to comical purposes, is achieved by Frank Margerin in *Tranches de brie* (1998: 7) in which we take the position of two squabbling children on the back seat, looking forward to the disconcerted parents and onto the open road, although the view is partially blocked by a bobbling toy ballet dancer hanging from the mirror.

Broader switches from a *plan général* to a *plan américain* and then even to a *gros plan* form part of the framework of visual narrative. A *plan général* sets the overall scene, before homing in on specific characters, or, in the case of the *gros plan*, specific features of specific characters, or indeed a close-up that gives prominence to a particularly important dialogue. Such techniques open Jean-Marie Poiré's *Le Père Noël est une ordure* [Father Christmas is Pure Filth] (1982), as the camera projects an aerial shot of the city lights, before concentrating on a single street scene and then the individual character, Gérard Jugnot's Father Christmas. In the final *bande* of our *Astérix* example we saw an example of such usage as the views became wider with the starting of the games, before focusing on individuals. As a general rule, any bande dessinée that needs to 'set the scene' before telling the specifics of the given tale will draw upon virtually the same visual techniques as those used by filmmakers.

But there is still much that separates the images of a BD from those of cinema. A BD is a series of static images with the intermittent narrative 'contained' in the *blancs intericoniques* and although it is possible for a film to use jump-cuts, this will have a deliberately jarring effect. Even the most conventional BD can use its *blancs* to create elements of ambiguity, or humour by suggesting 'off' action, such as excessive violence taking place between the *cases*. As stated previously, the static quality of the BD also means the reader can pause to reflect upon certain images. As a result it is possible to create large 'descriptive' *cases* or single *case planches*, as in the final page of *Tintin au Congo* where the natives are left with the memory of Tintin through the objects that remind them of him, such as the film projector he has left behind, or the iconic statues they have erected.

In such cases the detail is the essence of the creation rather than merely its 'background'.

As well as the technical level, it is also useful to compare BD and cinema on a historical level. If we class Rodolphe Töpffer as a precursor rather than an inventor of bandes dessinées (a subject to be discussed at length in the chapters on the history of the BD), we find that the form as we now know it sees an important stage of development towards the end of the nineteenth century: R.F. Outcault's *Yellow Kid* and other USA imports of the same period are often cited, but image-based magazines such as *Le Rire* [Laughter] were also starting to flourish in France. The same era saw the birth of the moving image, with the Lumière brothers' 'documentary'-style films, including the workers leaving the factory and the train pulling into its station, and Georges Méliès's fantasy creations, the best known of which is his *Voyage dans la Lune* [Journey to the Moon] (1902). The so-called Golden Age of American film, the 1930s and 1940s, corresponds to that of the superhero comic strip, and both had an important influence on their corresponding forms in France. As with literature, postwar cinema saw challenges to conventions, with French productions leading the way.

The *Nouvelle Vague* came into being during the late 1950s, although the title was journalistically attributed and the movement was not self-created, nor did it ever have a manifesto. The work of the leading exponents – François Truffault, Jean-Luc Godard and Alain Resnais – was characterised by low-budget improvisation on the level of script, lighting and location, thereby creating the impression of closeness to 'everyday' reality. Unlike large studio productions, the director took overall control and thus responsibility, a notion summarised by the expression *cinéma d'auteur*. Although the *Nouvelle Vague* by no means ousted blockbuster productions, it did make the general public aware of alternative possibilities, and, above all, made it clear that cinema could function as an art form and not just as a commercial enterprise.

It is in the push for artistic acceptance that BD productions take on the precepts of the *Nouvelle Vague*. This entails a time gap given that, as stated, the BD did not emerge as a self-aware form until the 1960s to 1970s, almost a generation on from the emergence of New Wave cinema. Furthermore, it was not really until the 1980s and 1990s that a number of independent movements such as Ego Comme X, Éditions Amok or L'Association came to the fore in artistic terms. To take this latter example, L'Association was founded in 1991 by Jean-Christophe Menu and Lewis Trondheim after they had met four years earlier at the prestigious *Bande dessinée, récit et modernité* conference at Cerisy-la-Salle in Normandy.

L'Association provided an outlet for independent artists, initially publishing the journal *Lapin* [Rabbit] and albums on small print runs. In the first (January 1992) issue of *Lapin*, for example, four pages by

David B observing a typical day in the rue des Rosiers (the centre of Paris's Jewish quarter) and an autobiographical piece by Menu recounting a Scandinavian excursion accompany works by Blutch, Killoffer, Duffour, Lewis Trondheim, Fabio, Mattt Konture and Stanislas, all up-and-coming taboo-breaking artists.

It was from 1991 that L'Association put out its first books, Menu's preferred term as he sees 'album' as linked rather to 'bédé' and indicative of the pejorative aspects of mainstream publishing. In *OuPus 1* Menu summarises this attitude:[10]

> Jamais le fossé entre 'BD' apparente, presque toujours standardisée, stéréotypée et supermarchiée, et la bande dessinée souterraine, souvent créative, intelligente et fertile, ne s'était autant creusé. (9)
>
> [Never has the divide between high-visibility 'BD', that is almost always standardised, stereotyped and made for supermarkets, and underground bande dessinée, that is often creative, intelligent and fertile, been so deep.]

L'Association has since published seven distinct collections, as will be discussed further in the chapter on Contemporary BD. The collections are disparate, but linked through themes of introspection, or simply as works that challenge expectations. We have already highlighted certain parallels between one of L'Association's outputs, the publications of OuBaPo, and modern trends in the novel. In many ways the link between L'Association (and publishers like it) and New Wave tendencies in cinema is even more flagrant: the promotion of an independent BD *d'auteur*; limited budget productions; an everyday subject matter intended to provoke reflection on the nature of our existence rather than escapism (see Fig. 10, Chapter 2); and a certain international perception as the flag bearer of cutting-edge productions that underline the new medium's blossoming potential.[11]

The comparison between BD and cinema also operates on the level of transfer between individual works in much the same way that we find an increasing number of BDs adapting novels.[12] With cinema, however, the process tends to function in the opposite direction: a successful BD or comic, from *Superman* and *Batman* to *Barbarella*, is taken over by the film producers. More generally, the overall movement – novel to BD, BD to cinema – with its shift towards the visual, can be seen as a microcosm of the current direction of Western culture.

Film adaptations of bandes dessinées should be distinguished from *dessins animés* or cartoons, a cultural entity in their own right and a subject worthy of a full-length study, although none currently exists in English. Sylvain Chomet's 2003 *Triplettes de Belleville* [Belleville Rendezvous] provides the variety of locations, action adventures and character intrigue we might associate with numerous mainstream cinema productions, whilst adding a fluid whimsical touch through the striking pastel artwork. This creation is very different from the *dessin animé* adaptations of *Tintin* or *Astérix* adventures, of which just a few examples are the 1969 *Tintin et le Temple du Soleil* [Tintin and the Temple of the Sun], *Astérix le gaulois* [Asterix the Gaul] of 1967, *Astérix et Cléopâtre* (1968) and *Astérix chez les Bretons* [Asterix in Britain] of 1986. These tend blandly to follow the plot of the BD, often losing much of the subtlety of the original – effects of case size variations, imaginative *bulles*, use of the *blancs intericoniques* – without always emphasising the additional possibilities of the moving image form.

But not all cinema adaptations are uniquely concerned with transferring a successful BD synopsis to the large screen and, by implication, to a larger audience. In some cases, such as *Tintin et le mystère de la Toison d'Or* [Tintin and the Mystery of the Golden Fleece] (1960, directed by André Barret and Jean-Jacques Vierne) and *Tintin et les oranges bleues* [Tintin and the Blue Oranges] (1964, directed by Philippe Condroyer), it is the spirit of the Tintin adventures that was to be reproduced, with the plots themselves a unique creation without previous album equivalents. The use of actors rather than cartoons was reminiscent of the early Tintin events staged by *Le Petit Vingtième* [The Pocket Twentieth Century], such as the arrival of Tintin, played by a local Brussels schoolboy, at the Brussels Nord station following the success of the 1929 album, *Tintin au pays des Soviets* [Tintin in the Land of the Soviets]. In other cases, such as Alain Resnais's *I Want to Go Home* (1989), the BD influence is more latent, recreating the style of the bande dessinée in general, with jumps into fantasy worlds, 'thought bubble' sequences and general references to the culture of comics from both sides of the Atlantic.

At the time of writing, the most high-profile and indeed successful BD-based film is Alain Chabat's 2002 *Astérix et Obélix: Mission Cléopâtre,* whose entry figures in excess of 14 million put it second only to the comedy wartime epic *La Grande Vadrouille* (1966).[13] Starring Gérard Depardieu and Christian Clavier, *Mission Cléopâtre* is effectively the sequel to *Astérix et Obélix contre César* [Asterix and Obelix against Caesar] (1999, directed by Claude Zidi), which stuck closely to the plot of the first Goscinny and Uderzo album, and, for that reason, was considerably less effective. The strength of *Mission Cléopâtre* lies in the use it makes of the specificity of cinema: fast dance sequences are intermingled with special effects and visual references to pillars of the cinema tradition such as *Star Wars*. As with the first film, the viewer enjoys the familiarity of star recognition, and here Depardieu and Clavier are joined by a further host of household names (Jamel Debbouze, Monica Bellucci, Gérard Darmon, Edouard Baer etc.). The film takes the base elements from the 1965 album *Astérix et Cléopâtre*, but updates it with references to mobile phones, the thirty-five-hour working week and popular songs.

Certain of the original BD references are dropped from the film. The use of hieroglyphs to represent the Egyptians' speech (and perhaps a reference to the notion of 'phylactères') cannot be reproduced, and the leitmotif reference to Pascal's *pensée* regarding Cleopatra's nose is played down. Above all, the front cover, and to a certain extent the album as a whole, is effectively a pastiche of the 1963 Elizabeth Taylor and Richard Burton blockbuster, *Cleopatra* (directed by Joseph Mankiewicz), which by 2002 would no longer have been a familiar reference. The process has therefore come full circle as a film updates a BD that originally updated a film.

In both of these cases, the novel and the cinema, iconoclastic movements have shaped French (and, to a certain extent, world) culture from the latter part of the twentieth century. The *Nouveau Roman* has added the notion of visuality to the text by emphasising the *non-dit* and the work of the reader's imagination in creating the final effects. In the case of the *Nouvelle Vague*, much of the impetus behind the creation of a *cinéma d'auteur* was to give film the type of artistic recognition accorded to the written text. It is not surprising that the newly self-aware bande dessinée should follow in the footsteps of both of these movements, perhaps as the text and image form that could provide completeness where previous creations had gaps.

It would of course be possible to provide further examples of bandes dessinées that draw upon the tradition of the novel, that function through cinema techniques, or both. The exact relationship between the forms, if broached fully, could give rise to many an article or chapter, and indeed has already done so, at least in French and with respect to the cinema.[14] In the present context it is enough to be aware of the questions and possibilities, and now hopefully to realise, in the light of this first section of the book, that what may appear to be a simple comic strip in French in fact draws upon a multitude of technical devices and fits firmly within the broader cross-Channel cultural framework.

Before being attributed to the bande dessinée, the appellation of Ninth Art was briefly applied to that of French gastronomy.[15] Although one might compare the concepts behind *Nouvelle Cuisine* with those of the *Nouveau Roman* or the *Nouvelle Vague* (a discussion that takes us well beyond our subject in hand), it is significant that French cooking has become a way of life recognised for its quality worldwide, whereas the bande dessinée aspires to artistic status but is less often tasted beyond its place of creation. In the hope of redressing Anglo-Saxon taste buds, and having whetted our palate with the BD's functional context, it is time to explore the historical development within which such techniques ripened, as we enter the main course of this mixed-media feast …

Notes

1. Caumery was the pen name of scriptwriter Maurice Languereau. The full name of the artist was Émile-Joseph Porphyre Pinchon.
2. The following analysis draws upon Chapter 12 (pp. 138–51, in particular 146–48) of my *Text/Image Mosaics in French Culture: Emblems and Comic Strips* (Aldershot: Ashgate, 2005). *Text/Image Mosaics* includes reproductions of pages 15, 44 and 53 of the Daeninckx/Tardi *Le Der des ders*. For an introductory overview and analysis of *Le Der des ders*, see also Allen Douglas and Fedwa Malti-Douglas, 'Tardi and Daeninckx: Comic Strips, Detective Novels and World War I,' *International Journal of Comic Art* 5.1 (2003), 134–46. The novel is available in English as *A Very Profitable War*, trans. Sarah Martin (London: Serpent's Tale, 1994).
3. On pp. 31–32 of 'Entretien avec Umberto Eco' [Interview with Umberto Eco] that forms the first section (pp. 8–33) of Henri Tissot, *Le Mouvement pop* (Lausanne: Éditions Grammont, 1975).
4. Again, much of the analysis that follows is taken from my *Text/Image Mosaics in French Culture: Emblems and Comic Strips* (see footnote 2 above), which includes illustrations of *Le Garage hermétique*. See also Matthew Screech, 'Jean Giraud/Moebius: *Nouveau Réalisme* and Science Fiction', *The Francophone Bande Dessinée*, ed. Charles Forsdick, Laurence Grove and Libbie [Elizabeth] McQuillan (Amsterdam: Rodopi, 2005), pp. 97–113.
5. The *ligne claire* or clear line style will be discussed further in the chapter on the BD's twentieth-century history.
6. The Lécroart example features on page 8 of *OuPus 1* (Paris: L'Association, 1997). It should be noted, however, that an American predecessor, *Eight Comics in One*, had been created by Ed Subitzky for *National Lampoon Magazine* in 1977. For further examples, related bibliography and analysis of the various constraints imposed by OuBaPo on its members, see my chapter on Contemporary BD.
7. Here, therefore, I would agree with Groensteen when he underlines the importance of the visual to the modern BD (see *Système de la bande dessinée*, p. 10). I would still maintain, however, that despite its development towards the visual and away from the textual, the bande dessinée remains a hybrid creation. Once the text becomes entirely redundant, as Groensteen seems to suggest, the bande dessinée will have evolved into something else.
8. A further example of BD/*Nouveau Roman* overlap will be explored as a case study in my chapter 'Cultural Studies and Beyond', where I analyse the narrative experimentation of André Juillard, an artist who acknowledges the influence of Alain Robbe-Grillet.
9. The translation given traditionally, *The 400 Blows*, does not convey the sense of the original title, which is nearer to 'to sow one's wild oats'.
10. Menu's article, 'Ouvre-Boîte-Po' (pp. 9–12), is part of the preliminary literature. The title is a play on 'ouvre-boîte', a tin-opener.
11. For a general overview and analysis of independent BD of this type, see Bart Beaty, *Unpopular Culture: Transforming the European Comic Book in the 1990s* (Toronto: University of Toronto Press, 2007). The first chapter (pp. 17–43) in particular concentrates on the work of L'Association. As stated, its output and influence will be discussed further in our chapter on contemporary BD.
12. For a listing of cinema productions based closely on comics of all national traditions, see 'Bande dessinée et cinéma,' pages 1585–695 of Claude Moliterni, Philippe Mellot, Laurent Turpin, Michel Denni and Nathalie Michel-Szelechowska, *BDGuide 2005: Encyclopédie de la bande dessinée internationale* (Paris: Omnibus, 2004).

13. This could be beaten by the 2008 *Astérix aux Jeux Olympiques* (directed by Frédéric Forestier and Thomas Langmann), which is now the most expensive European production to date. However, critical reception has been less than enthusiastic, and final entry figures may well not reflect the extra expenditure. *La Grande Vadrouille* was released in English with the title *Don't Look Now ... We're Being Shot At!* Literally the title means 'The Great Stroll'.
14. See, for example, Jean-Pierre Tibéri, *La Bande dessinée et le cinéma* (Izy: Regards, 1981), as well as the special issues of *Cinéma 71* (159, September 1971), *Cinématographe* (21, October 1976) and *Cinémaction* (no number, summer 1990) dedicated to the subject of cinema and BD.
15. The first issue of *La Gastronomie: Neuvième Art*, for example, appeared in 1952, and was often concerned with literary, artistic and social connections that could be made with the subject of cuisine. More practically orientated was *Le 9eme Art Français: La Revue de l'Élite Culinaire*, the journal of the 'Grand Prix de la Patisserie Française', whose first issue was in June 1954. It should be noted that song has also laid claim to the title: see, for example, Angèle Guller, *Le 9e Art: Pour une connaissance de la chanson française contemporaine (de 1945 à nos jours)* [The 9th Art: Towards an Understanding of French Contemporary Song (from 1945 to the Current Day)] (Brussels: Vokaer, 1978).

Part II

THE CHRONOLOGICAL APPROACH

CHAPTER 4

PRE-HISTORY: FROM BAYEUX'S TAPESTRY TO TÖPFFER'S TEACHINGS

The Notion of a Pre-History to BD

Having opened the previous part of this book by stating that the term 'bande dessinée' did not come into use before the 1950s, it may seem strange to follow with a chapter whose subtitle suggests it will begin with an eleventh-century strip. Taking our definition of bande dessinée as a 'French-language mixture of images and written text that together form a narrative' it is, as we have suggested, possible to include such disparate cases as illuminated medieval manuscripts, early illustrated printed books and pre-Revolution engravings. Chronologically, critics have gone as far back as the cave drawings in Lascaux, although it is difficult to attribute a narrative to these with certainty, and they cannot be classed as 'French-language'.

Notwithstanding such reservations, numerous are the critics – particularly, but not exclusively, from the 1970s and 1980s – who begin their works with a history of the BD that they take back to the Middle Ages and beyond: the catalogue to the first high-profile bande dessinée exhibition, *Bande dessinée et figuration narrative* (1967),[1] does precisely this, as did the *Origines et avenirs de la bande dessinée* [Origins and Future Paths of the Bande Dessinée] exhibition that was held during the 2005 Angoulême festival. Interlude examples include Gérard Blanchard's 1969 *La Bande dessinée: Histoire des histoires en images de la préhistoire à nos jours* [The Bande Dessinée: The Story of Stories in Pictures from Prehistory to Today],[2] Francis Lacassin's seminal *Pour un 9ème Art: La Bande dessinée* [For a Ninth Art: The Bande Dessinée] of 1971,[3] J.-B. Renard's *Clefs pour la bande dessinée* [Keys to the Bande Dessinée] (1978),[4] Annie Baron-Carvais's 'Que Sais-Je?' volume of 1985 and Thierry Groensteen's 1996 work for 'Les

Essentiels Milan',[5] to name but an important handful, all of which refer to forms from over a thousand years ago. The inclusion of these references says as much about the twentieth-century development of the BD as it does about the form's medieval antecedents: the need to justify and valorise the bande dessinée by association with a legitimate history of culturally acceptable forms is part of its own intellectual coming of age.

The works mentioned above, and the numerous others in a similar vein, tend to imply a linear development that has resulted in the bande dessinée as we know it today. Illuminated manuscripts led to illustrated printed books, which led to illustrated journals and then to the children's publications that nurtured the modern BD. In so much as it is impossible to put a definitive starting date to the bande dessinée or claim it has a single inventor – we will come to discuss the flaws in the critical attempts to attribute this accolade to Rodolphe Töpffer – this system has a certain logic. The bande dessinée must have come from somewhere and each stage of its development results from earlier influences.

Nonetheless, at many stages along the chain it is difficult to pinpoint a direct cause-and-effect link. It is perhaps more useful to think in terms of parallel mentalities, an overriding way of viewing the world that puts text and image together. David Kunzle in *The Early Comic Strip* outlines many of the forms,[6] from lives of saints in incunabula to Jacques Callot's pictorial account of the miseries of war and William Hogarth's narrative engravings, that have created a storyline through a mixing of the visual and the textual. Although Kunzle divides his work into very broad chronological categories there is no sense of sequential movement, of one form leading to the next, until we finally reach Mickey Mouse.

The aim of this chapter is to provide an overview of the types of text/image forms that have been and are still an intrinsic part of France's cultural make-up. Although, like Kunzle, we will follow a scheme that is vaguely chronological, starting with some of the earliest illuminated works, there will be no attempt to create a BD timeline. The pre-history of the BD is precisely that, a pre-history: we are not examining examples of the bande dessinée as we know it, but rather trying to grasp a tradition of text/image forms, one that is easier to outline than to explain, but a tradition that is arguably of the same mindset that now expresses itself through *Tintin*, *Astérix* and the other wonders of the Ninth Art.[7]

Early Illuminations

Text/image forms are to be found throughout the various manifestations of Western art from earliest times onwards, but to catalogue these exhaustively would be impossible: we depend on the few artefacts that the past has handed down to us, often with little

Figure 13. 'Textual Archway'. *Codex medicinalis*. Late eighth or early ninth century. Fols 23v–24r. Glasgow University Library MS Hunter 96 (T.4.13).

information on provenance or intended usage. If we go back more than a thousand years it also makes more sense to talk in terms of a Western tradition rather than specific national forms: Latin still conveyed the culture of Europe and the countries as we know them now were not yet defined.

Notwithstanding such caveats, a specific example can at least provide some awareness of the way in which early texts had a visual base. Glasgow University Library MS Hunter 96 (T.4.13) is a late eighth- or early ninth-century collection of medical writings produced in what is now southern France or possibly northern Italy. Written in a pre-Carolingian script, it includes an extensive list of drugs and plants and an overview of various medical conditions and how to treat them. Although, in theory at least, a text is no more than a symbolic system, a way of representing communication that has no innate value in itself – it might be compared to modern banknotes in this respect – already we can see that this is not the case in practice and that a layer of its value comes not only from its semantic meaning, but rather from its visual *éclat*.

Folios 23v and 24r, for example (Fig. 13), announce the start of a new section through visual brilliance. Folio 23v is a double archway, perhaps a representation of the new beginning facing the reader, embellished in a careful red, green and white crossover pattern. The facing folio lends physical importance to the text by making the opening letters larger and, here also, drawing attention through the use of red and green colour patterns.[8] From the very beginnings of the tradition of Western text, therefore, we find the text itself is manipulated so as to create meaning through physical appearance, thereby ensuring that the visual plays a central role.

The visualising of the textual comes to be expressed directly through the phenomenon of illuminated initials. To take the early example of a set of Anselm's treatises created (probably) in Flanders in the mid-twelfth century (Glasgow University Library MS Hunter 244 [U.4.2]), we find an initial 'S' taking on the form of a lion (fol. 2v), a 'G' is represented through two intertwined dragons (fol. 71v) and an 'A' takes the form of several dogs acrobatically forming a pyramid (fol. 82v). There seems to be little correlation between these beasts and the treatises themselves, but the Romanesque delight in the visual is already overpowering what should be the basis of this document, the words of the text.

A Parisian example from a century later, a Vulgate Bible probably produced by the Mathurin workshop (Glasgow University Library MS Hunter 338 [U.8.6]), displays equal visual exuberance in the creation of pictorial initials. The letter 'L' on folio 457r runs the length of the column, immediately drawing the reader's attention to the section of which it signals the beginning. The elongated back of the 'L' is decorated in pink, blue and green-crossover, with the tail of a fantastic winged creature leading us to the seat of the letter, wherein we see Matthew the Evangelist working at a book. Not only does the visual dominate, as throughout this carefully crafted illuminated manuscript, but here we also get a sense of a process of text/image interaction: the image of Matthew relates to the text as a whole, and the book he holds refers us to the actual word – 'Liber' [Book] – of which the illumination is the first letter.

The figurative scenes to be found largely in illuminated letters were to expand to occupying large panels, often centrally positioned at strategic points in the book. Glasgow University Library MS Hunter 373 (V.1.10), a *Vie de Cesar* [Life of Caesar] from late fourteenth-century Paris, opens not only with a delicate blue and gold decorated letter 'C' but also a central frame showing Caesar – dressed in fourteenth-century garb! – surrounded by his courtiers and warriors. The overall visual presence is enhanced by the ivy-leaf pattern that fills the margin and, in many cases, an elaborate binding of hardwood, velvet and brass bolts and decorative studs (often the original binding has been lost, but one such example survives in MS Hunter 385 [V.2.5], an early fifteenth-century version of a Gaston de Foix text). The book was more than a vessel for communicative text; it had become an art object per se whereby the overall effect was a visual and textual experience.

In such cases the visual 'attention grabbers' might be limited to the binding and the initial page, or pages, of particular importance. As productions became more luxurious, these images were to become more frequent, more detailed, and an increasingly central part of the overall production. In the 1467 French version of Giovanni

Figure 14. 'Manutius and Phocinus'. Giovanni Boccaccio. *De Casibus virorum illustrium*. 1467. Fol. 104v. Glasgow University Library MS Hunter 372 (V.1.9).

Boccaccio's *De Casibus virorum illustrium* [The Fall of Princes] (Glasgow University Library MS Hunter 371–372 [V.1.8–9]), as well as the detailed gold and blue initial letters and use of red lettering for important summary sections, the illustrated headers to each of the work's books, as in the elaborate Wheel of Fortune of volume 1 folio 1r or the story of Manutius and Phocinus of volume 2 folio 104v (Fig. 14), have reached a further level of sophistication: characters from the story – in this case Boccaccio himself addressing the protagonists – are carefully modelled with individual features; background details such as the books on the table or the contours of the hills amidst the trees bring the images to life; and the margin foliage boasts a variety of flowers that go right up to the border of the vellum.

It is an art that by this time is becoming almost formulaic. Other manuscripts, such as the *Chroniques de Saint-Denis* (Glasgow University Library MS Hunter 203 [U.1.7], third quarter of the fifteenth century), use exactly the same layout for 'star' pages. Folio 7r, a view of fortified Paris, has the main image in a boxed area with curved upper boarder, two columns of text and a foliage motif that goes to the edge of the page.

As well as the layout, the images themselves were also to become formulaic, with artists of stock scenes, particularly religious ones, able to follow pre-set models available in the producing workshop. The resulting ease (comparative at least) of production led to further proliferation of pictures and emphasis upon the non-textual elements of what a priori were textual works. A Book of Hours, for example, is a compendium of devotional texts for private use, often to be kept on the owner's person for consultation at specific hours of the day. In the case of the *c.*1460 Flanders volume that is now Glasgow University Library MS Euing 4, we can imagine the owner being enchanted by the scenes from the life of the virgin, such as the birth of Jesus, which would greet him or her when turning to the appropriate prayer. Here also the text would be rendered more attractive by the careful blue and gold illuminated initials and the exquisitely patterned line-fillers.

What becomes apparent, therefore, from this snapshot of early Western, or indeed French, culture, is an interaction with the image that increasingly takes the text beyond its literal representative value to create an overall effect, an attractiveness that makes of the book an object of delight, this delight being dependent on visual elements. The visual enhancement can come as a result of non-referential decorative elements, or through pictures directly related to the text. In terms of the modern bande dessinée, such works are no more than a part of the general culture of the image that will go on to include illustrated works of all kinds, but it is important to note that this culture of the image within the domain of the text exists from the earliest times.

In the discussion thus far I have made no mention of the notion of image-based narrative, a concept central to the modern BD, but just a few examples, again taken from the collections of Glasgow

University Library, can give an indication that the visual mindset of the pre-print era included the notion of storytelling through pictures. On the simplest of levels, illuminated illustrations, whether in initial letters or as larger chapter headings, might include 'before and after' scenes. In the above-mentioned 1467 *De Casibus virorum illustrium*, in parts a pseudo-historical anthology of grisly stories, the depiction on folio 104v of the second volume is divided into two sections (Fig. 14). As stated, the upper section shows Boccaccio – as one might expect he is a central figure throughout the illuminations as the work unfolds – addressing Manutius and his followers. The lower panel effectively tells the story as we see the subsequent murder of Manutius and his entourage by Phocinus.

The *Cent nouvelles nouvelles* [The Hundred New Stories] in its unique manuscript form, MS Hunter 252 (U.4.10), has one hundred miniatures, thereby providing an illustration for each *nouvelle*. As well as giving a detailed portrait of (often intimate) domestic life in late fifteenth-century provincial France – we have scenes of musicians, soldiers, churchmen, sailors, animals and of course lovers – the artist also manages to create a feeling for the narrative within the individual pictures. To take the example of the eighty-second illustration (folio 172v), analysed by Alison Adams in her 1992 *French Studies* article on MS Hunter 252,[9] we see a finely composed pastoral scene in which the lovers are entwined amidst the undergrowth with a further two characters behind them, the shepherd in the tree and the shepherdess making a daisy chain. When we read the text we discover that the two couples are one and the same: having made love, the shepherdess tries to convince the shepherd to re-perform the feat, but after such exertions he is happy to swing in the tree.

This is an example of the visual technique that Lew Andrews, in *Story and Space in Renaissance Art*,[10] labels 'continuous narrative'. His main examples are taken from painting of the Italian Renaissance, but the phenomenon exists throughout the French tradition in both manuscript and early printed forms. In short, artists or engravers would portray several elements of a story within a single image, generally placing later events in the background. To the modern mind the contradiction of an individual character that reappears and faces his earlier self may seem peculiar, and indeed a sign of a primitive medieval world-view. In fact, if we are able to suspend belief as far as perspective is concerned and accept the illusion of a three-dimensional world represented on a two-dimensional plane, why not suspend believe on the level of time-based perspective and accept that a multiple-instant 'reality' can be portrayed in a single frame?

An understanding of this notion is closely linked to an understanding of the mentality that underlies today's bande dessinée. When we view a *planche* we see the same characters several times in one place yet are able to allow this to represent the passing of time. In most cases we are helped by a physical and mental divider as provided by the *cadrage* of a *case*, but it is interesting to note that the removal of such boundaries and the return to a conspicuous continuous narrative, as in the Fred cat example cited in the previous section (Fig. 6, Chapter 2), has recently been seen as cutting-edge innovation in BD technique.

Early Modern representations, as we have noted in the case of the Boccaccio example (MS Hunter 372 [V.1.9], Fig. 14), can also use separating boundaries as an alternative to continuous narrative, and further examples of this are to be found in the *Cent nouvelles nouvelles* manuscript. The miniature to the forty-eighth story (folio 112r) shows, on the left, an outdoor couple with the woman refuting the man's advances and, on the right, an interior scene of a couple reclined on a bed, although her head is turned away from his. The story is that of a suitor in love with a newly married woman whose repeated requests for a kiss are refused. He eventually coaxes her into spending the night with him, but she still will not kiss him despite their sexual intimacy. Her explanation is that whereas she has made promises to her husband with her mouth, which therefore must not be touched, the same is not true of the other parts of her body!

A golden pole is ostensibly part of the decor for the cut-away bedroom scene, but in practice it serves as a divider between the illumination's two scenes, the overall result being an image that serves the function of two modern-day *cases*. Another example of this phenomenon comes in the illustration to the eighty-fifth story (folio 175v), where the rooms of the house provide rudimentary dividers that create a three-scene pictorial narrative. In the bottom-left section we see the central character, the blacksmith, working in his shop. The story develops with the discovery of the priest in bed with the blacksmith's wife (top left) and the subsequent punishment of the former (top right).

In the case of the *Miroir de l'humaine salvation* [The Mirror of Human Salvation], another Glasgow manuscript from the second half of the fifteenth century (Bruges, 1455; MS Hunter 60 [T.2.18]), the division of each of the forty-two chapter illustrations into smaller boxes once again compartmentalises events described in the text and leads us to expect a link between them, perhaps in terms of narrative evolution. This is effectively the case, although via the terms of reference of the religious preoccupations of the time. In general, of the smaller boxes, the full-colour one represents a scene from the New Testament, with the grisaille and gold illustrations referring to prefiguring moments from the Old Testament. To take the example of folio 43v (Fig. 15), the left-hand colour '*case*' shows the Virgin vanquishing the devil. Three Old Testament women who overcome evil prefigure her: Judith killing Holofernes, Jael killing Sisera and Tomyris killing Cyrus. The work's central concern with the doctrine of the Fall and of Redemption is therefore explored through the visual bringing-together of Old and New Testament events.[11] A primitive form of pictorial narrative exists in that the pictures thus provide a chronologically ordered series.

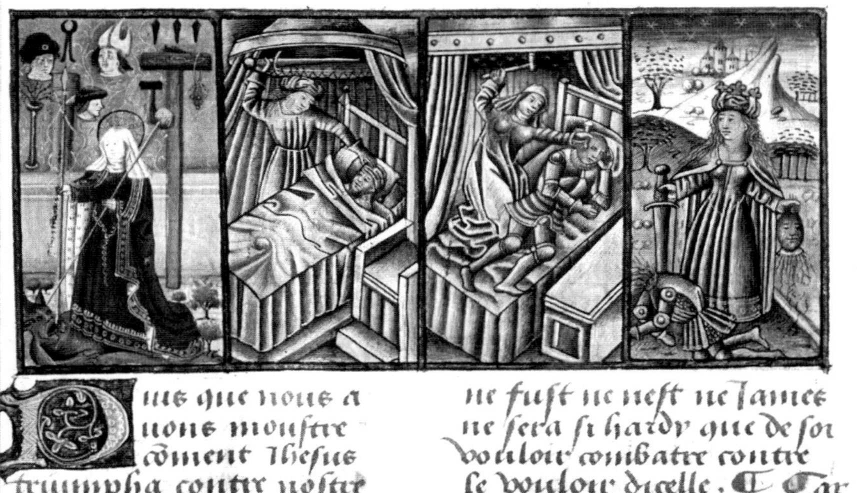

Figure 15. 'Women Vanquishing Evil'. *Miroir de l'humaine salvation*. 1455. Fol. 43r. Glasgow University Library MS Hunter 60 (T.2.18).

Related images in a chronological order that evokes a story underpin our final manuscript example, an early sixteenth-century illustrated translation by Clément Marot of Petrarch's *Visions* (Glasgow University Library SMM 2).[12] The text of the six visions, each of which relates to the central theme of earthly decay, has been separated over two pages, with the additional accompanying illustration on the facing folio. In accordance with the poem, these represent the 'before' and 'after' stages of events: a sea-bound ship that flounders, a tree struck down by lightning, a woman's beauty lost by a snake bite… It is through the layout of the manuscript that the visual narrative gains prominence and overshadows the words of Petrarch's original text. The artistry used to convey the passing of time and decay therewith associated is all the more noticeable for the fact that it is born of a medium of choice: printing was by now available, but the use of manuscript achieves visual brilliance.

This is no more than a brief survey based on a sample of Glasgow University Library's manuscript collections. It is intended to provoke awareness, or maybe just remind the reader, of the fact that text/image interaction can be traced back to the earliest forms of written culture. A text (in French at least) has rarely been 'just a text', an arbitrary system of non-representative signs, but in practice its format has added visual elements that play a primary role in the creation of meaning and effect. This might, quite simply, be on the level of *mise en page*, with larger letters or decorative frameworks indicating important sections, or, as time evolves, greater intricacy with a central pictorial element that increasingly tends towards chronological presentation of event-based narrative.

Printed Picture Books

The advent of print can be seen as the first step in a trend towards text-based culture, a movement not to be reversed until the onset of cinematographic and television images in the twentieth century. Given that moveable type allowed for different words and word patterns to be constructed and reproduced almost ad infinitum, whereas the early woodblocks could provide but a single picture, and one far more rudimentary than the manuscript masterpieces, one might be tempted to ask why images came to early print. It may be that despite the technical limitations the early woodblocks were still enough of a novelty to attract an eager public. Or, more simply, the image-based mentality of the pre-print era would not cease to exist with the initial spread of the new invention. Whatever the explanation, printed text/image productions thrived from the earliest times.

Often cited as the first printed comic strips are the various renderings of the woodblock Bible commonly referred to as *Biblia pauperum* or 'Bible of the Poor'. A manuscript appendix suggests that Glasgow University Library's copy (Hunter Ds. 2. 4.) was executed 'between the years 1420 and 1435', although it may in fact have been nearer to the 1460s and thus contemporary with the more sophisticated techniques of Gutenberg's moveable type, whilst still updating the various manuscript versions that had circulated from the twelfth or thirteenth century onwards. The new method involved the carving of a series of single-sheet woodblocks, which, when bound together, would effectively form a book. Although the *Biblia pauperum* were generally produced in Germany or the Netherlands, they were widely circulated in French-speaking countries.[13]

Each sheet of the *Biblia pauperum* consists of three strips: the top layer provides an interchange between two prophets relating to the themes of the central depictions, with accompanying texts briefly explaining the subject matter; the middle strip portrays key scenes from the scriptures with the common aim of demonstrating how events of the Old Testament prefigure those of the New; finally, the lower strip presents a further exchange between the prophets and adds summarising motto-like titles for each of the images. To take the specific example of block 10 (Fig. 9, Chapter 2), the central New Testament theme of the temptation of Christ is flanked by two scenes from Genesis: Esau selling his birthright for soup and Adam and Eve succumbing to the serpent's temptation. The theme of temptation is reinforced in the two exchanges that play upon biblical citations. In the top section the prophets state: 'They tempted me, they mocked at me with scorn' and 'The thought is unnatural, as if clay were to oppose the potter'. The bottom exchange refers closely to the central scene: 'I have slain all your enemies' and 'My enemy has looked at me with terrible eyes'.[14]

As we can see, therefore, the *Biblia pauperum* was not a Bible, but rather extracts of the Bible juxtaposed so as to create their own narration, nor would such new technology have been intended for the poor. Avril Henry gives the term as dating to 1769, whilst underlining its inappropriateness.[15] Whatever the misnomer, the work remains an interesting precursor of the comic strip in that it unites several elements that until this time had generally only been found individually. The mixture of text and image is central, with the 'action' presented both through the titular labels (*récitatifs*?) and the bandeau speech bubbles. The blocks as a whole operate through strips, and within the strips the use of columns creates a system of individual frames, or, in the case of the Esau scene, two sub-frames so as to separate Esau's return from hunting and the offering of the soup by his brother Jacob. Above all, and as we have already seen in the case of the *Miroir de l'humaine salvation* (Fig. 15), the central concept of elements of the Old Testament that look forward to those of the New implies an overarching narrative, a universal 'one step inevitably leading to the next'.

The *Biblia pauperum* was not the only early printed work to tell a story through a mixture of text and image, but it is as good an example as any for slightly closer analysis. Other possibilities cited by David Kunzle include the *Ars moriendi*, Dances of Death and Ships of Fools.[16] The *Ars moriendi* [Art of Dying] or *Art au morier* in the French rendering, of which the first versions were produced in the third quarter of the fifteenth century, used images to tell the life of Christ and thus prepare the reader for his own death in the light of eternal salvation. It was a tradition that saw an element of renewal in the seventeenth century with text/image works such as M. de Chertablon's *La Maniere de se bien preparer a la mort* [The Way to Prepare Oneself Well for Death] (1700).

Printed Dances of Death, generally dating from Guy Marchant's 1485 *Danse macabre*, but of which Hans Holbein's *Les Simulachres et historiées faces de la mort* [Images and Illustrated Facets of Death] (first version 1538) is maybe best known,[17] portray Death as a skeletal character who presents himself to various stereotypes of life's functions – the king, the pauper, the soldier, the priest, the surgeon – with the overarching narrative being that of our own eventual demise and the humility that this should teach us.

Sebastian Brandt's *Stultifera navis* or *Ship of Fools*, originally published in Basle in 1494, wherein the guiding theme, rather than Death, is that of human folly, similarly provides a form of character-based narrative through the various exploits of the central Fool figure. Although the work originated in German, French versions were soon produced and quickly became popular. What these early works have in common is that like the *Biblia pauperum* they are not just illustrated stories, but a narrative in its own right expressed through images that are nonetheless text dependent. One further point is that central characterisation underpins the narrative, be it the characters of the Bible, the Christian figure, Folly or Death.

Such works rely on general 'truths' – the inevitability of Death, the omnipresence of human Folly, the veracity of the scriptures – for the subject matter of their narrative. Two precise events, the assassination of Henri III in 1589 and that of Henri IV in 1610, provided the material for more specific storytelling through a proliferation of single-sheet engravings, many of which are now in the BnF's *Série Qb1: Histoire de France en Estampes*.[18] In the case of the 1589 engraving by Roland Guerard and Nicolas Prevost of Paris, the accompanying text outlines the main events of the drama:

> Figure de l'admirable & divine resolution de F. Jacques Clement Jacobin, de son arrivée à S. Clou pres Paris, accedz aux Gardes, & addresse au Roy, devant lequel s'agenoüillant luy donne un coup de cousteau, dont à ceste occasion est soudain tué, & son corps porté mort devant le Roy, ayant esté mis blessé au lict, après le decedz duquel fust ledict F. Clement mort, martyrisé, tire à quatre chevaulx, puis bruslé.

> [Figure of the admirable and divine resolution of Father Jacques Clement, a Jacobin, of his arrival at St Clou near to Paris, of his reaching the guards and addressing the King, before whom he knelt and in so doing stabbed him, whereupon he was immediately killed and his dead body brought before the King, who had been carried wounded to his bed, and after whose death the said Father Clement died, was martyrised, drawn by four horses, then burnt.]

These events are depicted at various points of the engraving, with the doorways acting as *case* dividers (cf. the *Cent nouvelles nouvelles* examples discussed above) between the arrival of Clement, the assassination, and, in the background, the deathbed scene.

The assassination of Henri IV in 1610 provided the material for a similar single-sheet engraving (Fig. 16), although in this case the *case* dividers are less obvious, despite the narrative action again following a general anti-clockwise trajectory, from the stabbing by Ravaillac in the foreground, to his arrest and three-stage execution. This is a further example of the general phenomenon of 'continuous narrative' that Lew Andrews has explored in *Story and Space in Renaissance Art* (see above), showing again how the Early Modern mind can suspend belief concerning the depiction of temporal progression in a way not dissimilar to the mechanics of reading a modern BD *planche*.

It may be the specific drama of these events that lends itself to a step-by-step exposition, with actions dominating words and thus favouring a pictorial narrative in stages, perhaps in the same way that modern equivalents, such as the assassination of Kennedy or the attack on the Twin Towers, have espoused picture-based storytelling either through film or comic strips.[19] Kunzle cites the examples of the regicide prints (though does not mention the full riches of *Série Qb1*), before suggesting, however, that, thereafter, pictorial narrative was to die out in France:

Figure 16. 'The Assassination of Henri IV'. 1610. From *Série Qb1: Histoire de France en Estampes*. Bibliothèque nationale de France, Département des Estampes.

> The popular print, the imagery of social and political satire, floushed in France throughout the seventeenth century, expiring during the latter half of the reign of Louis XIV. I have found, however, no picture stories or narrative strips from this period. The indications are that most of those we have reviewed originated with Dutch or German publishers and were distributed, copied or adapted by the French, who were never, at this time or later, much concerned with graphic narrative. (52)

Kunzle has maybe overlooked some later examples, such as a number of *Série Qb1* prints from around 1680 that tell the story of La Voisin, the infamous enchantress who was at the heart of the scandalous Affair of the Poisons, or a series telling the life of Henri de la Tour d'Auvergne, Vicomte de Turenne (1611–1675). This later example (Fig. 17), like many in *Série Qb1*, provides individual vignettes, each with a descriptive accompanying text, thereby creating an overall effect not unlike that of the *images d'Épinal*, a subject of discussion for later in this chapter. Furthermore, it may just be a question of a transfer of format for such narrative elements, namely the switch from *feuilles volantes* or loose leaves to book publications: to take but one example, Marc de Vulson's *Les Portraits des hommes illustres* (1650) is effectively a text/image narrative in book form telling the history of France, with Vulson using engravings and accompanying texts to present the biography of the great men (including Joan of Arc, Marie de Medicis and Anne d'Autriche!) from the Abbé Suger up to Louis XIII.[20] That said, omissions are inevitable

Figure 17. 'The Life of Turenne'. 1675. From *Série Qb1: Histoire de France en Estampes.* Bibliothèque nationale de France, Département des Estampes.

in any attempt to provide comprehensive coverage of picture narrative in Early Modern Europe, a task that Kunzle achieves admirably given its magnitude.

My aim is to shift the angle of view slightly and to underline not so much the individual instances – although these are of course interesting and important – but rather to consider, albeit briefly, the history of a mentality that coupled image with text in a way akin to that of the modern bande dessinée.[21] As we saw in Chapter 2, Thierry Groensteen has preferred to view the BD as an essentially visual form. Harry Morgan also discusses the relative roles of text and image at length in his *Principes des littératures dessinées*,[22] in particular in the fifth chapter on 'Les Rapports texte-image' [Text-image relations] (pp. 87–125). Morgan concurs with Groensteen, whilst suggesting that text/image relations are not specific to the BD and that the visual workings of a BD can be hard to distinguish from those of an illustrated Victorian novel:

> Nous avons vu ques les rapports texte–image dans une BD sont strictement les mêmes que les rapports texte–image dans un roman illustré; il n'y a pas de rapports texte–image qui seraient spécifiques à la BD. (118)
>
> [We have seen that the text–image relations in a BD are exactly the same as the text–image relations in an illustrated novel; there are no text–image relations that could be specific to the BD.]

Figure 18. 'La Fin nous faict tous egaux'. Gilles Corrozet. *Hecatomgraphie.* Paris: Denis Janot, 1540. Fol. Diiiiv. Glasgow University Library SMAdd. 385.

In Chapter 2 above I have differed from Groensteen in arguing for the essentially hybrid nature of the bande dessinée, without any shortcoming being implied in the hybrid element. Like Morgan I would suggest that a hybrid format of this type is not necessarily unique to the BD, but rather part of a long tradition. I would, however, go considerably further back than the Victorian illustrated novel, and will pay particular attention to one broad phenomenon, that of the emblem and related forms. In general terms, the emblem was a tripartite mixture of text and image consisting of picture, motto or title, and *subscriptio* or explanatory text.

In an ideal world the emblem picture does not make sense without the text, and vice versa. It is the conjunction of text and image that provides the key to the puzzle, as in the example of Figure 18, one of the one hundred emblems that make up Gilles Corrozet's *Hecatomgraphie* (1540). Our eye falls upon the image, centralised within the ornate frame, although the significance of the figure is not entirely clear. Is it the room that is important, or the man, or the game, or the contents of his hands? The motto, 'La fin nous faict tous egaux' [The End Equals Us All Up] seems self-explanatory but unrelated.

It is the explanation given in the *subscriptio*, namely that life is like a game of chess with pieces of all values ending up in the same bag at the end, that brings the two together and creates the overall effect.[23]

Corrozet's *Hecatomgraphie*, together with works by Guillaume de La Perrière (*Le Théâtre des bons engins*, 1540, *La Morosophie*, 1553) and the early translations of Andrea Alciato's *Emblematum liber* (the first version in French was 1536) marked the beginning of the emblem tradition in France.[24] It was here that it particularly flourished, even if the first version of Alciato's work, from which the genre takes its name, was produced in Augsburg in 1531. Alison Adams, Stephen Rawles and Alison Saunders's two-volume *A Bibliography of French Emblem Books* (1999–2002) notes over 650 editions of French emblem books, probably more than any other tradition. The bibliography stops at 1700, although the tradition did not die out until the early-to-middle years of the eighteenth century. Furthermore, associated forms, such as the Dances of Death mentioned above, courtly devices, manuscript creations pre-dating 1531 or Francesco Colonna's *Hypnerotomachia Poliphili* [Dream of Poliphile] of 1499 (first French version, 1546) with its enigmatic mixture of text narrative and integrated woodblocks, mean that the phenomenon was truly a mainstay of Early Modern culture.[25]

For our purposes the *aetas emblematica*, or Emblematic Age, as it has been called, is particularly relevant for the mindset it implies. The putting together of text and image was seen as natural not only in the hundreds of emblem books and related publications, but also in the décor of palaces and triumphal arches, in royal entries and flag-bearing processions and within the spheres of the academy arts of the time. Just as today the bande dessinée can been seen as one element in a wider hybrid visual way of life, one that includes advertising and the internet, so in the Early Modern period France was a European leader in a culture that readily expressed itself through pictures. To understand the bande dessinée as a phenomenon it is not enough to catalogue instances of comparable productions, but rather we should be aware of the wider cultural conditions, via precedents, that make it what it is.

We should also be aware of the specificities of each period's culture of the image, although on closer inspection these may be less marked than one might assume. A primary objection would be that it is the recounting of narrative that underpins the bande dessinée, a notion absent from the 'standard' emblem book, which is, on the contrary, a heterogeneous compilation of single instances. When we look a little closer matters do not appear as clear-cut. Even in the earliest of emblem books, examples of progression within a single picture are relatively frequent. In emblem 73 of La Perrière's *Morosophie*, for example, we see a castle atop a rocky island with a figure, hand to mouth, in the foreground. The text explains that just as the rock stops the advance of the water, so reason can stop the foolish chatter of one's tongue. Essentially the emblem provides a playful visualisation of a moral metaphor, but as such it includes an element of progress from one set of givens to the next. Apart from 'foreground' and 'background' there are no formal separators within the picture, but such is in keeping with the medieval and Renaissance phenomenon of 'continuous narrative' discussed above.

This technique occurs commonly within the *Morosophie*, as well as other early emblem books. The blooming and fading of a rose is placed next to the figure of youth passing to old age (*Morosophie*, emblem 87), the idiot attempts to pull out a horse's whole tail rather than applying gradual methodology (*Le Théâtre*, emblem 55), the squirrel advances using its tail as a sail just as we should use all facilities available to us (*Hecatomgraphie*, fol. Kiiv), and so on. In other instances the text recounts a fable with the image encapsulating a key moment. In Guillaume Gueroult's *Premier Livre des emblemes* (1550),[26] emblem 22, 'Trop enquerre n'est pas bon' [To Inquire Too Much is Not Good] tells the story of an insistent investigator who quizzes a wrongdoer regarding the number of women he has seduced. The wrongdoer ends up admitting the latter's wife to be one of his conquests, thus the motto 'Car s'enquerant on oyt: / Ce qu'on ne voudroit point' [For when we inquire we hear / what we do not want]. The woodcut shows us the investigator and the various other characters, although the same image is also adapted to emblem 28, 'En putain n'ha point de foy' [Never Trust a Whore].[27]

One could argue that Gueroult's work is effectively a collection of illustrated fables and as such is only an emblem book in title. But like fables that bear that name – and let us not forget that all seventeenth-century editions of Jean de La Fontaine's *Fables* were illustrated – and related phenomena such as Dances of Death or editions of Renaissance hieroglyphs, what matters is not so much whether we can shoehorn them into retrospective definitions of the 'true' emblem, but rather that they are part of a clear phenomenon that put text with image. Within these parameters, we will find that there is no such thing as a static text/image form, as either the different parts of the image, or the explanatory text, will inevitably formulate ideas via a clearly identifiable series of steps.

This progression of ideas develops towards a recognisable narrative as the form develops, and in particular as the emblems are more commonly grouped around a theme. Herman Hugo's *Pia desideria* [Pious Desires] (1624), which appeared in French as *Les Pieux désirs* from 1627, traces the journey of the soul as it advances from desperation to exaltation in the love of God. Another Jesuit collection, the *Imago primi saeculi Societatis Iesu* [The Image of the First Century of the Society of Jesus], published in 1640 to celebrate the Society's centenary, tells of its history from birth to worldwide influence. One of the most famous secular collections from the end of the seventeenth century, Dominique Bouhours's *Les Entretiens d'Ariste et d'Eugene* [The Discussions between Ariste and Eugene] (from 1671) takes place over a series of six days with the passing of time as a central theme.[28]

A comparative element for consideration is the extent to which the bande dessinée as we know it plays with conventions of narrative, and in so doing echoes the earlier text/image mentality. Some of today's cutting-edge works, such as Moebius's *Garage hermétique* or the iconoclastic creations of the Requins Marteaux group,[29] deliberately install sequences that appear not to follow a global thread, and wherein the joy of the creation lies in the interrelation of the individual pieces rather than in overall storytelling coherence. Once we are aware of this, the parallels between the mentality of the first emblematic age and modus operandi of the current BD seem all the more pertinent.[30]

As well as the question of narrative, that of characterisation may appear to separate the mindsets of the visual culture of the Early Modern period and that of today. But again a closer look suggests that the emblematic hero, in various guises, can often hold the work together. In the case of political works such as Martinet's *Emblemes royales a Louis le Grand* [Royal Emblems for Louis the Great] of 1673, or Claude-François Menestrier's device-based *Histoire du Roy Louis le Grand* [History of King Louis the Great] of 1689, the main character is the Sun King himself. In Marc de Vulson's *Les Portraits des hommes illustres* (1650, see above), the numerous characters from the Abbé Suger onwards tell the story of France's history.

Perhaps the best example of emblematic characterisation comes from the vogue for love emblems that marked the culture of Europe from the early years of the seventeenth century. Even if the majority of these collections came from the Low Countries' printing outlets, France also produced some volumes, and, furthermore, most publications included French text and were clearly popular in France. Amongst the leading works were Daniel Heins or Heinsius's *Quaeris quid sit amor* [You May Ask What Love Is] and *Emblemata amatoria* [Emblems of Love] (both from the first decade of the seventeenth century), the anonymous *Thronus Cupidinis* [Cupid's Throne] (*c.*1617 onwards) and Otto Van Veen or Vaenius's *Amorum emblemata* [Emblems of Love] (1608) and *Amoris divini emblemata* [Emblems of Divine Love] (1615), although a good many others existed, as Mario Praz indicates.[31]

Van Veen's *Amorum emblemata*, issued in several versions so as to include Dutch, Latin, English, Italian, Spanish and French texts, explores the theme of love through 124 emblems with an angelic Cupid acting as guide and chief protagonist. The second emblem (Fig. 19), one of the most famous, partly due to its appearance in the background of Johannes Vermeer's *A Lady Standing at the Virginal* (*c.*1672–1674, London, National Gallery), shows our Cupid holding up the figure '1' and trampling all other numbers. The text, under the motto 'Une seule' [Only One], explains that true love is for one person

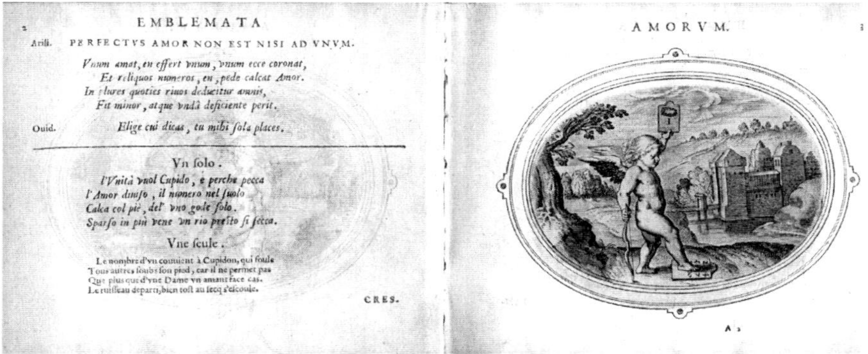
2

EMBLEMATA

Arist. PERFECTVS AMOR NON EST NISI AD VNVM.

Vnum amat, en effert vnum, vnum ecce coronat,
Et reliquos numeros, en, pede calcat Amor.
In plures quoties riuos deducitur amnis,
Fit minor, atque vndâ deficiente perit.

Ouid. *Elige cui dicas, tu mihi sola places.*

Vn solo.

l'Vnità vuol Cupido, e perche pecca
l'Amor diuiso, il numero nel suolo
Calca col piè, del' vno gode solo.
Sparso in più vene vn rio presto si secca.

Vne seule.

Le nombre d'vn conuient à Cupidon, qui foule
Tous autres soubs son pied, car il ne permet pas
Que plus que d'vne Dame vn amant face cas.
Le ruisseau departi, bien tost au secq s'escoule.

CRES.

AMORVM. 3

A 2

Figure 19. 'One Love'. Otto Van Veen. *Amorum emblemata*. Antwerp: Hieronymus Verdussen, 1608, pp. 2–3. Glasgow University Library SM 1050.

alone, just as a stream that divides will dry out. As we explore the volume we find Cupid holding a chameleon to represent his willingness to adapt to his lady's whims ('Selon que veut Madame' [According to Madame's Desires]), or trampling the trappings of riches and nobility since love holds sway over rank ('Amour sur tout' [Love above All]).

Secondary characters include Fortune who throws both honey and bile at the lovers ('Tout commun' [All Together]) but who also favours the brave ('Fortune aide aux hardis'), Hercules who achieves his brave deeds thanks to love ('Amour source de vertu' [Love a Source of Virtue]) or even the hare and the tortoise, who show the value of steady love ('Continuer fait gaigner' [Perseverance Leads to Victory]). Here, as in other books of love emblems, much of the collection's charm resides in the recognition of engraver Cornelius Boël's central figure and the way we find him adapted to love's diverse facets. The reader flips through the emblems to see how Cupid will adapt to new situations in much the same way that a modern reader might buy a serialised bande dessinée in eager anticipation of the hero's latest exploits. We do not doubt that all will end well for Tintin or Astérix; the pleasure comes with seeing how the authors adapt them to fit new situations.

French examples of love emblem collections from later decades include the *Théâtre d'amour* [The Theatre of Love] (no publishing details, probably *c.*1620), which shares many of the themes of Heinsius and Van Veen's works but boasts the peculiarity of copperplate engravings including carefully scripted text, or the licentious *Centre de l'amour* [Centre of Love] (published 'chez Cupidon', often undated but *c.*1680) whose double entendres would titillate even the most demanding of *Fluide Glacial* enthusiasts. Emblem 88, for example, 'Entre Amis, tout doit estre commun' [Between Friends All Must be Shared], shows what appears to be a respectable monastery scene, with a nun at the table and a monk entering by the right-hand door, but the text tells a different story:

Ouy, j'y consens de tout mon coeur,
Que sans mystere & sans scrupule
Le Frere visitant sa Soeur
Entre en sa petite cellule.

[Yes, I consent whole-heartedly,
that without mystery and without scrupule
the Brother visiting the Sister
Should enter her private quarters.]

When we now look closer at the image we see that there is indeed narrative progress, as the top left background features a bed shared by a couple! As stated above, love emblems are by no means unique, but they are a taste of the flavour of the general mentality of an age whose central culture readily played upon the interaction of text and image.

This 'Emblematic Age' appears to have died out sometime around the mid eighteenth century. We can quantify the decline in the emblem book through publication statistics, but perhaps more telling is that within the emblem books (and other works like them) that were published the space given to pictures decreases, and the image becomes illustration rather than an integral component of the communication process. Why this should be so is open to conjecture, and indeed such conjecture is at the base of my *Text/Image Mosaics in French Culture: Emblems and Comic Strips*. In short, one can see the onset of print as leading to a switch from oral and visual culture – the stained glass windows of the great cathedrals – to a textual one, although the transition was by no means immediate. It is the interim period that creates a hybrid culture, one whereby text and image interact. If we follow the hypothesis through, it was the end of the nineteenth century that saw the next major shift in cultural mentality, as the newly explored image – photography, cinema and, later, television – started to encroach upon a text-based mindset, creating once again a hybrid cultural mentality, of which the bande dessinée is now a prime example.

The Age of (Textual) Reason

That the status of the image changed as the Early Modern period progressed is undeniable; indeed it would be peculiar were the mindset of a society not to evolve over a period of 300 years. In terms of the culture of the image, as indeed with most cultures, the progress was presumably gradual, perhaps initiated by certain events or technological changes, but not a switch that took things from black to white overnight. Nonetheless it is difficult for the historian not to succumb to providing analysis that satisfies a retrospective need for classification, seeking out key turning points that may not have been seen as such at the time.

What we can note are certain instances that demonstrate how the status of the image has changed by a given historical moment. That is not to say that the image has died out, or even that text/image interaction no longer exists, but rather that it has changed its way of operating. This may be further from the text/image culture of today's bande dessinée than certain previous manifestations, but it may also put new emphasis on other 'BD-related' elements.

If the notion of direct text/image interaction becomes more discrete by the middle years of the eighteenth century, by contrast the self-contained narrative image, individually or in sequence, has gained an important place in posterity. Best known of these are works of the English tradition, and in particular the character-based narrative engravings of William Hogarth (1697–1764).[32] The *Rake's Progress* (1735, with reworkings up to 1763), for example, consists of eight prints (originally eight oils, now in the Sir John Soane's Museum in London) in which we see the eponymous Tom Rakewell moving through society following his miserly father's death, only to be plagued by hangers-on, marry for money and still finish in the debtor's prison, and subsequently the madhouse. Each of the plates includes a host of background details that complete the story of the Rake's activities – the love letters to the pregnant Sarah Young whom he is paying off in plate 1, a lightning strike pointing to a gambling house in a later version of plate 4 – with the result that the story, and the humour, is clear from the images alone, although a verse text adds moral comment.

In the case of *Before* and *After* (1736), two prints depicting a enthusiastic suitor and then the resulting dishevelled couple, Hogarth acknowledges his debt to the tradition of love emblems through the image of Cupid framed on the background wall, firstly about to let off a rocket, and then with his munition spent! Although Hogarth is generally cited as the father of the narrative print, the tradition is a European one that, like all cultural formulations, involves a heavy degree of interchange.

This point is particularly pertinent to the case of a near contemporary of Hogarth, Thomas Rowlandson (1756–1827), best known for his exaggerated caricatures and, in our context, for his frequent portrayal of speech through 'bubbles'. One such example is *Reform Advised* ... (*c.*1790), a satire of the French Revolution that includes an element of narrative via the three '*case*' progressions from 'Reform Advised' to 'Reform Begun' and finally 'Reform Compleat'. 'Reform Advised' shows visiting French Revolutionaries telling a corpulent and indulgent John Bull, via speech bubbles, that he is too fat; below this, in 'Reform Begun', John Bull is now starving and complaining of his lot to Revolutionaries; finally 'Reform Compleat' shows the Revolutionaries trampling the English stereotype underfoot. The subject matter is not arbitrary, as Rowlandson spent much time in Paris and was widely appreciated in France; indeed he may well have been a key influence upon Revolutionary prints (see below).

It is likely to have been direct contact with the French tradition of the *danse macabre* (see above) that inspired Rowlandson to produce *The English Dance of Death*, originally serialised from 1814 to 1816 and then reprinted in two volumes (London: Rudolph Ackermann, 1816). Rowlandson provides illustrations to William Combe's text, which updates the Holbein version by applying the theme specifically to the England of the time. 'The Sot', for example (facing p. 97 of volume I), shows Death mocking the angry wife as he wheels her husband away from the country pub, since now that he is 'dead & drunk' she no longer holds sway over him. Although this may initially seem like a clear-cut case of illustration rather than text/image interaction, the context of the Dance of Death tradition adds a level of ambiguity, as does the inclusion of brief text, and the sense of a narrative journey as we visit the different facets of English society.

The narrative journey is a key feature of the work for which Rowlandson and Combe had achieved notoriety, *The Tour of Doctor Syntax* (1812).[33] The first volume gives us Dr Syntax 'In Search of the Picturesque', the second 'In Search of Consolation' and the third 'In Search of a Wife'. Although each of the three volumes' eighty illustrations is accompanied by a dozen or so pages of Combe's verse, a glance through the list of plates – 'Dr Syntax setting out', 'Dr Syntax stopped by Highwaymen', 'Dr Syntax loses his Money on the Race-Ground' etcetera – suffices for us to grasp the story and it would indeed be possible to 'read' the work simply by skipping from picture to picture.

The title page of each volume bears the five-line quote from Horace's *Ars poetica* [Art of Poetry] that opens with 'Ut Pictura, Poësis erit' [As is painting, so is poetry], an immediate indication that the work claims to situate itself within the tradition of text/image interaction, with neither the text nor the image claiming supremacy. In practice we cannot doubt the primacy of the text as the title page also makes it clear that the work is 'A Poem by William Combe'; however, the Rowlandson plates must have been a key focus of attention and a major selling point.

Doctor Syntax, which appeared in a French version from 1821,[34] is of particular interest to the student of the French comic strip since it is a generally understated precurser of Rodolphe Töpffer's *histoires en images*, labelled by Thierry Groensteen and others as the first bandes dessinées. The similarities with Töpffer's *Le Docteur Festus* (1829) are striking, and indeed have been noted by Groensteen in *Töpffer: L'Invention de la bande dessinée* and in his introduction to the Seuil reprint edition.[35] But we can also compare the Tours of Dr Syntax with the various peregrinations of Töpffer's other creations. Travel, often in the quest of love, is the mainstay of the plot, but the numerous ups and downs are contrived to the point of reaching the burlesque. So too are the characters, in the rich variety the authors place before us, from dairymaid to learned savants, but also in their

Figure 20. 'Syntax's Return'. William Combe and Thomas Rowlandson. *The Tour of Doctor Syntax*. London: Nattali and Bond, 1817. Volume I, facing p. 253. Glasgow University Library BD6-f.1.

Figure 21. 'Cryptogame and Elvire'. Rodolphe Töpffer. *Histoire de Monsieur Cryptogame 1845*. In *Le Docteur Festus: Histoire de monsieur Cryptogame: Deux odyssées*, ed. Thierry Groensteen. Paris: Seuil, 1996. No pagination. Vignettes 36–38.

individual traits, be it undying love or unbridled bad humour, and in the physical aspects the two artists attribute. It is perhaps here that the influence of Rowlandson is most obvious:[36] the elongated lanky features of the male leads, the exaggerated expression of emotion, the capturing of movement at a set instance. This should be clear from a brief glance at Rowlandson's depiction of Syntax's initial return (Fig.

20, facing page 253 of volume I), compared, for example, with a scene featuring Monsieur Cryptogame and Elvire (Fig. 21, vignette 37) or, more generally, the opening page of *Mr. Crépin* in which Crépin looks lovingly at his wife and family, and Syntax's amorous exchange with Widow Hopefull (facing page 131 of volume II).

Rowlandson is remarkable for his connections with and possible influence upon the French text/image tradition, yet he receives no more than passing mention in Kunzle's *The Early Comic Strip*, and is generally ignored in French accounts of the BD's antecedents. Other artists, such as Richard Newton (1777–1798), Henry Bunbury (1750–1811), George Woodward (*c.*1760–1809), James Gillray (1757–1815) and George Cruikshank (1792–1878) are discussed by Kunzle, who gives a vivid picture of the growth of a new trend of caricature in England towards the end of the eighteenth century. The French tradition will also have a large part to play in the European development of the form through the emergence of artists such as Gustave Doré, Cham, Gill and Henri Daumier, creators whose work will be discussed in the next chapter with regard to the journals they helped to popularise.

The work of Hogarth and Rowlandson might be contrasted, in the context of the French tradition, with the set-scene paintings of Jean-Baptiste Greuze (1725–1805), although the immediate difference is that they are single-copy paintings, not prints for distribution. *La Malédiction paternelle: Le Fils ingrat* [The Father's Curse: The Ungrateful Son] (1777, Paris, Louvre) can function independently as a genre painting that tells a story, that of the moment of departure of the eponymous son: it has its characters, particularly the son and the father, but also the siblings, the mother, and the waiting accomplice; and the posture of the protagonists, including their outstretched arms, suggests movement – that of the son's departure – in the way that a BD with 'swish lines' might. Once we include the title it is possible to piece together a story, namely the son who against the wishes of his father has decided to leave the family home in order to seek his fortune in the wider world. When put with its sister painting, *La Malédiction paternelle: Le Fils puni* [The Father's Curse: The Son Punished] (1778, Paris, Louvre), the works form a two-*case* strip as we learn of subsequent events: the dishevelled son returns – the movement is accordingly now from right to left – to find his aged father dying and the family in disarray.[37]

Greuze had intended to extend the technique to twenty-six *cases* in a series of paintings telling the story of Bazile and Thibaut, Bazile being generous – he gives his last scrap of bread to a beggar – whereas Thibaut is haughty, cruel and cowardly. After various travels, Thibaut will murder and die in gaol while Bazile marries happily.[38] Greuze could well have intended to provide a 'serious' version of Hogarth's narrative sequences. Perhaps the reason for the project not coming to fruition was that the plan was for a large, and thus expensive, series of individual pieces, which would not have enjoyed the widespread popularity offered to Hogarth by the distribution of prints. This is one of the main areas of difference between the work of Greuze and our notion of the modern bande dessinée – apart from the titles there is no text, but above all these are individual artefacts rather than consumer culture – but it is interesting to note the importance of visual narrative within 'high art' at this time.

An extra dimension is added to these paintings when placed in the context of Denis Diderot's commentaries for his series of *Salons*, or musings on the art shows of his time. Diderot produced nine such works between 1759 and 1781, and although they were not widely distributed, they do bear witness to a mentality that still coupled images with text. For example, in his commentary on Greuze's *Jeune fille qui pleure son oiseau mort* (1765, Edinburgh, National Gallery of Scotland) that takes up several pages of his *Salon de 1765*, Diderot makes the 'real' story behind the painting explicit, namely that the object of the girl's tears is not the dead bird, but rather the loss of her virginity of which it is a symbol.[39]

The eighteenth century is not the only time to produce 'high' art that tells a story; indeed one could argue that all paintings, from Jean Cousin's *Eva Prima Pandora* [Eve the First Pandora] to Edouard Manet's *Déjeuner sur l'herbe* [Luncheon on the Grass] have at least an implicit level of narrative. Nor is this period the first to produce paintings that when placed together tell a story; indeed Peter Paul Rubens's *Medici Cycle* (1622–1625, Paris, Louvre) is effectively the narrative of Marie de Medici's life told through the twenty-four paintings. The eighteenth century differs, in France at least, in that it sees a rise in the prominence of paintings of everyday life – genre paintings – and, as stated above, a marked tendency towards caricature. Elements portrayed are exaggerated, be it in terms of movement and gesture or physiognomy. Whether this can be linked to the changing status of the text and the move towards text forms or image forms, rather than hybrids, is a matter for speculation. Perhaps the accessibility of text via print allowed it to take on an elevated communicative role, thereby leaving a demand for visual art with a wider spectrum of tone.

The same caricature-based traits are to be found in non-salon productions, principally the printed broadsheets that the new presses had made comparatively easy to produce. These updates of the popular images known from at least the sixteenth century – see for example the prints taken from the BnF's *Série Qb1: Histoire de France en estampes* cited above – were the first stages of what were to become the *images d'Épinal*, to use the umbrella term. Denis Martin, in *Images d'Épinal*,[40] points to the 1760 *Frise des douze apotres* [Frieze of the Twelve Apostles] as an early example of the genre, although it is primarily a static portrait of the apostles, a widely distributed devotional piece, as was often the case.

Another vein of caricature common at the end of the eighteenth century, for obvious reasons, were the prints depicting various aspects of the Revolution. Antoine de Baecque estimates that there are approximately 600 pro-Revolutionary caricatures dating from spring 1789 to summer 1792 still in existence,[41] although as might be expected from 1793 to 1794, at the height of the Terror, caricature seems to have disappeared in France.[42] The prints vary in style and refinement, but a fairly typical example is *Le Gourmand* of 1791, in which we see the scene in the Varennes inn in which the fleeing royal family took refuge.[43] Background images displayed on the wall of the inn give us the narrative progression, from the fall of the Bastille and the upturning of the king's power to the universal adulation of the revolutionary ideal, while the main-stage characters tell the immediate story: it is Marie-Antoinette's vanity and above all Louis's gluttony that are stopping them escaping. The print has many of the recognisable qualities of the modern BD – speech bubbles, narrative, comic characterisation – but it can also be assimilated with the political cartoon. As we shall see in the following chapters, the two forms are often hard to separate and the works of Martin Veyron and Georges Wolinski, to name but two, will bear modern witness to the continued high degree of overlap.

Les Images d'Épinal

It was in 1796 that Jean-Charles Pellerin founded the printworks in Épinal (in the Vosges *département*, about 70 km from Nancy) that bore his name. The *fabrique Pellerin* was to become synonymous with all *images d'Épinal*, and, by extension, all forms of nineteenth-century popular prints. Denis Martin identifies four main periods in the development of the *imagerie d'Épinal*: the foundation and initial growth under Jean-Charles Pellerin (1796–1822), modernisation and expansion under his son Nicolas Pellerin (1822–1854), the switch from woodcuts to lithographs and further expansion under Nicolas's son Charles (1854–1877), and finally, industrial factory-style development under Georges, Charles's son, until the outbreak of war prior to decline in the face of twentieth-century technologies (1887–1914).[44]

Initially the Pellerin printworks specialised in playing cards, moving on to religious subjects, and then current affairs such as the glories of Napoleon. By the boom years of the second half of the nineteenth century, subject matter had expanded to include country scenes and interior décor, animal lore, fairy tales, popular songs and moral tales, with a constantly increasing tendency to the telling of a story. It would appear that in general the *images d'Épinal* were single-sheet prints that were sold as such, presumably for display, although by the time of the popular press (see next chapter) there was much overlap with the more widespread distribution of pictures via periodicals.

One of the most popular and most frequently imitated images that the early Pellerin works produced was the *Degrés des âges* [Steps of the

Ages] print (*c.*1820), a theme that in itself had been passed down through the ages. In the Pellerin version each age of Man is portrayed on steps that rise until life starts to decline. The multiple images, almost like a series of *cases*, are central, but the labelling text clarifies the message, explaining the progress through the grand narrative of life as we go full circle from infancy to the childish imbecility of old age, with the only central constant being God in judgement.[45] In other cases, such as an 1827 *Calvaire de Jérusalem* [Jerusalem Calvary], the Renaissance technique of continuous narrative is resurrected as the background to the carrying of the cross and shows both Christ's birth and his crucifixion. The junction of more than one print can also form a narrative, as in the *Départ du soldat* [The Soldier's Departure] and accompanying *Retour du soldat* [The Soldier's Return] (both pre-1814). The two prints match the technique of Greuze's genre series, but the pro-war propaganda and the heavy style (in both the woodcut and accompanying verse) lack the subtlety of *Le Fils ingrat* and *Le Fils puni*. Finally, the narrative can be extended through a long series of individual prints, as in those of the life of Napoleon, each recounting a single event, such as the *Bataille des Pyramides* [The Battle of the Pyramids] (print dated 1830), *Le Retour de l'Île d'Elba* [The Return from the Island of Elba] (1833), the *Bataille de Waterloo* (1821–1822) or the *Tombeau de Napoléon* [The Tomb of Napoleon] (1832).[46]

It is not hard to see the similarities between these images and those of the emblematic age analysed above, be it in terms of the *Ars moriendi* images of Christ's life, or the biographical histories produced from Vulson's portraits of 'Great Men'. Maybe the *images d'Épinal* were the popular continuation of the fashion for emblems, one that has been overlooked by history, as they were no longer innovative in the way that the early text/image mixtures were. This continuation/throw-over theory would be supported by the fact that the desire for popular narrative prints could remain a constant to be satisfied in largely the same manner, as by the early years of the nineteenth century the essential elements of print technology had not changed that much from those of the sixteenth century. The importance assigned to the *image d'Épinal* in many twentieth-century histories of the bande dessinée – that the subject should be given its own section here is in recognition of this fact – tends to overlook the historical context, namely that the popular printed image has existed since printing itself (a quick glance through the BnF's *Série Qb1* bears witness to this). What differs, however, is the status accorded to the image, whether it is part of a mainstream cutting-edge culture that intrinsically mixes text and image, as appears to have been the case at the time of the emblem, or whether the image is a secondary support, which only comes into its own through the high-art narratives of academy painters such as Greuze.

With new technologies, such as the lithograph and the industrialisation of print production, the *image d'Épinal* came to embrace the text/image narratives that were also proving increasingly popular in the newly booming journals of the latter two-thirds of the nineteenth century. As we shall see in the next chapter, these narratives, with their detailed division into numerous boxes (thus essentially *cases*), were much nearer to what we now recognise as BDs. For the time being, however, the point to be noted is that the nineteenth-century proto-bandes dessinées, those so often quoted as being the true descendants of the form, were very much part of an overall text/image mentality whose full context goes back considerably further.

Rodolphe Töpffer: *'L'Inventeur de la BD'*?

Rodolphe Töpffer (1799–1846) was at his most productive just as these technological changes were taking place. But to single out one individual is to deny the notion of a general cultural movement that progresses in step with social changes, and in that sense the critical hagiography of Töpffer – more on that below – is little more than an easy solution to the complex question of the evolution of a mentality. But Töpffer is interesting as a case study, a representative of his time, an emblematic figure that remains with the habits of the past whilst showing important signs of the trends to come.[47]

Rodolphe Töpffer, second son of the painter Adam Töpffer, earned his living as master, and then also proprietor, in a Swiss boarding school. During his lifetime, and for a hundred years or so following it, he was best known to the outside world for his travel accounts, generally published between 1832 and 1842 and describing excursions in the mountains. These were originally books of notes and sketches made whilst exploring with his pupils, and many of these reports have remained in manuscript form since being bequeathed to Geneva's main library, the Bibliothèque Publique et Universitaire. From 1832 onwards his cousin, Jacques-Julien Dubochet of Paris, published the first *Voyages en zigzag* [Journeys in a Zigzag], with their immediate success leading to numerous reprints, some posthumous, and distribution on a wider scale.

Although Töpffer's travel writings cover many destinations – the Alps of course, but also Milan, Chamonix, the baths at Lavey, the Swiss countryside – the style is often similar, mixing personal circumstances with observation of general life, whilst introducing detailed description of both the human and environmental décor. Töpffer brings his work to life through caricatural tales, which are matched by the interspersing of sketches. These include the members of his own parties (often his schoolchildren), the natives encountered as well as the fellow tourists, and the more specialised roles, which are often the subject of detailed anecdotes. Amongst these we find innkeepers, smugglers, customs officers, guides and members of the priesthood. The illustrations exaggerate features to comic effect, whilst remaining clearly recognisable, as in the Englishman who forbids fellow travellers to speak unless spoken to first.[48]

The link with the English caricaturists, whose influence Töpffer acknowledges in a letter to Sainte-Beuve,[49] operates both in terms of style and of content, particularly with regard to Rowlandson. As stated above, the light touch of both caricaturists in their portrayal of the diverse beings that populate a traveller's encounters immediately attracts attention, and although these are text-based works, the reader who flicks through the images, as one inevitably does, will build up a memory-store related to the narrative.

Viewed in this context, Töpffer is a figure of his time, but by no means an inventor of a new genre, as Groensteen and others have labelled him. His key works, at least as far as his contemporary audience was concerned, were textual narratives, to which further spice was given through the addition of humorous illustrations. It was not until Paul Chaponnière's largely overlooked *Caricatures töpfffériennes* of 1941 that Töpffer's proto-BDs, as we now see them, received any depth of critical attention. Chaponnière underlines this fact in his first chapter:

> Les meilleurs biographes et critiques de Töpffer n'ont accordé le plus souvent à ses albums de caricatures qu'une assez légère attention. Ils ne pouvaient sans doute les ignorer, mais feignaient de ne voir là que l'amusement d'un écrivain occupé d'ailleurs à de plus nobles travaux. Sainte-Beuve ne cache pas qu'il les trouve d'un goût assez médiocre; Gaullieur reproche à leur auteur de se livrer à un bas comique, de ne point songer à l'amélioration des mœurs; l'abbé Relave montre quelque gêne à les louer, et seuls peut-être les Allemands Friedrich Vischer et Ernst Schur ont pris le soin de leur consacrer une étude attentive et méthodique. (15–16)

> [The best biographies and critics of Töpffer have generally only given scant attention to his albums of caricatures. They must undoubtedly have known about them, but gave the impression that all that was to be seen in such albums was the plaything of a writer who had more noble work to occupy his attention. Sainte-Beuve does not hide the fact that he finds them in somewhat mediocre taste; Gaullieur criticises the author for giving in to a low comic style and for not aiming at improving mores; Abbot Relave is reluctant to praise them, and it is possibly only the Germans Friedrich Vischer and Ernst Schur who took the trouble to study them with attention and method.]

But the view of a Töpffer in keeping with his time rather than as a ground-breaking precursor does not mean that he, and his time, are not of interest to the historian of the bande dessinée. The new technology of the 1830s was particularly suited to popularising the illustrated narrative: the lithograph made the reproduction of images feasible on a wide scale (Töpffer had mastered the technique of *autographie*, one similar to the lithograph), and the production and distribution of mainstream journals provided an outlet. Illustrated extracts from the *Voyages en zigzag* appeared in the high-selling *L'Illustration* from 16 December 1843 and *Les Nouvelles genevoises*, a collection of some of Töpffer's most popular works, featured from 21 December 1844. Similar illustrated voyages, such as Albert Aubert's *Voyage au long cours à travers la France et la Navarre: Récit philosophique, sentimental et pittoresque* [Travelling through France and Navarre the Long Way Round: A Philosophic, Sentimental and Picturesque Récit] were frequent.[50] The technology was, once again, to change the status of the image, and Töpffer was, at least as far as recent critics are concerned, in the right place at the right time.

In 1998 in *Forging a New Medium* Thierry Groensteen backed up his defence of Töpffer as originator of the modern comic strip:[51] 'The invention of printing killed the comic strip, because printing requires a durable separation between text and picture. It would take several centuries before the Genevan Rodolphe Töpffer (1799–1846) reinvented the comic strip, about 1830' (1998: 109).

Such schematisation should perhaps be viewed in the context of a barrage of French criticism eager to give the bande dessinée an immediate home-grown pedigree, as opposed to American centenary celebrations of *Yellow Kid* in 1996. My overview, on the contrary, has pointed to a rich history of text/image interaction largely fostered by the gradual influence of the new medium of print, with French culture at the forefront. By the end of the eighteenth century the new medium was no longer new, but the image had been subordinated, or elevated in its own right, rather than abandoned. A shift in emphasis was to occur once again with the onset of the industrial era.

Notes

1. The catalogue's authors are Pierre Couperie, Proto Destefanis, Edouard François, Maurice Horn, Claude Moliterni and Gerald Gassiot-Talabot. The exhibition took place at the Musée des Arts Décoratifs in Paris. The Musée des Arts Décoratifs published the catalogue.
2. (Verviers: Marabout).
3. (Paris: 10/18).
4. (Paris: Seghers).
5. Both Baron-Carvais and Groensteen's works are entitled *La Bande dessinée*. Both were published in Paris by PUF and Milan respectively. 'Que Sais-Je?' refers to Michel de Montaigne's motto ['What Know I?] and is the subtitle of a series of short popular guides on all aspects of world knowledge and culture.
6. *The Early Comic Strip: Narrative Strips and Picture Stories in the European Broadsheet from c. 1450 to 1825: History of the Comic Strip Volume 1* (Berkeley: University of California Press, 1973). The second volume, on the nineteenth century, will be discussed below and in the next chapter.
7. Most of the examples that follow have been taken from the Special Collections Department of Glasgow University Library. The choice has

partly been based on practical expediency since much of my research was carried out while based in Glasgow. Nonetheless the collections of Glasgow University Library do offer an exceptionally rich and varied overview of early text/image forms, with the works readily available for first-hand examination. Other libraries would generally not boast the completeness of these collections, or alternatively might not permit ready access to such treasures. Furthermore, the depth of knowledge, accessibility and willingness to help that staff at Glasgow University Library's Special Collections take as givens have played a key role in the research process.

For further information on many of the works discussed, see Nigel Thorp, *The Glory of the Page: Medieval & Renaissance Illuminated Manuscripts from Glasgow University Library* (London: Harvey Miller, 1987).

8. Further images of this and of many of the other works mentioned in this section can be accessed via the University of Glasgow Library's website (www.lib.gla.ac.uk), which in turn leads to the pages of their Special Collections Department. The site includes a number of virtual exhibitions.
9. Alison Adams, 'The *Cent Nouvelles Nouvelles* in MS Hunter 252: The Impact of the Miniatures', *French Studies* 46.4 (1992), 385-94. Images taken from the *Cent nouvelles nouvelles,* including folio 172v, can be accessed in the pages of University of Glasgow's Special Collections website (via www.lib.gla.ac.uk). See in particular *The World of Chaucer* virtual exhibition.
10. *Story and Space in Renaissance Art: The Rebirth of Continuous Narrative* (Cambridge: Cambridge University Press, 1998).
11. Much of this information is taken from the virtual *Treasures from Two Millennia* exhibition and September 2000 Book of the Month that feature on the University of Glasgow's Special Collections website. See also Adrian Wilson and Joyce Lancaster Wilson, *A Medieval Mirror: Speculum humanae salvationis, 1324–1500* (Berkeley: University of California Press, 1985).
12. This manuscript is November 1999 Book of the Month in the University of Glasgow's Special Collections website.
13. On these points see Avril Henry's *Biblia pauperum* (Aldershot: Scolar, 1987), a facsimile edition based upon the Dresden copy. Her introduction, notes and transcriptions are to be consulted for a thorough introduction to the work.
14. The translations are those of Avril Henry, taken from page 67 of her *Biblia pauperum.*
15. *Biblia pauperum,* p. 3.
16. See David Kunzle, *The Early Comic Strip.* In particular chapter 1, 'The First Century of Printing: Religious Propaganda (c. 1450–1550)', pp. 11–39, should be consulted.
17. The characteristic woodcuts are by Hans Holbein the Younger, although the 1538 (Lyon: Melchior and Gaspar Trechsel) edition is often attributed to the authorship of Jean de Vauzelles. A facsimile edition with introduction and translation by Werner L. Gundersheimer is available under the title of *The Dance of Death* (New York: Dover, 1971).
18. As one might expect, this is held in the Département des Estampes. The series is also available on microfilm. It appears to have been assembled sometime in the nineteenth century, although the series is not closed and constant additions are made.
19. Examples of September 11 depictions in comic art form include Art Spiegelman's *In the Shadow of No Towers* (London: Penguin Viking, 2004) and, more recently and in French (despite the title), Fabrice Colin and Laurent Cilluffo's *World Trade Angels* (Paris: Denoël Graphic, 2006).

20. Charles de Sercy in Paris published the 1650 edition. Further editions followed in 1664, 1667, 1668, 1672, 1673, 1690 and 1699. For more examples of the move towards narrative via the medium of Early Modern book publications, see chapter 11 of my *Text/Image Mosaics in French Culture: Emblems and Comic Strips* (Aldershot: Ashgate, 2005). The subject will also be discussed briefly below with particular reference to emblem books. On general patterns of publication history, see Roger Chartier, 'Publishing Strategies and What the People Read, 1530–1660', which is chapter 5 (pp. 145–82) of *The Cultural Uses of Print in Early Modern France* (Princeton: Princeton University Press, 1987).
21. The notion of 'parallel mentalities' as underlying both Early Modern text/image forms (in particular emblem books) and today's bande dessinée is central to my *Text/Image Mosaics in French Culture*.
22. (Angoulême: Éditions de l'An 2, 2003).
23. The *Hecatomgraphie* does not in fact follow the 'standard' tripartite structure in that the facing page contains a fourth element, a longer explanation in verse. The 1544 version of the work is available in a facsimile edition by Alison Adams (Geneva: Droz, 1997). The title means 'One Hundred Pictures'.
24. *Le Théâtre des bons engins* (Lyon: Denis Janot, [1540]) means 'Theatre of Good Devices', *Morosophie* (Lyon: Macé Bonhomme, 1553) means 'Foolish Wisdom' and *Emblematum liber* (first edition, Augsburg: Heinrich Steiner, 1531) translates as 'Book of Emblems'.
25. For an introduction to the French emblem and its context, a subject that has been explored at length in its own right, see Daniel Russell, *The Emblem and Device in France* (Lexington, KY: French Forum, 1985). For further works on the French emblem, see Laurence Grove and Daniel Russell, *The French Emblem: A Bibliography of Secondary Sources* (Geneva: Droz, 2000).
26. (Lyon: Balthazar Arnoullet). The title, 'The First Book of Emblems', implies the existence of a sequel, but the nearest we have to this is a 'second book' of animal descriptions.
27. This emblem tales the tale of a whore in a paternity suit, whom the defence asks to walk across a bed of roses. When she cannot identify the thorn that has pricked her, the paternity suit is thrown out.
28. The question of progress towards narrative in the developing emblem book and associated forms provides the central topic of chapter 11, 'From Moveable Mosaic…' (pp. 124–37) of my *Text/Image Mosaics*. It is for that reason that I only give limited examples of the phenomenon here.
29. The group's title is a play on the term for 'hammer shark' and the colloquial use of 'marteau' [hammer] to imply madness. Their work will be discussed briefly in Chapter 7 on contemporary BD.
30. Again, this is a question that I discuss at some length in *Text/Image Mosaics*, and so I am merely touching its surface here. See chapter 12, '… To Moving Images' (pp. 138–51).
31. See Mario Praz, *Studies in Seventeenth-Century Imagery* (Rome: Edizioni di Storia e Letteratura, 1964 [first edition 1939–1947]), in particular pp. 83–134 ('Profane Love') of chapter 3.
32. On the role played by Hogarth, Rowlandson (see below) and other English caricaturists in the development of the modern comic strip, see Paul Gravett, 'The Cartoonist's Progress: The Inventors of Comics in Great Britain', in *Forging a New Medium: The Comic Strip in the Nineteenth Century*, ed. Pascal Lefèvre and Charles Dierick (Brussels: VUP UP, 2000 [first edition 1998]), pp. 79–103. This volume will be discussed further in our next chapter. See also Kunzle, *The Early Comic Strip*.
33. The edition consulted is that of Nattali and Bond of London, 1817. This is a three-volume version of the eight-part serialisation, also of 1817. The first *Dr Syntax* volume appeared in 1812, although the London publisher

Rudolph Ackermann had used Rowlandson's *Dr Syntax* plates in his *Poetical Magazine* as early as 1809.

34. M. Gandais, *Le Don Quichotte romantique, ou voyage du Docteur Syntaxe à la recherché du pittoresque et du romantique; poëme en XX chants, traduit librement de l'anglais et orné de 26 gravures* [The Romantic Don Quioxote, or the Journey of Doctor Syntax in Search of the Picturesque and Romantic: A Poem in XX Verses, Translated Freely from the English and Decorated with 26 Engravings] (Paris: chez L'Auteur et Pélicier, 1821).
35. Thierry Groensteen and Benoît Peeters, *Töpffer: L'Invention de la bande dessinée* [Töpffer: The Invention of the Bande Dessinée] (Paris: Hermann, 1994). Rodolphe Töpffer, *Le Docteur Festus: Histoire de monsieur Cryptogame: Deux odyssées* [Doctor Festus: The Story of Mr Cryptogame: Two Odysseys], ed. Thierry Groensteen (Paris: Seuil, 1996). This work is part of a three-volume collection of Töpffer reprints. For further details, see the final section of this chapter and the opening section of the next chapter.
36. It is an influence that Töpffer acknowledges, as will be discussed below. Töpffer's *histoires en images* will be considered in the opening section of the next chapter.
37. These paintings are reproduced on the Louvre's website (www.louvre.fr).
38. A summary of Greuze's description for these twenty-six paintings is given in *Greuze et Diderot: Vie familiale et education dans la seconde moitié du XVIIIème siècle* [Greuze and Diderot: Family Life and Education in the Second Half of the Eighteenth Century] (Clermont-Ferrand: Musées de Clermont-Ferrand, 1984), pp. 107–12. The work is a catalogue of a 1984 exhibition. The text (no author is given) notes on page 112 that the project was published in the *Annuaire des Artistes et des Amateurs* [The Artists and Art Lovers Yearbook], 1861, pp. 265–73.
39. This painting is reproduced on the National Galleries of Scotland website (www.nationalgalleries.org). The gallery uses *A Girl with a Dead Canary* as the painting's English title. Diderot's *Salons* are available in a four-volume set (Oxford: Clarendon, 1957–1967) edited by Jean Seznec and Jean Adhémar. John Goodman has provided a two-volume annotated and illustrated translation of the Salons of 1765 and 1767 under the title of *Diderot on Art* (New Haven: Yale University Press, 1995).
40. (Quebec: Musée du Québec, 1995). This is the catalogue of a Musée du Québec exhibition of that year. See also Nicole Garnier-Pelle, *L'Imagerie populaire française II: Images d'Épinal gravées sur bois* [French Popular Imagery II: Woodcut *Images d'Épinal*] (Paris: Réunion des Musées Nationaux, 1996). This is the catalogue of the extensive collections held by the Bibliothèque nationale de France and the Musée National des Arts et Traditions Populaires. The trailblazer studies on the *images d'Épinal* were Champfleury's *Histoire de la caricature moderne* [The History of Modern Caricature] (Paris, E. Dentu, [1865]) and *Histoire de l'imagerie populaire* [The History of Popular Imagery] (Paris: E. Dentu, 1869). For a general introduction to the subject see also Jean Mister, François Blaudez and André Jacquemin, *Épinal et l'imagerie populaire* (Paris: Hachette, 1961).
41. Antoine de Baecque, *La Caricature révolutionnaire* (Paris: CNRS, 1988), p.13. See also the companion volume by Claude Langlois, *La Caricature contre-révolutionnaire* (Paris: CNRS, 1988). Michel Vovelle's five-volume *La Révolution française: Images et récit: 1789–1799* (Paris: Messidor, 1986) is also an important source of visual iconography. For a scholarly overview in English, see the Imaging the French Revolution site (http://chnm.gmu.edu/revolution/imaging/). This is a joint project of George Mason University's Centre for History & New Media and the University of California, Los Angeles's Department of History. On post-Revolutionary prints and English interchange (to be compared with the

earlier case of Töpffer and Rowlandson discussed above), see Caroline Rossiter, 'Early French Caricature (1795-1830) and English Influence', *European Comic Art* 2.1 (2009), 39-62.

42. This assumption is based on a survey of the *Série Qb1: Histoire de France en estampes* at the BnF's Département des Estampes. This series is a particularly rich source of revolutionary prints.
43. The print is reproduced on pp. 178–79 of Antoine de Baecque's *La Caricature révolutionnaire*, with analysis on p. 181.
44. *Images d'Épinal*, pp. 53–57. Again, for general background to the *images d'Épinal*, see the works by Martin, Garnier-Pelle, Champfleury, and Mister, Blaudez and Jacquemin cited above.
45. For an illustrated analysis of the Ages of Man theme, see Daniel Russell, 'Emblems and the Ages of Life: Defining the Self in Early Modern France', *Emblematica* 14 (2005), 23–53.
46. All of these prints are illustrated and catalogued in Denis Martin's *Images d'Épinal.*
47. In recent times there has been quite an industry of criticism on Töpffer. See, for example, David Kunzle, *The Early Comic Strip: The Nineteenth Century: History of the Comic Strip Volume 2* (Berkeley: University of California Press, 1990); David Kunzle, *Father of the Comic Strip: Rodolphe Töpffer* (Jackson, MS: University Press of Mississippi, 2007); Thierry Groensteen and Benoît Peeters, *Töpffer: L'Invention de la bande dessinée;* Thierry Groensteen, ed., *Les Origines de la bande dessinée* [The Origins of the Bande Dessinée], *Le Collectionneur de Bandes Dessinées* special number ['hors série'] (no. 79, 1996); [Geneva, Musées d'Art et d'Histoire], *Rodolphe Töpffer: Aventures graphiques* [Rodolphe Töpffer: Graphic Adventures] ([Geneva]: [Musées d'Art et d'Histoire], 1996); Danielle Buyssens, Jean-Daniel Candaux, Jacques Droin and Daniel Maggetti, eds, *Propos töpffériens* [Remarks about Töpffer] (Geneva: Société d'Etudes Töpffériennes, 1998); Daniel Maggetti, ed., *Töpffer* (Geneva: Albert Skira, 1996).
48. This image appears in *L'Illustration* IV 95 (21 December 1844), p. 253. It is an extract from the *Nouvelles genevoises* [News from Geneva], an author-illustrated collection of Töpffer's prose fiction and selected travel récits. This first illustrated edition (Paris: Garnier, 1876) is available in a 1998 facsimile (Geneva: Slatkine).
49. The letter is dated 29 December 1840. An extract is given on p. xiii of Groensteen and Peeters, *Töpffer: L'Invention de la bande dessinée.*
50. This example appeared from 7 December 1844. The Albert Aubert in question was presumably the Parisian bookseller who created and issued pirate versions of M. Jabot. We should also note, as has often been stated, that a version of *M. Cryptogame* appeared in *L'Illustration* from 25 January 1845. This will be discussed further in the next chapter.
51. 'Töpffer, the Originator of the Modern Comic Strip', in *Forging a New Medium*, pp. 105–14. This, Kunzle's chapter on Töpffer (pp. 28–71) in *The Early Comic Strip: The Nineteenth Century*, and Kunzle's recent monograph, *Father of the Comic Strip: Rodolphe Töpffer*, are the main pieces on Töpffer in English.

CHAPTER 5

THE NINETEENTH CENTURY: PHOTOS, FUNNIES AND FILMS

Töpffer Again

The placing of Rodolphe Töpffer astride two chapters – the BD's prehistory, to a certain extent its legitimising mythology, and the nineteenth century, the period that saw the growth of the form as we know it – is quite deliberate. Although, as we have seen, Töpffer 'Inventor of the BD' is an appellation founded on retrospective historicism and probably no more pertinent than a claim for either Queen Mathilde or Ugg the Lascaux caveman to be *mater/pater et princeps* of the genre, the work of Töpffer is important as an indication of the mindset that was current by the 1830s. It was a mindset that was starting to put text with image in a way that, once again, no longer necessarily implied subordination. Töpffer is particularly significant for the awareness he shows of this phenomenon, as expressed in the much-quoted opening words of the 'Annonce de l'histoire de M. Jabot' [Advance Notice for the Story of M. Jabot] that originally appeared in 1837:[1]

> Ce petit livre est d'une nature mixte. Il se compose d'une série de dessins autographiés au trait. Chacun de ces dessins est accompagné d'une ou deux lignes de texte. Les dessins, sans ce texte, n'auraient qu'une signification obscure; le texte, sans les dessins, ne signifierait rien. (167)
>
> [This little book is of a mixed nature. It is composed of a series of drawings reproduced following their autograph state. Each of the drawings is accompanied by one or two lines of text. Without the text the meaning of the drawings would be obscure. Without the drawings the text would be meaningless.]

In the same 'Annonce' Töpffer also emphasises the hybrid nature of the work in terms of its tone, mixing the light-hearted with the serious. But he appears to put entertaining style before philosophical content, referring to *M. Jabot* as a work that,

> parlant directement aux yeux, s'exprime par la représentation, non par le récit. Ici, comme on le conçoit aisément, les traits d'observation, le comique, l'esprit, résident dans le croquis lui-même, plus que dans l'idée que le croquis développe. [...]
> Somme toute, M. Jabot est un livre amusant, médiocrement imprimé, fort cher, et à sa place dans un salon surtout. (170–71, 172)
>
> [speaking directly to the eyes, expresses itself through representation, not through the récit. Here, as soon becomes clear, the observation of details, the comic elements, the spirit of the thing, all lie in the sketch itself, rather than in the ideas developed by the sketch. [...]
> [In short, M. Jabot is an amusing book, of mediocre print quality, that is rather expensive and above all at home in a salon.]

Here, and elsewhere, Töpffer is at pains to underplay any notion of his *histoires en images* as a serious endeavour. There is a good dose of comic modesty, but it is also the indication that he himself was not prepared to claim the invention of a worthy new genre.

Notwithstanding, several of his works show a precursory preoccupation with what we might now label as image theory. In a lengthy 1836 two-part article entitled 'Réflexions à propos d'un programme' [Reflections on a Programme] Töpffer discusses the merits of William Hogarth in the context of the *images d'Épinal* long before Champfleury's analysis.[2] In his 'De la plaque Daguerre' [On Daguerre Plates] (1841),[3] with the subtitle of 'Le Corps moins l'âme' [The Body without the Soul], Töpffer discusses the status of photography, condemning its 'realism' as lacking artistic nuance. Töpffer is willing to engage with the new visual culture of his time, albeit somewhat conservatively; nonetheless his reference to Cartesian-style body and soul duality in the context of text/image forms is another example of the way in which he reinforces notions of the past. Claude-François Menestrier, one of the leading analysts of the emblem, had used these terms in his *L'Art des emblemes* (Lyon: Benoist Coral) of 1662.

The *Essai de physiognomonie*, a tract that appeared in 1845,[4] expands on the idea that physical appearance, and its ensuing representation, is indicative of moral character. Again, the broad notion in itself was not new, and had indeed been discussed and illustrated by Charles Le Brun in his 1702 *Méthode pour apprendre à dessiner les passions* [Method for Learning to Draw the Passions].[5] This is the posthumous publication of a 1668 address given to the Académie Royale de Peinture et Sculpture and includes an 'Abregé d'une conférence de Monsieur Le Brun sur la phisonomie' [Summary of a Paper by M. Le Brun on Physiognomy]. Töpffer, however, applied such theories not to 'high art' but to caricature. As well as a general apology for *littérature en estampes* (once again holding Hogarth up as example), the result is a manual, illustrated in Töpffer's distinctive style, demonstrating the expressive possibilities that careful manipulation of fine line traits can produce. Viewed today, the work appears remarkably fresh and entirely relevant to an understanding of one of the key features of bande dessinée production.

The works of Töpffer that are now best known – *M. Jabot, M. Crépin, M. Pencil, M. Vieux Bois, Docteur Festus, Histoire d'Albert, M. Cryptogame* (see Fig. 21, Chapter 4) – exemplify the interdependence of text and image. These are the seven stories now seen as precursors to the bande dessinée that appeared during Töpffer's lifetime, with a further adventure, *M. Trictrac*, remaining in manuscript form.[6] The order of publication, between 1833 and 1846, was that of the above listing, although composition differed, with *M. Cryptogame* the first creation around 1827.

Töpffer compiled these stories as a pastime to amuse his pupils, but following the encouragement of Johann Wolfgang von Goethe, to whom some of the manuscripts had been passed, he then released them for publication.[7] This was initially on a very limited scale – approximately 400–500 copies in general – although a certain amount of success was obtained by word of mouth. His distance from Paris, upon which a centralised nineteenth-century print industry was heavily dependent, doubtless hindered the success of Töpffer's *histoires en images*. This was to change to a certain extent through a strong working relationship with his cousin, the Parisian publisher Jacques-Julien Dubochet, and, more specifically, as a result of the serialisation of *M. Cryptogame* in *L'Illustration*, the journal for which Dubochet was responsible, as from 25 January 1845.[8] Nonetheless the 'bandes dessinées' never outshone Töpffer's other publications in and around his lifetime, although he was to see a considerable amount of success, one that included having his strips imitated/pirated and even translated.[9]

Each adventure is presented through a series of vignettes, generally three or four per oblong page, but possibly a single image or alternatively more than a dozen. Beneath each picture a few words, or lines, of calligraphic text advance the narrative, without being purely descriptive. Together they form a close narrative sequence, and differ from many previous image narratives, such as the genre paintings of Greuze, in that they provide considerably more 'frames per second'. As the titles tend to suggest, the stories are based on a central character, whose various peregrinations, be it in search of love (*M. Jabot, M. Vieux Bois*), freedom from love (*M. Cryptogame*), knowledge (*Dr Festus*), or domestic fulfilment (*M. Crépin*), provide the mainstay of the plot.

The tone is always burlesque and caricatural, and is much easier to see than to describe, as in the scene in which M. Cryptogame attempts to placate the angry Elvire (Fig. 21, Chapter 4). A certain amount of humour is derived from the discordance between the pseudo-lofty tone of the text ('Elvire satisfaite redevient intéressante et tendre' [Elvire, now satisfied, becomes fetching and tender once again]) and the contradictory nature of the accompanying images, whereby we see Cryptogame as less than satisfied. The text does explain and contextualise the pictures, but it is the *relationship* between text and image that gives the work its bite. The humour comes from *seeing* M. Cryptogame's amusing dismay, and playing it against the words, rather than having it spelt out for us. The speed of the narrative varies, and, as in the modern BD, the size of the *case* and the relative roles of text and image create the interplay between action and description.

Nonetheless Töpffer is far from unique in putting word with image in this way. Firstly, there may well have been numerous thus-far-undiscovered authors in corners of the French-speaking world who were composing private manuscripts of pictorial narratives. More significantly in terms of tangible cultural history, prior to *M. Cryptogame*'s 1845 debut in *L'Illustration* (the periodical's context will be the subject of a section below) it was entirely normal to find similar compositions within the journal's pages.

In general such caricatural strips provide Voltaire-style exaggerations of exotic events and places, whereby any potential unease is diffused by the grotesque humour. The 1843 version of *La Péri*,[10] a ballet that charmed 'la perfide Albion', gives the outlandish story of the ottoman Achmet and his attempts at distraction, with the text interspersed with caricatural illustrations giving the narrative in sequence. Alternatively, travel takes the characters to the exotic. This is exemplified in Albert Aubert's *Voyage au long cours à travers la France et la Navarre* (mentioned in our last chapter) that appeared in regular episodes from 15 June 1844.[11] Cham's 1843 *Impressions de voyage de M. Boniface* tells of Boniface's adventures following his flight to England in an attempt to avoid military service.[12]

This last feature appeared as a preview of Cham's album within the 'Publications illustrées' [Illustrated Publications] section. *L'Illustration* included tasters of the work of some of the most important caricaturists of the day, such as J.-J. Grandville, whose 'Cent proverbes' [One Hundred Proverbs] were single-frame play on words visualising well-known dictums.[13] Cham, the pen name of Amédée Charles Henri de Noé (1818–1879), was a regular contributor, both through hero-based adventures, such as those of M. Boniface, to be compared with his earlier Monsieur Lajaunisse (published separately from 1839),[14] as well as thematic caricatures, such as seaside visits, the hunting season or the grape harvests,[15] which still effectively told a story of a particular time and place.

As to whether Töpffer composed his 'strips' before those of Cham et alii is largely immaterial. It was the medium, the high-profile illustrated journal, that created the phenomenon, and in this respect Töpffer's work was just one of the many 'variétés' to be listed in the end-of-volume index. If we are, however, to single out individuals, the role played by Jacques-Julien Dubochet is likely to have been decisive, for it was he, in practical terms, who drew upon the possibilities of the new technology of the lithograph so as to bring together the text/image talents of the time. His family bonds with Töpffer mean he may well have had access to his early scribblings, or alternatively he could have discussed his knowledge and admiration for narrative caricature with his cousin, perhaps unwittingly providing the inspiration for what in hindsight was to become Töpffer's hallmark.

Another important figure in the diffusion of these 'proto-BDs' was the publisher Gabriel Aubert, who was responsible for *La Caricature* (from 1830), as well as various 'pirate' versions of Töpffer's works. Leonardo De Sá points to the animosity felt by Töpffer towards Aubert,[16] but one can imagine there being a certain amount of complicity given that Aubert worked closely with Dubochet. It also seems likely that Gabriel Aubert was related in some way to the Albert Aubert responsible for the *Voyage au long cours à travers la France et la Navarre* strip (see above). More research is needed on the links between those responsible for the early creation, and perhaps more importantly, propagation, of what we now see as the nineteenth-century bande dessinée.

L'Illustration grew to be the most prominent of the outlets for the work of Cham, Grandville, Aubert and Töpffer, but also for other illustrators who were to achieve renown throughout the new industrial era: Gustave Doré, Honoré Daumier, Benjamin Rabier and Caran d'Ache (pen name of Emmanuel Poiré), as well as lesser-known authors such as Job and Vernier. This book will not deal with any of these in individual detail, as the importance of the nineteenth-century caricaturist is generally recognised – see, for example, *Forging a New Medium* and *The History of the Comic Strip: The Nineteenth Century* cited below – and works are available with relative ease in English.[17] This chapter instead will aim to give the general picture, with an overview of the changes in visual culture that made the modern BD possible.

Prior to *L'Illustration*'s prominence, it was the late 1820s and early 1830s that saw the creation of the first illustrated journals distributed on an industrial scale, starting with *La Silhouette* (founded 1829), *La Caricature* (1830) and *Le Charivari* [The Discordant Din] (1832). However primitive they may seem today, in all of these publications, as we shall discuss below, a main point of attraction was the satirical images that functioned by reference to the accompanying text. It was not a coincidence that the image should achieve such renewed prominence at exactly the time when photography was also taking its first steps as a fledgling art.

In what way, however, does the text/image mindset that was starting to blossom at this period differ from, say, children's illustration in the so-called Age of Reason? As ever, a mindset by its nature is hard to define and even harder to explain, but certain empirical observations can be related to the question. As with the Renaissance, when the invention and spread of print technology was rapidly followed by a vogue of emblem-related publications relying upon the *interaction* of text and image in order to function, so the nineteenth century saw the development of key visual technologies at the same period as text/image forms, including a revival of the emblem book, became popular and fashionable. The nineteenth century differs from previous ages in that the technology involved mass production on a scale previously unknown, not just in the sphere of heavy industry but also in terms of the spread of information.[18]

To reiterate, it is through a general exploration of artistic milieu that this present study differs from the excellent works on the nineteenth-century beginnings of the BD-related artist by Philippe Kaenel, by David Kunzle, and by Pascal Lefèvre and Charles Dierick. Kaenel in his *Le Métier d'illustrateur 1830–1880: Rodolphe Töpffer, J.-J. Grandville, Gustave Doré* presents authoritative sections on the artists in question. Kunzle's *The History of the Comic Strip: The Nineteenth Century* continues the project of his first volume,[19] this time providing important discussions of Töpffer, Cham and Daumier, but also Nadar, Gustave Doré, Léonce Petit, and the tradition of caricature not only in France but also Germany and England. The work edited by Lefèvre and Dierick, *Forging a New Medium: The Comic Strip in the Nineteenth Century* (Brussels: VUP University Press, 2000 [first edition 1998]), provides chapters on the main European traditions of caricature-based narrative. In all three cases, however, the mainstay of the research is channelled very specifically through individual 'great men'.[20]

Nonetheless, *Forging a New Medium*, and other general works from art history backgrounds,[21] have demonstrated a willingness for English-language scholarship to engage with questions of text/image expression in nineteenth-century France as precursory to the modern comic strip.[22] In this respect the period differs from the subject matter of other sections of this current chronology; however, there has been little or no attempt to provide a more general BD-related framework for the artists now seen as pioneers. Lefèvre and Dierick summarise the critical situation in the final sentence of the introduction to *Forging a New Medium*:

> This book has no ambition to close discussion about the 19th century comic strip once and for all. The intention is rather to encourage international and cross-cultural research into this often neglected subject. Although further research is needed (there are still a lot of countries to be 'excavated'), we are beginning to understand that the development of the comic strip in the 19th century was crucial, not only as regards the history of the comic itself, but also in the development of a new more democratic society in the West. It is not coincidental that the comic strip flourished in the 19th century, because it is related to larger social, scientific and artistic developments. (22)

Our present chapter will centre on three of the major social, scientific and artistic developments: photography, the satirical popular press and then the moving image. As stated, I will take a very different view from that of the *l'homme et l'oeuvre* school that heralds individual great men – Töpffer, but also cited are Christophe, Wilhelm Busch and R.F. Outcault – as inventors of the BD, in the same way that Thomas Edison invented the phonogram and Alexander Graham Bell invented the telephone. It is my priority, before considering clearly perceivable landmarks of the twentieth-century BD – even if it was not to get its current label until the 1950s it was nonetheless recognisable at least from the 1920s – to look at the *context* that saw the early development of the form as we know it today.

Photos

The zeal with which France has appropriated the invention of the bande dessinée is not a new phenomenon. In a letter dated 6 April 1847 Alfred Bouard tells Henry Fox Talbot that, 'En France on a fait de la découverte de Mr Daguerre une chose en quelque sorte nationale' [In France Mr Daguerre's discovery has been made into a sort of national phenomenon].[23]

In 1827 Nicéphore Niépce reproduced a print on a metal plate by a process of light sensitivity, thereby inaugurating the mechanism that would lead to Louis-Jacques-Mandé Daguerre's 1839 announcement of his process of capturing images via the use of iodine on a silver plate, the creation of the 'daguerreotype'. The story of the discovery and gradual improvement of photographic techniques is one that bears witness to the growth of cultural phenomena through a series of linked defining instances, an evolution rather than a single 'eureka' moment. It is a story that involves interchange (sometimes less than happily) between Niépce and Daguerre in France, David Octavius Hill and Robert Adamson in Scotland and Henry Fox Talbot, an Englishman travelling throughout Europe.

It is interesting to note that in 1834, the year following Töpffer's M. Jacob, Talbot was also in Geneva conducting photographic experiments. Talbot's correspondence shows that he also spent considerable time either in France or in contact with French events as he closely followed Daguerre's progress, improving on his methods by dint of the fact that his Calotype process, which he unveiled in 1841, used negatives, thereby allowing multiple copies to be made of a given image. In 1844 Talbot published *The Pencil of Nature* through Longman, Brown, Green, and Longmans of London.[24] This was the first collection of photographic images.

The Pencil of Nature is of interest to us for the insight it gives into the assumptions underpinning the culture of the image at the time, assumptions that the twenty-first-century onlooker might not always take for granted. On an immediate level it is significant that Talbot felt the need to publish the showpiece collection of his photos with text, with the images followed by one or two sides of explanation and comment. This explanation could be on technical matters associated with the new process, both as used in the plate in question and with respect to further possibilities, but it could also contextualise in a wider cultural sense. To take the example of Plate X, that of 'The Haystack', Talbot makes the following points:

> One advantage of the discovery of the Photographic Art will be, that it will enable us to introduce into our pictures a multitude of minute details which add to the truth and reality of the representation, but which no artist would take the trouble to copy faithfully from nature.
>
> Contenting himself with a general effect, he would probably deem it beneath his genius to copy every accident of light and shade; nor could he do so indeed, without a disproportionate expenditure of time and trouble, which might be otherwise much better employed.
>
> Nevertheless, it is well to have the means at our disposal of introducing these minutiæ without any additional trouble, for they will sometimes be found to give an air of variety beyond expectation to the scene represented.

Talbot is at pains to give his new art as artistic a presentation as possible, as he makes clear in the text that accompanies Plate VI, 'The Open Door': 'The chief object of the present work is to place on record some of the early beginnings of a new art, before the period, which we trust is approaching, of its being brought to maturity[.]'

It may also be that in the context of a high-quality artistic production it was felt that images alone would not be sufficient, perhaps serving as illustrations with nothing to illustrate and therefore lacking *gravitas*. Ironically, it is of course the photos that are the mainstay of the work, which means that effectively Talbot is reversing the then traditional roles by using text to support image. The dynamics become ambiguous and as a result a sort of interdependence is achieved. Although *The Pencil of Nature* has no form of narrative progression, it is indicative of the type of text/image relationship that will be a defining element of the kindling precursors to the modern BD.

It is indeed important to stress the often-overlooked fact that *The Pencil of Nature*, despite being a showcase for new scientific techniques, is very much an *artistic* production, a view that was far from taken for granted. Töpffer in his 'De la plaque Daguerre' (1841), for example, goes to some length to condemn photography as lacking in artistic nuance. But if we take the case of Talbot's ladder image (Fig. 22), we can see that what may appear to be a rustic arrangement of randomly chosen objects is in fact laden with symbolic significance, as indeed Mike Weaver has convincingly demonstrated in his introduction to *Henry Fox Talbot: Selected Texts and Bibliography* (Oxford: Clio, 1992):

Figure 22. 'The Ladder'. Henry Fox Talbot. *The Pencil of Nature*. London: Longman, Brown, Green, and Longmans, 1844, plate XIV. Glasgow University Library Photo A 18.

> Emblematically, the ladder represents the leading idea of a countenance looking upwards. It appears in the Bible as Jacob's ladder; in alchemy as a ladder of experimental ascent from which it is all too easy to fall; and in freemasonry as symbolic of the progress of the soul. As an emblem it signifies ascent towards the light. In the work of Ramon Lull (1232–*c*.1316), the ladder of ascent refers to the philosophical rungs by which man climbs eventually to God [.] (12)

The new technology is therefore provoking interest in the image, but contextualisation is paramount. The image does not stand alone as an imitator or a reproducer of the outside world – that would be the role of the secondary art of illustration – instead its resonances convey morals and deeper meaning. As such, early photography has the same aspirations as academy painting. Talbot often makes the comparison, and does not hesitate to conclude in favour of his new photographic art, as in the text that accompanies 'The Haystack' (see above), but he must have been aware that stylistically it was hard for early photography to rival the subtleties of a master painter. His new visual art form could, however, achieve serious standing when imbued with weighty references and published alongside book-form text.

In France one of the main figures truly to exploit photography as an art form was Gaspard Felix Tournachon, better known as Nadar (1820–1910). Originally Nadar worked as a caricaturist for such publications as *Le Charivari* (see below), *La Revue Comique* (founded 1848) and the *Journal Pour Rire* (also founded 1848), before taking to photography in 1853 as a financial enterprise. Indeed his photographic portraiture fed into his continued caricaturing, including in his own publication, the *Petit Journal Pour Rire* (founded 1856) and its spin-off publications.

Nadar's bohemian lifestyle gave him the connections that enabled him to become a latter-day photographer to the stars, with portraits of the likes of Charles Baudelaire, Honoré de Balzac, Charles Philipon, Honoré Daumier and Gustave Doré. Nadar emphasised the advantages of an informal style of portraiture, without retouches or carefully posed sitting, but rather one that captured, or even created, the *essence* of his subject. This was furthered by his use of series photography rather than single takes, giving a form of evolution to our view of the sitter. As such his photos strove to the same end as his caricatures, which by the exaggeration of certain details and the use of sequential framing aimed to provide the stories beyond the physical appearance.[25]

His 1886 portrait of the acclaimed chemist Michel-Eugène Chevreul on his hundredth birthday, for example, consisted of a series of twenty-seven photographs each to be accompanied by a quote from the sitter. It is through the mixture of text and image, the twists of the various poses and Nadar's ability to capture the old man's vivacity through facial expressions that we end up with a lively enactment of the scientist's endearing old age. An opposite effect had been achieved with similar means in Nadar's portrayal of Môssieu

Figure 23. 'Nadar'. André Gill. 1867. *French Political Caricatures.* Glasgow University Library Hx 133/18/51.

Réac, who first appeared in *La Revue Comique* from 1848.[26] Môssieu Réac is an opportunist, as we see in his electioneering techniques, whereby he promotes his own candidacy by pretending to be working class, until recognised by members of the hustings and forced to explain that he means he is a working-class landlord! As with the adventures of Töpffer's creations, the exaggerated physiognomy and the discordance between text and image create much of the humour, but Nadar is now bringing caricatural strips to the portrayal of current events. Ironically, Nadar's style is often best captured in the portraits of him by others, as in the 1867 caricature of his ballooning antics by André Gill (Fig. 23).

Beyond the particular case of the overlap in Nadar's interests, the relevance of such concerns to the development of the bande dessinée lies in the fact that a specific technological advance was changing the status of the image. The photographic (or caricatural) image could be the first point of attraction per se, but it also functioned within a context involving further media, with the framing of the image achieved by something other than the literal gold-painted frame that presented the viewer with the Davids and the Ingres on the walls of the Louvre.[27]

Funnies[28]

It was the newly growing popular press that was to further this changing role of the image. Once again production technology had its part to play as the development of mechanical presses from about 1830, but also composition techniques through Adrien Delcambre's automated process (1849), as well as the industrialisation of paper fabrication, made wide-scale print publications affordable, thereby creating what Frédéric Barbier has called 'la seconde révolution du livre' [the book's second revolution].[29] From the second quarter of the nineteenth century, England had seen the publication in serialised form of certain novels, such as Charles Dickens's *Pickwick Papers*, that effectively created the phenomenon of the illustrated magazine. In France Charles Philipon introduced *La Silhouette* in 1829, which proved to be a prototype for the highly successful *La Caricature* (1830) and *Le Charivari* (1832).

Both combined satirical text with image – *Le Charivari* appearing daily – and, like *L'Illustration* that was to follow (1843), included the works of such illustrators as J.-J. Grandville and Honoré Daumier. *Punch* was to pursue a similar format in England from its launch in 1841. By the turn of the century *Le Courrier Français* [French Correspondence] (1884), *Le Sourire* [The Smile] (1899) and *Le Rire* (1894) were just some of the many titles in which illustration – often of a saucy nature – played an important role. In such cases the uses of images – fine-line illustrations, caricatures, or later photographs –

generally appeared to complete or support the texts to which they referred.[30] In practice, however, the prominent positioning of the images, the sense of instant recognition and reader identification they espoused, and their capacity to grab attention immediately meant that the journals could not have survived on text alone.

It is important to stress this contextual development, as caricatures per se had, as we have seen, existed for some time, be they Greuze's scenes of life, the *images d'Épinal*, or the various other productions to which David Kunzle refers in the two volumes of *The Early Comic Strip*. The culture of the new popular press was, however, on a par with the interchange of roles that Talbot and his peers were unwittingly introducing with their early collections of photographs: the image, that for a century and a half or so had been the secondary element in print expression, was now de facto playing the leading role, albeit one which was still dependent upon the context of the written word. Furthermore, the journals' serialisation format and the thematic repetition thereby engendered provided a sense of evolved continuation, a sort of overall narrative beyond that of the individual features.

These points should seem clearer with the aid of specific examples. By the middle of the century already existing publications had progressed and new ones had arisen. In 1835, for example, *Le Charivari*, whose subtitle boasted it to be the 'Journal publiant chaque jour un nouveau dessin' [The Journal that Publishes a New Sketch Each Day] only provided a single full-page illustration (on the third of its four sheets), generally with an additional textual explanation on the facing page. By 1850 things were considerably different, as is clear from the case of *L'Illustration*, founded in 1843. Although it was the best known of such illustrated publications,[31] it had plenty of rivals, whose very names generally underlined the selling point: *Le Monde Illustré* [The Illustrated World] (1857), *L'Univers Illustré* [The Illustrated Universe] (1858), *Le Journal Illustré* (1864) and so on. All of these probably took *The Illustrated London News* (1842) as base model. *L'Illustration* was a luxury production of sixteen folio pages per number with a cover price, 75 centimes, that limited it to the well off.

In a typical mid-century number, volume XV no. 362 of Saturday 2 February 1850,[32] closely packed pages of text giving weekly news alternate with illustrations of a temple in Lambaesa, scenes from a Parisian play and a feature article on England's curiosities, in particular advertising ploys such as sandwich men. The back page provides a short feature on the Seal of California and a rebus. Overall, the majority of the pages are by now illustrated or even image-dominated. This issue has no topical cartoons, such as the one by Vernier on *Les Étrennes* [New Year's Gifts] telling the story of a household's New Year celebrations by contrasting the social conditions of its various members,[33] but it does have the *Aventures de M. Verdreau* by Stop (Fig. 24).[34]

To all intents and purposes this strip boasts the very attributes by which Töpffer has been crowned father of the bande dessinée: thin-

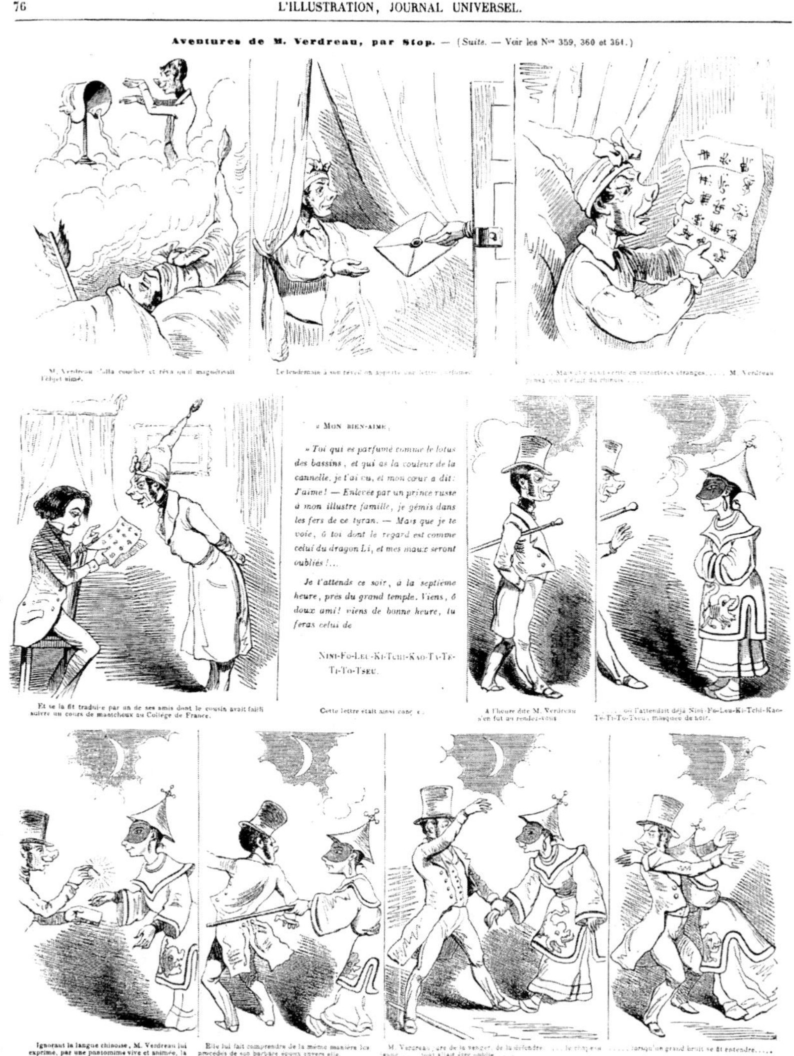

Figure 24. 'Les Aventures de M. Verdreau'. *L'Illustration*, Vol. XV, no. 362 (2 February 1850), p. 76. Private collection.

line caricature drawings, narrative development, *cases* and an interdependence of text and image. Stop, however, is mentioned in none of the main dictionaries of the BD. He may of course have just been a vulgar imitator of the Swiss schoolmaster, although it is by no means sure that he would have had direct access to his work. But even if he were a spin-off, his proto-BDs were constantly reaching an audience of approximately 18,000 a week. Similar works in cheaper publications such as *Le Journal Illustré* could sell up to 105,000. Thus to reiterate the opening section of this chapter, Töpffer is the name that has been pushed to posterity, but we should be aware that creations drawing upon the principal elements of what is now the bande dessinée were, by the 1850s, a settled form of widespread popular culture.

The general trend to an image-based culture for the masses did not decline. In a typical *illustré* at the end of the century, *Le Courrier Français* of 24 February 1895 (issue 8, year 12), the reader is immediately drawn in by Adolphe Willette's front-cover illustration, a slightly saucy view of Carnaval et les Cendres [Carnival and the Ashes], picking up once again on the Dance of Death tradition but in a Mardi Gras context. Carnival, carrying a naked woman drinking heartily from the bottle, addresses an on-looking skeleton to express disapproval at the less spicy Ashes of the Innocent. Page 2 includes various poems and page 3 reproduces a Beardsley portrait of Mantegna. News of concerts and theatre activity follows, before one in a series of illustrations of everyday life, here two women chatting, by Hermann Paul. A double centre-page spread illustrates the Châtelet production of *Don Quichotte*, with the next pages providing a text, *Les Liens du sang* [Blood Ties] by Yves le More, illustrated by a Beardsley print, and followed by a photograph of a project for a monument in honour of Jean-Antoine Watteau. Page 10 includes a further illustration by Zo d'Ana and page 11, the final page before that of the announcements and advertisements, gives a playful poster design for the 'Cabaret de l'Âne Rouge' [The Red Donkey Cabaret] by M. Gras. In a general artistic affairs publication such as *Le Courrier Français* there may be little that can be directly assimilated to the bande dessinée or even prototype illustrated narratives, but the predominance of the image, in a variety of forms and styles, now cannot be doubted.

In addition to the numerous illustrated journals that prospered by the end of the nineteenth century, it would appear that individual prints were also available, presumably sold as *feuilles volantes* or single flysheets to be mounted and used for decoration. This is the case of Glasgow University Library's collection of French political cartoons from the years following 1870 (call number HX 133), now housed in nineteen boxes and depicting prominent political figures, as well as such personalities as Victor Hugo, Gustave Doré and Nadar (see Fig. 23). To a certain extent these individually available sketches continue the tradition of popular imagery associated with the *images d'Épinal*.

Individual 'strips' were of course to be found, and the cases cited in this chapter, be they from Cham, Töpffer, Aubert, Vernier or Stop, bear witness to this. Others were to join the ranks. Caran d'Ache (pen name of Emmanuel Poiré, 1859–1909) specialised in image-only satirical narratives, including anti-Dreyfus, or on occasions generally anti-Semitic pieces, such as his *Carnet de chèques* [Cheque Book], an album in the shape of a cheque book that refers to cheques supposedly given as bribes in the Panama Canal scandal of the time (1892).[35] Benjamin Rabier (1864–1939) is recognised for his animal strips, such as his 1906 image-narrative of Jean de La Fontaine's *Fables* and, later, his intelligent duck character, Gédéon (1923). Although often associated with children's literature, Rabier, like Caran d'Ache, made his career via the illustrated press for adults.[36] These are the names to be found in twentieth-century histories of the BD, although such accounts generally do not make it clear that their works were individual facets of a much wider renewed culture of the image.

Illustrated publications for children have always existed and are particularly noted from the eighteenth century, but again it was not until the late nineteenth century that technology allowed the phenomenon to become widespread. Publications such as *Mon Journal* (1881), *Le Petit Français Illustré* (1889) or *Le Noël* [Christmas] (1895) mixed short textual stories with tips for the readers and abundant illustration, both of fictional imaginings and current fashions and events. In short these journals were creating a youth version of the *illustrés* that had seized the 'grown-up' market. By the early twentieth century magazines such as *Les Belles Images* (founded 1904) or *Jeunesse Illustrée* [Illustrated Youth] (1903), with print runs of approximately 100,000 copies, were flaunting their visual aspects, as these particular titles suggest. It is worth underlining, therefore, that the rise of the popular illustrated press for children followed on from that for adults, not vice versa, and if the origins of the modern bande dessinée are to be found in the culture of the image espoused in the nineteenth century, then suggestions that the genre grew from children's literature should be rethought.

Nonetheless, illustrated productions for children played an important role in the text/image culture of the time. To take a typical example of *Les Belles Images*, that of 16 February 1905 (number 44 of year 2): of the twelve pages, nine are image-based. Seven of these form *histoires en images*, with an additional page for rebuses and the back cover a cut-out of a grocery. The format of the *histoires en images* is the standard Épinal style, namely four rows of three picture-bearing rectangles with the text below each one. The stories tell of burlesque family travels (*L'Héritage de la famille Cassonade* by 'G. Ri'), the fears that dominate Aristide Froussard's life, or a story full of pathos in which a sailor finds and saves his long-lost son (*Le Petit mousse*).[37] In the case of *L'Héritage de la famille Cassonade*, the cover story, the repeated exaggerated characters, such as the top-hat-bearing M. Cassonade, and the break-neck sequel of unlikely events – a train crash, a shipwreck, adventures of South American savages – echo back to the style of Töpffer, while the subject matter foreshadows Hergé's *Tintin au Congo*.

By the time of this copy of *Les Belles Images*, further technological advances were adding a new dimension to pictorial expression. As with the first stages of photography, the early attempts to produce motion pictures are of interest in that they provide a window to the status of the image. Whereas early photography, at the beginning of what we can now see as the industrial and technological revolution, was a pioneering indicator of increased interest in the image, not just as a scientific gadget but also in terms of social and artistic credibility, it would appear that the motion picture consolidates and builds upon the image's already-acquired standing.

Films

The early projections by the Lumière brothers are now recognised as a landmark in the history of modern culture, as indeed befits the initial moments of what is becoming the principal art form of the twenty-first century. Nonetheless, as with photography the invention is more of a development than a single instance. Motion pictures were the natural progression from magic lanterns, Zoetropes, serial and high-speed photography. Furthermore, here again it is easy to confuse a retrospective view in the light of current developments and the innovation as it appeared in context. A brief overview of some of the influences on the material of early filmmakers will suggest that although technologically they were stretching the boundaries of the presentation of the image, in terms of content they were, by the end of the 1800s, very much a *reflection* of the image-related spirit of the time.

The initial non-public showing in Paris on 19 March 1895 of the 45-second film of workers passing through the factory gates allowed Auguste and Louis Lumière not only to show off the technology that provided the illusion of movement, but also to present a manipulation of a street scene in the way that contemporary illustrations would have produced.[38] The Lumières made certain 'characters' appear on camera, loop around the set and then reappear front-stage, thereby creating the impression of a faceless mass, in keeping with the industrial subject, and reinforced by the fact that the 'actors' had clearly been told not to look at the camera. The illusion of depth is given by the diagonal shots, with the occasional close-up to provide specific detail. As with early photography, posterity has tended to view this production in terms of technological advancement, often overlooking the artistic attainment.

The diagonal shot to create depth marks another well-known 1895 production, the train arriving at the station in La Ciotat. The movement is then contrasted with the more static angles as passengers disembark. The subject matter is thoroughly modern (cf., for example, Émile Zola's *La Bête humaine*), going far beyond the simple 'portrayal of reality' that is often used to label the Lumières' productions. The contrast between the static station scenes and the cutting movement of the train's arrival underlines the power of the new transport, a power

Figure 25. 'Train Entering the Station'. Christophe. *La Famille Fenouillard*. Paris: Armand Colin, [1893], p. 11. Bibliothèque nationale de France NUMM-106164.

that must have been felt at early projections when members of the audience reportedly fled the room! The effects achieved by the Lumière brothers can be compared with those produced by Christophe (Georges Colomb, 1856–1945) as part of his popular *Famille Fenouillard* [Fenouillard Family] series that appeared in *Le Petit Français illustré* in 1890, to be reissued in album form in 1893 (Fig. 25).[39] The principal contrast between the cutting angle of the train's movement and the closer shot of passengers on the platform is so similar that one must wonder whether the influence might have been direct. In any case, as one might expect, trains were one of the most popular subjects of the *illustrés*, which at this time would eagerly report the expansion (and associated disasters) of the new rail network. In many ways, therefore, the Lumière brothers were just giving further movement to the image-based impetus of the popular press.[40]

Similar overlap occurs with many of the 'gags' in early films. The Lumières's *L'Arroseur arrosé* [The Waterer Watered] (1895), whereby a boy standing on a hosepipe stops it working, only for the water to be released when the 'arroseur' places his face to the nozzle, was well known to readers of the *illustrés*. One such example is again the work of Christophe, and was published in the *Petit Français Illustré* of 3 August 1889, although several other versions had appeared in the *images d'Épinal* format.[41]

Georges Méliès, although largely overlooked for much of the twentieth century, has regained public interest amongst historians of the cinema, who now recognise his Montreuil studios as being the world's first. He is also credited with the creation of many of the special effects we now take for granted – substitution effects, slow motion, double-takes, superimposition – but as with the Lumière brothers his subject matter, and to a certain extent his techniques, were often a reflection of the way in which certain images were being presented in popular journals. Méliès's 1902 *Voyage à la Lune* [Journey to the Moon], for example, could be compared with an 1896 (9 May) *L'Illustration* feature giving photos of the Moon, or even Benjamin Rabier's *Le Voyage dans la Lune du nain Hans Krutten* [The Dwarf Hans Krutten's Journey to the Moon].[42] Méliès's cinematographic trickery, based on his early career as a magician, might remind us of the numerous 1890 features on magicians, or, more specifically, a strip by Luc that appeared on 5 June wherein the main character carries his detached head in his hands. Similarly early films such as Romeo Bosetti's *L'Agent a le bras long* [The Long-Armed Policeman] (1909), featuring a policeman whose arms physically extend, have all the zany flavour of the early strips.

These are but a few examples, but enough, hopefully for the point to be clear. Whereas the technology of photography changed the status of the image, celluloid built upon an already acquired status, using the same topics, angles of approach and framework, but by its very nature it made explicit a key factor thus far only hinted at in most paper-based productions: narrative progression.

The New Era of the Image

The beginnings of the Modern era, the period that saw the industrial revolution in the aftermath of the 1789 Revolution – in other words the period that roughly corresponds to the nineteenth century – was also the time that saw the modern development of the image in a popular context. In terms of the bande dessinée, although we can find numerous examples that conform to our definition of the form ('a French-language mixture of images and written text that together form a narrative'), they are not yet self-aware components of a genre. Nonetheless this period is important because it saw the rise and predominance of the conditions that allow for the BD as we know it: a culture whereby the image had become part of popular codes of reference and could function hand in hand with the text.

As with the 'Gutenberg Revolution' that changed cultural norms in the Early Modern period, so in the nineteenth century certain technological advances were the catalyst for the new culture of the image. Photography promised new possibilities, with the foundling art seeming to reproduce external reality, not just represent it. But the process of discovery was a gradual one and as such the early photographic image, despite the scientific advances behind it, was still part of the artistic climate of the time. Works such as Talbot's *Pencil of Nature* and Nadar's caricature-like photographic portraits elevated the image and helped create an environment in which further text/image productions could prosper.

These came on a widespread and popular level through the illustrated journals that had started to form in the same decades as the first photos were unveiled. Again print technology allowed early satirical cartoons to reach a large audience, and their success and resulting impact was to be measured by the fast-growing number of imitators. Illustrations, with captions, were to be provided in France by the likes of Cham, Daumier, Doré and then Rabier and individual pictures could be matched by page-spreads of themed drawings, or, later, related series of images with text explanations below each box. Such *histoires en images* are often what we think of in terms of the modern proto-bande dessinée, but their initial usage was above all a spin-off from caricatures.

With early photography, therefore, new possibilities for an image-based culture had opened up; possibilities that developed through the medium of print from the 1830s onwards, meaning that by the time of the first motion pictures the role of the image was no longer peripheral or subordinate. Early films drew upon the stock of now accepted image culture, be it the portrayal of power through the arrival of the railways or the slapstick gags of everyday life, and added the movement that gave such images further dimension. Such a process of evolution makes it hard to identify 'stars' of a genre that was in the process of embryonic development, but in order to understand the 'stars' that came as the BD could be identified it is important to grasp the process that took us from a text-dominated culture to one whereby the text and the image could once again function interdependently.

It is in this context that John Grand-Carteret founded *Le Livre et l'Image* [The Book and the Image] in March 1893. Grand-Carteret (1850–1927) was a visionary of multiple interests, including work, amongst other things, on the 1883 Rousseau exhibition, on emblems, and on the history of eroticism in art and literature. He showed a particular interest in caricatures from a number of national traditions.[43] Although short-lived, *Le Livre et l'Image* was one of the few journals openly to state self-awareness of the new image culture. In the preface to the first issue of the new publication (March–July 1893) Grand-Carteret underlines the newly found coupling of text with image:

> Le Livre et l'Image! C'est-à-dire ce qui se lit et ce qui se regarde; ce qui parle à l'imagination, ce qui s'adresse aux yeux; la langue littéraire et la langue graphique. [...] Des études littéraires présentent, en quelques pages, la caractéristique d'une idée ou d'une période; des images

> viennent éclairer le texte, restituant sous leur forme réelle et tangible les objets dont on parle. [...] [A]ujourd'hui, le document triomphe, et l'on peut affirmer que le XXe siècle verra se réaliser la grande révolution dont nous voyons les premiers germes: la langue graphique, l'Image, marchant de pair avec la langue littéraire, l'Ecriture. (1–2)
>
> [The Book and the Image! Namely, that which can be read and at which we can look; that which speaks to the imagination and addresses the eyes; literary language and graphic language. [...] Literary studies present, in a few pages, the characteristics of an idea or of a period; images then light up the text, and return the objects under discussion to their real and tangible form. [...] Today the document is triumphant, and we can be sure that the twentieth century will see the completion of the great revolution whose first seeds are already visible: graphic language, the Image, going hand in hand with literary language, Writing.]

Grand-Carteret is describing the very cultural circumstances that allowed for the BD as we now recognise it. By the end of the nineteenth century the culture of the image had its stock themes and techniques and an increasing association with narrative progression, but above all it could feasibly operate on an equal standing with the text.

Notes

1. I have consulted this 'Annonce' as it appears in the following volume: Rodolphe Töpffer, *Mélanges* [*Varia*] (Paris: Joël Cherbuliez, 1852). A facsimile reprint of the *Mélanges* also exists (Paris: Phénix, 1999). This 'Annonce' and several other of Töpffer's theoretical texts are also re-edited in Thierry Groensteen and Benoît Peeters, *Töpffer: L'Invention de la bande dessinée* (Paris: Hermann, 1994). The 'Annonce' is on pp. 161–63, where its original 1837 publication, namely on pp. 334–47 of *Bibliothèque Universelle de Genève* [Geneva Universal Library] 18 (June 1837), is indicated.
2. This article, signed 'R.T.', originally appeared in the *Bibliothèque Universelle de Genève* 1 (January 1836), 42–61 and 2 (April 1836), 314–41. Extracts of the article are given on pages 144–60 of *Töpffer: L'Invention de la bande dessinée*. Champfleury published his *Histoire de la caricature moderne* in 1865 (Paris, E. Dentu).
3. In his *Mélanges*, pp. 233–82. Daniel Grojnowski has provided a 2002 critical edition of the work, *De la plaque Daguerre: À propos des Excursions daguerriennes* (Cognac: Le Temps qu'Il Fait).
4. The first edition of this work, signed 'R.T.', was in *autographie* form from Schmidt of Geneva. It is available in a modern print version prefaced by Thierry Groensteen ([Paris]: Kargo, 2003) and is also reproduced, again in modern print, on pp. 184–225 of *Töpffer: L'Invention de la bande dessinée*.
5. (Amsterdam: François Van der Plaats). A 1982 facsimile edition is available (Hildesheim: Georg Olms Verlag).
6. Although the published *histoires en images* have been re-edited from the 1970s onwards, most accessible of the French versions is the 1996 three-volume collection produced by Thierry Groensteen for Seuil of Paris:

Monsieur Jabot: Monsieur Vieux Bois: Deux histoires d'amour [M. Jabot: M. Vieux Bois: Two Love Stories] (vol. 1), *Monsieur Crépin: Monsieur Pencil: Deux égarements de la science* [M. Crépin: M. Pencil: Two Scientific Distractions] (vol. 2), *Le Docteur Festus: Histoire de monsieur Cryptogame: Deux odyssées* (vol. 3). For *M. Trictrac*, see Philippe Kaenel's facsimile edition (Paris: Favre, 1988). An annotated English translation of the *histoires en images* has now been produced and edited by David Kunzle: *Rodolphe Töpffer: The Complete Comic Strips* (Jackson, MS: University Press of Mississippi, 2007). For an indication of secondary work on Töpffer, see the final section of our preceding chapter.

7. Originally Töpffer's 'strips' were published in *autographie* form by Schmidt of Geneva.
8. For a general history of the publication of Töpffer's works, see Philippe Kaenel, *Le Métier d'illustrateur 1830–1880: Rodolphe Töpffer, J.-J. Grandville, Gustave Doré* [The Illustrator's Profession 1830-1880: Rodolphe Töpffer, J.-J. Grandville, Gustave Doré] (Paris: Messene, 1996). The chapter on Töpffer is on pp. 125–78. See also David Kunzle, *The Early Comic Strip: The Nineteenth Century: History of the Comic Strip Volume 2* (Berkeley: University of California Press, 1990). Kunzle's chapter on Töpffer is on pp. 28–71. On the specific question of Goethe's reception of Töpffer's sketches, see David Kunzle, 'Goethe and Caricature: From Hogarth to Töpffer', *Journal of the Warburg and Courtauld Institutes* 48 (1985), 164–88. Both these pieces are updated in David Kunzle, *Father of the Comic Strip: Rodolphe Töpffer* (Jackson, MS: University Press of Mississippi, 2007).
9. On the pirate editions, see Leonardo De Sá, 'Aubert, le "pirate" qui a inventé les albums de bandes dessinées' [Aubert, the 'pirate' who invented the bande dessinée album], *Le Collectionneur de Bandes Dessinées* 108 (2006), 32–33. On English (1840–1841) and American (1842) versions of Töpffer's *histoires en images* see Robert Beerbohm and Doug Wheeler, 'Töpffer en Amérique', *9e Art* 6 (2001), 10–21.
10. Volume II, no. 40, 2 December 1843, pp. 213–14. The copies of *L'Illustration* that I have consulted are those of the BnF, where a complete run (1843–1955) is available on open access.
11. Volume III, no. 68, pp. 249–50.
12. Volume II, no. 43, 23 December 1843, p. 269.
13. On Grandville's 1828–1829 caricature of society *Les Métamorphoses du jour* [The Metamorphoses of the Day], see Noelle P. Bradley, 'Masks that Reveal: Social Inequality in J.-J. Grandville's *Les Métamorphoses du Jour* (1828–1829)', *International Journal of Comic Art* 8.1 (2006), 1–16.
14. See Alfredo Castelli, 'Monsieur Lajaunisse: Première bande dessinée française' [M. Lajaunisse: The First French Bande Dessinée], *Le Collectionneur de Bandes Dessinées* 108 (2006), 22–28.
15. 'Les Bains de mer en France' [Sea Bathing in France], pp. 408–09 of volume III, no. 78, 24 August 1844; 'Les Chasses' [Hunting], pp. 24–25 of volume IV, no. 81, 14 September 1844; 'À propos des vendanges' [On the Wine-Harvest], pp. 88–89 of volume IV, no. 85, 12 October 1844. Cham and Töpffer corresponded in the 1840s, with Töpffer, indisposed by ill health, asking Cham to produce a version of *Monsieur Cryptogame*. See Michel Kempeneers, 'Cham: Un Pionnier oublié' [Cham, A Forgotten Pioneer], *Le Collectionneur de Bandes Dessinées* 108 (2006), 29–31. See also the important section on Cham that David Kunzle provides in chapter 3 of his *The History of the Comic Strip: The Nineteenth Century*. Much of this piece explores the comparison between Cham and Honoré Daumier.
16. See Leonardo De Sá, 'Aubert, le "pirate" qui a inventé les albums de bandes dessinées'.

17. See, for example, Beatrice Farwell, *The Charged Image: French Lithographic Caricature 1816–1848* (Santa Barbara: Santa Barbara Museum of Art, 1989); David S. Kerr, *Caricature and French Political Culture 1830–1848: Charles Philipon and the Illustrated Press* (Oxford: Oxford University Press, 2000); Judith Wechsler, *A Human Comedy: Physiognomy and Caricature in 19th Century Paris* (London: Thames and Hudson, 1982). Of the individual artists, Daumier and Doré are most frequently explored in English. See, for example, Bruce Laughton, *Honoré Daumier* (New Haven: Yale University Press, 1996); Heinrich Schwarz, 'Daumier, Gill and Nadar', *Gazette des Beaux Arts* 19 (1957), 89–106; Joanna Richardson, *Gustave Doré: A Biography* (London: Cassell, 1980); Thierry Groensteen, 'Gustave Doré's Comics', *International Journal of Comic Art* 2.2 (2000), 111–20.
18. On this subject see Harold Innis, *The Bias of Communication* (Toronto: University of Toronto Press, 1964 [original ed. 1951]).
19. *The Early Comic Strip: Narrative Strips and Picture Stories in the European Broadsheet from c. 1450 to 1825* (Berkeley: University of California Press, 1973).
20. In *Forging a New Medium* the 'great men' considered include the Dutchman Willem Bilderdijk (discussed by Nop Maas), William Hogarth and Thomas Rowlandson (Paul Gravett), Rodolphe Töpffer (Thierry Groensteen) and Wilhelm Busch (Hans Ries). Kunzle does also provide important sections on the popular journals, such as *Revue Comique*, *Journal pour Rire* [The Journal for a Laugh], and *Le Chat Noir* [The Black Cat].
21. In addition to the work of David Kunzle, see the publications cited in footnote 17 above.
22. One might, however, argue that as the editors of *Forging a New Medium* are Belgian and the work resulted from an international conference held in Brussels, English is in fact only the language of convenience, rather than an indication of academic interest outwith the established francophone channels of BD criticism.
23. For this and the rest of Henry Fox Talbot's correspondence, see the site of the William Henry Fox Talbot project (www.foxtalbot.arts.gla.ac.uk).
24. The work was originally published over two years and in six fascicules. The copy I have consulted is in a single volume, that of Glasgow University Library (Special Collections Photo A 18). A facsimile edition edited by Larry J. Schaaf is also available (New York: Hans P. Kraus Jr., 1989). On Talbot, see H. J. P Arnold, *William Henry Fox Talbot: Pioneer of Photography and Man of Science* (London: Hutchinson Benham, 1977); Mike Weaver, *Henry Fox Talbot: Selected Texts and Bibliography* (Oxford: Clio, 1992).
25. For Nadar's works see Philippe Néagu, ed., *Nadar: Tome 1: Photographies* and Jean-François Bory, ed., *Nadar: Tome 2: Dessins et écrits* [Nadar: Volume 2: Drawings and Writings] (Paris: Arthur Hubschmid, 1979). This latter volume provides comprehensive reproductions of his sketches, including those of Môssieu Réac, discussed below (see, for example, p. 766 for the election piece). See also the catalogue of the 1990 Paris Maison de Balzac exhibition, Loïc Chotard, *Nadar: Caricatures et photographies* (Paris: Paris-Musées, 1990). In English, James H. Rubin's *Nadar* (London: Phaidon, 2001) gives a clear and well-illustrated introduction to his photographic work, including the portrait of Chevreul discussed below.
26. On *Môssieu Réac*, see chapter 4 of David Kunzle's *The History of the Comic Strip: The Nineteenth Century*.
27. For more on the social context of early photography, with often specific reference to Talbot, see Carol Armstrong, *Scenes in a Library: Reading the Photograph in the Book, 1843–1875* (Cambridge, MA: MIT, 1998).
28. This subtitle is primarily alliterative. Many of the publications to be discussed were principally current-affairs based and thus far from

humorous, even if illustrative caricatures almost by definition were satirical and thus intended to inspire laughter.

29. In 'L'Industrialisation des techniques' [The Industrialisation of Printing Techniques], pp. 57–67 of Henri-Jean Martin and Roger Chartier, eds, *Histoire de l'édition française: Tome III: Le Temps des éditeurs: Du Romantisme à la Belle Époque* [The History of Publishing in France: Volume III: The Age of the Publishers: From Romanticism to the Belle Époque] (Paris: Promodis, 1985). The volume as a whole should be consulted for the background to technological developments in printing at this time, as well the broader question of the rise of the journal in the nineteenth century.
30. Michel Melot cites *Le Journal Illustré* as being the first daily to include a photo, one by Nadar on 5 September 1886. See Michel Melot, 'Le Texte et l'image', on pp. 286–312 of Henri-Jean Martin and Roger Chartier, eds, *Histoire de l'édition française: Tome III: Le Temps des éditeurs: Du Romantisme à la Belle Epoque*. On photojournalism in the USA but with analysis that often is relevant beyond the American context, see Michael L. Carlebach, *The Origins of Photojournalism in America* (Washington: Smithsonian Institute Press, 1992).
31. On *L'Illustration*, see the catalogue of the 1987 Paris, Musée Carnavalet, exhibition in the paper's honour: Krishnâ Renou, *Journal Universel: L'Illustration: Un Siècle de vie française* [The Universal Journal: Illustration: A Century of French Life] (Paris: Paris-Musées, 1987). See also David Kunzle, '*L'Illustration*, journal universel 1843–1853', *Nouvelles de l'Estampe* [News on Engravings] 43 (January 1979), 8–19.
32. It should be noted that Dubochet is no longer publisher. Subscriptions are now to be sent to A. Le Chevalier, and the back page bears the signature 'Paulin'.
33. This appears in volume XV, no. 358 (Saturday 5 January 1850), p. 13.
34. The final sequence of this series appeared in number 363 of volume XV, dated Saturday 9 February 1850.
35. See Thierry Groensteen's catalogue of the CNBDI's 1998 exhibition, *Les Années Caran d'Ache* [The Caran d'Ache Years] (Angoulême: CNBDI. 1998). *Carnet de cheques* is available in a 2000 facsimile edition from Corsaire of Orleans. No editor's name is given. See also David Kunzle's *The History of the Comic Strip: The Nineteenth Century*, in particular pp. 178–80.
36. On Rabier, see François Robichon, *Benjamin Rabier: L'Homme qui fait rire les animaux* [Benjamin Rabier: The Man who Makes the Animals Laugh] (Paris: Hoëbeke, 1993). For a selection of his *histoires en images* see Edouard François and Pierre Couperie, eds, *Benjamin Rabier* (Paris: Pierre Horay, 1982).
37. 'G. Ri', author of '*The Cassonade Family's Inheritance*', is a play on words evoking 'j'ai ri' or 'I laughted'. 'Froussard' is a familiar term for one who is often frightened. 'Le Petit mousse' means 'The Little Sailor Boy'.
38. For a recent copy of the Lumière brothers' work, see the 1999 DVD by Kino of New York, *The Lumière Brothers' First Films*.
39. Christophe, *La Famille Fenouillard* (Paris: Armand Colin, [1893]). The extract discussed is on p. 11. Christophe is now considered one of the pioneers of the *histoire en images*: in addition to the *Famille Fenouillard*, his *Sapeur Camembert* [Fireman Camembert] and *Savant Cosinus* [The Learned Cosinus], also from the final years of the nineteenth century, continue to enjoy popularity. See François Caradec, 'Christophe', *Le Collectionneur de Bandes Dessinées* 100 (2003), 14–19.
40. See also the final pages (377–78) of David Kunzle's *The History of the Comic Strip: The Nineteenth Century*, wherein he concludes by examining the parallels between the growth of the railways and that of the early comic strip.

41. Lance Rickman explores this subject in '*Bande dessinée* and the Cinematograph: Visual Narrative in 1895', *European Comic* Art 1.1 (2008), 1–19. The article has five illustrations, including the Christophe example.
42. Rabier's tale is reproduced (without pagination) in Edouard François and Pierre Couperie, eds, *Benjamin Rabier.*
43. For further information on John Grand-Carteret, see the appropriate entry in M. Prévost, Roman d'Amat and H. Tribout de Morembert, eds, *Dictionnaire de biographie française* [Dictionary of French Biography], 18 vols. (Paris: Letouzey and Ané, 1985). See also the 'Afterword' (pp. 51–53) that follows the first section of my *Text/Image Mosaics in French Culture: Emblems and Comic Strips* (Aldershot: Ashgate, 2005).

CHAPTER 6

THE TWENTIETH CENTURY: THE RISE, FALL AND RISE OF THE BD

A Rollercoaster Century

The twentieth century, for most people, is the century of the bande dessinée. It saw the culture of the *histoire en image* continue to flourish, generally (but certainly not always) in children's publications, and expand under the influence of American imports. It saw the darker years of wartime suppression followed by the censorship inflicted in France via the 1949 Law on Children's Publications. But it also saw the switch to an art form for grown-ups following the cutting-edge inspiration of 1960s icon *Pilote* magazine. And each bump of the rollercoaster ride saw its own mini bumps ...

Naturally enough, most histories of the BD concentrate, sometimes almost exclusively, on this period. Patrick Gaumer and Claude Moliterni's *Dictionnaire mondial de la bande dessinée* [World Dictionary of the Bande Dessinée],[1] one of the mainstream reference works, intersperses its main dictionary entries with eight sets of colour plates telling the chronological history of the form. The first set, 'Les Pionniers: De 1833 à 1908' [The Pioneers: From 1833 to 1908], briefly overviews nineteenth-century precursors starting with Rodolphe Töpffer, but the seven remaining sections sit firmly in the twentieth century. Of the six 'Musées imaginaires' [Imaginary Museums] that from 2003 formed the Centre National de la Bande Dessinée et de l'Image's semi-permanent display of its collections, one is on the theme of history:[2] after a brief section on the period 1830–90, most of the 'museum' concentrates on the years from 1890 to 1960, leaving post-1960 to its own contemporary 'gallery'. Matthew Screech's *Masters of the Ninth Art*,[3] a pioneering monograph in English, functions via case studies concentrating on eleven artists, the earliest of whom, Hergé, started production in the 1920s. Ann Miller's remarkable *Reading Bande Dessinée: Critical Approaches to the French-Language Comic Strip* gives an overview of the BD's history from the nineteenth century onwards, but she deliberately concentrates her analysis on post-1990s creations.[4]

As a result, the current section of this book may appear understated, as I see no need to duplicate the generally reliable minutiae of such highly illustrated tomes. With respect to Hergé, André Franquin, René Goscinny and Albert Uderzo, Moebius, Jacques Tardi, Marcel Gotlib, Claire Bretécher, Régis Franc, Alejandro Jodorowsky and François Bourgeon, my comments will generally be little more than passing as Matthew Screech has provided the English-language reader with full analysis of the artists' lives and works.[5] Nonetheless what this current study can do is to present a graspable overview of the patterns of development in the BD's progress whilst bringing to the newcomer's attention some of the names, events and attitudes that have marked the bande dessinée's passage to status of Ninth Art.

Rise

Histoires en images

Starting in 1905, one of the most popular publications for girls was *La Semaine de Suzette* [Suzette's Weekly], although like *Les Belles Images* it largely restricted its target to a bourgeois audience. Amongst the best-loved features were the adventures of the Breton maid Bécassine in which her stupidity invariably was at the base of a misunderstanding with comic results. The pictures were largely figurative representations, with Bécassine's facial features limited to a line for her nose and eyebrows and dots for eyes (see Fig. 11, Chapter 3). Nonetheless these were enough to create reader recognition, as became clear from the number of spin-off products such as dolls, games and general paraphernalia that became available from an early stage. To assign Bécassine the role of first BD 'star' would have all of the faults of retrospective historicism that we can associate with the elevation of Töpffer's heroes. But in the case of Bécassine we have a 'star' who was widely recognised as such in her own time. Unlike Töpffer, Pinchon and Caumery, Bécassine's initial creators, were aware that they were working within a firmly based cultural context. What in the 1830s was an *air du temps*, had become, by 1905, a specific genre (or at least a literary and artistic form) in all but name.

Like many of the *histoires en images* of the early twentieth century, each episode would consist of a number of sequential images, generally between nine and sixteen to a page, each with an explanatory text below, although Pinchon was one of the first to vary *case* sizes, as we see in the circles of Figure 11 (Chapter 3). In the issue for 21 February 1918, part of the *Bécassine mobilisée* [Bécassine's Call Up] story, we learn of the house move from Paris to Versailles, with the general background of the displacement of First World War troops.

Almost in Hollywood style, Pinchon sets the scene with recognisable situations, before posing a problem – the exploration of Versailles – and providing a humoristic punchline as Bécassine mistakes the château and its gardens for her new abode.

The *Semaine de Suzette* ran from 1905 to 1960, although Bécassine, resurrected by Jean Trubert in 1959, lived into the 1960s, and has, more recently, seen several unflattering parody editions (e.g., *Pétassine*).[6] Of the *histoires en images* it was the Breton maid who

Figure 26. 'Les Pieds Nickelés'. *L'Épatant*. No. 1004 (27 October 1927), p. 8.

perhaps had the greatest impact – certainly in hindsight, as can be seen from the quantity of centenary paraphernalia released in 2005, but also in terms of contemporary reception, again judging from the associated products quickly made available; however, stylistically she was just one of many kindred productions.

Some of these were continuations from the late nineteenth century, as in the works of Christophe, Caran d'Ache or Benjamin Rabier, which we have discussed briefly in the previous chapter. In general the popular illustrated press, publications such as *Le Rire* (1894–1908), *Les Belles Images* (1904–1936),[7] or *L'Épatant* [Astonishing] (1908–1939) gave prominence to the various characters, aimed at the young but also at the not-so-young, whose movements were contextualised by the text beneath them. Louis Forton's *Les Pieds Nickelés* (Fig. 26), first seen in *L'Épatant* in 1908, were a typical example, one that has recently also seen a nostalgic revival in popularity. This can be attributed to Forton's ability to mix register to comic effect in the retelling of the trio's misadventures, as well as the universal appeal of the characters' mischief.[8]

On a les bulles?

For many a historian of sequential narratives a defining element that separates bande dessinée from storytelling by illustration is the use of speech bubbles, *phylactères*, or, simply, *bulles*. I have not included this as a prerequisite of the definition (reminder: 'a French-language mixture of images and written text that together form a narrative') as many a modern BD, not to mention the form's embryonic creations, do extremely well without them, and if anything the current tendency is taking us away from bubbles (more of that in the next section …). Nonetheless one of the clear characteristics of the BD's development in the early part of the twentieth century is a shift to an almost standard use of *bulles*.

The use of speech bubbles, or at least *bulle*-like bandereaux, can be traced back to the Middle Ages (see Fig. 9, Chapter 2), although the phenomenon is most often noted in the context of English satirical sketches by the likes of Thomas Rowlandson (1756–1827).[9] In more modern times speech bubbles were an accepted feature of American syndicated strips at the turn of the century. Of these, R.W. Outcault's *Yellow Kid*, a series that from 1895 recounted the adventures of a waif and his peers in the fictional Hogan's Alley in New York, is probably the first to make dialogue by bubbles an integral part. Cultural crossovers and, to a certain extent, early imports – for example *Bicot* (aka *Perry*, Winnie Winkle's brother) and *Pim-Pam-Poum* (aka *The Katzanjammer Kids*) – would have meant that *bulles* were not unknown in France, although it would appear that their existence was not accepted as commonplace until even the 1950s. Jean de Trignon, in his *Histoire de la littérature enfantine de Ma Mère l'Oye au Roi Babar*

(1950) gives us a description that suggests that speech bubbles were still to be regarded with caution:

> On vit naître des hebdomadaires de formats variés, dont les textes hachés et presque inexistants se réduisent à des interjections, parfois même à un point d'exclamation, placés dans les phylactères. Des filles blondes et des cow-boys sortis de films américains émettent ainsi de sortes de nuages ou de banderoles où s'inscrivent des mots sans suite. C'est le sabotage de tout art et de toute littérature. Une mise en page fiévreuse acheva de donner une impression de désordre et d'anarchie. (174–75)
>
> [We saw the birth of weeklies in various formats. Their texts, placed in *phylactères*, were cut up and almost non-existent, reduced largely to interjections, sometimes even to an exclamation mark. Blonde girls and cowboys, straight out of American films, thus emitted some sort of cloud or *bandereau* in which senseless words were written. It is the sabotage of all art and of all literature. A fever-stricken *mise en page* completed the impression of disorder and anarchy.]

That is not to say that French versions of the phenomenon did not exist before 1950. The earliest 'modern' French speech bubble is possibly one by Caran d'Ache that appeared in *L'Illustration* of 14 April 1894. Better known are the adventures of Alain de Saint-Ogan's *Zig et Puce* which featured in *Le Dimanche Illustré* [Sunday Illustrated] from 1925. Zig and Puce are two children, accompanied by Alfred the Penguin, whose travels take them across the globe, expressing themselves through *bulles* as they go. Like a *Bécassine* for boys, *Zig et Puce* was to become a cult phenomenon with a range of spin-off products. Like Bécassine herself, these continue to satisfy a nostalgic market today, crowned perhaps by the use of Alfred the Penguin as the mascot for the early awards at the Angoulême festival.[10]

Tintin starts his adventures

It was at this time – 1929 to be precise – and in the context of such conditions that Hergé published the boy scout's first adventure, *Tintin, reporter du 'Petit Vingtième', au pays des Soviets* [Tintin, the Petit Vingtième's Reporter, in the Land of the Soviets].[11] Like Bécassine, the mainstay of middle-class Catholic values for girls that *La Semaine de Suzette* espoused, or indeed many of the characters born of weeklies with a particular axe to grind (such as *Coeurs Vaillants* [Valiant Hearts] for Catholic boys, from 1929, *Vaillant* [Valiant] for families with communist ideals, from 1945, and others), Tintin reflected the values of his publication. He appeared in *Le Petit Vingtième*, the children's supplement of the right-wing Brussels newspaper *Le Vingtème Siècle* [The Twentieth Century], which under the auspices of the Abbé Wallez defended Christian capitalism. Tintin's trip to the

Soviet Union was based therefore on hearsay and dubious propaganda, largely with reference to Hergé's reading of a single anti-communist publication, Joseph Douillet's *Moscou sans voiles: (Neuf ans de travail au pays des Soviets)* [Moscow without Veils: (Nine Years of Work in the Land of the Soviets)] (1928). But it was enough for the intrepid reporter to be able to unmask Soviet power abuses and communist cruelty before escaping by plane, car and train to Brussels via Germany.

Stylistically *Tintin* has much in common with *Zig et Puce*: clear-cut line drawings, simple division of *cases* within a *planche* (generally, but not always, four by three), serial publication resulting in a series of cliffhanger moments, young boys and their talking animal as centre-stage protagonists... Why then has Saint-Ogan, despite his career success, largely been relegated to French museum exhibits, nostalgia drives and subsections of BD histories, whilst Hergé has spawned an international library of publications and re-editions that literally sell in the millions? As with Töpffer, one might point to the fickleness, for good or for bad, of retrospective analysis. But if the two highly popular series were neck and neck when they first appeared, perhaps the difference is that Tintin, like other Belgian superheroes Jacques Brel, Hercule Poirot and Johnny Hallyday, has known how to evolve and, above all, reflect the issues of the day, whilst using whimsical aspects of the medium of expression to keep a happy distance. Thus Tintin could charm as he (implicitly) aided the Nazis in the 1942 *L'Étoile mystérieuse*, provide a giant step for man- (and dog-) kind as he went to the moon in 1953 and 1954 (*Objectif Lune* and *On a marché sur la Lune*) and help us to auto-deconstruct with the self-reflexive *Tintin et l'Alph'Art* (posthumously in 1986).[12]

Needless to say, this book is not another volume in the homage to Hergé, although one could almost, and almost will, trace the development of the bande dessinée in step with that of its best-selling creation, without wishing to imply that BD is now dead. For this section it is enough to know that the *Tintin* of the 1920s and 1930s was in keeping with many of the trends of the would-be genre as a whole: adventures in far-flung lands – Africa in *Tintin au Congo* (1931), China in *Le Lotus bleu* (1936), Scotland in *L'Île noire* (1938) – that simplify the exotic and overemphasise Otherness, the creation of Manichean 'goodies' and 'baddies', and breakneck adventure winning the day over verisimilitude. Above all, publication was episodic and journal-based, with albums following on largely as a by-product.

Whilst exemplifying the BD (or proto-BD) *air du temps*, Hergé was also innovative, albeit unwittingly, in his implementation of the *ligne claire* or 'clear line' style, one which retrospectively has become his trademark.[13] Favoured by the initial monochrome format, the *ligne claire*, as its name suggests, uses stark black outlines both for the characters and for surrounding objects, avoiding any blurring effects. The addition of colours in the reworkings of the 1940s and in the later albums allowed the style to gain further emphasis by dint of the use of stark primaries. The result is that characters, places and objects are easily recognisable and classable and, as Numa Sadoul has stated, 'c'est parce que la ligne était claire que les idées étaient claires' [it is because the line was clear that the ideas were clear].[14] The style has left its mark on later BD productions, such as Edgar-Pierre Jacobs's *Blake et Mortimer* series and, more recently, André Juillard's *Le Cahier bleu* [The Blue Notebook] (to be discussed in the next part of this book). On a wider level, the *ligne claire* can be seen as influencing the mainstays of Pop Art, such as Roy Lichtenstein and Andy Warhol, thereby implicitly putting BD at the centre of the Cultural Studies debate (again, more on this, and postwar *Tintin* more generally, in Part III, 'The Cultural Phenomenon').

Belgicité?

The mention of Belgian superheroes raises another question central to any history of the BD: that of the role played by *le plat pays* in the development of the bande dessinée.[15] One might be tempted to bypass the issue by referring to 'franco-belgian' creations, or indeed simply ignoring it, just as some histories of English literature throw in Oscar Wilde and Sir Walter Scott or certain commentators include Bryan Adams and Céline Dion as USA pop stars. Indeed when the specifics of the cultural output under analysis are not subject to the specifics of individual and separate national traditions, that might be justifiable, if explained. In the case of Belgian bandes dessinées one could perhaps argue that the unifying factor is the French language and the market target is largely France. On the other hand, is it by chance that the distinct style of the *style atome* (more on this later) coincided with the Brussels world fair? And the differences between France and Belgium in wartime conditions, and in postwar legislation, inevitably made for distinct creational contexts.

This aside does not provide answers to such questions, but it does allow us to be aware of issues as we put forward another viewpoint on Hergé's rising success in the 1920s and 1930s, namely that he was at the base of the Belgian school of bande dessinée production, whose importance was heralded by the popularity of the *Petit Vingtième*, but, above all, from 1938 onwards, by the influence of *Spirou* magazine.[16]

Enfin Mickey vint ...[17]

By 1934, therefore, the bande dessinée had the beginnings of a distinct literary and artistic form, even if it had not been labelled as such and despite the general hostility of commentators leading up to this time. One example, taken from Marie-Thérèse Latzarus in *La Littérature enfantine en France dans la seconde moitié du XIX siècle* [Children's Literature in France in the Second Half of the Nineteenth

Century] (1924), is typical in that it attacks both the form and the content that implicitly comes as a result:

> Les illustrations des journaux d'enfants de notre époque sont grotesques par leurs couleurs, et de mauvais goût par leur inspiration. Elles reproduisent, fréquemment, des scènes d'ivrognerie ou des pugilats. Elles ridiculisent des difformités ou des disgrâces physiques. Il n'est pas rare d'y voir des écoliers, tirant la langue à leur maître, ou des enfants, jouant de bons tours à leurs parents. (158)
>
> [The illustrations in today's children's journals are grotesque in their colours and inspired by bad taste. They often reproduce scenes of drunkenness or fighting. They mock deformities or physical blemishes. In their pages it is not rare to see schoolchildren who stick their tongues out at their teacher or children playing pranks on their parents.]

Nonetheless, to judge by the by-products and the front-page advertising, it was increasingly the *histoires en images* that were selling the periodicals. But despite the innovations of Caran d'Ache and then Hergé and Alain de Saint-Ogan, most of the strips were still four-by-three narratives with descriptive texts below the images. Weekly print runs of such illustrated journals were generally around 50,000 (although there were some exceptions), with the main titles, according to Alain Fourment, performing as follows between 1930 and 1934:[18]

Les Belles Images
(Weekly, much emphasis on fictional *histoires en images.* See also our discussion above.)
Between 86,628 (1930) and 38,525 (1934)

Bernadette
(Weekly for Catholic girls of rural background. Lasted until 1972.)
195,000 in 1930

Cadet Revue
(Fortnightly. Alain de Saint-Ogan was chief editor and major contributor.)
9,000 in 1933, 25,000 in 1934

Coeurs Vaillants
(Weekly for Catholic boys. Included *Tintin.*)
90,000 in 1930

Jeunesse Illustrée
(Weekly. Included *histoires en images* by Benjamin Rabier.)
Between 98,350 (1930) and 40,583 (1934)

We should also add publications such as *Cri-Cri* (1911–1937) and *L'Épatant* (1908–1939), both selling around 50,000 copies a week, which followed the same sort of format without being specifically aimed at children, and thus not included in Fourment's statistics.

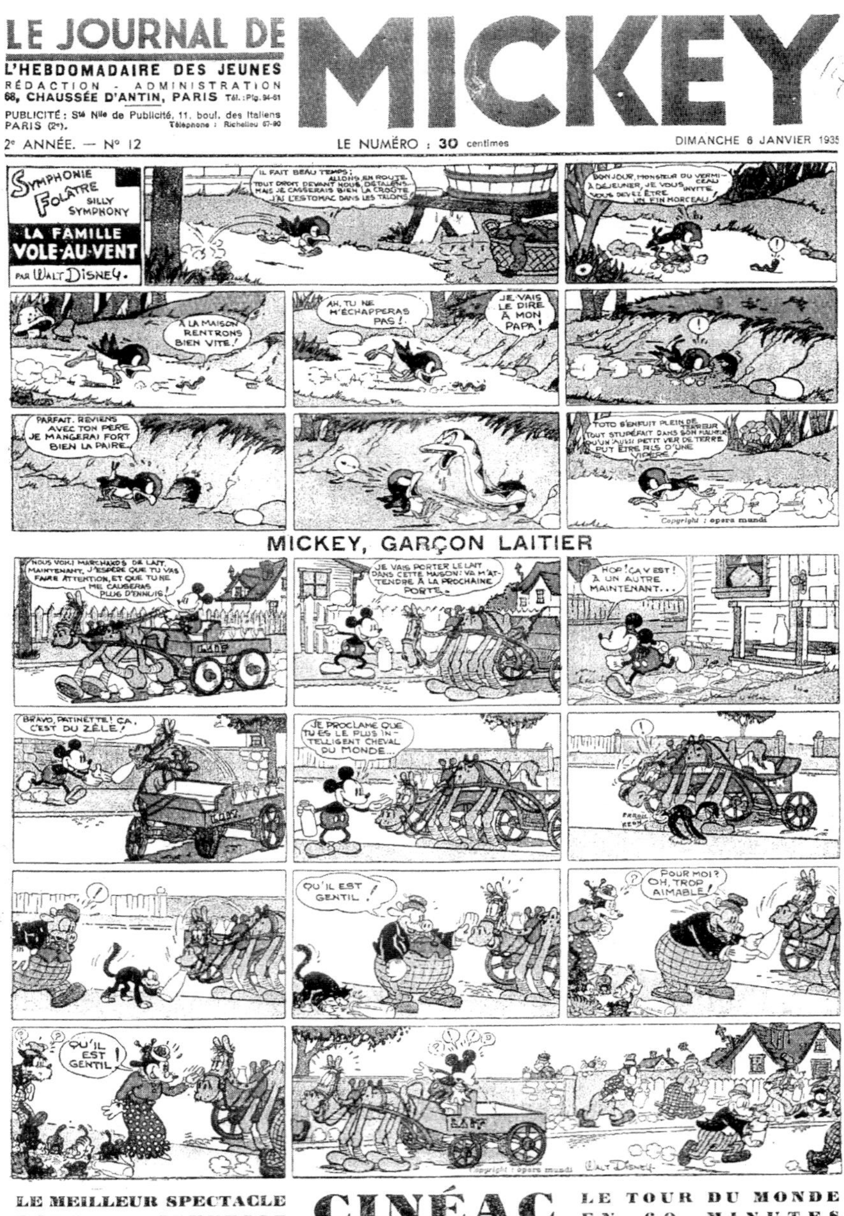

Figure 27. 'Silly Symphony and Mickey'. *Le Journal de Mickey*, No. 12 (6 January 1935). Front cover.

All was to change with the arrival of *Le Journal de Mickey*, the brainchild of Paul Winckler, with the silent backing of Hachette. Via his Opera Mundi syndicate that he had set up in 1928, Winckler bought the rights to American strips that were appearing in the dailies or Sunday supplements. His flagship strips were those of the up-and-coming Walt Disney, who had been producing Mickey Mouse cartoons since 1928, but Winckler also drew upon other works, including those by Harold Knerr (*The Katzenjammer Kids*/*Pim-Pam-Poum*), Alex Raymond (*Jungle Jim*/*Jim la Jungle*) and Brandon Walsh (*Little Annie Rooney*/*Les Malheurs d'Annie*). The sellers had nothing to lose by making the strips available to a wider audience, and Winckler had a deep pot of high-quality material with little more than translation charges as overheads. Stylistically Winckler was well ahead: the repetitive monochrome of strips that might appear in publications such as *L'Épatant* (Fig. 26), with little background detail and a heavy reliance on miniscule text, could not compete with the variety, colour, attention to detail and exoticism of Winckler's imports (Fig. 27). The former was the leftover of the dying Épinal printworks, the latter the new age of Hollywood.

But such exoticism was not without drawbacks. One can imagine the mishaps of Bécassine, such as when she mistakes a chèvre cheese for the animal itself, appealing because they touched the realm of the readers' daily existence. Similarly Tintin, for all his far-off travels, was nonetheless a boy scout from Brussels seeing the world through the same optic as his audience. The gasoline-guzzling automobiles, the high-tech refrigerators and the sky-scraping cityscapes that populate the 1930s world of Mickey and friends must have been as alien as Flash Gordon's intergalactic habitat. Winckler's stroke of genius was to assimilate these imports to French life by placing them in the context of a journal that was Gallic through and through.

To take a typical early issue of *Le Journal de Mickey*, number 12 from 6 January 1935, of the eight pages, four had imported colour strips: the leading Disney features on the front cover (*Symphonie Fôlatre* [Silly Symphony] and *Mickey, garçon laitier* [Mickey the Milkboy]), a centre spread of four light-hearted features and an adventure serial, *Les Malheurs d'Annie*, on the back page. These were balanced in the interspersed black and white pages by Claude Davière's serialised novel, *Le Secret du Templier* [The Templar's Secret], a pre-*Da Vinci Code* treasure chase firmly situated throughout France; news of Onc' Léon's *Club Mickey* with individual replies to letters in the 'Petite Correspondance' (e.g., 'Kiki: Je te crois que tu peux tutoyer ton vieil onc' Léon. Entendu pour Rochefort' [Kiki, I expect you can say 'tu' to your old Uncle Léon. Message received for Rochefort]); jokes based on French puns; and competitions with the previous results and the names of winners.

It was the framework of the journal, therefore, that allowed the readers to assimilate the imported strips to their own culture. Mickey was Frenchified by the texts, but also by the interaction with Onc' Léon, and the participation via competitions and related activities. The now famous *Club Mickey* that are a feature of France's most popular beaches allowed Winckler to take his characters into three dimensions. Even if the children of the 1930s did not catch the references to USA culture, Mickey and friends were still as much a part of their daily experience as might have been Bécassine and Tintin.

The long-term success of Winckler's enterprise can be seen in the endurance of *Le Journal de Mickey*: it is still going strong, and were it not for breaks brought on by the war could be the oldest 'comic' in Europe.[19] More generally, the journal is indicative of the special relationship France has with Disney culture in general, even if this includes a certain element of intellectualising love-hate. As I will discuss below, *Le Journal de Mickey* pre-dated Disney journals in all countries – including the USA – except Italy, and, more significantly, enjoyed success on a scale not seen elsewhere. From its full launch in October 1934 (a pilot issue had been circulated in June) *Le Journal de Mickey* broke all sales records, averaging approximately 400,000 copies a week.

The knock-on effect redefined the bande dessinée. It soon became difficult for 'old-format' (see Fig. 26) publications to compete, and indeed many disappeared or reformatted. Casualties included *La Jeunesse Moderne* [Modern Youth], *Le Petit Illustré*, *L'Intrépide* [Intrepid], *Cri-Cri* and *L'Épatant*, all of which folded, or took on new names and styles, between 1936 and 1939. On the other hand, a new wave of Mickey-clones invaded the news-stands. In some cases these were sister productions from Winckler aimed at slightly different audiences – *Robinson* (1936) for older boys or *Hop-Là!* (1937), also for slightly older children – but more generally they were competitors looking for a slice of a clearly lucrative market.[20]

L'Aventureux [Adventurous] (1935) was a slightly cheaper publication from Cino Del Duca's Éditions Mondiales [World Editions], although the quality of its paper and print were also considerably lower. It constantly supplied new imports, providing well over fifty new strips in five years, almost all adventure-based, as the journal's title implied. *Hurrah!* (1936), also by Del Duca, provided a similar format based upon American escapism, and again used imports to the exclusion of all other works.

The Offenstadt brothers' SPE (Société Parisienne d'Édition [Parisian Publishing Company]) house, many of whose 'old format' journals had been hit by the arrival of Winckler's publications, provided *Junior* (1936) and *L'As* [The Ace] (1937), both of which gave prominent placing to imports, whilst still keeping some French productions, often, in the case of *L'As*, even the old-style *histoires en images*.[21] *Junior* stood out, literally, due to its extra-large format, which in turn meant the *cases* were larger and more eye-grabbing. It followed the *Journal de Mickey* formula of interspersing strips with fictional text, reader participation and general-knowledge sections, although even this showed leanings towards the USA, as in the editorial article explaining the phenomenon of baseball.[22] Above all, it was through such publications that such favourites as Brick Bradford, Superman, Madrake the Magician and Red Ryder became household names in France, albeit as Luc Bradefer, L'Homme d'Acier, Mandrake Roi de la Magie and Cavalier Rouge.

Although sales of the new arrivals were considerably higher than the *histoires en images* publications they had effectively replaced – *Hurrah!* reached 250,000 and *Junior* 200,000 – none came near to toppling *Le Journal de Mickey*.[23] One reason may have been that the original was perceived as the best, even if it was slightly more expensive. But to accredit *Le Journal de Mickey*'s success uniquely to such an advantage is to underestimate Winckler's achievement. Publications such as *L'Aventureux* and *L'As* could attract readers with the sophisticated artwork and risqué exoticism, but they generally provided strips and only strips, and as such were unlikely to create a following, a feeling of attachment and involvement, in short a *French* cultural phenomenon in the way that Winckler had done through the context he had given his imports.

Retrospectively (again as history inevitably is, sometimes highly problematically) the 1930s saw a boom in the culture of the bande dessinée. What had been a culture of the narrative image in a textual context became the culture of the narrative image that we now unquestionably identify with the BD. Again from a distance this can easily be seen as the so-called Golden Age of the American strip invading France. Whatever their French names, it was Mickey Mouse and Donald Duck, Tarzan, Flash Gordon, Little Orphan Annie and Pete the Tramp who were keeping the youth of France on bated breath each week. It was they who made speech bubbles and onomatopoeia the *lingua franca*, albeit in translation. But that does not mean that the bande dessinée is an American invention. Far from it.

Disney detractors often overlook the unique Frenchness of the movement's catalyst, *Le Journal de Mickey*. This is an understandable error given the careful silence kept by the force behind it, Hachette, and given the current status of the Disney Corporation as upholders of the American Dream, but an error nonetheless. When Paul Winckler launched his new journal the format was entirely of his own invention. Disney had first released Mickey in 1928 for *Steamboat Willie*, the seven-minute cartoon, but the ensuing strips (1930) were only syndicated and no such *Mickey's Journal* existed in the United States, and would not do so until 1935 when *Mickey Mouse Magazine* was founded. Even the English version, *Mickey Mouse Weekly*, only came into being in 1936. The only comparator would have been the Italian *Topolino*, which had appeared on the last day of 1932, but the main 'Disney' strips were crude copies by Italian artists. Above all, *Topolino* was not the immediate social phenomenon that the French version was: by the end of 1934 Italian sales had never gone beyond 50,000.[24]

Winckler's innovation came in that he updated and turned around the blossoming French tradition of the independent illustrated journal for children. Comics in North America would be syndicated as strips to appear in different newspapers from the *New York Daily News* to the *Los Angeles Times*, or they would appear in special Sunday supplements, but children's weeklies, like print news media in general, did not exist on a national level. In 1934 Paul Winckler gave Mickey and Donald a status in France that they could not have achieved in America. *Le Journal de Mickey* gave America's cartoon artwork the national platform it did not get at home, but in so doing it created a cultural phenomenon that was unique to France.

Fall

The phenomenon that *Le Journal de Mickey* had created came into its own after – and to a certain extent as a result of – a double bout of vilification based on fervent anti-Americanism. From a retrospective and ideological angle the period that followed the boom of the 1930s can be seen as the dark years of the bande dessinée, but it nonetheless provided the conditions that made the final crowning of the Ninth Art possible.

Nazi supremacy

Most of the journals that had developed by the outbreak of war continued with varying degrees of success, although they were generally forced to move south into the Vichy zone. *Le Journal de Mickey* and *Robinson*, for example, continued from Marseilles between 1940 and folding in 1944; *Hurrah!* and *L'Aventureux* survived in Vichy from 1940 until 1941; and *Coeurs Vaillants* and *Âmes Vaillantes* [Valiant Souls] (the girls' version of the latter) continued in Lyon from 1940 until 1944.[25] In general the journals could carry on as before, providing content remained politically innocuous, although the shortage of supplies, such as paper, led to increasing, and eventually insurmountable, practical difficulties. Likewise in Belgium the Nazi invasion caused a number of publications to stop production – sometimes explicitly, as in the case of *Spirou*, which refused to accept German control and so ceased publication in 1943.

In Brittany one publication, *O Lo Lê*, the self-acclaimed 'Journal illustré des petits Bretons' [Illustrated Journal for Young Bretons], flourished from 1940 to 1944. Although its main remit was the promotion of Breton culture with a view to independence, its underlying right-wing stance suited the occupying powers. On the front page of issue 20 (27 April 1941), for example, the journal sends its wishes to the venerable [*vénéré*] Maréchal Pétain, thanking him since, 'en demandant l'armistice en juin dernier, [il] a sauvé la France du désastre où les forces du mal l'avaient entraînée' [by asking for the armistice last June, [he] saved France from the disaster into which the forces of evil had led her]. In number 35 (11 August 1941), in reply to a bilingual French and Breton good-wishes card the journal had sent, we read Pétain's letter expressing his affection for Brittany.

Like *Le Journal de Mickey* the publication offered a mixture of textual stories, reader participation and image-based narratives. In a reasonably typical issue, number 9 of 9 February 1941, we are immediately drawn to the front-page *Corsaire des îles* [Pirate of the Islands], a historical strip telling of the struggles of a Breton sailor. On the following pages traditional Épinal-style *histoires en images* tell of Breton lore (e.g., *Le Dragon du Menez Arè*). These are interspersed with illustrated fiction (*Les Loups de Coatmenez* [The Wolves of Coatmenez]) and carefully directed fact (*Une Grande & belle histoire: celle de notre Bretagne* [A Great and Beautiful Story: That of our Brittany], *Surcouf: le Roi des Corsaires* [Surcouf: King of the Pirates]). Reader participation includes competitions, a call for letters and the possibility of Breton language lessons. From number 64 onwards (15 March 1942) a major selling point was the serialisation of *Tintin chez les Soviets*.

In many ways *O Lo Lê* is a throw-over from the pre-Mickey era. Its similarity with *Coeurs Vaillants* lies not only in its frequent coverage of Catholic events (saints' days, Breton pardons, anniversaries) but also through a layout, such as the traditional four-by-three bubble-less illustrated story, that pays homage to the traditions of the past. Much the same can be said of the Paris-based and equally Pétainiste *Fanfan la Tulipe*, although that only survived until 1942, having lasted less than a year.

More forward looking, stylistically at least, was the other children's journal available in occupied France, the masterpiece of Nazi indoctrination with which I opened this book, *Le Téméraire* (see Fig. 1, Chapter 1). As Pascal Ory has shown,[26] pseudo-scientific texts would point to the superiority of Aryan blood as compared to that of the Jews or to the magnificence of 'Chevalerie moderne' [Modern Knighthood] epitomised by the 'École de Jeunes Chefs en Allemagne' [School for Young Leaders in Germany], with fictional stories telling of the courageous Irish struggle against English domination or the anti-terrorist (i.e., Resistance) police work of Tom le Flic [Tom the Cop]. Humorous but largely non-politicised strips would juxtapose such texts thereby providing a counterbalance, but on other occasions it was the bandes dessinées that supplied the implicit ideological message.

Published from 116 rue Réaumur in Paris, *Le Téméraire* appeared in thirty-eight fortnightly numbers from 15 January 1943 to 1 August 1944. According to figures held by the Police de Paris, sales went as high as 200,000 and, as copies would be shared, we can reasonably assume that each issue had as many as half a million readers. This may not seem much for a captive audience given that *Le Journal de Mickey* had averaged 400,000, but *Le Téméraire* had the greatly reduced catchment area of occupied (i.e., non-Vichy) France.

Figure 28. 'The Central Spread'. *Le Téméraire*, No. 26 (1 February 1944), pp. 4–5.

An overview of a single issue can give a clear idea of the format and themes of *Le Téméraire* given that the journal's set-up saw no variation until the last few issues, and then the changes were minimal. The title page of our chosen issue, number 26 of 1 February 1944, introduces the theme of the issue, Tibet. Other themes included the Ancient Egyptians, Atlantis, The Year 2000, Ireland, Insects, Prehistoric Man, and so on. On pages 2 and 3 illustrated texts would expand on the theme of the title page and it was here that some of the most blatant Nazi propaganda would be put forward. In the issue on Blue Beard we learn of the primitive Judaic rite of slaughtering children. The issue on Ireland makes a point of underlining the perfidiousness of the English, against whose oppression one should struggle.

The top of page 4 bore the 'comic' adventures of *Le Professeur Fulminante et le docteur Vorax* by Erik. As can be seen from Figure 28, the 'baddy' is distinguishable by his Semitic features. The bottom of the page would have a fictional text, often based on folklore. The top of page 5 gave the adventures of *Marc le Téméraire* by Josse, a spy story in which the villains were often English, American or Russian. Comic strips by Vica filled the bottom of page 5, thereby creating a parallel effect with that of Erik's. Vica's were some of the journal's most politically overt works, presenting negroes as savages (albeit likeable) of little more than animal intelligence; or, in the 1 July 1944 issue, the hero's parrot addresses a USA embassy conference on the Allied bombings with the words 'Assassins, vous voulez donc tuer tout le monde?' [Assassins, so you want to kill us all?].

On page 6 appeared a follow-up story, which was generally a fictional adventure with the English or Americans once again invariably the villains. Page 7 was the reader-participation page, based on the format of that of the *Journal de Mickey* (or, previously, that of *Coeurs Vaillants*) and centring on the activities of the 'Cercle des Téméraires'. Page 7 also included factual trivia sections, *Police moderne*, a type of solve-it-yourself whodunnit, crosswords and competitions, all of which encouraged active participation on the part of the readers.

Finally, the back cover provided the adventure series *Vers les mondes inconnus*, first of all by Auguste Liquois then by Raymond Poïvet. Here again, the villain, 'Goul roi des Marais' (see Fig. 1, Chapter 1), a reference to the Jewish district of Paris, has clear Semitic features, whereas his accomplice Vénine (cf. Lénine) wears a Star of David on his headgear. Meanwhile the 'goodies' conform to the Aryan ideal of tall svelte figures invariably with blue eyes and blonde hair.

It is hard not to let the hard-line Nazi ideology cloud our judgement of *Le Téméraire*, or, as has been the case for most of the histories of the BD (at least until recently), underplay its importance. Artistically *Le Téméraire* was of the highest quality, as the success of the later careers of its contributors might indicate. In terms of format *Le Téméraire* provided a clever, well-balanced mixture of text and narrative image, of humour and adventure, of information, participation, and fantasy fiction. Ironically, the key to its success lay in the fact that the journal took the formula that had worked for *Le Journal de Mickey*, refined and updated it, and added a final alluring element, that of the themed issue.

The success and importance of *Le Téméraire* lies initially in the influence it bore upon a decisive generation of young minds. Such things cannot be quantified, but could early indoctrination at the hands of *Le Téméraire* account for the success of the far right in France today? More tangible is the influence the journal had on postwar publications both in terms of format and artists employed. Virtually all of *Le Téméraire*'s team continued on to highly successful careers in the BD world, with some, such as Raymond Poïvet, Eugène Giroud or Étienne Le Rallic (who also contributed to *O Lo Lê*), becoming well-respected establishment figures. In terms of format, it became normal for the high-flying postwar publications to adopt *Le Téméraire*'s set-up, namely the familiar mixture of BDs, textual features and participation elements, with the added characteristic of issues by theme.

As we will see below, each of the postwar journals had its own angle, its own star strips and its own format, but the basic template was the formula that *Le Téméraire* had mastered and which in turn had been largely modelled on the success of *Le Journal de Mickey*. Just as *Le Journal de Mickey*, despite its reliance on American content, was a very French phenomenon, so we should not 'credit' *Le Téméraire* to the Germans. With the exception of Vica, an immigrant of Ukrainian descent, the artists were all French, as was the management.[27] There is nothing to indicate that the publication received any aid from the occupying authorities, apart from implicit approval.

As such, *Le Téméraire* is an outstanding example of the bande dessinée's value as a cultural phenomenon and a key to wider issues in French Cultural Studies, in this case the tricky question of the nature and the effect of wartime collaboration. Despite its technical excellence, it is not hard to see why *Le Téméraire* has largely been excluded from accounts of the BD's progress, both in terms of the poor pedigree it gives the Ninth Art, but also as another example of an awkward page in France's history. Nonetheless it should not be overlooked, and even if it is generally impossible to ascertain exact levels of influence, all the indications are that *Le Téméraire* was an important milestone in the development of the bande dessinée, and indeed postwar French culture in general.

La Loi du 16 juillet 1949

Before the war, pressure-group attitudes to the fledgling bandes dessinées were generally hostile, based on the view that the ideas espoused were leading children astray. The real target of such attacks was not *La Semaine de Suzette* or *Âmes Vaillantes* (for Catholic girls), but the new wave of imports that, by their introduction of foreign mores, could lead the youth of France away from traditional values. From 1936 union pressure had also been applied to introduce protectionist laws in favour of French artists. When the movement regained momentum after the war, this time enjoying the support of the governing Communist Party, Winckler became one of the main targets of attack, with the communist *député* André Pierrard going as far as to assimilate imported strips in general, and Winckler in particular, to a pro-Hitlerite American press.[28] A new law was being prepared and its twelfth clause would specifically require a limit on the amount of imported material that could be published.[29]

As it happened, the twelfth clause did not materialise, although the act did specifically state that all imported material aimed at children required the approval of the *Ministre Chargé de l'Information* or Information Minister. Nonetheless the nature of the law was enough to make sure imports were reduced, as its main clause, the second, effectively described American strips as they were perceived by a hostile public:

> **Art. 2** Les publications visées à l'article premier [i.e. 'destinées aux enfants et aux adolescents'] ne doivent comporter aucune illustration, aucun récit, aucune chronique, aucune rubrique, aucune insertion présentant sous un jour favorable le banditisme, le mensonge, le vol, la paresse, la lâcheté, la haine, la débauche ou tous actes qualifiés crimes ou délits ou de nature à démoraliser l'enfance ou la jeunesse.
>
> [**Art. 2** The publications that are the object of the first article [i.e. 'those aimed at children and adolescents'] must not contain any illustration, story, column, feature or article that presents in a favourable light banditry, lies, theft, idleness, cowardice, hatred, debauchery or any act designated as a crime or misdemeanour or whose nature might harm the morality of children or youths.]

With such a law in place it would now be easy to repel the undress of Tarzan ('débauche'), the double life of Superman and Clarke Kent ('le mensonge') or the daily non-activity of Goofy ('la paresse').

It is worth pausing briefly to compare the 1949 law with its transatlantic counterpart, 'The Comics Code', instituted in 1955. Just as France had seen a rising number of books and newspaper articles speaking out against the perceived ill-effects of *histoires en images*, and specifically, imported comic strips, so it was a high-profile publication, Fredric Wertham M.D.'s *Seduction of the Innocent: The Influence of 'Horror Comics' on Today's Youth* (1954) that sparked the backlash in America.[30] Wertham's (pseudo-)scientific study concentrated on the horror and crime subsections of comics, claiming that they could either disturb children mentally, and/or lead to crime by imitation. His sixth chapter concentrates on the latter, with the title 'Design for Deliquency: The Contribution of Crime Comic Books to Juvenile

Delinquency'. In it he cites twenty-two cases of juvenile delinquency, of which the following is the third:

> A boy of eleven killed a woman in a holdup. When arrested, he was found surrounded by comic books. His twenty-year-old brother said, 'If you want the cause of all this, here it is: It's those rotten comic books. Cut them out, and things like this wouldn't happen.' (Of course, this brother was not an 'expert'; he just knew the facts.) (151)

The discourse is remarkably similar to that propagated in France, generally by parties claiming to represent educators or psychologists. Alphonse de Parvillez in *Que Liront nos jeunes*? [What Will Our Youth Read?] (1943) had gone to extremes in connecting illustrated publications with violent crime: 'À Juilly, deux petits bergers massacrent une famille de cinq personnes. On trouve dans leur chambre une abondante provision d'illustrés' (36) [In Juilly two little shepherd boys massacre a family of five. In their room an abundant provision of illustrated journals is found].

Jacqueline and Raoul Dubois in *La Presse enfantine française* (1957) were to imply the same sort of cause and effect, despite absolving the *illustrés* of total responsibility:

> Nous savons tous que l'illustré ne porte pas seul la responsabilité du passage des jeunes devant le tribunal pour enfants ... (4)

> [We all know that illustrated journals do not bear unique responsibility for those youths that end up in children's court ...]

> L'enfant assis sur le rebord d'un trottoir n'emportera pas un livre: il lira facilement un illustré, si peu éducatif soit-il. (4)

> [The child who hangs out on the pavement will not pick up a book: he will easily read an illustrated journal no matter how little its educational content.]

One of the more extreme cases was a tract by D. Parker and C. Renaudy, *La Démoralisation de la jeunesse par les publications périodiques* [The Harming of the Morality of Youth by Periodical Publications] (1944), which includes 'les Petits Journaux illustrés' as 'littérature pornographique'. The inside cover summarises areas of concern: 'publications périodiques' come after cinema, but before prostitution, immorality in the workplace, and alcoholism. This was ten years prior to Wertham's seventh chapter, '"I Want to be a Sex Maniac": Comic Books and the Psychosexual Development of Children'.

The main difference is that in the United States the resulting 'Comics Code', initiated after a number of Senate hearings, was to be self-regulated by the Comics Magazine Association of America (founded a year previously in 1954). The terms of the Comics Code were similar to those of clause two of the 1949 law – essentially, sex, excessive violence and the victory of anti-authoritarian 'evil' could not be portrayed – but the important distinction was the political subtext behind the restrictions. Whereas in France nothing concrete had come of the protests until the law was pushed forward by the Communist Party, with, ironically, heavy support from Catholic pressure groups, the uniting factor being an anti-Americanisation ticket, in the USA there was far less motivation in terms of party politics, although moral censorship did tend to be the domain of the right. And whereas the effect in the United States was to cut the comics production line, slash sales and effectively ostracise the genre, the same was not at all true in France.

Once again it was *Le Téméraire* that had shown the way forward, again somewhat ironically, for those faced with the new communist law. For practical as well as ideological reasons *Le Téméraire* could not use American imports, but it had used French artists to plug the gap. André Licquois and Raymond Poïvet's *Vers les mondes inconnus* was in many respects a calque on *Flash Gordon*, with a subtext that was pertinent to France of the time. Similarly Jean Ache's *Biceps, le costaud sentimental* [Biceps, the Sentimental Muscle Man], a strip telling of the eponymous caveman's adventures that was unusual in its elongated form, was effectively a reformulation of Vincent T. Hamlin's *Alley Oop*. Faced with a law that de facto put a stop to imports, the post-1949 publications merely continued along the path forced upon them by the necessities of the war: in-house productions that picked up on the successful techniques of the prewar imports, be they through intergalactic battle or domestic comedy, whilst adding a French touch.

One such example is the *Pionniers de l'Espérance* [The Pioneers of Hope] series that ran from 14 December 1945 in *Vaillant* (see below) to 26 September 1973 in *Vaillant*'s successor, *Pif*. Its authors, Roger Lécureux and Raymond Poïvet, effectively continued the intergalactic struggles that Auguste Liquois and then Poïvet had created in *Vers les mondes inconnus*, although this time the protagonists of the Espérance (the space ship from which the series got its name) are decidedly multicultural. Indeed in keeping with *Vaillant*'s communist stance, prominent place was given to Chinese and Russian members of the expedition. Similarly, in the back-page feature of *Coq Hardi* [The Courageous Cockerel] (again, see below), *Guerre à la Terre* [War with Earth], Liquois now presented the French and the English as struggling to save the planet against a Martian force aided by the Japanese! Such 'recycling' can be noted as a practical response to the needs of postwar censorship, but it also bears witness to the inherent polyvalence of the bande dessinée, whose hybridity allows it to re-form textually whilst keeping a trademark graphic style.

Postwar to 1959

Ideology-based bande dessinée journals dominated the initial postwar period. *Vaillant*, the top-selling weekly sponsored by the Communist Party, owed its origins to *Le Jeune Patriote* [The Young Patriot], a clandestine resistance publication, and went on to become *Pif* and then *Pif-Gadget*, the latter remaining popular until well into the 1970s and early 1980s, as well as enjoying a 2003 rebirth. Pascal Ory has demonstrated how a typical issue of 1940s *Vaillant* mirrored the set-up of *Le Téméraire*: a themed front page; two pages of textual non-fiction; a centre spread in which adventure stories and comedy strips create a symmetrical effect by their diagonal positioning; two pages of reader-participation texts; and *Les Pionniers de L'Espérance* on the back cover.[31]

Vaillant became a pillar of 1950s French culture, selling as many as 210,000 copies a week.[32] The now familiar mixture of fictional texts, reader participation sections and bandes dessinées continued to have a communist touch to it, with, for example, translations of Russian tales such as *Le Portrait* by V.-J. Chichkov, in which the villain is a tyrannical 'koulak',[33] or pleas to send teddy bears to the children of striking dockers.[34] Of the bandes dessinées, some of the most popular were *Pif le Chien* [Pif the Dog], originally by José Arnal, a canine version of Mickey, and *Placid et Muzo*, a bear and fox duo, also by Arnal. In general their adventures gently undermined laziness and capital gain in favour of collective effort. Similar themes underlay adventure serials, such as *Mister Bep*, a Robin Hood-style Wild West millionaire of humble origins, or *Yves le Loup* [Yves the Wolf], a medieval fantasy. The ex-*Téméraire* team still featured strongly, as in Gire's comedy parrot *Père O.K.* (an animal previously favoured by Vica),[35] or Cézard's *Arthur le fantôme justicier* [Arthur the Justice-bringing Ghost].

Ideologically opposite was *Coeurs Vaillants*, the Catholic publication for boys from the well-established Fleurus publishing house, and the representative of the second faction of the 1949 law alliance. The similarity of the names was unfortunate and indeed there are anecdotes of confused priests recommending the communist *Vaillant* to their flock! Once again, and to add to the priests' confusion, it was using very much the same kind of formula to promote its bandes dessinées. In the postwar series – *Coeurs Vaillants* had originally existed from 1929 to 1944, before re-forming in 1946 – the front cover would carry a BD adventure story such as *La Mission de Ralph*, *La Dette du Sioux* [The Debt of the Sioux] or *Le Chrysanthème de Jade* in which the latest techniques in terms of colour, variation in *case* size and cinematographic viewing angles were invariably showcased. The journal as a whole provided a well-balanced and symmetrical mixture of light-hearted and adventure BDs (including *Tintin*), letters, advice to readers (e.g., 'Comment faire une boîte pour une collection d'insectes' [How to make a box for a collection of insects];[36] 'Les 36 trucs du campeur: Une petite croix pour mettre dans la tente' [36 tricks the camper knows: A little cross to put in your tent][37]) and texts. Of the latter the serialised story continued, such as *Le Révolté de Bethléem* [The Rebel from Bethlehem], which appeared towards the end of 1954 and told of the adventures of Jobal, Hillel and Asbahmeh at the time of Herod.

But as in the case of *Vaillant*, non-fictional texts had become more common and these would often underline the required political and religious stance. To take the example of a typical issue, number 43 of 24 October 1954, on pages 2–3 an article on the French pole-vaulter Victor Sillon appears alongside an account of the plight of Asian refugees, a description of the longest suspension bridge in Europe planned for near Le Havre and an analysis of the Bible's stance on miracles. A retrospective of the journal's achievements from 21 March 1954 points to its 'héros', its 'consignes' [advice], its 'articles scientifiques' and its 'reportages', and bears the motto-style title,

> Depuis 25 ans ...
> Coeurs Vaillants a aidé des millions de garçons à vivre en Chrétiens et à servir leur pays.[38]
>
> [For 25 years ...
> Coeurs Vaillants has helped millions of boys to live as Christians and to serve their country.]

Other important BD journals of the immediate postwar period each offered a specific twist with a particular market in mind. *Fripounet et Marisette* was a Fleurus production, with the Catholic values familiar to readers of *Coeurs Vaillants*, but aimed, via its subject matter, at rural children. Similarly, *Âmes Vaillantes*, also from Fleurus, was specifically for girls, and would reflect the publishing house's conservative viewpoint in the ambitions it offered: girls and women feature as companions and housewives aspiring to serve the menfolk. *Coq Hardi*, for which the artist and Resistance hero Marijac was largely responsible, offered boys adventure stories, often revelling in the wartime victory in much the same way that *The Eagle* was to do in England from 1950. Ironically, the main strips, at the beginning at least, were all produced by members of the ex-*Téméraire* team, namely Eric, Étienne Le Raillic, Raymond Cazanave and Auguste Liquois. Cino del Duca's *L'Intrépide* initially sold particularly well,[39] as it attempted to recreate the flavour of the prewar import journals using French artists working in the American style.

The bande dessinée of the 1950s was also remarkable for its absences, namely the journals that were lost during the war and did not manage to start up again in the new market. Casualties included *L'Aventureux*, *Junior*, *Robinson*, *L'As* and *Hop-Là!*. Initially the most noticeable loss was *Le Journal de Mickey*, but this did successfully

Figure 29. 'Mickey plays European Football'. *Le Journal de Mickey*. New Series no. 27 (30 November 1952). Front cover.

reappear, in an updated format, in 1952. Paul Winckler reinstituted the prewar formula that mixed fictional texts, reader participation – in number 27 of 30 November 1952 Onc' Léon tells us that the Club Mickey now has several tens of thousands of members – and general information, whilst including several important changes. The format was now tabloid, with more pages – sixteen for number 27, a typical issue – and increased and more sophisticated use of colour. Of the sixteen pages, ten are bandes dessinées, plus a feature front cover (see Fig. 29). Above all, all of the familiar strips are now produced 'par les studios français de Walt Disney' [Walt Disney's French studios]. This was undoubtedly linked to the drop in 'contextualising' content as the new strips could provide the readers with French affinities: in number 27 we find the popular series *Mickey à travers les siècles* [Mickey through the Centuries] wherein Mickey explores the history of France, Goofy hunts bears in a play on the French expression 'Dingo vend la peau de l'ours',[40] and the front cover shows Mickey and Donald playing European football.

This was also the period that saw the regrowth of publications from Belgium, starting with the weekly return of *Spirou* in 1946 (it had initially returned in 1944), vaunting its wartime stance against the invader and expanding by wide-scale distribution throughout France. In many ways the journal's format was that of the French counterparts, a tabloid mixture of texts, reader participation and bandes dessinées, with emphasis on the latter, and indeed the French and Belgian editions differed only in the advertisements when these were carried. Nonetheless the benefit of hindsight, once again, allows us to identify a distinctive style, now known as that of the *École de Marcinelle*, Marcinelle being the suburb of Brussels from which Dupuis, *Spirou*'s publisher, operated. Elements of the renewal have also been classed with the label *style atome*, a reference to the optimistic modernism of the 1958 world exhibition and its leitmotif the Atomium. 'Star' strips such as Morris's *Lucky Luke*, André Franquin's eponymous bellboy *Spirou* or, later, *Gaston la Gaffe* (1957),[41] or Peyo's *Schtroumpfs* [*Smurfs*] (1958), show the *ligne claire* stylistic lucidity popularised by Hergé, making for larger-than-life caricatures that nonetheless retain a feeling of realism.

Drawing upon the success of the early *Tintin* adventures that had appeared in serial form in *Le Petit Vingtième* and *Coeurs Vaillants* before being released as albums,[42] in 1946 Hergé launched the spin-off journal, *Tintin*. This too transferred on to the French market (1948), although here there were some content differences between the two editions. As one might expect, the *ligne claire* was the journal's trademark, although in general its realism was accentuated well beyond *Spirou*'s younger, more humour-based strips. As well as *Tintin*, two further examples are outstanding: Jacques Martin's *Alix*, a historical adventure set in Roman times whose sumptuous and meticulously researched decors are a prime example of the bande dessinée's visuality serving pedagogical purposes, and Edgar-Pierre Jacobs's tales of Francis Blake and Philip Mortimer, a strip somewhere between *Tintin* and *Indiana Jones*, whose rebirth in 1996 (cf. Fig 7, Chapter 2) is generally cited as being the catalyst for the BD's economic revival at the end of the century.[43]

The success of *Spirou* and *Tintin* may be accounted for in terms of Belgian specificity: if such journals did well at that particular time was it not because the success of *Tintin* had encouraged the culture of the BD, whereas in France the subtext of the 1949 law was to have the opposite effect? Alternatively, it could be quite simply that paper was less of a scarce commodity due to postwar restrictions that had been set in France. On the other hand, it could be argued that both publications conform admirably to the requirements of the law, showing no hints of loose morality or evil-doing, and, perhaps more pertinently, employing a high percentage of home-grown talents. Once again it is hard to quantify abstract notions such as national specificity as being at the root of cultural developments, but if we avoid the question of origins and look at that of effect, an undeniable conclusion is that of a notion of the BD as being a particular Belgian entity whose Golden Age is generally traced to the 1950s.

We have classified this period as that of the fall of the BD, a low period marked by the influence of Nazi collaboration in the form of *Le Téméraire* and restriction and ignominy at the hands of the 1949 law. Although ideologically it is hard to argue with a negative assessment of the period, aesthetically this judgement is misleading. The bande dessinée as it now stands, the Ninth Art that is a French national asset, still bears the influence of this time in terms of format and style. It was *Le Téméraire* that mastered the format that was to become the norm, and it was the pillars of *Le Téméraire* – Poïvet, Gire, Matt, Erik, Licquois – who went on to become the pillars of the postwar BD. The 1949 law, whatever its motivation, had the effect of creating a specifically French art form, even if imported influences were essential. Again in hindsight it is not surprising that histories of the BD underplay the importance of the influences, but the glory days that followed could not have come about without them.

Rise

A new direction with a new Pilote

On 29 October 1959 a new journal, *Pilote*, hit the news-stands. It was the brainchild of René Goscinny, Albert Uderzo and Jean-Michel Charlier, who, according to Charlier's account in *Le Livre d'or du journal Pilote* [The Golden Book of the Journal *Pilote*],[44] had met in a Brussels café to instigate a declaration of authors' rights; as a result were sacked by their respective editors, and so set up their own creation, a sort of *Paris Match* for children, with the backing of Radio Luxembourg. The name, apparently, was in reference to the notion of leadership, although it may not be a coincidence that one of the most popular initial characters, Michel Tanguy, was a fighter pilot. The journal's success was immediate, with early numbers of *Pilote* selling between 200,000 and 300,000 copies and attracting national media attention.

The new journal followed the tried and tested formula of the post-*Mickey* publication – the familiar mixture of textual features, reader exchanges and, increasingly, bandes dessinées – but it added an unfamiliar irreverence. The readers' letters, for example, included spoofs, such as the episode in which a group of 'bricoleurs inpénitents' [unrepentant odd-jobbers] create an aeroplane out of matchsticks.[45] Even the overall format cried out to the passer-by, initially through its larger size (28.5 by 38.5 cm), but also through its cover montage of photos, BD extracts and zany titles.

Once again, however, what appeared as cutting-edge innovation was in fact a renewal of the past and external sources. The use of a large format to stand out from the crowd had worked in the 1930s for *Junior*, and the stunning cover art as a front was a prime feature of *Le Téméraire*, but also of the 1950s array of cheap magazines each providing complete, often imported, stories – examples include *Audax*, *Aventures Film* and *Météor* from the Tourcoing publishing house Artima – as well as of the postwar *Journal de Mickey*. Perhaps most significant, however, was the renewed influence of American artwork as a template for French creation, in this instance the model being *Mad*.

Just as the founders of *Pilote* had grown up with the influence of *Le Journal de Mickey*, *Junior* and, presumably, *Le Téméraire*, so the sway of the American satirical best-seller was far from coincidental. René Goscinny, born in 1926, had lived in the United States from 1945 until 1951 and spent a considerable period of time working with Harvey Kurtzman, Will Elder, Jack Davis and John Severin, the main figures behind the creation of *Mad*.[46] *Tales Calculated to Drive You Mad*, as was its full original title, first appeared in 1952 with the subtitle 'Humor in a Jugular Vein'. The format, and specifically the early cover illustrations, parodied the popular horror comics, whilst the features would lampoon television, cinema, popular fashions and celebrity figures.

The irreverent tone in general and the self-aware introspective mockery in particular had clearly rubbed off onto the early *Pilote*. Issue 231 (26 March 1964), for example, shows an opened telegram with the words 'desolé stop avons perdu dessin couverture de pilote numero 231 les imprimeurs' [sorry stop have lost cover sketch pilote number 231 the printers]. Speech bubbles below exclaim 'ooh!' 'mais ... mais ... c'est épouvantable' 'c'est du sabotage' and 'que ... va-t-on faire? ...' [ooh! but ... but ... it's awful / it's sabotage / what ... shall we do?]. In the 1 April issue of 1961 (number 75) the journal's heroes, including Astérix and Obélix, Michel Tanguy and Barbe-Rouge, promise Jacques Le Gall that he will finally be portrayed in colour. In fact he is a black silhouette until he turns the tables, washes, and transforms himself to colour and all others to black and white. The strip is signed 'Ozredu' and 'Ynnicsog'! Early numbers would mock work scenes, or the everyday life of France – the anachronisms of *Astérix* to this end are famous – whereas more direct satire, such as of politicians and pop stars, was to become commonplace in the 1970s.

It is ironic, or perhaps inevitable, that a journal whose birth had the Algerian war as background should come of age in par with the events of 1968. In keeping with the spirit of the time, the authors of *Pilote* organised a take-over by way of a protest against what was seen as Goscinny's de Gaulle-esque running of the journal. The insurrection culminated in a hastily assembled meeting in a café on the Parisian rue des Pyramides, to which Goscinny rushed on foot because there was no petrol available. Publication halted for three weeks, after which Goscinny resumed at the head of the editorial team despite having threatened to resign. The new-look *Pilote*, to be decided each week by a meeting of all staff, was to include sections on current affaires with, by implication, an older target audience. It was from then on that the expression 'le phénomène *Pilote*' became current and sales rose further.

A quick comparison between an early issue of *Pilote*, number 32 of 2 June 1960, and one following the post-1968 changes shows how the journal itself had grown up, but, more importantly, stands as a microcosm of the BD's coming of age. The 1960 issue emphasises the education of youth, implicitly through the subtitle, 'Le Grand Magazine illustré des jeunes' [The Great Illustrated Magazine for Youth] and more explicitly through the information pages: several pages give short pieces, such as a discussion of the danger of grand prix racing or a report of a freak tornado, whilst extended articles explore subjects in greater depth, for example the ethnographic review of snake charming that picks up on the front cover photo. The centre spread *Pilotorama*, a popular feature, here gives a schematic illustration of a working mine.

Of the thirty-two pages, thirteen are bandes dessinées, including one traditional *histoire en images*, a historic account of Charette, a royalist martyr in 1796. Leading strips by J.M. Charlier – *Le Démon des Caraïbes* [The Demon of the Caribbean] and *Michel Tanguy* – Antonio Parras – *Ivanhoe*, based on Walter Scott's tale – and Goscinny and Uderzo – *Jehan Soupolet* and *Astérix* – mix humour and adventure, education and fantasy, whilst appealing to the eye through bright colours and styles that rarely stray far from the clarity of the *ligne claire*.

By issue 572 of October 1970 *Pilote* had become 'Le Journal qui s'amuse à réflechir' [The Journal That Has Fun Thinking]. The format is now reduced in size, but it stands at sixty pages, of which fifty are bandes dessinées or bande dessinée related. Apart from the cover and adverts, the remaining pages comprise a spoof article on the BD artist Fred, two pages reviewing cars, films and books, and a further two pages on fashion from shoes to motor scooters. The style of the BDs is more eclectic, ranging from a *Mad*-style article offering adverts featuring society's losers ['minables'], *gros nez* or 'red nose' satire by Reiser, sci-fi bordering on the psychedelic by Mézières and by Fred (cf. Fig. 6, Chapter 2, from the previous issue), *Magic City* a *histoire en images* in the style of the Sergeant Pepper artwork, and Gotlib's self-reflexive *Rubrique-à-brac*,[47] but also more traditional favourites such as *Lucky Luke* and *Astérix*. Gone are the competitions and the reader participation: the creators are now the stars, many strips including a small portrait of the artist.

Tu Bandes?

The post-1968 era of *Pilote* was marked by a number of breakaway publications which took the bande dessinée in directions – generally via direct sexual or scatological reference – that would not have been possible in Goscinny's administration, but the fact that the general premise of humour based upon zany parody remained the central strand pays tribute to the influence of *Pilote*. The main case in point is *L'Écho des Savanes* [The Savanna Echo], founded in May 1972 by Claire Bretécher, Marcel Gotlib and Nikita Mandryka, all three of whom had had leading roles in *Pilote*'s production.

The enthusiast who consults one of the numerous BD histories or dictionaries and learns that *L'Écho* took *Pilote* one step further and led the bande dessinée towards its status as a serious art form, will, when consulting early issues of the journal, be surprised on several counts. Firstly, although the cover attracted the eye with bright colours and outlandish designs in the manner of *Mad*, the journal itself was spartan in its fifty-two black and white pages initially almost entirely the work of Bretécher, Gotlib and Mandryka. This was perhaps to be expected, but one should be aware that the initial 'home made' appearance was a far cry from the panache of *Pilote*'s production. Secondly, the publication broke from the formula of text, reader participation and BDs to turn almost exclusively to the latter. This may have been for practical reasons given the expertise of the contributors, but it did suggest that satire could be exclusively bande dessinée based, an important fact given that *Mad* had moved away from comic strips in the aftermath of the Comics Code.

There were a few non-BD exceptions amongst the early pages of the *Écho*, such as a *roman photo* or photo strip featuring the three founders (issue 2, pp. 25–28), or the 'Appel de 343 Hommes' [The Call to Arms from 343 Men] that appeared on pages 2 and 3 of issue 7. In what is a direct satire of appeals for women's rights, and in particular the 1971 *Manifeste des 343* [The 343's Manifesto] published in the *Nouvel Observateur* [New Observer] whereby 343 women declared they had had an illegal abortion, the *Écho*'s male protest calls for 'la masturbation libre' [free masturbation] and invites protestors to send a postcard to RTL stating 'Je déclare m'être branlé' [I declare that I have wanked]. Signatories include Mick Jagger, Alfred E. Neuman (the cartoon boy who represented *Mad*), Alain Robbe-Grillet, Mao-Tsé Toung and, as an honorary member, Claire Bretécher.

This is a good example of the way in which the *Écho* might surprise the neophyte reader (then and now), namely through the extent to which the early journal was dominated by explicit sexual, or generally taboo, humour. The opening page of number 2, for example, draws the life of the artist, summed up by the phrase 'je montrais mon cul à tous les passants' [I showed my arse to all who passed by]. The same issue contains an eleven-page strip by Gotlib in which the central character walks through a local wood only to witness the sexual exploits of various characters of folklore: Red Riding Hood and the wolf copulating, M. Seguin in a long-term relationship with his goat, Snow White and the dwarfs enjoying an orgy, Tarzan as a gay exhibitionist and so on. It is easy to see how, again with hindsight, *L'Écho des Savanes* could be dismissed as a crude fanzine, but that would be to overlook the genuine social satire in many of the strips, and a development that was to give early free rein to artists such as Moebius, Robert Crumb and René Pétillon. Perhaps for an Anglophone the clearest comparison would be with *Viz*, which, significantly, did not appear until seven years later in 1979.

Judging by the poor quality of the paper, the almost exclusive use of monochrome and the lack of high-profile advertisers, one can imagine that the influence of early issues of *L'Écho*, like that of the early *Viz*, was limited. Even by 1980 Les Éditions du Fromage, as Mandryka, Gotlib and Bretécher's publishing venture was known, was only announcing a capital of FF 21,000, but it was announcing a capital as a limited company and the situation had undoubtedly evolved: *L'Écho des Savanes* had expanded to eighty-four pages, including an increased number of photographs and colour illustrations. This was coupled with a greater diversity of strips, from the historical to the sociological, and a lower percentage of explicitly sexual content.

L'Écho des Savanes is important as the first of a series of publications in the same vein, each with their own specific twist, but which, when viewed together, form a group indicative of a shift in the values and possibilities of the BD. In terms of the satirical values that came with a lampooning of institutions, coupled with a taboo-shattering directness, one can point to the influence of publications such as *Hara-Kiri* (1960), its heir *Charlie-Hebdo* [Charlie Weekly] (1970) or even *Le Canard Enchaîné* (1915).[48] What was new in the case of *L'Écho* and other post '68 BD dissidents was that the bande dessinée alone could be used to such ends.

From early 1975 *Métal Hurlant* was produced by Les Humanoïdes Associés, with Moebius and Philippe Druillet at the head.[49] The work's remit was BD for a mature audience with a specific interest in science fiction, and although the format had much in common with that of *L'Écho*, the quality of the production was more sophisticated, with a good percentage of colour pages and a number of advertisers, such as Casterman and J'ai Lu, that would indicate a higher profile.

In a typical early issue, number 28 of April 1978, of the one hundred tabloid-size pages seventy-two were BDs, divided amongst ten leading strips, which whilst still generally following the 'à suivre' format now extended well beyond the single- or maybe double-page contribution. The *ligne claire* is absent, with styles underlining experimental *case* sizes, fantasy and narrative disjunction: two examples are Moebius's *Garage hermétique* (discussed in our second chapter) and Frank Margerin's *Guy Leclerc*, an intergalactic everyman spoofing *Flash Gordon*, who, in this instance, forgets to fill the space ship with petrol.[50] The remaining pages provide adverts, a running 'robot' theme and reviews of the latest records, films and books.

Just as *Mad* had set the tone for *Pilote*, so *Fluide Glacial* (first issue also 1975) picked up on the raunchier aspects of the American underground commix movement. More general and less sci-fi than *Métal Hurlant*, *Fluide Glacial* specialised in zany social parody, such as Gotlib's *Superdupont*, a French non-superhero, or Christian Binet's *Les Bidochon*, the now cult rendition of the eponymous Robert and Raymonde Bidochon's couch potato antics.[51] *Fluide Glacial* stands apart as one of the few postwar journals still to publish today, having braved the economic crisis of the end of the century.

Alternatively, *Ah! Nana* (1976) used similar taboo-breaking sexual directness but to promote a militant feminist viewpoint.[52] Published by Les Humanoïdes Associés, in many ways *Ah! Nana* drew upon the same formula as *L'Écho*, mixing BDs, *romans photos*, themed dossiers (e.g., Nazism, female child sex, homosexuality, sado-masochism) and reports on cinema, TV, art and book events. The difference was that the editorial team and artists were predominantly female, including contributions from Chantal Montellier, Marie-Noëlle Pichard, Agnès Varda and Trina Robbins. Despite reaching a level of incision that is still a landmark for the popular expression of French feminism, *Ah! Nana* was short-lived: it survived only nine issues, the last in September 1978, folding soon after having received an 'adults only' label.

By the 1980s the bande dessinée was set up as an adult organ, even if most dictionaries and histories of the BD point to Jean-Claude Forest's 1962 Barbarella as the watershed character. Barbarella did indeed create a cult symbol of sexiness through a level of undress that suggested the 1949 law no longer held sway, but much of her notoriety was linked to Jane Fonda's 1968 cinema portrayal. It was through publications such as *L'Écho*, *Hara-Kiri* and *Métal Hurlant* that the 'adult' bande dessinée obtained a higher profile and took an increasing share of the everyday market, with the front covers on news-stands clearly proclaiming the move to manhood. Indeed the bande dessinée had moved on, but this was surely because the *Pilote* schoolboys of 1959 had left the classroom and were now wanting something a little spicier.

Fall within a rise

The expansion period that enjoyed the expressive freedom of the bande dessinée's newly found adulthood was short-lived as the form fell prey to wider social and economic changes. From the early 1980s the trade crisis that had stifled American growth also hit France, with unemployment going from approximately 4 per cent in the mid-1970s to over 10 per cent a decade later.[53] Leisure industries, such as publishing, particularly suffered and many of the weeklies that had heralded the new way forward ceased to be. Having switched to a monthly format in 1974, *Pilote* published its last number in February 1986. *L'Écho des Savanes* moved to Albin Michel in 1982 and took on a new format with a greater emphasis on overt eroticism. *Métal Hurlant* folded in 1987.

The decline of the journals has, however, been counterbalanced by a rise in album publications: whereas 1974 only saw 139 new albums, in 1982 this had more than tripled to 446.[54] This may be a reflection of the bande dessinée's new status as a valid form of expression in its own right, one that no longer needed the legitimising context of a journal in order for it to appeal. Alternatively, it may be that in the world of instant-access television and videos the notion of eagerly awaiting the next episode of a serialised strip was no longer realistic. Or maybe it is just that as the trend continues the schoolboys of the 1960s are now the middle management of the twenty-first century, pocket money has become disposable income, and album sales, at an average of between €10 and €20 per publication, are far more lucrative than counting on regular journal purchase.

Consecration of the Ninth Art

Indeed recent figures suggest that the financial slump of the 1980s is over as BD sales continue to rise. The number of new albums and editions published has increased steadily from the latter years of the twentieth century onwards, going from 878 (1997) to approximately 4,318 in 2008.[55] But the current success of the bande dessinée is not just a marketing concern. In 1982, as part of the newly elected socialist government's push towards greater public appreciation of French culture, Jack Lang, the then Minister of Culture, announced his 'Quinze Mesures pour la bande dessinée' [Fifteen Measures for the Bande Dessinée]. These included plans for revision of the 1949 law, the creation of bodies to aid with the practical side of publishing BDs, and encouragement for the translation of bandes dessinées. Above all, in the context of the *grands travaux* a scheme was to be initiated for the creation of a national BD centre. This Angoulême project was officialised in 1984, with an intended opening of 1988, although it was finally delayed until 1990.[56] As well as getting national and international media attention, the measures consecrated the BD as an art form – the term 'Neuvième Art' or Ninth Art had been in circulation since the mid-1960s – and, moreover, a French art form.[57]

Histories of the Ninth Art tend to overlook the fact that in 1989, a year before the actual launch of the French national centre, the Centre Belge de la Bande Dessinée (CBBD) also opened in the regenerated Victor Horta Art Nouveau Waucquez building (1906) in central Brussels. Like its Angoulême counterpart it includes ample exhibition space as a showpiece for its collection of original *planches*, a library that fulfils leisure and research functions, and a specialist bookshop. Despite the prestigious location and the initial in-pouring of state money, however, much has been made of the Centre's gradual shift toward the status of a commercial tourist attraction, rather than a flagship establishment for a national art.[58]

The unveiling of the French national centre, the Centre National de la Bande Dessinée et de l'Image (CNBDI, Fig. 30) followed in 1990 under the architectural auspices of Roland Castro, who adapted the disused Champigneulles brewery on the banks of the Charente in Angoulême (115 kilometres northeast of Bordeaux). Originally the building included a library, cinema and museum, but the museum is now an exhibition space, with a new national museum planned in close proximity and due to open in 2009. Since September 2007 the CNBDI and the projected new museum have become part of a broader complex, the Cité International de la Bande Dessinée et de l'Image (CIBDI), that also includes an artists' residency ('Maison des Auteurs').

Angoulême had been chosen on account of the success of the town's annual BD festival, held on the last weekend of January every year since 1974, and also in reference to the School of Art that had started to specialise in the teaching of the BD. From one point of view, these were perfectly reasonable criteria, although the form's detractors would soon comment that the placing of the BD in a provincial town of 43,000 inhabitants was a way of differentiating the bande dessinée from other, more traditional, cultural forms whose high-profile institutions were Paris-based *grands travaux*, such as the extended Louvre or the Bastille Opera.

Whether or not the bande dessinée, even today, can boast the cultural status of Academy art, ballet or opera is open to debate. And indeed that debate, including the related question of the evolution of the bande dessinée's critical reception and associated status, will be the subject of the opening chapters of Part III of this book, 'The Cultural Phenomenon'. What is clear is that what was a pastime for children subject to the wrath of educators is indeed now the centre of an industry of critical analysis. The festival itself continues to flourish,[59] having received the patronage of presidents and film stars, with the thirty-sixth gathering in 2009 attracting some 220,000 visitors over its four days. The bande dessinée now regularly draws front-page newspaper attention and prime-time television; has its own section in *Livres de France*;[60] and often provides the overall best-seller of French publications. That said, as we have seen in the Introduction to this book, the CNRS, France's main research body, still does not recognise the BD as a valid academic discipline and although many scholars will talk enthusiastically about their passion for BD, it is a passion that remains a hobby as the number of French university-based academics specialising in the field can be counted on one hand.

Figure 30. 'CNBDI or National BD Centre, Angoulême'. Photo 2007.

A Century of Events

This brief summary of the twentieth-century development of the bande dessinée, in other words the very period generally associated with the form's growth, has pointed to a century of events: the development of the early *bulle* through *Zig et Puce*, the advent of the *Journal de Mickey*, *Le Téméraire* and the wartime turnaround, the 1949 law and its aftermath, the *Pilote* years, *L'Écho des Savanes* and the breakaway into adulthood, the CNBDI and the consecration of the Ninth Art. The methodology appears very different from that of the previous chapter where the emphasis was on the gradual development of a cultural climate, that of the image, rather than individual defining moments.

One could conclude that the BD did not become a self-aware form until the twentieth century, a fact that this methodology implicitly underlines. The difference between the chapters also has the advantage of demonstrating variety in the approaches that can be applied to the study of the BD, although in this case it would be difficult to imagine a twentieth-century outline that does not identify key moments. But it is a question that should not be overlooked. The very notion of a century-based approach is problematic, as the world did not suddenly change on 1 January 1901; nonetheless the format of a book requires chapters in order to maintain structural coherency.

Perhaps the answer is to ask the reader to 'suspend belief', to accept the information and analysis contained within these sections, whilst remaining aware that the history of the bande dessinée is rich enough to sustain numerous other methods of approach.

Notes

1. (Paris: Larousse, 1994 and 2000).
2. Apart from the 'Musée d'Histoire' [Museum of History], the Angoulême exhibition comprises the 'Museum d'Histoire Naturelle' [Museum of Natural History], the 'Musée d'Ethnographie' [Museum of Ethnography], the 'Galerie d'Art Contemporain' [Gallery of Contemporary Art], the 'Musée des Sciences et Techniques' [Museum of Science and Industry] and the 'Musée des Beaux Arts' [Fine Art Museum]. The *mise en scène*, by Lucie Lom, is a playful attempt to categorise (or at least to underline the problems of categorisation) the different aspects of the BD via interconnected spaces with cardboard cut-out museum façades. The exhibition is outlined in Thierry Groensteen and Gaby Scaon, eds, *Les Musées imaginaires de la bande dessinée* (Angoulême: Éditions de l'An 2, 2004).
3. *Masters of the Ninth Art: Bandes Dessinées and Franco-Belgian Identity* (Liverpool: Liverpool University Press, 2005).
4. *Reading Bande Dessinée: Critical Approaches to the French-Language Comic Strip* (Bristol: Intellect, 2007).
5. The *Astérix* series will, however, be considered at some length in the 'Best-sellers' section of Chapter 7 on the contemporary BD, and the works of several of Screech's authors have been given some analysis in the first part, 'What is a Bande Dessinée?', of this book.
6. 'Pétasse' is a derogatory slang term for an intellectually and culturally challenged young lady. On Bécassine see Marie-Anne Couderc, *Bécassine inconnue* [Unknown Bécassine] (Paris: CNRS, 2000) and, more specifically, Charles Forsdick, 'Exoticising the *Domestique*: Bécassine, Brittany and the Beauty of the Dead', *The Francophone Bande Dessinée*, ed. Charles Forsdick, Laurence Grove and Libbie [Elizabeth] McQuillan (Amsterdam: Rodopi, 2005), pp. 23–37.
7. See once more the discussion in the previous chapter, as well as below.
8. A glance through one of the encyclopaedias of the bande dessinée will give an idea of the style and background of many of the *histoires en images* characters. See, for example, Patrick Gaumer and Claude Moliterni, *Dictionnaire mondial de la bande dessinée*; Henri Filippini's thematic (e.g., adventure characters, sci-fi characters, humorous characters etc.), *Dictionnaire encyclopédique des héros et auteurs de BD*, 3 vols. (Grenoble: Glénat, 1998–2000); Claude Moliterni, Philippe Mellot, Laurent Turpin, Michel Denni and Nathalie Michel-Szelechowska, *BDGuide 2005: Encyclopédie de la bande dessinée internationale* (Paris: Omnibus, 2004). No such work, however, is yet available in English. Specifically on Louis Forton, see Maurice Dubourg, 'Louis Forton et Les Pieds Nickelés: Essai de chronologie' [Louis Forton and the Pieds Nickelés: A Chronological Essay], *Le Collectionneur de Bandes Dessinées* 35 (1982), 17–23.
9. On the 'pre-history' of the speech bubble, see Laurence Grove, 'Emblems with Speech Bubbles', *Visual Words and Verbal Pictures: Essays in Honour of Michael Bath*, ed. Alison Saunders and Peter Davidson (Glasgow: GES, 2005), pp. 89–103.
10. On *Zig et Puce* see issue 48 (1985) of *Le Collectionneur de Bandes Dessinées*, which has a main section dedicated to them. See also chapter 2 of Jean-

Jacques Gabut, *L'Âge d'or de la BD: Les Journaux illustrés 1934–1944* [The Golden Age of BD: Illustrated Journals 1934–1944] (Paris: Catleya, 2001).

11. As stated above, our analysis of the *Tintin* series will be fleeting, as it is one of the rare areas of the bande dessinée that has spawned considerable criticism in English. Mathew Screech's *Masters of the Ninth Art* includes an important section on Hergé (pp. 17–51) and offers a substantial related bibliography. Ann Miller's *Reading Bande Dessinée: Critical Approaches to French-Language Comic Strip* privileges *Tintin* as the only pre-Second World War work to be given extended analysis (pp. 201–14), this in the context of psychoanalytic approaches. We will also return to *Tintin* for the first of our case studies in the chapter 'Cultural Studies and Beyond'.
12. The dates given here and in the paragraphs that follow are for the first album publication. The first album publication of *Tintin au pays des Soviets* was in 1930. The published English titles are *The Shooting Star* [*L'Étoile mystérieuse*], *Destination Moon* [*Objectif Lune*], *Explorers on the Moon* [*On a marché sur la Lune*], *Tintin and Alph-Art* [*Tintin et l'Alph'Art*], *The Blue Lotus* [*Le Lotus bleu*] and *The Black Island* [*L'Île noire*].
13. The term *ligne claire* was originally coined by Joost Swarte, the Dutch designer, illustrator and comics artist.
14. Quoted on video format available via the Tintin official site (www.tintin.be).
15. Here I am deliberately separating Belgian bandes dessinées from the production in Flemish, a rich tradition that is not within the scope of this study.
16. For an overview of the twentieth-century history of the bande dessinée in Belgium, see Pascal Lefèvre's chapter, 'La Bande dessinée belge au XXe siècle' [Belgian Bande Dessinée in the Twentieth Century] on pp. 168–207 of Charles Dierick, ed., *Le Centre Belge de la Bande Dessinée* (Brussels: Dexia, 2000). On the question of 'belgicité' with specific reference to *Tintin*, see Anna Soncini Fratta, ed., *Tintin, Hergé et la 'Belgité'* (Bologna: CLUEB, 1994). *Spirou*, and in particular its postwar success, will be discussed further below.
17. Much of this section draws upon and updates material presented in my 'Mickey, *Le Journal de Mickey* and the Birth of the Popular BD', *Belphégor* [www.dal.ca/~etc/belphegor] 1.1 (2001).
18. Alain Fourment, *Histoire de la presse des jeunes et des journaux d'enfants (1768–1988)* [History of Youth Press and Children's Journals (1768–1988)] (Paris: Eole, 1987). These statistics appear on p. 409 as part of an appendix coving the period 1925 to 1985. On p. 167 Fourment also quotes Paul Winckler as claiming that when *Le Journal de Mickey* was launched no other journal went beyond 50,000 copies, as compared with his, at 500,000. Although not 100 per cent reliable, Fourment's work does provide a good general overview of the development of children's journals in France, many of which were BD related.
19. That accolade would appear to belong to Scotland's *Dandy*, whose first issue appeared in 1937. *Topolino*, the Italian Disney-based journal, was founded in 1932, but broke for the war and also became *Tuffolino* for a short while.
20. This section will give no more than a brief presentational overview of a subject which is the object of a fully documented and highly illustrated study: Jean-Jacques Gabut, *L'Âge d'or de la BD: Les Journaux illustrés 1934–1944*.
21. On the SPE, see *Le Collectionneur de Bandes Dessinées* 35 (1982), which has the subject as its main theme.
22. On p. 2 of the 23 October 1937 issue.

23. *Le Journal de Mickey*'s nearest rivals were fellow Winckler productions, such as *Robinson* which also reached 400,000. These figures are based on the works cited by Alain Fourment and by Jean-Jacques Gabut.
24. On European equivalents of *Le Journal de Mickey*, see *Le Collectionneur de Bandes Dessinées* 105 (2005), which has the subject as its main theme.
25. On wartime *illustrés*, see issue 14 (1978) of *Le Collectionneur de Bandes Dessinées*, which is a special number on the subject.
26. The main work on *Le Téméraire* is Pascal Ory's monograph, *Le Petit Nazi illustré: Vie et survie du Téméraire (1943–1944)* [The Little Nazi Illustrated: The Life and Afterlife of Le Téméraire (1943–1944)], first published in 1979, with a new expanded edition (Paris: Nautilus) in 2002. See also issue 14 (1978) of *Le Collectionneur de Bandes Dessinées*, which is a special number on wartime *illustrés*. See also chapter 10, 'Where Have All the Nazis Gone?' (pp. 107–17) of my *Text/Image Mosaics in French Culture: Emblems and Comic Strips* (Aldershot: Ashgate, 2005). Much of this section draws upon and updates this chapter.
27. On Vica, see Clare Tufts, 'Vincent Krassousky: Nazi Collaborator or Naïve Cartoonist?', *International Journal of Comic Art* 6.1 (2004), 18–36.
28. An unusual accusation given that Winckler had had to flee France because he was Jewish. Could Pierrard have been putting *Le Journal de Mickey* and *Le Téméraire* in the same basket due to the similarities in their format?
29. On this subject, see specifically Thierry Groensteen, 'La Mise en cause de Paul Winckler' [Paul Winckler Under Fire], *'On Tue à chaque page': La loi de 1949 sur les publications destinées à la jeunesse* ['They Kill on Every Page': The 1949 Law on Publications Aimed at Youth], ed. Thierry Crépin and Thierry Groensteen (Paris: Éditions du Temps, 1999), pp. 53–60. The volume as a whole should be consulted for a background to and analysis of the law, as well as for the text of the law itself, which is reproduced in an annex (pp. 237–44). For a detailed overview of the conditions leading to the 1949 law and its ensuing effect with specific reference to children's publications, see Thierry Crépin, *'Haro sur le gangster!': La Moralisation de la presse enfantine 1934–1954* [Shame on the Gangster!: The Moralisation of the Press for Children 1934–1954] (Paris: CNRS, 2001). See also Thierry Crépin, '1950–1954: La Commission de surveillance entre intimidation et répression' [1950–1954: The Surveillance Commission: Between Intimidation and Repression], *9e Art* 4 (1999), 21–27, and Thierry Groensteen, 'C'était le temps où la bande dessinée corrompait l'âme enfantine ...,' [It was the Time when the Bande Dessinée Corrupted the Souls of Children ...], pp. 14–19 of the same publication.
30. On the context of *Seduction of the Innocent*, see Bart Beaty, *Fredric Wertham and the Critique of Mass Culture* (Jackson, MS: University Press of Mississippi, 2005). Beaty persuasively argues that Wertham's intentions were more liberal than generally portrayed, that he did not wish to have comics banned or burnt, but rather was in favour of a more effective system of censorship.
31. See *Le Petit Nazi illustré: Vie et survie du Téméraire (1943–1944)*, pp. 88–90.
32. For an overview of the journal's history and contents, see Henri Filippini, *Histoire du journal et des éditions Vaillant* [The History of *Vaillant* the Journal and its Publications] (Grenoble: Glénat, 1978).
33. Number 476, 27 June 1954.
34. Number 455, 31 January 1954.
35. Literally 'Father O.K.,' but the sound is that of 'Perroquet' or 'Parrot', the animal featured as the strip's main character.
36. Number 1 of 1954 (3 January).

37. Number 34 of 1954 (22 August).
38. Number 12 of 1954.
39. This is not to be confused with a prewar (1910–1937) Offenstadt production of the same name.
40. 'Vendre la peau de l'ours avant de l'avoir tué', literally 'to sell the bear's skin before having killed it', equates to the English counting of unhatched chickens. 'Dingo' is the French version of 'Goofy'.
41. On Franquin and his creations see chapter 2 (pp. 52–74) of Matthew Screech's *Masters of the Ninth Art*. Franquin took over the *Spirou* series from Jijé, who in turn had taken over from his creator Rob-Vel. A 'gaffe', as in 'Gaston la Gaffe', is a blunder.
42. These were the main journals to carry *Tintin*. Others, such as *Le Soir* [Evening News] of Brussels also serialised his adventures. Again, on Hergé, his creations and his associates, see chapter 1 (pp. 17–51) of Matthew Screech's *Masters of the Ninth Art*.
43. The1996 album, *L'Affaire Francis Blake* [The Francis Blake Affair] (Paris: Dargaud), was the work of Ted Benoît and Jean Van Hamme. Jacobs died in 1987.
44. (Neuilly-sur-Seine: Dargaud, 1980), p. 16. No author's name is given to this work. For the history of *Pilote* see also Patrick Gaumer, *Les Années Pilote: 1959–1989* [The *Pilote* Years: 1959–1989] (Paris: Dargaud, 1996). For lucid introductions in English, see Wendy Michallat, '*Pilote*: Pedagogy, Puberty and Parents', *The Francophone Bande Dessinée*, ed. Charles Forsdick, Laurence Grove and Libbie [Elizabeth] McQuillan (Amsterdam: Rodopi, 2005), pp. 83–95; Elizabeth McQuillan 'Between the Sheets at *Pilote*: 1968–1973', *International Journal of Comic Art* 2.1 (2000), 159–77. Both scholars have completed PhD theses on *Pilote* or with important sections on *Pilote*, which although less accessible are well worth consulting: Wendy Michallat, '*Pilote* Magazine and the Evolution of French *Bande Dessinée* between 1959 and 1974', Diss., University of Nottingham, 2002; Elizabeth McQuillan, 'The Reception and Creation of Post-1960 Franco-Belgian BD', Diss., University of Glasgow, 2001.
45. In issue 265, 19 November 1964.
46. On the style and history of *Mad*, see Maria Reidelbach, *Completely Mad: A History of the Comic Book and Magazine* (Boston: Little, Brown and Company, 1991). See also Roger Sabin, *Comics, Comix & Graphic Novels: A History of Comic Art* (London: Phaidon, 2002 [first published 1996]).
47. The title is a play on words between 'rubrique' or 'column' and 'bric-à-brac'.
48. Literally 'the enchained duck', but a reference to the popular use of 'canard' to mean 'newspaper'.
49. See Chapter 3, 'Formal Specificity', for a brief introduction to Moebius and his work. See also chapter 4 (pp. 95–127) of Matthew Screech's *Masters of the Ninth Art*.
50. 'Guy Leclerc' is a play on 'Guy L'Éclair', the French title for 'Flash Gordon', whilst referring to the popular Leclerc supermarkets.
51. *Les Bidochon* will also be discussed further in our next chapter, 'Contemporary BD'.
52. The title is a play on pejorative slang for a woman, a rough equivalent of 'bird'. The question of the expression of feminism through BD will also be discussed in the chapter 'Cultural Studies and Beyond'.
53. These are the figures of the Institut National de la Statistique et des Études Économiques (L'INSEE) or National Institute for Statistics and Studies of Economics, as given on their website (www.educnet.education.fr/insee/chomage).

54. See the 'Dossier BD' (pp. 79–104) of *Livres Hebdo* [Books Weekly] (21 January 1985, number 4 of that year), specifically p. 80. It should be noted that the number of new albums then fell until the early 1990s.
55. See the 'Dossier BD' (pp. 64–91) of *Livres Hebdo* 761 (23 January 2009), specifically p. 72.
56. The *Quinze Mesures* were updated on 24 January 1997. The *Mesures Nouvelles* [New Measures] can be consulted on the Ministry of Culture's website (www.culture.gouv.fr/culture/actual/misfred2.htm). See also Elizabeth McQuillan, 'The Reception and Creation of Post-1960 Franco-Belgian BD'.
57. In 1964 under the title of *Neuvième Art: Musée de la bande dessinée* [Ninth Art: The Museum of Bande Dessinée] Morris and Pierre Vankeer had initiated a series in *Spirou* that examined key landmarks of the form's history. The term became widespread when Francis Lacassin entitled his seminal 1971 study *Pour un 9ème art: La Bande dessinée* [For a Ninth Art: The Bande Dessinée] (Paris: 10/18).
58. On the CBBD, see Dierick, *Le Centre Belge de la Bande Dessinée*.
59. In recent years this has been despite journalistic predictions that it would flop.
60. Literally 'Books of France', this monthly presents authoritative listings and analysis of the current publishing industry in France.

CHAPTER 7

CONTEMPORARY BD: INNOVATORS, BEST-SELLERS AND PRIZE-WINNERS

Another Method of Approach

That this book should be written only nine years into a new millennium is methodologically fortuitous as it allows for a chapter on the current century whilst making a chronological approach unfeasible. But with 1,293 albums newly published in 2001,[1] the first year of the century, alone – without forgetting the fact, as we shall see, that some of the most influential works in the twenty-first century are those published in the 1980s and 1990s, or beyond – to provide a full overview, or even a nod of the hat, to every BD author would be impossible. The avid reader could of course consult the dictionaries and general works that pepper the footnotes of this current book,[2] but nothing replaces a trip to the local *bédéthèque*, to the Fnac, to a nearby BD festival or even a bookshop web search, all of which will provide an idea of some of the latest creations and continuing favourites. From there readers can choose their own directions …

Such caveats notwithstanding, it is possible to give some indication of the current state of the bande dessinée, at least at the time of writing in 2009. My aim is to provide a balance between the works which cram the supermarket shelves and top the charts for incoming euros, sometimes at the expense of artistic subtlety, and those that are perhaps more adventurous, creative and foreseeing, but which might not appeal to a wide-scale audience, and so arguably have less overall impact.

Twenty-first-century Innovators

Marketing success and/or academic accolade do not necessarily crown all the worthy representatives of an artistic form, as current-day cultural icons from Cyrano de Bergerac to Vincent Van Gogh remind us only too well. Unfortunately a selection of 'likely to lasts' will inevitably be more of an indication of the values of 2009, many of which are successful continuations from previous decades, rather than a definitive list of the good and the great, even if such were desirable. Nonetheless one of the main aims of this current work is to give the English-language reader an insight into some of the facets of the foreign world of bande dessinée, and as such it is worth starting this chapter by pointing out a few possibly unfamiliar works that are generally considered household names in France today.

Tranches de vie

It can be argued that everything from sweet wrappers to soap operas provide a *tranche de vie* or slice of life,[3] a sociological insight to the values of the world that produced such artefacts. In some cases, however, the artist consciously aims to portray the society around him or her. This is not the same thing as having a political axe to grind, but as there is no such thing as a neutral image (or text), any portrait will reflect the *parti-pris*, even if it is subconscious, of the artist.

Claire Bretécher has generally denied claims that she is the flag-bearer of feminist bande dessinée.[4] Nonetheless, as a woman artist producing subversive (sometimes gently, sometimes not so gently) works from the late 1960s and 1970s, she inevitably reflects her unique position. Her strips, as published in the *Nouvel Observateur* from 1973, reflect the anguishes of the thirty-something middle class, and her leitmotif characters – Agrippine and Cellulite – broach problems that are specific to women, whilst keeping a universal appeal that has lasted well into the twenty-first century.

To a certain extent Cellulite, the medieval princess with the twentieth-century angst, is an Astérix for the modern woman. In *Les Angoisses de Cellulite* [Cellulite's Anguishes] (1974), for example, we see her dealing with enthusiastic and not-so-enthusiastic suitors, interacting with an impatient father, leaving her bedroom in a mess and doing her best not to get out of bed before vespers. Agrippine, her modern counterpart despite having a name that echoes Racinian tragedy, shows similar preoccupations – physical appearance, gossip and boys – although both the character and audience are adolescent. In all such cases the humour pertains to a female subject matter, but this in itself does not make Bretécher any more feminist than, say, the editors of *Cosmopolitan* magazine. Bretécher is not concerned with the 'male gaze' (and neither, it would seem, are her androgynous characters), with an attempt to tackle serious questions of social injustice, or with a claim to analyse and differentiate the male and female psyches. But the very fact that Bretécher presents a female viewpoint in a milieu that is such a male bastion, both in terms of artists and subject matter, is in itself noteworthy.[5]

In many ways it is the series that does not have a specific female lead, *Les Frustrés*, that best characterises Bretécher's work. Thirty-somethings muse over their physical appearance (see Fig. 3, Chapter 2), the 'in' cultural activities, their sex life or the effect of the media, as in the discussion in which Xavier emphasises his distaste for television as a corrupt genre that overemphasises appearance and sound-bites, only for us to discover, in the final *case*, that the discussion is taking place on a chat show.[6] Here, as throughout, Bretécher uses a regular *case* set-up with minimal visual variants. The 'action' is all words, and as such a reflection of the bourgeois life portrayed. Form and content of bande dessinée overlap in a style that by its minimalism provides a counterbalance to the exuberant visual experimentation often associated with avant-garde BD.

It is hard to imagine a *tranche de vie* artist in greater contrast to Claire Bretécher than Philippe Vuillemin, best known for his *Sales blagues* [Dirty Jokes] which have appeared regularly in album format since 1987.[7] As the title suggests, these compilations visualise coarse, often politically incorrect, jokes, but the appeal is not necessarily in the often-predictable punch line. Vuillemin paints an exaggerated 'warts and all' picture of the everyday anguishes and fantasies that envelope his characters, such as the time-damaged women of mature age on the beach who reminisce for the era when they wanted to look like Brigitte Bardot, only to point out that they now do look like her, or the quidam who frantically attracts the attention of the faithful at Lourdes by screaming 'je marche' [I'm walking] – unfortunately it turns out to be because someone has stolen his car.[8] Like Robert Crumb, S. Clay Wilson, or other exponents of the American Underground, Vuillemin does not shy away from explicit sex and/or violence, although this is generally a vehicle for the carefully noted expressions, background details and tics of a world that is a grotesque version of our own.

A toned-down version of Vuillemin's parade of social exclusions peppers the work of Frank Margerin, although Lucien, Ricky Banlieue and their associates crave belonging in their marginalised *banlieue* world.[9] Margerin's style is semi-realist, a sort of non-Superman of the suburbs, and the effect is enhanced by the fact that many of the characters are based on close friends or family of the author.[10] We see them in everyday activities, such as listening to Johnny Hallyday records, trying to entice women or attempting get-rich-quick schemes, all of which lead to a reasonably guessable punchline. In one strip, 'Les "Anti-Noël"', for example, Lucien and friends indicate that they will boycott the excessive consumerism of Christmas, only to end up organising an 'anti-Christmas' party whose trappings – foie gras, crèche, neatly wrapped presents and champagne – are a caricature of a generic French yuletide.

The strip ends with the friends about to boycott New Year ...[11] Here and elsewhere Margerin's tone is warmly humoristic, even, ironically, when he refers to such subjects as social or racial exclusion, and at no stage do our *banlieusards* offer any threat to the social status quo.

Christian Binet's *Les Bidochon*, who have starred in nineteen albums by 2009 having originally transferred from *Fluide Glacial*, have some of the direct coarseness of Vuillemin's subjects, whilst underlining a sharp social edge in keeping with Bretécher's works. The eponymous couple, Robert and Raymonde, are the French 'everyman' and 'everywoman', obsessed with television and petty consumerism. In the same way as Bretécher's creations, at the other end of the social scale, make us feel uneasy as we recognise aspects of ourselves, so we sympathise with the Bidochons' predicaments, despite the fact that we all hope to avoid affinities. In the first album, *Roman d'amour* [Love Story] (1980),[12] we see them squabbling over the correct usage of the term 'chiottes', (slang for 'toilets', singular according to Raymonde, plural for Robert), the fact that Raymonde uses Robert's razor, or Robert's noisy eating habits. Perhaps more than the spin-off figurines, the film (Serge Korber, 1996) or the stage show, the influence of the series is best gauged by the fact that the title has now entered the language, *un bidochon* being the equivalent of a *beauf* or an American redneck.[13]

Politically aware

Perhaps it is the humorous element that allows us to keep our distance when reading the above works. Although there is serious topical comment to be found in Bretécher and Margerin's pieces, as indeed is de facto the case for political cartoonists such as Georges Wolinski, Martin Veyron and René Pétillon (all to be discussed below), the social or political stance is not generally what makes these works memorable. In the case of albums where humour and satire are absent, we are more inclined to read them as *engagé*, even if the cause in question can be largely undisputed.

Such is the case for *Jo* by Derib (1991), an album in which the eponymous heroine becomes HIV positive as a result of her first sexual experience, a one-night stand. The moral of the story, that AIDS can hit anyone and safe sex at all times is essential, is further documented in an appended 'questions and answers' dossier, to which are added letters of encouragement from Jack Lang and L'Abbé Pierre. It is an album in which Derib puts the advantages of the bande dessinée medium to full use, as we see in the central *planche* where Jo learns of her condition (Fig. 5, Chapter 2): variations on *case* size and shape allow Derib to switch between narrative explanation, which is largely verbal (bottom-right *case*) and the pictorial, with a *gros plan* on Jo's face to display overcoming emotion.

Jo has nonetheless been criticised as a naïve portrayal that avoids broader, and possibly uncomfortable, questions of sexual morality and social acceptance.[14] Slightly more controversial is Lax's *Chiens de fusils* [Gun Dogs] (1996), in which we see the conflict in Northern Ireland from the viewpoint of a young Catholic boy progressing into the IRA Although visually the documentation, such as Lax's reproduction of the various sectarian murals, is stunning, a reader from one of the countries involved might find the complexities of the conflict betrayed by a Manichean oversimplification. Nonetheless Lax demonstrates a willingness to use the medium so as to take a stand on difficult issues – a proof, if it were needed, that the bande dessinée is far from being 'comic'.

The inclusion of works from the 1990s in a subsection of 'Twenty-first-century Innovators' is quite deliberate. These are undoubtedly the BD of 'today', a medium that uses its very specific text/image interchange to tackle the issues of our time, thereby giving them immediacy and appeal that can persist even when our view on the subject matter has evolved. In some cases, as in the socially aware *Tendre banlieue* [Sweet Suburbs] albums by Tito (more on this in the 'Cultural Studies and Beyond' chapter), a series can develop so as constantly to reflect the burning issues of the time. However, just as any attempt in twenty-first-century cinema to tackle attitudes to AIDS or Northern Ireland politics would inevitably have *Philadelphia* (Jonathan Demme, 1993) and *In the Name of the Father* (Jim Sheridan, 1993) as the initial point of reference, so *Jo* and *Chiens de fusils* stand as two of the audacious building blocks that have made today's BD an acceptable medium through which to broach social and political issues.

It is the work of Chantal Montellier that in many ways exemplifies the bande dessinée as such an ongoing tool for political dissidence. From the 1970s and throughout the 1980s her *Andy Gang* series was groundbreaking in its portrayal of social injustices, in particular the violent excesses of a right-wing police organisation. Montellier has continued to challenge, perhaps not always subtly, any concept of a police state through strips such as *Shelter* (1979) and *Le Sang de la Commune* [The Blood of the Commune] (1982, with Pierre Charras). That this is an ongoing process was to be seen in the success of her 2005 *Les Damnés de Nanterre*, a work short-listed for the Angoulême *Grand Prix* in which Montellier reconsiders the case of Florence Rey and Audry Maupin, two disillusioned left-wing activists at the centre of a 1994 police chase that resulted in five deaths. Montellier's style is initially comparable to that of Jacques Tardi, although at times she almost touches a level of photo-realism, providing added shock value to the starkness of the subjects she approaches.[15]

Graphic classics

Some of the most intriguing works of the current era shine not so much through plot or potential message but purely in terms of artistic dynamism. Again, the thin-line drawings of Tardi or even Hergé could come under this category, as could many of the most popular multi-album series, headed by Jean Van Hamme's *XIII* (to be discussed briefly below).

A leading example is Glénat's 'Collection Vécu' [Lived Collection] with its major venture *Le Cycle des 7 Vies de l'épervier* [The Cycle of the 7 Lives of the Sparrowhawk], which spans history from the Renaissance to the Revolution in nine series (by 2009) of between five and eleven volumes. The scriptwriters and artists, of whom Patrick Cothias and André Juillard are best known, intermingle recurrent historical characters in overlapping plots that create a sense of ongoing non-completion on a par with modern-day soap operas or even nineteenth-century novels. These works often exemplify the duality of the BD form, whereby the fast-moving narrative forms a partnership with a graphic precision that evokes the static atmosphere of historical places and costumes in a way that even the most lavish film could not. The exoticism comes from the precise recreation of a bygone time although historical accuracy is rarely a forte and is easily sacrificed to doses of action and eroticism.[16]

Arguably the popularity of such a style can be traced back to the rebirth of *Blake et Mortimer* in 1996. Upon its release *L'Affaire Francis Blake* (Brussels: Éditions Blake et Mortimer), scripted by Jean Van Hamme with artwork by Ted Benoit but based upon the characters that Edgar-Pierre Jacobs had first created in 1946, sold approximately 700,000 albums and in many ways marked the turning point in the bande dessinée's post-recession fortunes.[17] Although Jacobs's original adventures reflected the time of creation, the post-Jacobs *Blake et Mortimer*, of which there have been five volumes between 1996 and 2004,[18] have tended to return to the 1950s. Beyond the nostalgia appeal, one can see how the fine-line drawings (e.g., Fig 7, Chapter 2) both recreate the atmosphere of a bygone era in keeping with the precision of an Art Deco style, and provide an element of realism through period detail that allows the reader to contemplate the key *cases* in the way one might enjoy dissecting an old photo of a familiar place.[19]

Popular experiments

The examples cited above, and they are just a few chosen from an increasingly expanding pool, give pride of place to technical virtuosity, but often to the detriment or even exclusion of experimentation, be it in terms of artwork or more general approaches to the medium. André Juillard, a pillar of the graphic classics who has worked on both *Le Cycle des 7 Vies de l'épervier* and post-Jacobs *Blake et Mortimer*, spans the gap with *Le Cahier bleu* (1994, second edition 2003), an album that uses intricate graphics to question modes of narrative. *Le Cahier bleu* will be discussed at length as one of our case studies in the 'Cultural Studies and Beyond' chapter. This analysis will be accompanied by a section on the work of Marc-Antoine Mathieu, whose self-reflexive playfulness is also a model of narrative experimentation.

As will be noted later in this chapter, it is the partnership of François Schuiten and Benoît Peeters that has done most to popularise the notion of BD as ground for formal experimentation. The *Cités obscures* series bursts into the multi-dimensional through web guides, walk-through exhibitions and stage productions, thereby suggesting that bande dessinée reaches ultimate fulfilment when it no longer limits itself to the textual two-dimensionality we associate with the physical page. The experimentation is increasingly visual, once again taking us towards Thierry Groensteen's theory of the BD as an essentially image-based medium.

It is fitting that Groensteen should have been one of the inaugurators of the OuBaPo movement, one that implicitly explores the potential of image-domination in the BD, even if its direct reference is the literary world of the later postwar period.[20] Just as OuLiPo – the Ouvroir de Littérature Potentielle – imposed constraints on its authors in order to push the boundaries of literary formal experimentation,[21] so the self-conscious aim of OuBaPo – Ouvroir de Bande Dessinée Potentielle – is to do the same for the bande dessinée. The project was originally formulated and initial examples produced at the 1987 bande dessinée conference at the prestigious Cerisy-la-Salle centre in Normandy, but it was not until 1997 that the Paris-based L'Association (see below) started its *OuPus* series with *OuPus 1*.

It was in *OuPus 1* that Groensteen presented OuBaPo's unofficial manifesto through the leading article, 'Un Premier bouquet de contraintes' [A First Bouquet of Constraints] (pp. 13–59), which dominates the volume and catalogues the type of limitations with which OuBaPo authors could challenge themselves. There are essentially two categories: 'Génératrices', or works that create meaning, and 'Transformatrices', or works that transform meaning. Within the 'Génératrices' category we find BDs that can be read upside-down, back to front (thus palindromes), via the folding of the page (an exercise that had been a popular feature of *Mad* magazine, the 'Fold In') or in multiple directions, as in the Étienne Lécroart strip of Figure 12 (see Chapter 3). The 'Transformatices' category generally involves the implantation of *cases* by other authors, as in Lewis Trondheim's earlier *Moins d'un quart de second pour vivre* [Less Than a Quarter of a Second to Live] (1991; see below), or the removal of certain *cases* in order to create a different but equally valid final work.

OuPus 3: Les Vacances de l'OuBaPo (2000, and thus the second volume) reproduces examples, based on the volume 1 categories, that had been published individually in *Libération* throughout the previous summer. That the strips should have appeared in a mainstream daily, even if it is one that tries to portray itself as anti-establishment, bears witness to a level of public attention that would be almost unthinkable in the English-language presses. Further volumes were less high profile: *OuPus 2* (2003) continues the exercises (in particular of the 'Transformatrices' type) of volumes 1 and 3, whereas *OuPus 4* (2005) is a collection of strips created in performance manner between physically distanced artists at two simultaneous BD festivals, Bastia and Luzern. Unfortunately, *OuPus 4* as a whole has the trappings of a parlour game between pals who could not be together rather than an incisive literary experiment with a creative final product.

The work of OuBaPo is playful and fun to dip into, but it does become overtly self-conscious, often repetitive, and generally with the format desperately overshadowing the content. These works are a long way from the novels of Georges Perec, Raymond Queneau or Jacques Roubaud that can be read per se for the beauty of their plot, linguistic humour and overall structure, all of this regardless of the literary limitations that are being surveyed. OuBaPo pieces are short individual strips, with as yet no full-length album produced by an individual author, although works by Étienne Lécroart and by Jochen Gerner, despite not being published under the official aegis of OuBaPo, do go some way to achieving this. The *OuPus* volumes mark the new maturity of a form that can explore its full potential, one that can question its very nature in terms of text/image roles, sequentiality and the relationship between specifically visual elements, but which still leaves one with the final impression that it is trying a little too hard to make a point.[22]

L'Association and associates

L'A.A.N.A.L., or, in more polite terms, L'Association pour L'Apologie du Neuvième Art Libre [The Association for the Apology for a Free Ninth Art], came into operation as a result of *Lynx à tifs*,[23] a 1970s periodical fanzine aimed at questioning the editorial policy of the mainstream publishing houses. The driving force behind these initiatives was Jean-Christophe Menu, who in 1990 shortened the title to L'Association and began to concentrate on books rather than fanzines. In *Plates-bandes*,[24] a retrospective of L'Association's achievements in its first ten years that also functions as manifesto, Menu sums up his aims:

> la dimension de *dissidence* est essentielle dans la fondation de *L'Association. L'Association* n'aurait probablement pas existé si un certain nombre d'Auteurs, très différents, ne s'étaient pas retrouvés à cette époque avec deux principaux points communs: d'une part le désir d'utiliser la Bande Dessinée comme moyen d'expression au sens absolu du terme (disons de nécessité intérieure plus que d'*aptitudes* extérieures); d'autre part le constat que le contexte professionnel du moment n'était absolument pas en mesure de satisfaire à ce désir. (25)
>
> [the dimension of *dissidence* is essential in L'Association's foundation. L'Association would probably not have existed if a certain number of authors, who were very different from each other, had not found themselves with two principal points in common at that time: on the one hand a desire to use the Bande Dessinée as a means of expression

> in the absolute sense of the term (let us say from interior necessity rather than from exterior *aptitude*); on the other hand a realisation that the professional context of the time was in no way apt to satisfy that desire.

The specific brunt of Menu's attack is the standardised format of a forty-eight-page hardbound colour album – '48CC' or '48 couleur cartonné' – which tends to encourage standardised genres such as westerns, science fiction, or, worst of all, fantasy adventure ('48CC/HF/KK' or '48 couleur cartonné/heroïc-fantasy/kaka' according to Menu). Most of the examples cited below in the 'Best-sellers' section of this chapter come under the '48CC' format, whereas works published by L'Association give the author free rein regarding format and number of pages, although colours are generally not permitted. The monochrome rule encourages artistic expression, but the cost-saving element is not completely irrelevant.

In terms of content L'Association's publications tend to be introspective and reflection-based. David B. in *Le Cheval blême* [The Bleak Horse] (2000) explores the inner world of nightmares, whereas works by Marjane Satrapi, Julie Doucet or Menu himself are directly autobiographical. L'Association publishes eight separate collections (including 'Hors Collection') whose style and format reflect those of the authors, be it 'Ciboulette', which comes closest to the novel, 'Mimoulette' for works nearer to the spirit of underground commix, or 'Éprouvette' for theoretical works. The other collections are 'Éperluette' for more standard album formats (this was the first series), 'Côtelette' for a general literary style and 'Patte-de-Mouche' for small formats, the BD equivalent of a *court métrage*. 'Espôtelle' was inaugurated at the end of 2007 as a bridge between 'Ciboulette' and 'Côtelette'.[25] By January 2008 L'Association had published approximately 250 volumes.

As well as being instrumental in the creation of OuBaPo and in the financial and literary success of Marjane Satrapi, L'Association was responsible for *Comix 2000*, a 2,000-page volume for the year 2000 uniting artists from several continents with the guiding theme of the twentieth century and the proviso that all strips be free of text so as to impose no language barriers. Although this project was ambitious and groundbreaking it did hit financial difficulties, provoking Menu to explain the background situation in a widely circulated e-mail. That much of the critical discussion relating to L'Association, its works and its policies, should bypass traditional journalistic channels – L'Association notoriously has no press service – in favour of websites (e.g., discussions on ActuBD at www.actuabd.com) or e-mail polemics related in the pages of *Plate-bandes* or *Éprouvette* (L'Association's theoretical journal) in itself bears witness to an outlook that shuns mainstream norms.

Beyond publications that actually bear the stamp of L'Association, Menu's dynamism has diverted the course of bande dessinée through its knock-on influence.[26] Fabrice Neaud's autobiographical *Journal* series published by Ego Comme X, to take a leading example, explores the traumas of gay life in small-town France, a subject matter that was previously either taboo or ignored. Neaud uses the medium to full effect, and is at his strongest when nuances of the image express twinges of emotion and personal priorities, allowing him to reflect upon the world around him. In the section where he considers a fleeting lover's rejection of the notion of homosexuality (Fig. 10, Chapter 2), Neaud uses a (hypocritical?) standardised *case* system for a non-standardised emotion system but underlines the blurring of feeling through the blurring of styles.[27]

Other dissident or exploratory voices such as those of Manu Larcenet or Christophe Blain (both discussed below) are published by the mainstream houses, but in the specialised collections that are now available, for example Dargaud's 'Poisson Pilote' or Casterman's 'Écritures'. Although Menu is often less than complementary regarding such 'spin-off' series (some of his fiercest attacks feature in the pages of *Plates-bandes*), their existence suggests that the contemporary BD has matured on a par with other popular forms, and in particular cinema, whereby a certain tension, but also an interchange, and even occasional overlap, is inevitable between the cutting-edge innovators and the big-business best-sellers.

Best-sellers

According to *Livres Hebdo*, the best-selling BD productions of the opening years of the twenty-first century were the following:[28]

2008 Zep, *Titeuf 12: Le Sens de la vie* [Titeuf 12: The Meaning of Life] (Grenoble: Glénat, 2008).
495,400 copies sold.[29]

2007 Jean Van Hamme and Jean Giraud, *XIII 18: La Version irlandaise* [XIII 18: The Irish Version] (Paris: Dargaud, 2007).
286,300 copies sold.[30]

2006 Zep, *Titeuf 11: Mes meilleurs copains* [Titeuf 11: My Best Friends] (Grenoble: Glénat, 2006).
570,800 copies sold.[31]

2005 Albert Uderzo, *Le Ciel lui tombe sur la tête* [Asterix and the Falling Sky] (Paris: Éditions Albert René, 2005).
1,305,300 copies sold.[32]

2004 Zep, *Titeuf 10: Nadia se marie* [Titeuf 10: Nadia Gets Married] (Grenoble: Glénat, 2004).
835,200 copies sold.[33]

2003 René Goscinny and Albert Uderzo, *Astérix et la rentrée gauloise* [Asterix and the Class Act] (Paris: Éditions Albert René, 2003).
865,900 copies sold.[34]

2002 Zep, *Titeuf 9: La Loi du préau* [Titeuf 9: The Law of the Playground] (Grenoble: Glénat, 2002).
892,600 copies sold.[35]

2001 Albert Uderzo, *Astérix et Latraviata* [Astérix and the Actress] (Paris: Éditions Albert René, 2001).
2,288,065 copies sold.[36]

Other top-sellers in recent years have included Stéphane Deteindre's *Joe Bar Team*, reworkings of Morris's *Lucky Luke*, such as those by Laurent Gerra and Achdé, further adventures in the *Blake et Mortimer* series originally created by Edgar-Pierre Jacobs, including two albums by André Juillard and Yves Sante, and various previous volumes in the *XIII* saga, by Jean Van Hamme and William Vance.[37]

The *Joe Bar Team* series, published by Vents d'Ouest of Issy les Moulineaux near Paris, provides a playful *Titeuf*-style exploration of youth preoccupations, this time for older teenagers and with a central motorbike theme. The Morris and Jacobs reworkings remind us that BD 'classics' will always feature amongst the best-sellers, as Uderzo has shown by continuing the *Astérix* series and as would undoubtedly be the case for *Tintin*, were it not for the fact that Hergé's estate expressly forbids any further albums.

Even the French are sometimes surprised by the importance of the BD within the book market. In 2007 the two final volumes of the *XIII* series took ninth (volume 18) and eleventh (volume 19) places in the overall best-sellers list for the year, this despite not being released until 13 November. Nonetheless the scale of their success was limited compared with other performances in recent years. In 2004 six of the ten overall best-sellers were bandes dessinées. In 2008 *Titeuf 12* was a close second in the overall best-sellers list, as was the 2004 *Titeuf 10*, that fell behind Dan Brown's *The Da Vinci Code* by just over 20,000 copies, having been on the market more than five months less.[38] In 2005, however, *Le Ciel lui tombe sur la tête* was clear overall best-seller, beating *Harry Potter et le prince du sang-mêlé* [Harry Potter and the Half-Blood Prince] and the newly released paperback edition of *The Da Vinci Code* into second and third respectively. In 2006 *Titeuf 11* similarly outsold Dan Brown's paperback edition to claim top overall spot, despite not being available until 12 October. *Astérix et la rentrée gauloise* had taken second place in 2003, this time to *Harry Potter et l'Ordre du Phénix*. And it is significant that in terms of sales in their respective years of release *Astérix et Latraviata* was considerably more than a quarter of a million copies ahead of *The Da Vinci code* and *l'Ordre du Phénix* put together.

Titeuf

Philippe Chappuis (born 1967 in Geneva) takes his pen name of Zep from the English heavy metal band Led Zeppelin of which he has been a fan since childhood. Having done pieces for various fanzines from his teenage years, Zep opened the door to fame in January 1993 with the publication of the first *Titeuf* album, *Dieu, le sexe et les bretelles* [God, Sex and Braces], published, like the albums to follow, by Glénat.

Titeuf, whose name is in reference to the shape of his head ('petit oeuf' or 'small egg'), is a schoolboy of between eight and twelve years old living with his parents and younger sister and socialising through his school friends. These come in a range of shapes, sizes and ethnic backgrounds, from the Hispanic Ramon and Muslim Maxime, to the overweight Hugo, the nerdy lisp-ridden Jean-Claude and general sidekick Manu. The love interest is Nadia, who, as might be expected, shows a greater degree of maturity, which may be the reason for her rejection of Titeuf's awkward advances. The action takes place in and around school, home and related activities, in a non-specified setting presumably intended to create affinities with the equally standard environment of the average reader.

The albums, all in the 48CC format (see above), consist of a series of associated episodes, generally of little more than a *planche*, each with its own build-up and punchline, and vaguely related to the central theme. *Titeuf 12: Le Sens de la vie*, for example, includes the leitmotif of Titeuf's father's depression and the associated feeling that life has no meaning. In one *case* (p. 25) a thought bubble shows the father imagining his head as formed from excrement thereby indicating his self-view of worthlessness. In the case of *Titeuf 10: Nadia se marie*, the plot revolves around Titeuf's discovery that Nadia is living with someone – predictably he turns out to be her cousin – and his subsequent attempts to win her over. Individual episodes see Titeuf assimilating taking a girl out to taking a dog out (the plastic bag he brings along is to pick up her droppings), or coming to terms with bumping into his father's ex-fiancée (he asks his dad if he really did kiss her on the mouth). In *Titeuf 11: Mes meilleurs copains* the central theme is Titeuf's interaction with his friends in the light of his impending departure for America. He 'bravely' torments school bullies before we, and he, are allowed to realise that Titeuf's father is moving to an American company, but the family are going no further than across the road. Thereafter we see the friends discussing cosmetic breast surgery, admiring the delights of the female body via a naked Barbie doll, and comparing Halal, Kosher and Christian ('Jésus, il peut pô manger de soupe, il a des trous partout!!' [Jesus can't eat soup, he's full of holes!!]) menus in the canteen. In this, and in albums 1 to 9 and 12, the separation between the episodes is explicit, as each of the strips has its own title. Further single-strip episodes are available in the journal *Tchô*, the title being Titeuf's catchphrase greeting, with *Titeuf*, as one would expect, being the leading strip in a latter-day parallel with the *Tintin* journal of the 1950s.

The style of *Titeuf* is in keeping with a tradition of episodic gags often associated with the Marcinelle school from which such characters as André Franquin's *Gaston la Gaffe* emerged. Just as the subject matter is recognisable both in terms of environment and events (Gaston is an office boy, Titeuf is a schoolboy), so the framework is based upon that which we know well, namely four strips of rectangular *cases*. Within these parameters Zep provides elements of variation, using elongated *cases* and an uneven *cadrage,* and he produces characters that fit well-known stereotypes, whilst giving comical exaggeration to their demeanour as well as to their appearance, one that draws upon overemphasised body parts, simplistic facial features and emphatic use of pastel colours. The style alone alerts us to the content, one that is familiar but amusingly distorted, with no hint of any threatening or disturbing undertones.

In terms of subject matter, *Titeuf* owes much of its success to its ability to tap into the social concerns of its time without becoming overbearing. In *Mes meilleurs copains*, published shortly after the 2006 riots, we see a burnt-out car, with Manu explaining 'c'est le malaise des gens' [it's because people are ill at ease]. Titeuf subsequently attributes a neighbour burning his leaves and flambé bananas at family dinner to similar malaise! The series also succeeds in evoking slightly taboo preoccupations of the target audience without becoming offensively vulgar. Scatological jokes are popular, for example Titeuf spanking his baby sister only for her nappy to burst with the contents splattering him, or a prank in which a friend is pulled away from a urinal so as inevitably to shower himself. Zep also alludes to potentially awkward subjects, such as explaining Maxime's brown skin in terms of genes and chromosomes, but here again the tone remains light. In short, Zep willingly opens the dialogue on adult matters, but avoids giving any answers.

Above all, (pseudo-)sexual references are there to amuse the young or pre-teenagers, without going so far as to incur the parent's wrath: when the replacement teacher bends down below his desk, his slightly-shaven head, together with its reflection, looks like a hairy backside; Titeuf concludes that the photos in Hugo's *Playboy* are fake because 'y z'ont oublié les boules' [they forgot the balls]; when in a dream Titeuf goes on an internal journey through Nadia's body in search of her love neurone, we see a section with her breasts, clearly marked 'nichons' [tits], in plant pots next to a watering can and fertiliser. Direct sexual references have been followed up and contextualised by a health education volume produced by Zep and his partner Hélène Bruller, *Le Guide du zizi sexuel* [The Guide to the Sexual Willy] (2001), a work that also hit the best-sellers list.

Perhaps *Titeuf*'s greatest impact is by linguistic association, through the fact that Zep has pinpointed the mannerisms of a generation and in turn influenced further development. 'Chais pô' [dunno] and 'tu pues du slip' [stinky pants] are now commonplace in playgrounds, as is the general grammatical ellipsis practised by Titeuf and his friends.[39] Other expressions, such as 'momosexual' (a 'cute' mispronunciation and thus misunderstanding of 'homosexual') create linguistic cults that are more directly social, although again Zep stays well clear of any polemic. Like Hergé and Bretécher, Zep has a trademark script, which as well as being recognisable adds to the aural effect: like the playground slang, the lettering is sloppy and informal, but clearly understandable.

Just as *Astérix* was noted as being a phenomenon in the 1960s, so the same is true of *Titeuf* in the early years of the twenty-first century. Sales of course indicate that the *Astérix* phenomenon lives on, although *Astérix* is in no small part nostalgia-based and increasingly orientated towards adults, even if they are the grown-ups who were children of the *Pilote* era. *Titeuf* indubitably captures the mood of modern pre-teens and teenagers, or at least those of a relatively stable environment, and will mainly only appeal to adults by association, namely to parents or those working with the children. But maybe in thirty years' time *Titeuf* will have evolved with its audience: after all, those who were pre-teens when *Dieu, le sexe et les bretelles* came out are now well into adulthood ...

In any case, a walk through a French, Belgian or French-Swiss town of the first years of this century is enough to confirm *Titeuf*'s status as a phenomenon. As well as the usual figurines, T-shirts and posters we find cosmetics, plasters, biscuits, ice-creams, restaurant menus, board games and video games, stationery, bicycles, satchels, sweets, and so on. Beyond the high street, *Titeuf* has been adapted into illustrated book form by Shirley Anguerrand; the TV animation adaptation shown on FR3 is increasingly popular; Titeuf has featured on Swiss stamps; and exhibitions thrive. These often play on *Titeuf*'s mixture of youth appeal yet mainstream acceptability, as in the case of the hugely successful 2007 display at the Paris Villette science centre, *Zizi sexuel: L'Expo* [Sexual Willies: The Exhibition], a sex-education exhibition, based on the book by Zep and Bruller, for nine- to fourteen-year-olds.

Titeuf's success seems to increase with its success, as familiarity is very much part of the attraction. We recognise the foibles in Titeuf and enjoy sharing them, just as previous generations first tasted such enjoyment when reading about and effectively making friends with Spirou, Agrippine, Ricky Banlieue or indeed Astérix and Obélix. *Titeuf*'s humour is repetitive and often predictable, the albums are mass produced at low cost, and the artwork is stereotyped, all of which places it at the opposite end of the spectrum from some of the experimental bandes dessinées that we explore throughout this book. *Titeuf* maybe gives the BD, as an art form, a bad name, but no more than does, by similar argument, *Harry Potter* for the modern novel or *Ninja Turtles* for animation. *Titeuf* is a continuation of the bande dessinée's postwar grass roots, roots that are embedded in early *Tintin* and *Astérix*, and that have, originally at least, succeeded in appealing to children in quest of figures who may not provide role models, but do provide light-hearted audience identification.

XIII

The success of the *XIII* series (published by Dargaud) is international and has known spin-offs that include scratch cards and PC games. It is a good example of the ongoing adventure series – by 2007, when the final volume appeared, there were nineteen *XIII* volumes, the first having been published in 1984 – that provides clear line graphic realism coupled with snappy dialogue and narrative suspense, here based on the central motive of the mysterious main character who can only be identified by his 'XIII' tattoo. Jean Van Hamme (born 1939 in Brussels), the scriptwriter, specialises in the type of popular scenario that might be compared to the plots of Ian Fleming or John Buchan, having also worked on the *Largo Winch* adventure series (the eponymous character being a millionaire playboy), as well as the 1980 cult-thriller *Diva* (directed by Jean-Jacques Beineix).

The formula has brought success – financial at least – to dozens of continuing historical, sci-fi and fantasy series, many of which push the violent or sexual elements to the extremes. To a certain extent the francophone BD world echoes that of Hollywood films as recurring core features provide the necessary elements to ensure mainstream sales. The importance of these sales should not be overlooked, a point worth emphasising to anglophone readers for whom even the best-seller lists of comics – with a few exceptions, notably the work of Art Spiegelman – can represent a subgenre well separate from the overall cultural money-spinners.

Astérix the BD giant

The opening two *planches* of *Astérix le Gaulois* appeared in the first issue of *Pilote* on 29 October 1959. The whole adventure was released in album form in 1961 with a print run of 6,000.[40] The second album, *La Serpe d'or* [Asterix and the Golden Sickle] (1962) had a print run of 20,000 and the third, *Astérix chez les Goths* [Asterix and the Goths] (1963) 40,000.[41] The success continued with the release of twenty albums between 1964 and 1976, all of them firstly serialised in *Pilote*, which in 1965 reflected the success by adopting the subtitle of 'Le Journal d'Astérix et d'Obélix'. After René Goscinny's death following a heart attack in November 1977 Albert Uderzo continued the series on his own and has produced ten further albums between 1979 and 2005.[42]

In addition to translations into 107 languages, the series has seen a number of full-length animated films and associated publications, spin-off merchandise too numerous to mention, its own theme park and three blockbuster movies, the second of which, *Astérix et Obélix: Mission Cléopâtre* (2002), starring Gerard Depardieu and Christian Clavier, has taken the all-time second place for cinema entries to a French film (the wartime epic *La Grande Vadrouille* is first). The third, *Astérix aux Jeux Olympiques*, based on the 1968 album and released in

January 2008, has attracted attention through the 'bling' aspect of its numerous appearances by stars, including Adriana Karembeu, Zinedine Zidane, Tony Parker and Michael Schumacher.

In hindsight it is easy to see the recipe for the phenomenal *Astérix* success: the basic principle behind each story is a simple conflict of 'goodies' and 'baddies' with the inbuilt bias of us identifying with the underdog 'goodies' since they are human in their shortcomings and French (one out of these two works for the exports). That in itself is not an original formula, but it creates the conditions that allow for *Astérix*'s originality. With each new album the reader delights in discovering how the formula is adopted to the new situation, this being in terms of the new pretext for adventure but also for the anachronistic references to modern life. Along the way verbal and visual gags add a timeless spice before we sit down to the banquet on page 48, a banquet for which our appetite has been whetted from page 1 onwards.

Each pretext for adventure must fit a given set of expectations whilst providing the context for innovation. As with classic Hollywood films, the tranquillity of the status quo must be disturbed by an outside element, the problem must then be recognised and a solution envisaged, which when attempted seems set to fail until a timely but 'unexpected' reversal occurs. And then there's the banquet. Within these parameters Goscinny and Uderzo set up a system of 'home' and 'away' adventures, each with their own advantages. 'Home' adventures might allow us to see an extra facet of the Gauls' village life, without its basic precepts being undermined. In *La Serpe d'or* (1962), for example, further variations on Panoramix (Getafix in English) the Druid's powers are introduced as well as additional members of the village. In other cases the 'home' adventures can explore specific aspects of domestic life, such as the housing boom that forms the backcloth to *Le Domaine des Dieux* [The Mansions of the Gods] (1971) or the obsession with show-business that is the context for *Astérix et Latraviata* (2001).

The 'away' adventures can take Astérix and Obélix to events that are of domestic interest, such as *Astérix aux Jeux Olympiques* released the same year as the 1968 Winter Olympics in Grenoble, or *Astérix et Cléopâtre*, a pastiche of the Elizabeth Taylor/Richard Burton blockbuster that appeared in *Pilote* from 1963, a few months later than the film's first showing. More often, however, they allow for the trademark humour based on the gently mocking stereotypes of different regions, races or nationalities. The Swiss are obsessed with tidiness, have holes in their cheese and provide discreet banking facilities (*Astérix chez les Helvètes* [Asterix in Switzerland], 1970), the Corsicans are insular and macho (*Astérix en Corse* [Asterix in Corsica], 1973) and the English stop battle for tea, lovingly tend their lawns and add tags – 'n'est-il pas' – to their statements (*Astérix chez les Bretons* [Asterix in Britain], 1966). For the anecdote, Goscinny received complaints from all nationalities portrayed with the exception of the English …[43]

The use of verbal tags, warm beer, double-decker buses, Swiss banks, the Statue of Liberty (*La Grande Traversée* [Asterix and the

Great Crossing], 1975), Belgians eating chips (*Astérix chez les Belges* [Asterix in Belgium], 1979) are all examples of the first-degree anachronisms that provide the central running gag upon which the series's success is founded. In terms of this adaptation of pseudo-historical context, best known are the characters' names, which conform to historical stereotypes in that the Romans end in '-us', the Gauls in '-ix', the Greeks in '-os' and so on, whilst providing a reference to the life of today when read out loud. Of the 325 character names, we all have our favourites, but some of the best known are 'Abraracourcix' the head of the Gauls' village, 'Numérobis' the Egyptian architect, 'Ipipourax' the rugby player, 'Zebigbos' the English chieftain, 'Grossebaf' the weighty Norman, 'Soupalognon y Crouton', the Spanish leader and 'Zérozérosix' the spy.[44]

Verbal dexterity can also be on the level of a simple gag – 'il ne faut jamais parler sèchement à un Numide', 'Je suis mon cher ami, très heureux de te voir'/'C'est un alexandrin'[45] – or a more complex cultural reference, such as when Latraviata receives a bust of Caesar, who then retorts 'Donner un César à une tragédienne? Mais c'est absurde!' [Give a Caesar to a tragedienne? But that's absurd!], a reference to the French equivalent of the Oscars, 'les Césars', the trophies in question being the work of the sculptor César. In such cases one can understand how *Astérix* has become an icon of Frenchness, although the translations, or rather adaptations, are generally fittingly imaginative, and have rightly been cited as model examples in the art. Goscinny was concerned that the spirit of the original should be conveyed and went as far as to check the English and Spanish versions (languages he knew well) personally.

Bande dessinée is of course a mixture of text and image and much of the appeal of *Astérix* comes from the visual. Uderzo's style has almost become the benchmark for humorous BD, a form of *ligne claire* with *gros nez* tendencies, with the brash use of colour and composition to emphasise the slapstick elements (cf. Fig. 4, Chapter 2). In terms of content it is again the anachronisms that have left their mark, with Uderzo famously introducing regular caricatures: the Beatles appear as a band of bards in *Astérix et les Normans* [Asterix and the Normans] (1966), Sean Connery is a spy in *L'Odyssée d'Astérix* [Asterix and the Black Gold] (1981), and Cléopâtre is not without similarity to Elizabeth Taylor. Other cameo appearances include Laurel and Hardy, Kirk Douglas, Dupond and Dupont from the *Tintin* series, and Jacques Chirac.

At other times full *cases*, or even a full page, can pastiche a cultural artefact. A sombre scene in *Le Devin* (1972) when a fish's entrails are under scrutiny mimics the *The Anatomy Lesson* by Rembrandt, and the convivial supper in *Astérix chez les Belges* refers to the Flemish tradition of the Middle Ages by imitating a Pieter Breugel depiction of a village feast. The pleasure comes in catching the reference, admiring Uderzo's technical prowess and relating its relevance to the anachronistic gag in question. On a few occasions the humour has been so specifically French as to require redrawing in the English version: in *Astérix et Cléopâtre* the French dice game for which the best roll is 4-2-1 had to be changed to three sixes; in the same album a newspaper strip showing *Isis de mon coeur* (a parody of a newspaper strip of the time, *Juliette de mon coeur* [My Heart for Juliette]) is adapted to *Pnuts* and made to resemble Charlie Brown; and in *Astérix chez les Helvètes* at a filling station (oats and water for horses!) the Antar petrol company's logo-character Antarix was reworked to show Michelin's Bibendum.

Much has been made of the possible significance of *Astérix*, a phenomenon that amounts to taking the anachronisms beyond individual wordplay or visual references and onto each album, or indeed the series, as a whole. Most popular is the view of Astérix as de Gaulle, the spirited underdog who uses his intelligence to fight off the invader. This can be a reference to the wartime occupation, or, more specific to Astérix's first appearance in 1959, France's then refusal to yield to American imperialism, including the pressure of NATO membership. The 'potion magique' could be France's independent nuclear deterrent, French *esprit vif*, or, quite simply, wine as opposed to the newly imported Coca Cola.

That de Gaulle was in the minds of the authors is clear from the full-page announcement for *Le Combat des chefs* [Asterix and the Big Fight] that appeared on the back cover of *Pilote* 260 of 15 October 1964. In a direct pastiche of the media techniques used by de Gaulle, Abraracourcix takes centre stage at the press conference he has called, briefly announces the news (the forthcoming serialisation of the new *Astérix* adventure) and leaves abruptly. On the other hand, both Goscinny and Uderzo have always been at pains to deny any direct political referencing. In a rare interview given in 1973,[46] Goscinny accounted for the success of *Astérix* as follows:

> Uniquement au fait que ça fait rigoler les gens. Pas à autre chose: toutes les exegèses [*sic*] qui ont été faites ne correspondent pas à la réalité, il n'y a rien à faire! Vous comprenez, on m'a trouvé toutes sortes d'intentions, on m'a accusé aussi de toutes sortes de turpitudes et, notamment, on m'a lié à la politique, alors que je n'en faisais et que je n'en fais pas … On m'avait en particulier posé cette question: 'Que ferez-vous quand De Gaulle aura disparu?' Eh bien! Quand De Gaulle a disparu, j'ai continué comme avant: disons que nos destinées n'étaient pas spécialement liées! (10)

> [Uniquely due to the fact that it makes people laugh. Not due to anything else: no exegesis that has been offered corresponds to the truth, it's as simple as that! You know, all sorts of intentions have been imposed upon me, I've also been accused of all sorts of misdemeanours, and, in particular, I've been linked to politics despite the fact that I was not involved in it at all and am still not … In particular I have been asked: 'What will you do once de Gaulle has

passed away?' Indeed! When de Gaulle passed away I carried on as before: let's say that our destinies were not particularly linked!]

Ah! Oui, la potion magique signifiant le général De Gaulle ... Oui, le gars qui a trouvé ça voyait De Gaulle jusque dans son potage! C'est formidable, n'est-ce pas? (16)

[Ah yes, the magic potion stood for General de Gaulle ... Yes, whoever found that saw de Gaulle wherever he looked! Isn't it marvellous?]

Goscinny was undoubtedly honest in his claim that *Astérix* has no intended political bias – in the same interview he points to the fact that he refused political parties across the spectrum use of the character – nonetheless that does not lessen the value of the series as an indicator of values of the time, in the same way that *Tintin au Congo* helps us to understand the mentality behind 1930s colonialism. *Astérix* can remind us of the excitement surrounding cultural and social events that marked their period – the Grenoble Winter Olympics or the release of *Cleopatra*, for example – but it can also reflect the broader world stage. *Astérix chez les Bretons* (1966) came out at a time when England was in the news on account of the World Cup, and, more generally, due to the worldwide influence of London-based 1960s culture. *La Grande Traversée* (1975) was just ahead of American bi-centenary celebrations. Uderzo admitted that *Le Grand Fossé* [Asterix and the Great Divide] (1980), with its motif of the village divided by a man-made ditch, was a direct reference to the Berlin Wall.[47] More recently, *La Galère d'Obélix* [Asterix and Obelix All at Sea] (1996), in which citizens of numerous countries literally end up in the same boat, can be seen as a reaction to the reinforcing of European links through the 1992 ratification of the Treaty of Maastricht.

The 2005 *Le Ciel lui tombe sur la tête* is as near to a self-referential bande dessinée that Uderzo comes, its subject effectively being a spoof of current world trends in BD. The tranquil life of the village is disturbed by the arrival of a Tadsylwien from a ball-like space ship, accompanied by a race of Superclones. They in turn are attacked by the evil Nagmas, for the situation only to be resolved by some effective mixing and distributing of potion by Panoramix, whereupon the aliens leave having removed all trace of events from the humans' memory. 'Tadsylwien' is a loosely veiled anagram reference to Walt Disney, admiration for whom Uderzo states at the end of the volume, the Superclones are the wholesome superheroes of America's Golden Age, and the evil Nagmas represent Mangas, whose current invasion is pushed back by the Gauls.

Despite topping the overall book sales for the year, a fact that was anticipated with certainty quite some while before the album's release, in general the work has not been well received. In many ways the album is adventurous, taking the series to the next external frontier, beyond Earth, whilst exploring the deepest internal frontier, the trappings of the medium itself. But the metaphor can be heavy-handed, and many of the popular hallmarks are missing, such as the evocative décor, the anachronistic jokes or even the sense of narrative progression that leads to the final banquet, which in this instance is in fact played out twice, before and after the aliens' departure.

Astérix is often further criticised more generally for representing the big-business, mainstream, predictable side of the bande dessinée world, perhaps an indication of the extent to which it is seen as encapsulating the form's success, a success that undoubtedly will be continued when Uderzo marks the fiftieth anniversary of *Astérix* by releasing a new album of unpublished short strips in October 2009. But this is nonetheless an evaluation that overlooks the innovation the series has brought: *Astérix* was the flagship strip of *Pilote* and as such was instrumental in bringing the bande dessinée into adulthood. It was the first French strip to export on a wide scale, but was nonetheless quintessentially French. The gags are neither sexual nor scatological, but appeal to sophisticated adult tastes. And whilst remaining simple and accessible to all, the verbal and visual aspects of the strip are so precise they are models for the technical possibilities of the Ninth Art, as indeed we have seen in our chapter on How a BD Works.

Grand Prix d'Angoulême

From the third festival (1976) onwards an Angoulême jury consisting of festival organisers, artists, journalists and CNBDI dignitaries has awarded prizes for the year's BD production. The similarity with Cannes, surely a deliberate attempt to confer some of the glory of the Seventh Art onto the Ninth, continues with presentations and acceptance speeches made from the balcony of the town hall. Although such ceremonies sometimes take on a grotesque allure of self-congratulatory back-slapping, the prizes do give a mainstream indication of trends in the bande dessinée without being based purely on economic factors.

The prizes were known as 'Alfreds', after Zig and Puce's companion penguin, from 1981 until 1989, when they became the 'Alph-Arts' in honour of the final unfinished *Tintin* album. The system was again reworked in 2004, resulting in categories for the best artwork ('dessin'), best script ('scénario'), best first album, best series, best fanzine and best youth (7–8 years and 9–12 years) productions, as well as the public's best album and the overall best album. A further change in 2007 removed the prizes for best script and artwork, whilst introducing six 'Essentiels d'Angoulême', in effect rewarding a larger number of Best Album runners-up without distinguishing specific merits. Most prestigious, however, is the *Grand Prix*, awarded to an individual author for his or her overall contribution to the art, with the recipient then chairing the following year's jury.[48]

The early twenty-first-century winners for Best Album and for the *Grand Prix* were as follows:

2009	*Meilleur Album:*	Winshluss, *Pinocchio* (Albi: Les Requins Marteaux, 2008)
	Grand Prix:	Blutch
2008	*Meilleur Album:*	Shaun Tan, *Là où vont nos pères* [The Arrival] (Paris: Dargaud, 2007)
	Grand Prix:	Philippe Dupuy and Charles Berberian
2007	*Meilleur Album*:	Shigeru Mizuki, *NonNonBâ* (Paris: Cornélius, 2006)
	Grand Prix:	José Muñoz
2006	*Meilleur Album*:	Gipi, *Notes pour une histoire de guerre* [Notes for a War Story] (Arles: Actes Sud, 2004)
	Grand Prix:	Lewis Trondheim
2005	*Meilleur Album*:	Marjane Satrapi, *Poulet aux prunes* [Chicken with Plums] (Paris: L'Association, 2004)
	Grand Prix:	Georges Wolinski
2004	*Meilleur Album*:	Manu Larcenet, *Le Combat ordinaire* [Ordinary Victories] (Paris: Dargaud, 2003)
	Grand Prix:	Zep
2003	*Meilleur Album*:	Chris Ware, *Jimmy Corrigan* (Paris: Delcourt, 2002)
	Grand Prix:	Régis Loisel
2002	*Meilleur Album*:	Christophe Blain, *Isaac le pirate: Les Amériques* [Isaac the Pirate: To Exotic Lands] (Paris: Dargaud, 2001)
	Grand Prix:	François Schuiten
2001	*Meilleur Album*:	René Pétillon, *L'Enquête corse* [The Corsican Investigation] (Paris: Albin Michel, 2000)
	Grand Prix:	Martin Veyron

2009: Winshluss, Pinocchio *(Les Requins Marteaux)*

The choice of Winshluss's *Pinocchio* as overall best album signals a certain coming of age for the medium: it is a work that functions by reference to its own traditions, playing upon and parodying them, creating humour and pathos that succeed through an implicit dialogue with a wider context. At first glance the book has the trappings of a childhood favourite: a large volume, sturdily bound, with a front cover whose bright colours, silver sparkle and plethora of details dance around the central Pinocchio figure (Fig. 31). It is the

Figure 31. 'Not a Book for Children'. Winchluss. *Pinocchio*. Albi: Les Requins Marteaux, 2008. Front cover. © Les Requins Marteaux.

closer look that underlines the disturbing details: Pinocchio is a confused robot whose name is aflame, he is surrounded by roses, but roses with prominent thorns, with a background of machinery that suggests inevitability and from whose cogs rise wailing ghosts. Further motifs point to the fickleness of fate, be it the double one on the dice, the sword marked 'deus ex machina' (next to dollar-laden flowers), or the plummeting eight-balls. This is no book for children.

Winschluss uses the framework of the well known Disney-adapted story to refer to many of the milestones of bande dessinée. The narrative does largely follow that of Carlo Collodi and Walt Disney, but here Pinocchio is an out-of-control robot who electrocutes Geppetto's wife when she tries to use his nose as a sex toy and Jiminy Cricket becomes Jiminy Cafard [Jiminy Cockroach] nesting inside Pinocchio's brain. The volume consists of interwoven episodes whose style echoes American strips of the 1950s, full page illustrative *planches* the like of which decorated early *Tintin* albums, *Mad*-style double-pagers with heavy type, the lurid colours of post-war Romance strips, delicate pastels, or, for Jiminy Cafard, the black and white sketches of *Pilote*'s Gotlib or later introspection by L'Association, these being the only pages to use speech bubbles. Further references to the tradition are made and upturned through the passing parade of characters, such as a military penguin who reminds us of Afred, Zig and Puce's companion, or Snow White, in this case gang raped by the 'Sept Salopards' [Seven Bastards].

The burlesque parody is nonetheless underpinned by biting satire as we see Geppetto trying to sell Pinocchio to the military as an arm of destruction, the fat factory owner at Stromboli Inc. turning child labour into profits and police brutality forcing Geppetto to sign a confession for the murder of his wife. Just as the form jumps from style to style, so the content portrays a variety of intertwining settings, characters and themes. The reader soon learns to look closer, to expect the unexpected, as the ideas raised are often incongruous with the apparently innocuous form, a process that in itself can be seen as a microcosm of *la nouvelle bande dessinée*.

As such *Pinocchio* picks up on much of the author's previous work. Winshluss (penname of Vincent Paronnaud, born 1970 in La Rochelle) was one of the instigators of *Feraille*, an iconoclastic review by the Requins Marteaux team whose strips and exhibitions would undermine everyday appearances with macabre humour.[49] In the *Supermarché Feraille* installation/exhibition whose venues included the 2002 Angoulême Festival, the visitor would find himself or herself amidst the shelves of a typical, albeit it slightly downmarket, supermarket of the current consumer age. Closer inspection revealed products such as 'Miettes de Dauphin' [Dolphin Crumbs] or 'Foie Gras de Chomeur' [Foie Gras of the Unemployed], the empty but labelled tins of which were available for purchase. The associated album, *Monsieur Feraille* (2001), a co-production with Cizo, with whom

Winshluss works frequently, includes references to Scooby Doo (Velma presents herself as Marguerite Duras), Betty Boop, Tintin, old-style adverts and 1950s comics, whilst constantly undermining awaited norms. In similar disconcerting style, the ghostly figures that adorn the cover of *Pinocchio* refer back to *Welcome to the Death Club* (2002), a bleak satire around the central theme of untimely and violent demise.

As much of *Pinocchio* was originally serialised in *Feraille*, it is no surprise that it should provide a continuation of Winshluss's previous style and themes. The upturned depiction of the traditions of graphic art that forms a central trend almost makes *Pinocchio* a work of metafiction, but one with a disconcerting darkness and subtle ambiguity. As we shall see, Angoulême has come a long way since 2003 when Régis Loisel's fantasy eroticising of another Disney classic, *Peter Pan*, was instrumental in the main award.

2009: Blutch

The bestowing of the *Grand Prix* upon an iconoclastic artist in the same year that Best Album is given to an anti-establishment publication marks a clear break for Angoulême, one of whose major awards would generally reflect mainstream preoccupations. Coupled with a joint French choice, again a break from the three previous years, the suggestion, as we head towards the end of the first decade of the new century, is that France leads the way in a form whose strength lies in dissidence and alternative thinking. A fitting message for 2009, the year of the fiftieth anniversary of New Wave cinema.

Blutch (penname of Christian Hincker, born 1967 in Strasbourg) is best known for his regular contributions to *Fluide Glacial*, many of which have subsequently appeared in album format. If anything his work is better suited to journal publication, as it tends to be episodic or even fragmentary, in constant evolution, and far from closure. His style reflects this, with its black and white pen-strokes that are rarely in keeping with traditional *case* and *planche* set-up, generally creating an impression of unfinished disorder. It is fitting that preferred publishers include art-house producers such as L'Association and Cornélius.

Blutch's tales often recount a distortion of the everyday, as in *Waldo's Bar*, the album of which appeared in 1992. The city setting and the parade of lovers and hustlers may seem familiar (cf. José Muñoz's *Le Bar à Joe* [Joe's Bar], see below), but elements of the surreal, such as a pig-faced playboy or a machine-gun-touting Tweety Pie leave the reader on the boarders of comprehension. Similarly *Vitesse moderne* [Today's Pace] (2002) tells of Lola the dancer's modern city lifestyle, whilst intermingling the rediscovery of her father and his sexual habits (bondage, cross-dressing) with an intervention from Omar Sharif and an obsessed suitor with cagouled accomplices. Such an atmosphere had been perfect for Blutch's *Péplum* (1998), whose inspiration is an extremely loose adaptation of Petronius's *Satyricon*.[50]

In line with 'New Wave' artists such as Dupuy and Berberian, Marjane Satrapi and Fabrice Neaud (see below and throughout this chapter), much of Blutch's most incisive work is self-reflexive or directly autobiographical. Childhood reminiscences underpin *C'était le bonheur* [Those Were Happy Days] (2005) and *Le Petit Christian* (2 volumes, 1998 and 2008), although the ambiguities of distant memories are preserved through the ecliptic style. In *Le Petit Christian* battling children become Wild West heroes and the characters of *Pif* and *Mickey* appear as childhood friends. In *Blotch* (2 volumes, 1999 and 2000, reissued in one volume in 2009) the profession of cartoonist is the subject of biting satire as we enter the world of what appears to be a popular artist of the early twentieth century, albeit one peppered with anachronisms given that Blotch, the anti-hero, works for *Fluide Glacial.* The work is constantly tongue-in-cheek, be it through the depiction of Blutch's heavy-handed gags or the spurning of a young artist named Georges Rémi. The surface tone may be the Parisian journalistic world of Guy de Maupassant's *Bel Ami*, but the reader is left with the feeling of having glimpsed a modern-day profession that is corrupt, cruel, sexist and racist.

It is in openly disjunctive, often non-narrative, works that Blotch attempts to seize key elements of our human condition whose nature is such as generally to deny depiction. *La Volupté* (2006) and, in particular *La Beauté* (2008) use pastel shades in their evocation of partially recognisable, sometimes Freudian nightmare-esque situations, such as a child crying out to his father to look as he dives in the water, or an office worker returning home, stripping naked, engaging verbally with his partner's vagina, only to be attacked by the lion he believes himself to be. These works, and Blutch's *œuvre* more generally, may at times be over-eclectic to the point of inaccessibility, but they remain true to the notion of beauty Blutch himself gives in the Foreword to the book of that name: 'Le non-dit, le sous-entendu, la respiration, le trouble, le mystère' [that which is unspoken, implied, breathed, disarming, mysterious].

2008: Shaun Tan, **Là où vont nos pères** *(Dargaud)*

As the work of an Australian artist of Chinese descent that operates without recourse to language-specific text (i.e., only occasional references to an incomprehensible sign system), *Là où vont nos pères* underlines not only the potential universality of the Angoulême Festival, but, more importantly, that of the form it champions.

Given that between 1986 and 2001 separate prizes were awarded for Best French Album and Best Foreign Album, it is interesting to note that in the immediate years following the abolition of distinction by nationality, the prize has been awarded to three Frenchmen (2002, 2004 and 2009), a Frenchwoman of Iranian descent (2005), an American (2003), an Italian (2006), a Japanese (2007) and an Australian (2008).

Since this current book is concerned with the bande dessinée rather than the world cultures of comics, I will limit my analysis of non-French authors to the role they play within the French tradition. The 2008 and 2007 awards in particular were intended to signal France's far-reaching outlook, rewarding consecutively two works from the other side of the planet for Best Album, and an Argentinian artist for the 2007 Grand Prix.

Shaun Tan (born Fremantle, Western Australia, 1974) generally works as an artist and children's illustrator, it being the emphasis on continuity between frames, with the suggestion of narrative, however ambiguous, that makes *The Arrival* a graphic novel rather than a picture book. Tan portrays the universal strangeness of migrant experience as the main character leaves his family with only a boat ticket and some cash in order to make his way in a land of imposing buildings, unknown creatures and hieroglyphic scrawls. The lack of recognisable writing allows us to share the alienation of the immigrant, suggesting that here, as elsewhere, when a graphic novel lacks text it is so as to create a lacuna, one that deliberately breaks with expectations.

The work can also be seen as following in the tradition of L'Association's *Comix 2000* (see above), a text-free international anthology intended to be boundary-breaking. Stylistically, Tan's pastel realism might be compared with that of André Juillard, but the work of Englishman Raymond Briggs also comes to mind, and the overall effect is that just as the experience evoked in *The Arrival* can be non-culture specific, so, in some ways, can the form of expression.

2008: Philippe Dupuy and Charles Berberian

Philippe Dupuy (born Sainte-Adresse, near Paris, 1960) and Charles Berberian (born Bagdad, 1959) are unusual in that as a duo they do not take up assigned roles of scriptwriter and artist, but rather each contributes on both fronts. Within a single *planche* the *cases* can switch from one to the other, often with no indication as to who is responsible for what. In their joint hands the bande dessinée has become a collaborative venture in the style of a mini-Renaissance *atelier*, whilst keeping the introspection and intimacy that we associate with the post-1990 *BD d'auteur*.

Dupuy and Berberian first started working together in 1983 in the context of fanzine work. Further collaboration saw them at *Fluide Glacial*, a number of journals for children and adolescents, various advertising and promotional campaigns including for Canal + and for the wine merchant Nicolas, book illustration, cartoons for mainstream press such as *Libération* and *The Washington Post*, volumes for L'Association, a short series of sketchbooks on cities of choice and, more recently, large-scale album-based releases for Les Humanoïdes Associés and Dupuis. Since 1998 they have also worked in an editorial capacity for Les Humanoïdes.

Henriette, the eponymous central character of their first successful series (in *Fluide Glacial* from 1985, in album form from 1988), in many ways updates Claire Bretécher's anguished heroines. Henriette is a slightly tubby teenager who lives with her insensitive parents, recounting an exaggerated but recognisable view of adolescent angst through the journal that gives the strips their structure. In the first album, for example, we see the mental tribulations of Henriette's flight from home, only for her to return before her un-noticing parents, who have been to the cinema and a restaurant, could have seen her good-bye note.

Similar analyses of the torments of the grown-up world mark the series that has brought Dupuy and Berberian widespread recognition: after starting as a serial in *Yéti*, *Monsieur Jean* has seen nine volumes between 1991 and 2005, seven of which form the main series. In the first album, *Monsieur Jean, l'amour et la concierge* [Monsieur Jean, Love, and the Concierge] (1991) we meet the title character, a thirty-something city-dweller whose unstable love life, past and present, appears as his main preoccupation, as well as being that of the concierge. The style is a caricatural version of the *ligne claire*, less exaggerated than the likes of Manu Larcenet and Christophe Blain (see below), but still a hybrid reflection of the subject matter's mix of comic distortion and biting social portrayal. Pastel-coloured flashbacks and variations in *case* and *planche* layout allow us to delve into the imagination of Monsieur Jean and appreciate the distorted anxieties that make for everyday traumas.

Such anxieties are transferred onto an autobiographical level for the 1994 *Journal d'un album* [Diary of an Album], whose publication by L'Association reflects its deeper introspection, represented through the black and white reduced *planche* format. The *Journal* chronicles the authors' lifestyle and creative process during the composition of the third *Monsieur Jean* album, *Les Femmes et les enfants d'abord* [Women and Children First] (1994), with each of the two providing pages detailing their own viewpoints. Much attention is paid to Dupuy's recovery from depression, but we also see the compositional process and the ups and downs of the BD industry. In the opening *planches*, for example, the regularity of the *cases* shows the banality of a conversation with a taxi driver, but a visual jump into *style indirect libre* portrays with humour the alienation a bande dessinée author feels (Fig. 32).[51]

In many ways Dupuy and Berberian are flagship authors not just for Angoulême but for the bande dessinée as a form in general. Both their compositional technique and their final output underline the hybrid nature of the BD, the specifics of which they draw upon to full effect. They provide psychological introspection in a social context, but always with humour, and through a multiplicity of approaches and of projects they appeal to a widespread audience without lessening their analytical substance.

Figure 32. 'BD Artist'. Philippe Dupuy and Charles Berberian. *Journal d'un album.* Paris: L'Association, 1994. No overall pagination. Section I, plate 7. © L'Association.

2007: Shigeru Mizuki, NonNonBâ *(Cornélius)*

The choice of a manga can be seen as paying homage to a tradition that is loved and respected in France, as well as being big business: 812 new manga releases were planned in France for between January and June 2007, the equivalent of approximately four out of six comic-related productions.[52] The influence is also cross-cultural, to the extent that certain artists, such as Frédéric Boilet, have produced 'manga-ised' BDs in Japanese style, namely French works that have the clear line style often associated with manga, that deal with East–West social questions, and that on occasion read from right to left.

Shigeru Mizuki (born Sakai-minato, 1922) is considered a master of horror mangas, one whose work constantly refers to spirits, ghosts and monsters of folklore, using these as a way-in to addressing the concerns of the human world. The eponymous NonNonBâ is a mysterious old lady whose stories of the supernatural will ignite the imagination of the young Shigeru, with whom she comes to lodge. The themes that Mizuki evokes, such as the recollection of past times, provincial life, the fleeting nature of happiness and the need to *carpe diem* could almost be inspired by canons of French literature such as Marcel Proust or André Gide.

2007: José Muñoz

Mizuki and Muñoz (born Buenos Aires, 1942) represent opposite geographic poles of the planet, with Angoulême between the two serving as a metaphorical bridge whereby bande dessinée becomes the lynchpin that joins the world's comic cultures.

Although Muñoz is an Argentinian artist now based in Italy who often works in partnership with scriptwriter Carlos Sampayo, a fellow Argentinian living in Spain, Muñoz is a key figure of the BD tradition in France. *Alack Sinner*, for example, a black tale telling of Sinner the detective's dealings with the margins of New York existence, was pre-published in 1975 in *Charlie Mensuel*, and then later in *[À Suivre]*. Sinner's meanderings allow us to consider the nature of exile – like the authors the character has fled Argentina – a feeling of almost existential non-belonging, and bitterness at social injustice. The second in the series, *Flic ou privé* [Cop or PI], published in album form by Casterman in 1983, was awarded that year's Angoulême prize for best album, and can be seen as a catalyst for a later artists – Jacques Tardi and Edmond Baudoin are but two examples – that reject the *ligne claire* precisely to suggest that life is not always clear cut, and that the violent ambiguities of society's underclasses can indeed be worthy of artistic portrayal.

Le Bar à Joe, published in album form by Casterman in 1981 with a new edition in 2002, continues this style, using blurred black and white strokes to evoke people and surroundings whose proportions are distorted often beyond recognition. Here the base setting is the struggling nightlife of the eponymous New York bar, one of Sinner's hang-outs, the exoticism of which would not have been lost to the readers of *[À Suivre]* in which the work was serialised from 1980.

Like the better-known Hugo Pratt, Italian author of the *Corto Maltese* series, under whom Muñoz studied, Muñoz's work is important in that it demonstrates the international quality of the bande dessinée, but very much within a context of French experimental distribution. If Muñoz is considered a key figure in 2007 it is surely because he has led the way for the open aesthetics and subject matter of *BD noir*, suggesting that the form in the twenty-first century has evolved into an object of global reflection in a manner comparable with the progress of French cinema and popular literature.

2006: Gipi, Notes pour une histoire de guerre *(Actes Sud)*

Published originally as *Apunti per una storia di guerra* in 2004 (Bologna: Coconino), *Notes pour une histoire de guerre* by Gipi (pen name of Gian Alfonso Pacinotti, born Pisa, 1963) can almost stand as the epitome of the latter-day evolution of Muñoz-style experimental BD, a style born of publications such as *Linus* in Italy and *[À Suivre]* in France that saw popularity in the last decades of the twentieth century.

Notes pour une histoire de guerre tells the story of three adolescent boys caught up in a fictional near-future war, one that is not specified but with visual references pointing to the countryside of the Balkans. The album traces the mental changes in terms of values and beliefs that the youngsters undergo, underlining that the effect of war, and presumably any social upheaval, goes far beyond the material loss involved. Gipi's style, like Muñoz's, uses monochrome and distorted proportion to steer his depictions firmly away from realism, but his touch is not black-dominated and therefore is less stark, and his characters have a physical simplicity that betrays their emotional depth.

Gipi's work was comparatively little known in France before its Angoulême award, but its introspective realism (despite the hypothetical subject) coupled with a contrasting and deceptive simplicity of trait is entirely in keeping with a new style of BD championed by authors such as Manu Larcenet (see below) and Étienne Davodeau, whose *Les Mauvaises gens: Une Histoire de militants* [The Wrong Type of People: A Story of Militants] (2005) portrays the daily anguishes of everyday people in postwar regional France.

2006: Lewis Trondheim

Lewis Trondheim (pen name of Laurent Chabosy, born Fontainebleau, 1964) has become an *incontournable* figure of the twenty-first-century BD scene, this through his links with avant-garde movements such as L'Association, his media presence, the general popularity of many of

Figure 33. 'Something Strange'. Lewis Trondheim. *Lapinot et les carottes de Patagonie*. Paris: Le Lézard and L'Association, 1992. Page 313. © L'Association.

his series, specifically *Donjon*,[53] and the prolific nature of his work, with his publications numbering well over one hundred.

Trondheim was a founder member of L'Association (see above) and is instrumental in the creations of OuBaPo,[54] indications that it is intellectual rather than graphic subtlety that drives his work. Indeed his *Moins d'un quart de second pour vivre* (1991), in which he creates a series of *bandes* based on starter *cases* imposed by Jean-Christophe Menu, prefigured the first *OuPus* volume by six years, whilst engaging in the very sort of experimental exercise that was to become the OuBaPo's *raison d'être.*

Working from leading contributions to L'Association's journal *Lapin*, Trondheim went on to publish the 500-page *Lapinot et les carottes de Patagonie* (1992), the work that first brought him mainstream attention.[55] Essentially an *exercise de style* from an artist who claims to be learning the BD trade, the work follows a three by four square *case* system in simplistic monochrome style, with the characters anthropomorphic animals (see Fig. 33), as they generally are throughout his work. The setting switches between fantasy and recognisable elements of modern-day France, with the mainstay gentle verbal humour. A further ten volumes of *Lapinot*'s adventures continue the mixture of register, background and tone (with humour nonetheless always present), but go on to vary form, including the use of colour for volumes published by Dargaud.

Experimental variation is also the mark of the hugely successful *Donjon* series, the most mainstream of Trondheim's work, of which the first volume, *Coeur de Canard* [Duck Heart], in reference to Herbert de Vaucanson the central duck character and guardian of the *Donjon*, appeared in 1998, a joint work with Joann Sfar published by Delcourt of Paris. The series' setting is a light-hearted reference to the fantasy world of Dungeons and Dragons, within which context gentle quips can be made about current-day society. The series is marked by its prolific vastness, consisting of three main cycles corresponding to times of the day, and three further sub-cycles, making a total of thirty-two albums up to January 2008. *Donjon* has involved joint work with some of the leading alternative (although increasingly becoming mainstream) BD artists – Sfar, but also Menu, Christophe Blain, Manu Larcenet et al. – and can almost stand as a practical *Who's Who* of current production.

Trondheim's further endeavours include works for children (*A.L.I.E.E.N.*, 2004), a manga-related work that sees life through the eyes of an eponymous fly (*La Mouche*, 1995), a text-free Father Christmas series (e.g., *Bonjour Petit Père Nöel*, 2000, artwork by Thierry Robin), autobiographical pieces (*Approximativement*, 1995, and *Désoeuvré* [Inactive], 2005),[56] and polemics on the status of the bande dessinée (e.g., pieces in L'Association's theoretical three-volume journal *Éprouvette*). He also publishes a BD blog entitled *Les Petits riens* [Little Bits of Nothing] (www.lewistrondheim.com/blog). His larger-than-life output is matched by a personality that includes announced and retracted retirements, disdain for journalists to whom he rarely gives interviews – he once famously referred to *Le Monde* as 'caca' – and a cavalier attitude to the suits-and-ties behind bande dessinée: at his Angoulême *Grand Prix* acceptance speech he goaded the sponsors Leclerc with plays on words referring to Carrefour, Mammouth, Casino and Auchan, namely their supermarket rivals.

On the negative side, Trondheim can be seen as a media manipulator who, having quit L'Association in 2006, has sold out to big business BD (despite the attack on Leclerc), and whose repetitive style shows little technical ability. Conversely, he has demonstrated the cerebral potential of the bande dessinée (perhaps out of necessity), and achieved a rarely found mixture of the immensely popular and the experimental. Like Serge Gainsbourg, whose limited singing ability did not stop him producing an eclectic output that challenged the norms of French *chanson*, Trondheim, although less scatological and sexual, uses a simplistic style and understated humour to promote serious reflection both on life in general and on the status of the BD as an art form.

2005: Marjane Satrapi, **Poulet aux prunes** *(L'Association)*

The work of Marjane Satrapi (born Rasht, 1969) is introspective and reflective, an exponent of the autobiographic mode championed by Lewis Trondheim, Jean-Christophe Menu and Fabrice Neaud, with a stark graphic quality that is nearer to caricature than representational realism. In short it is exactly the sort of experimental BD one might expect L'Association to champion, yet unlike most art-house productions it has become a best-seller, translating into several languages. As a female BD artist Satrapi is a rarity, yet her concerns are gender-based in a specific national and cultural context, that of an Islamic woman with a liberal upbringing, as she describes in *Persepolis* (four volumes, 2000–2003, also by L'Association, as well as a 2007 film), the chronicle of her development from childhood in Iran during and after the revolution that deposed the Shah.[57]

Poulet aux prunes tells the story of Nasser Ali Khan, Satrapi's great-uncle, a Teheran musician who in November 1958 decided life was no longer worth living. Through a series of flashbacks and flash-forwards Satrapi paints a picture of daily existence in Iran during the changes of the second half of the twentieth century. The idiosyncratic suicide as Nasser Ali Khan waits eight days to die – the final catalyst comes when he can no longer find a musical instrument through which to express his art – gives a poignant central framework that allows for touches of black humour. Sophia Loren, his sexual fantasy, appears in a plate of the eponymous *poulet aux prunes*, his culinary fantasy, as starvation sets in. His son breaks wind as the father bids farewell, reminding the latter of how little they have in common. His granddaughter gives birth having been too fat to notice she was pregnant ...

Poulet aux prunes is a microcosm of Satrapi's style, a deadpan mixture of pathos and humour, a work that affronts global issues whilst giving them an accessible personal touch, and lending much-needed moments of comedy to deflate the tension. The comparison can be made with Robert Zemeckis's *Forrest Gump* (1994), in which we see a chronicle of the twentieth century through the central character's eyes, or with the films of Ken Loach whereby bitter worlds of social deprivation are made watchable by interludes of almost slapstick humour. Satrapi's graphic style is at one with her overall effect as the restrained use of black and white shading sets the grim general tone, with the subjective personal viewpoint achieved by the blurring together of *cases* through lack of *cadrage*, or the underlining of marking moments, such as Nasser Ali Khan's funeral, by the use of a full-page image. The graphic tension is lightened by moments of fantasy, such as background details in a USA flash-forward, for example a T-shirt inscribed 'Fuck' or shops labelled 'Mickey', 'Bank', 'Music Shop'.

This style is encapsulated above all in the four volumes of *Persepolis*, but presumably by the time her talent had become known it was *Poulet aux prunes* that was eligible for the glamour prize. Furthermore it made sense to reward her in the same year as Georges Wolinski, thereby setting up clear elements of comparison and contrast.

2005: Georges Wolinski

Wolinski (born 1934) is also a childhood immigrant, in that he arrived in France in 1946 from Tunis, his birthplace, although his parents, a French/Italian mother and a Polish father, would have given him closer affinities to metropolitan France than to North Africa. His subject matter includes political questions specific to his place of birth, as one might expect from a commentator who was in his twenties at the time of the Algerian war, but this is very much within the broader context of a vast body of output that covers all aspects of social and political happenings relevant to France.

Most of Wolinski's career has been spent in journalistic circles, starting with the satirical magazine *Hara-Kiri* in 1960, before becoming chief editor of *Charlie Mensuel* in 1970. Both of these publications were outlets for satirical bandes dessinées (*Charlie Mensuel* specialising in introducing subversive US imports to France) within a context of humour and comment aimed exclusively at adults. Wolinski went on to contribute to *L'Écho des Savanes, Le Nouvel Observateur, Libération* and *L'Humanité*, thereby giving his left-of-centre political cartoons wide-scale exposure.

That Wolinski should be awarded a major Angoulême accolade raises the question of the link between political cartoon, for which the wider public best knows Wolinski, and bande dessinée. Clearly both are text/image forms, although the political cartoon generally has no notion of narrative progression. Wolinski's are typical of the genre in that he uses simple line forms to create exaggerated characters that generally rely on one or two features – for example Jacques Chirac's pointed nose or rimmed glasses – in order to render the 'characters' instantly recognisable. The text, often a single speech bubble, makes the point, as in a portrayal of a youthful Chirac crouched like a dog and licking Giscard's boots, with Giscard announcing 'Ce Chirac! On croît qu'il va mordre ... il lèche!' [That Chirac! You think he's going to bite you ... in fact he licks you!].[58] Wolinski's cartoons are also known for humour that is openly sexual, often bordering on the obsessive and explicit. Indeed taboos of all kind are his prey, as in the satire of bourgeois France in which a well-to-do couple are presented with their son-in-law to-be. As they cry, 'Notre fille fiancée à un nègre, juif, borgne, et boiteux' [Our daughter engaged to a one-eyed lame negro Jew] and 'Jésus Marie!', the daughter whispers to her suitor, 'Chéri, sois gentil, ne leur dis pas tout de suite, que tu es communiste' [Go gently darling, don't tell them straight away that you are a communist].

The same style and subject matter naturally underpin Wolinski's fully fledged bandes dessinées, which range, in literally dozens of albums, from political strips that originally appeared in newspapers, to erotic musings on the role of the sexes in modern society, or satirical adventure stories, again often erotic, as in the *Paulette* series, co-authored by Pritchard. In a typical example,[59] a businessman enters a hotel room with a prostitute who lovingly offers to sew his jacket, suggests Sunday lunch with the parents, and describes a dress that would please him. Having returned home he apologises for having had to work late. The final *case* reveals his wife waiting in an overtly sexual pose as she yells: 'Je n'en pouvais plus tellement j'avais envie de baiser. Vite! Vite! Vite!' [I couldn't hang on any more I was so desperate for a fuck. Quick! Quick! Quick!] and, 'J'espère que tu bandes, salaud!' [I hope you can get it up, you bastard!].

It is hard to imagine such sexual openness and widespread political incorrectness receiving mainstream critical acclaim in Anglo-Saxon countries. This could be attributed to a general difference in *mores*, or perhaps to the fact that the BD is an accepted adult genre in France and so will legitimately combine popular titillation with incisive social comment. Wolinski's award was in recognition of this, but also in homage to a pillar of bande dessinée whose four decades of service have helped raise it to its current status.

2004: Manu Larcenet, Le Combat ordinaire *(Dargaud)*

Like Marjane Satrapi's *Persepolis, Le Combat ordinaire* by Manu Larcenet (born 1969 at Issy-les-Moulineaux) is indicative of a new wave of introspective works whose subject matter is no longer fiction and fantasy but the joys, anguishes and mundane preoccupations of harsh reality, specifically that of the author's lived experience. Larcenet is slightly unusual in that, with the exception of a few youthful fanzine productions, he has always come through mainstream publishers: strips in *Fluide Glacial* from 1994 and in *Spirou* from 1997, and albums produced by Glénat, Delcourt and Dargaud.

Larcenet's early work for *Fluide Glacial* was generally *one-shot* shorter pieces often satirising popular culture, as in the case of his *Starsky & Freud* and *Alerte à Malibu* [Baywatch].[60] Larcenet has also worked on collaborative projects, such as with Jean-Michel Thiriet on albums of single cartoons in the manner of Gary Larson's *Far Side* for his *La Vie est courte* [Life is Short] series (Dupuis, 1998 onwards), or joint albums with Joann Sfar and Lewis Trondheim for the *Donjon* project. More recently Larcenet has created three albums in a similar graphic style to *Le Combat ordinaire*, but with Sigmund Freund, Vincent Van Gogh and Attila the Hun as the historically displaced main protagonists (Van Gogh, for example, paints the horrors of the First World War).[61]

The graphic style in question might appear unsophisticated at first glance, a *gros nez* effect with caricature characters in outline settings, a regular four-row *case* arrangement and brashly coloured backgrounds. Part of *Le Combat ordinaire*'s sophistication, however, lies in the dismantling of expectations, as the apparent simplicity of the artwork is a front for an account of the complex preoccupations behind Larcenet's daily life: the bonding with his brother (with whom, incidentally, he has co-authored several works) over soft drugs, the non-communication between himself and his parents, coming to terms with the physical anguish of panic attacks, his affinity with nature, lassitude with work as a photographer, accepting past acts of others (or not) as he discovers an elderly friend had committed crimes of torture in the Algerian war, and the need for commitment and sacrifice in a love relationship.[62]

Given the reflective nature of the work, apparently redundant *cases* can create the strongest effect, as in the silent fraternal bond shared at the breakfast table (Fig. 8, Chapter 2) or the views of the fields as Larcenet enjoys his surrounding countryside. One of Larcenet's fortes is also the switching between graphic styles, such as the use of a semi-realist view of the *cité* to provide an apt contrast between the dreary outside world and the internal fantasy escapism enjoyed by the two brothers (Fig. 8, Chapter 2). On other occasions Larcenet introduces full *planches* with a symmetric two-by-four case system, reduced to grey-tone colours and semi-realist line drawing. These allow for flashback moments of reflection, for instance on the psychology of his fear of motorways, his relationship with his parents, or his reticence regarding open sexuality.

The themes behind *Le Combat ordinaire* are, as the title suggests, everyday, and the dialogue concentrates on the protagonists' mundane moments. It is Larcenet's skill of composition that lets us into his world; he is a manipulator of unexpected images. As the main autobiographical character himself says (p. 35):

> Je ne connais rien de plus captivant que de faire des images … Quand tous les éléments de la nature s'ajustent, s'ordonnent, s'imbriquent … C'est une émotion sans pareille …
>
> [I know of nothing that is more captivating than to create images … When all the elements of nature fit together, organise themselves, interweave … It's an emotion that has no equivalent …]

2004: Zep

One can easily imagine the choice of Zep and Larcenet as main prize-winners being based on the contrast their joint selection creates. The *gros nez* styles are similar, although the effect of Larcenet lies in the surprise when one discovers that his work is precisely not slapstick for adolescents. *Titeuf*, as we have seen above, is an outstanding example in its field, but one wonders whether the award of *Grand Prix* to Zep was a conscious attempt to stay in touch with the popular marketing choice. If so, it was proven right by the unprecedented queues that greeted the 2005 *Grand Prix* exhibition in honour of Zep.

2003: Chris Ware, Jimmy Corrigan *(Delcourt)*

The choice of Zep may have also been in contrast to the 2003 selection of *Jimmy Corrigan* as best album. The work of Chris Ware, like that of Daniel Clowes or even Robert Crumb, stands as an example of the way in which American comix can challenge the norms of graphic and social expression and still receive mainstream critical acclaim.[63] In *Jimmy Corrigan* we see different stages of the eponymous main character's life from childhood to old age, with abrupt switches between time-frames also presenting the broader story of different male generations of the dysfunctional Corrigan family. As an analysis of psychological preoccupations of American society expressed through *ligne claire* minimalist semi-realism, *Jimmy Corrigan* could not be further from *Titeuf*.

As stated earlier, however, this is not the place for an analysis of the tradition and current state of American comics. There is quite enough meat in the francophone world to keep us going, and Roger Sabin has already dissected the English-language tradition admirably.[64] What is of interest to our purpose is the inclusion of an American work as the Best Album at Angoulême reasonably soon after the 2001 abolition of the specific Best Foreign Album category, although it was also significant that Robert Crumb should have been awarded the *Grand Prix* in 1999. The choice of *Jimmy Corrigan* signalled Angoulême as a truly international festival for an international genre, albeit headed by French creation. It could also be seen as an attempt to patch up differences that had arisen in 1996 over the question of the paternity of the BD – *Yellow Kid* or Töpffer – whilst acknowledging an exchange that included experimental artists on both sides of the Atlantic on an equal footing.

2003: Régis Loisel

Régis Loisel (born 1951 at Saint-Maixent, near Poitiers) initially became known for *La Quête de l'oiseau du temps* [The Quest for the Time Bird], a five-album series, with artwork by Loisel and scripted by Serge

Le Tendre, spread over more than twenty years. The first album came out in 1983, having appeared in serial form in *Charlie Mensuel* the previous year, but there had been an initial version consisting of twelve *planches* published in *Imagine* in 1975–1976. The last volume, which is in fact a 'prequel', first appeared in 1998.[65] The series is a heroic-fantasy adventure with the voluptuous princess Pélisse as central character and a plot based upon the search for the eponymous mysterious bird whose powers will overcome the cruel god Ramor.

Unlikely as it may seem, Loisel's other top-selling production, *Peter Pan* (six volumes up to 2004), in many ways functions along similar lines. According to Loisel the inspiration is more the Disney film of 1953 than the book by J.M. Barrie,[66] although his main characters of Peter Pan, Captain Hook and Tinkerbelle are common to both. Loisel, now responsible for artwork, scenario and colouring, tells the main story in the first two volumes (*Londres*, 1990 and *Opikanoba*, 1992, both from Vents de l'Ouest of Issy-les-Moulineaux), but his portrayal of some of the harsh realities of Victorian life seems entirely detached from Disney niceties. Once again the work delves into heroic fantasy, this time under the auspices of Clochette (i.e., Tinkerbelle), a lightly clad fairy whose wings are considerably overshadowed by her breasts, thereby adding an important dose of eroticism.

Loisel's forte is his graphic style, a detailed use of pastels to create the characteristics of people and places without ever letting us forget that this is fantasy and not photo-realism, while his play upon *case* size and camera angles exemplify many of the techniques outlined in the first section of this book. His selection for the *Grand Prix* at Angoulême recognised his immense popularity, highlighted by the sales of *Peter Pan: 5 Crochet* [Peter Pan: 5 Hook] that had reached 140,200 copies in 2002,[67] but it also rewarded a representative of a subgenre, the heroic fantasy epic, that occupies an increasingly important place in terms of bande dessinée production and sales.

2002: Christophe Blain, Isaac le pirate: Les Amériques *(Dargaud)*

Issac le pirate, like much of Larcenet's work, and indeed that of other leading artists of the nineties – David B., Johan Sfar, Lewis Trondheim – is part of Dargaud's 'Poisson Pilote' collection, a series aimed at bringing together artists who challenge the limits of the 'traditional' bande dessinée whilst offering mainstream production and distribution possibilities. Indeed Blain (born 1970 at Argenteuil) has worked with many of the Poisson Pilote team, including Sfar and Trondheim, for the *Donjon* series (see above).

In *Les Amériques* we meet Isaac Sofer, an eighteenth-century Parisian whose real interest lies in his artistic aspirations, and Jean Mainbasse, a harsh but likeable explorer-pirate. Against the loosely sketched backcloth of *ancien régime* France and its colonies, Blain shows us love tested by hardship as Sofer leaves Alice Jeannenet, his beloved, to make his fortune at sea; the building of friendship as the seafarers evolve together; preoccupations with the discovery of the newly widening world; and anguish before metaphysical questions such as the nature of the afterlife. In the first three of the subsequent volumes, *Les Glaces* [Ices] (2002), *Olga* (2002) and *La Capitale* (2004), Isaac and Alice drift apart as further lands, and relationships, are explored.

Figure 34. 'Eighteenth-Century Life'. Christophe Blain. *Isaac le pirate: Les Amériques*. Paris: Dargaud, 2001. Page 13. © Dargaud.

Despite a subject matter that could easily lend itself to photo-realism, Blain's style almost goes in the opposite direction with its naïve use of line strokes, making characters whose physical features are little more than stock cartoon attributes, although the background to their adventures often swarms with cameo details that bring the period to life (see for example Fig. 34). Colours can make an individual stand out against a descriptive background, lend brightness and exoticism to distant colonies, or provide the warm glow of fireside conviviality. It is interesting to note that these have been added by Walter & Yuka, and do not feature in the black and white 2003 reissue of the first three volumes (again by Dargaud), underlining once again the notion of the bande dessinée as a *metissage* bringing together the skills of several individuals. In terms of Blain's contribution, we can see his naïve style as reflecting the colonial painting that Isaac might have produced, or, more simply, a further example of the method exploited by Larcenet, albeit less introspectively: the characters lack physical depth precisely to underline the importance of the psychological portrayal.

2002: François Schuiten

With François Schuiten (born 1956 in Brussels) graphic realism gains the upper hand on psychological depth, although the primary interest lies in the way in which he playfully tackles questions of representation, literary convention and intertextuality. Schuiten's work has almost exclusively been in partnership: for instance with his brother Luc or with Anne Baltus, but most often with Benoît Peeters. As with the Régis Loisel/Serge Le Tendre collaboration, it was the graphic artist rather than the scriptwriter who received the Angoulême accolade, superficially adding fuel to Thierry Groensteen's hypothesis that the bande dessinée is a visual art rather than a hybrid form.[68] Schuiten, however, is in fact the perfect advocate for the bande dessinée as a multi-media creation.

The influence of Schuiten's family background of Brussels architects is to be seen in his speciality cityscapes, wherein Art Nouveau, baroque and skyscraper-minimalism come together to produce overpowering fantasy worlds. This, however, is not the fantasy of elves and goblins, but rather a futuristic parallel universe used to question the motives of twentieth-century urbanism, the shortcomings of which are exemplified in parts of Schuiten's home city. In the *Cités obscures* series (first published in *[À Suivre]* in 1982, then in album form from Casterman) Peeters and Schuiten have created a number of parallel cities, such as Brüsel or Pâhry, into which slip privileged and insightful individuals, for example the mysterious painter Augustin Desombres. Schuiten allows his fine-line graphic realism to mix with pure photo-realism and then photography itself, as in the *Écho des Cités* (Casterman, 2001), the chronicle of the newspaper that becomes obsolete with the advent of the photo. The final *planches* are photographs of the newspaper's deserted offices.

The self-referential creation is one of the many artifices explored by Schuiten in an output that constantly requires the reader to contemplate the nature of the product before him or her, to the extent that the unexpected becomes the norm or at times even contrived. In the first *Cités obscures* album, *Les Murailles de Samaris* [The Great Walls of Samaris] (1988), Franz discovers that the walls of the town are no more than a theatrical décor, moving cut-outs set to deceive and entrap him, a sort of *Truman Show* ten years before the Peter Weir film. In BD terms, it is a *trompe l'oeil* and a *mise en abyme* as the décor turns out to be the central character. In *L'Archiviste* (1987) we identify with Isidore's quest to explain the world around him, the strange tower housing his office, the rumours of a parallel world and the secrecy that surrounds such rumours as well as him, the Archivist. With Schuiten's final *planche* we come to realise that the book itself is the dossier that leads to the obscure parallel world and that we, the reader, are now in Isidore's place.

Throughout the *Cités obscures* fiction and history intermingle as Jules Verne and Leonardo da Vinci mix with Isidore and Desombres and the albums form a non-chronological corpus surpassing the individual works. Even in the bandes dessinées that are not part of the *Cités obscures* Schuiten explores new possibilities, as in *NogegoN* (with Luc Schuiten, produced in 1991 by Norma of Barcelona) where the final *planches* mirror the opening ones, with two narrative strands meeting in the middle of the album, thereby undermining the notion of a pre-set left-to-right reading.[69]

Schuiten and his collaborators are at the forefront of a post-1980s movement – other exponents, such as the OuBaPo artists, have been discussed above – that has grasped the specific potential of the bande dessinée as a vehicle for exploring theoretical issues of expression in a way that texts or images alone cannot do. In this context it is also important to appreciate the multi-media aspect of Schuiten's output, one that gives us seemingly traditional bandes dessinées and book illustration, but which goes on to include stage productions, films and film sets, websites and architectural *mise en scène*.[70]

2001: René Pétillon, L'Enquête corse *(Albin Michel)*

The 2004 film of *L'Enquête corse*, produced by Alain Berberian (not to be confused with Charles Berberien) and starring Jean Reno and Christian Clavier, underlines the hallmarks of Pétillon's work through its divergences from the original album. The plot of *L'Enquête corse*, essentially the attempts of Paris detective Jack Palmer to trace Corsican Mafioso Ange Leoni, provides a framework for a series of gags not unlike those Pétillon (born 1945 in Lesneven, Brittany) had published in *Le Canard Enchaîné* on the subject: a secretary receives a death-threat coffin through the post, only to reveal, in the next *case*, that she has a drawer full of them; the key trial defence witness, Figoli, routinely vouches he was playing cards with whomsoever happens to be accused of terrorism; an 'informer' meets Palmer in the middle of the night so as to satisfy his request, namely information as to the whereabouts of the toilets!

In cases where the humour is essentially verbal, as in these latter examples, Pétillon's caricatures give the outrageous a mundane touch through stoic expression, lack of movement, or a gently raised eyebrow. The humour is equally understated in the visual gags; indeed it is the lack of dialogue, as in the secretary who calmly places the latest coffin with the others, that provides the antithesis between the shock of the event and the reaction to it. A staccato progression from one *case* to the next underlines such dry humour while Pétillon's cartoon graphics and *gros nez* characters ensure the comic deflation of a potentially distressing subject.

This is difficult to achieve in a film, however much Clavier succeeds in rendering Palmer ridiculous. Instead Berberian's version substantially complicates the plot, gives Reno's macho Leoni centre stage and provides a sexy-comedy love element through the introduction of Leoni's sister, played by Caterina Murino. The audience's awareness of Pétillon's figures means their celluloid incarnations cannot be taken too seriously and certain gags do transfer (albeit falling slightly flat), but the film per se is inevitably a different creation from the bande dessinée.

Pétillon, like Wolinski, has succeeded in providing a bridge between political cartooning and the socially aware, but not too serious, bande dessinée. Previous Jack Palmer investigations, *Les Disparus d'Apostophes!* (1982) and *Jack Palmer et le top model* (1995),[71] provide the same detached wry reference to current affairs (the writer Jean-Edern Hallier had disappeared shortly before the former volume). As with Wolinski, Pétillon's career had spanned some forty years in a variety of publications, no doubt a consideration for his award of the 1989 *Grand Prix*.

2001: Martin Veyron

One might assume that Wolinski's 2005 *Grand Prix* was at least partly to rectify the anomaly of his mentee, Martin Veyron (born 1950 at Dax), having received the accolade four years previously. A glance at the work of both authors is enough for immediate affinities to be obvious: clear-line satirical trait with a pastel realism, a love of all things taboo and a recurrent eroticising of the female form. Veyron is less openly political, as his outlets, *Pilote* and *Écho des Savanes*, but also *Cosmopolitan* and *Lui*, would indicate.

Veyron's leitmotif character is Bernard Lermite, whose adventures started in 1977 in *L'Écho des Savanes* and went on to seven albums (also available in a two-volume *Bernard Lermite en complet*,[72] published by

Albin Michel) by the time of the Angoulême award. Lermite appears to be an everyday anguished thirty-something white male, but apparently normal situations lead to outlandish consequences, including chases across the opera stage, encounters with a serial suicider and a variety of plane crashes. Humour comes from the slapstick adventure, but also from dialogue – a taxi driver who when hailed comments, 'ça m'enerve qu'on me dise taxi à chaque fois, je sais bien que je suis un taxi' [it gets on my nerves that people keep yelling taxi at me, I know I'm a taxi] – and a reversal of social expectations, as in Bernard's success as a stripper being thwarted by the complaints of his mother in the audience. The almost obligatory presence of comically attractive women determined to shed their clothes adds a dimension of politically incorrect self-parody, although one might wonder if all readers are aware of the second-degree humour.

As in the case of Wolinski, the challenges of the politically incorrect provide a unifying thread to Veyron's work. In the introduction (p. 7) to *L'Amour propre ne le reste jamais très longtemps* (2001),[73] a best-selling album (originally a series in *L'Écho*) which the author himself playfully classes as pornographic, Veyron answers the question, 'Parlons des femmes, que représentent-elles pour vous?' [Let's talk about women, what do they represent for you?] with, 'un trou avec du poil autour' [a hole with hairs around it]. Such provocation was already present in the 1995 text-based collection *Politiquement incorrect* and the 1998 *Cru bourgeois*,[74] an album portraying the bourgeoisie as decadent, uncaring and naïve. In *Executive Woman* (1986) Veyron appears to present the modern world from the career woman's point of view, but the obsessions explored are still those of the insecure male: a debate centring on Mme Hette-Michard's success in streamlining the company goes no higher than 'C'est pas possible! Elle fait des pipes aux syndicalistes!' [It can't be true! She must be sucking off the union leaders!].

As well as BD author, Veyron is also known for illustrative creations, such as for the Futuropolis edition of Philippe Soller's *Portrait du joueur* [Portrait of the Gambler] (1991), numerous advertising productions and film work, including the cinema version of *L'Amour propre* (1985) and the popular Patrice Leconte comedy, *Circulez y a rien à voir* [Keep Moving, There's Nothing to See] (1983). One can easily see how in the 1970s and 1980s Veyron's work would have appeared daringly innovative, a taboo-free voicing of male anxieties with a generous dose of accessible second-degree humour.[75] The Angoulême award vocalised the admiration of a generation of thirty-something male BD fans, but it is hard to imagine it being repeated as the genre becomes increasingly experimental and heterogeneous, both in terms of form and content.

Where Now?

In 2006 Lewis Trondheim announced that he was leaving L'Association and would concentrate on a high-distribution collection, Delcourt's 'Shampooing', of which he is director.[76] Indeed of L'Association's founder members and de facto editorial team – David B., Killoffer, Mattt Konture, Jean-Christophe Menu, Mokeït, Lewis Trondheim and Stanislas – five are no longer involved. Mokeït left shortly after its foundation to concentrate on ventures in the plastic arts, and David B. (2005), Trondheim, Killoffer and Stanislas (all 2006) departed more recently, giving 'editorial differences' as a reason. These differences may be the very crux of L'Association's *raison d'être*, namely Menu's firmly asserted belief that creative BDs and big business are contradictory phenomena.

L'Association's possible decline may, ironically, be the proof of its success: L'Association (and associates) have made it clear that there is an alternative to *Astérix*, *Titeuf* and *XIII* and that even if on occasions the individual volumes produced might be overly abstract or lacking in subtlety – in short they try too hard to be avant-garde – the fact that they exist has created an irreversible step. Bande dessinée now stands as a vehicle for artistic expression, but associated recognition can come via the high-profile Angoulême awards, or indeed through the backing of mainstream publishers (albeit in specialised collections) capable of providing a wide level of support and distribution to promising artists.

In many ways L'Association, and outlets of a similar ilk such as Frémok or Les Requins Marteaux, provide a latter-day bande dessinée parallel with the historical development of the *Nouvelle Vague* in cinema, a comparison initially explored in our chapter 'Formal Specificity'. The *Nouvelle Vague* challenged the anonymous studio production through the *cinéma d'auteur* in much the same way as L'Association has promoted the status of BD author as total creator. The *Nouvelle Vague* produced films that led to reflection and introspection rather than just pure action. The techniques used were characterised by low-budget improvisation – on the level of script, lighting and location – thereby creating the impression of closeness to 'everyday' reality. Now that the value of such productions is a cultural given, fairly middle-of-the-road films frequently take aspects from the *Nouvelle Vague*: for all its airbrushing out of Paris graffiti, Jean-Pierre Jeunet's *Le Fabuleux destin d'Amélie Poulain* [released in English as '*Amélie*'] (2001) is recognised as a creation that plays around with camera angles and plot techniques. Similarly, 'alternative' bandes dessinées have an ever-increasing niche amongst large-scale publishers; in short it is no longer surprising to find BDs that experiment with *case* size, break the 48-page format and/or question our place in society, be it Tito's *Tendre banlieue* series for adolescents or Peeters and Schuiten's *Cités obscures*.

That said, L'Association, like the *Nouvelle Vague*, has not eliminated standard big-business productions. To return to Menu's terminology, the '48CC' and indeed the '48/CC/HF/KK' still dominate the market and the comment generally attributed to Voltaire to the effect that for every one good book we will find a hundred poor ones could undoubtedly be applied to the twenty-first-century bande dessinée. What sells, and thus the BDs that most people see, remain violent and erotic narratives, imports of varying qualities – increasingly mangas, but also USA hits such as *Calvin and Hobbes* – and the favourites new and old such as *Tintin* and *Titeuf*.

It is perhaps this juxtaposition of mainstream and art-house that has allowed the bande dessinée to become a national icon in a way that the commix, graphic novels or *fumetti* of other traditions have not. France has a tradition of top-sellers, but these are now challenged, or at least contextualised, by works that explore, question and reinvent. In the USA, to take but one example, the fact that commix are rarely mainstream best-sellers has meant that the Underground challenges the subject – society – but not the form of its expression.[77]

It is when we accept the bande dessinée as an integral part of francophone culture, an icon of French cultural uniqueness, that we no longer need to define and describe it but can examine what it tells us about the broader world-view. And that is where the next part of this book begins …

Notes

1. This figure is taken from Thierry Groensteen, *[Primé à Angoulême]: 30 ans de bandes dessinées à travers le palmarès du Festival* [[Prize winners at Angoulême]: 30 Years of Bandes Dessinées through the Festival Awards] (Angoulême: Éditions de l'An 2, 2003), p. 99. The number appears to be growing: at a 2005 BnF conference, Jean-Pierre Mercier gave the 2004 figure for new publications as 2,120. As we saw in the last chapter, the *Livres Hebdo* figure for new albums and editions in 2008 was approximately 4,318.
2. See, for example, the eighth footnote of the previous chapter, or, for works in English, the bibliographic information given in the Introduction.
3. This phrase is taken from a newspaper article that will be discussed in the Conclusion of this book. The question of how BD might be applied so as to better our understanding of French society forms the basis for brief sections in the chapter 'Cultural Studies and Beyond', where such themes as 'Sex and Sexuality' and 'BD and *Banlieue*' will include passing discussion of the works of Margerin, Tito, Bretécher and Montellier.
4. On Bretécher and Binet (see below), Elizabeth McQuillan's 2001 University of Glasgow doctoral thesis should be consulted: 'The Reception and Creation of Post-1960 Franco-Belgian BD'. On pp. 139–40 McQuillan explores the ambiguities of the label of feminism as applied to Bretécher. See also Elizabeth McQuillan, '"I Live my Body I am my Body": The Comic Bodies of Claire Bretécher', *Corporeal Practices*, ed. Hannah Thompson and Julia Prest (Bern: Peter Lang, 2000), pp. 91–103; Nhu-Hoa Nguyen, 'The Rhetoric of Parody in Claire Bretécher's *Le Destin de Monique*', *International Journal of Comic Art* 3.2 (2001), 162–74. For a more

general introduction to Bretécher's work in its social context, see pp. 165–70 of Matthew Screech's *Masters of the Ninth Art: Bandes Dessinées and Franco-Belgian Identity* (Liverpool: Liverpool University Press, 2005).

5. The situation was not unique to France. Roger Sabin broaches the subject of the often-misogynistic tone of the American underground that boomed from the late 1960s; see *Comics, Comix and Graphic Novels* (London: Phaidon, 2001 [first ed. 1996]), especially pp. 92–107.
6. This example is taken from *Les Frustrés 5* (Paris: Hyphen, 2001), p. 33. The strip originally appeared, however, in 1980.
7. The *Sales blagues* originally appeared in *L'Écho des Savannes.* Up to and including 2009, fourteen album volumes have been published.
8. These examples are taken from *Les Sales Blagues de L'Écho 6: Sucré ou salé* [The Echo's Dirty Jokes 6: Sweet or Sour] (Paris: L'Écho des Savanes/Albin Michel, 1996), p. 54, and *Les Sales Blagues de L'Écho 11* (Paris: L'Écho des Savanes/Albin Michel, 2003), [no pagination], respectively.
9. Margerin's work will also be discussed briefly in the context of Chapter 10, 'Cultural Studies and Beyond'.
10. See Thierry Groensteen's interview with Margerin ('Entretien avec Frank Margerin') published on pp. 8–17 of *Les Cahiers de la Bande Dessinée* 77 (1987). Margerin's summary of the models for his characters is on p. 11.
11. This example is taken from *Lucien 4: Chez Lucien* (Paris: Les Humanoïdes Associés, 1998), pp. 50–55.
12. (Paris: Fluide Glacial).
13. On *Les Bidochon* in general see Libbie [Elizabeth] McQuillan, 'Les Bidochon assujettis académiques', *The Francophone Bande Dessinée*, ed. Charles Forsdick, Laurence Grove and Libbie [Elizabeth] McQuillan (Amsterdam: Rodopi, 2005), pp. 159–74. See also Ann Miller, *Reading Bande Dessinée: Critical Approaches to French-Language Comic Strip* (Bristol: Intellect, 2007), wherein she discusses *Les Bidochon* in terms of Binet's farcical portrayal of petit-bourgeois aspirations (pp. 182–86).
14. See, for example, Murray Pratt, 'The Dance of the Visible and the Invisible: AIDS and the Bande Dessinée', *The Francophone Bande Dessinée*, pp. 189–200. Pratt points to the fact that *Jo* does not engage with issues such as homosexuality, drug taking or prostitution.
15. Montellier's work of a militant feminist leaning will be discussed briefly in the chapter 'Cultural Studies and Beyond', where a secondary bibliography will be provided.
16. For bibliographical information pertaining to the work of Juillard (some of it specific to *Les 7 Vies de l'épervier*), see the chapter 'Cultural Studies and Beyond'.
17. For an account of the making of *L'Affaire Francis Blake*, based largely but not exclusively on interviews with the artists, see Jean-Luc Cambier and Éric Verhoest, *Blake et Mortimer: [Histoire d'un retour]* [Blake et Mortimer: [The Story of a Comeback]] (Paris: Dargaud, 1996).
18. Two volumes by Van Hamme and Benoit, and a further three by André Juillard and Yves Sante.
19. The image of Hadrian's Wall (Fig. 7, Chapter 2) is that looking east about half a mile beyond Housesteads fort. It is probably taken from an edition of David Breeze's guides to the wall, published by Penguin and then English Heritage. Despite the general accuracy of the depiction, there are some elements of poetic licence: the road does not run that close to the wall, and the border between England and Scotland is several miles north of Hadrian's Wall.

    As we have seen, this particular *planche* also illustrates many of the formal techniques explored in our earlier chapters. In particular we can note the switch from general scene-setting *cases* to close up, text-based narrative, and the use of *contre-plongée* to emphasis a character's good standing, here as in our initial view of Cameron.

20. See Chapter 3, 'Formal Specificity', in the previous section of this book. Here both OuBaPo and L'Association are discussed in terms of other forms of avant-garde expression such as OuLiPo or New Wave cinema.
21. One such example is Georges Perec's *La Disparition* [A Void] (Paris: Denoël, 1969), in which the disappearance of the title ultimately refers to the letter 'e', which is entirely absent from the novel.
22. A special dossier on OuBaPo occupies pp. 72–99 of *9e Art* 10 (2004), and Ann Miller has dedicated an article to the subject: 'Oubapo: A Verbal/Visual Medium Is Subjected to Constraints', *Word & Image* 23.2 (2007), 117–37. See also chapter 3 (pp. 70–110) of Bart Beaty, *Unpopular Culture: Transforming the European Comic Book in the 1990s* (Toronto: University of Toronto Press, 2007).
23. Literally 'Lynx with Hair', the term plays upon a near homonym with 'laxatif'.
24. (Paris: L'Association, 2005). Again the title is a play on words, between 'flat strips', the literal meaning and 'flowerbeds', the overall expression.
25. The names originated from the typographical meanings of 'Éperluette' (the 'and' sign) and 'Ciboulette' (the 'or' sign), with 'Mimoulette', 'Côtelette' and 'Espôlette' as food-related plays on the '-ette' endings. 'Éprouvette' means 'test tube'.
26. In *Reading Bande Dessinée: Critical Approaches to French-Language Comic Strip*, Ann Miller gives a comprehensive overview of the post-1990s world of independent BD, as well as individual case studies of 'independent' artists including Baru, Marc-Antoine Mathieu, Manu Larcenet, Farid Boudjellal, Kamil Khélif, De Crécy and Chomet, Dupuy and Berberian, Lewis Trondheim, Julie Doucet, Marjane Satrapi and Menu himself. Pages 99–125 of Claude Moliterni, Philippe Mellot, Laurent Turpin, Michel Denni and Nathalie Michel-Szelechowska's *BDGuide 2005: Encyclopédie de la bande dessinée internationale* (Paris: Omnibus, 2004) also discuss the changes in BD publishing trends from 1990 to 2004. Above all, see Bart Beaty's *Unpopular Culture*, whose first chapter (pp. 17–43) analyses the development of L'Association, suggesting it to be the catalyst for post-1990s small-press comics throughout Europe.
27. Four volumes of Neaud's journal have appeared, published between 1996 and 2002 and covering the time period between February 1992 and July 1996. All are published by Angoulême-based Ego Comme X. The brief discussion of Neaud's work in the chapter 'Cultural Studies and Beyond' will indicate recent approaches to the *Journal* that have been formulated in English. This example is taken from *Journal 4: Les Riches heures* (2002), p.111.
28. Here, and in the analysis of Angoulême prize-winners below, I have started with the most recent (at the time of writing) and worked backwards. Although this arrangement is to a certain extent arbitrary, the aim is to emphasise that this is the chapter on Contemporary BD – that, if anything, it is synchronic rather than diachronic, and therefore 2008/2009 is at the top of the list.
29. *Livres Hebdo* 760 (16 January 2009).
30. *Livres Hebdo* 717 (18 January 2008).
31. *Livre Hebdo* 673 (19 January 2007).
32. *Livres Hebdo* 629 (20 January 2006).
33. *Livres Hebdo* 586 (28 January 2005).
34. *Livres Hebdo* 542 (30 January 2004).
35. *Livres Hebdo* 497 (17 January 2003).
36. *Livres Hebdo* 453 (18 January 2002).
37. Only the penultimate volume, *XIII 18: La Version irlandaise* by Van Hamme and Jean Giraud, has not been by Van Hamme and Vance.
38. *Titeuf 10* was released on 26 August. *The Da Vinci Code* was released on 3 March. The tables of best-sellers summarised in this paragraph are again based on the statistics of *Livres Hebdo*.

39. The question of BD and linguistics, with specific reference to *Titeuf*, will be discussed briefly in Chapter 10, 'Cultural Studies and Beyond'.
40. (Neuilly-sur-Seine: Dargaud). From 1980 onwards all albums have been published in Paris by Albert Uderzo's Éditions Albert René.
41. The figures are those given by René Goscinny as quoted in Aymar du Chatenet, ed., *Le Dictionnaire Goscinny* (Paris: JC Lattès, 2003), p. 101. Many of the other statistics given in the section are also taken from this invaluable source of background information on the output of Goscinny's career. On *Astérix* see also chapter 3 (pp. 75–92) of Matthew Screech's *Masters of the Ninth Art: Bandes Dessinées and Franco-Belgian Identity*. For discussion of *Astérix* in the context of national identity, see Ann Miller, *Reading Bande Dessinée: Critical Approaches to French-Language Comic Strip*, pp. 152–59. In French Nicolas Rouvière's *Astérix ou les lumières de la civilisation* [Asterix or the Lights of Civilisation] (Paris: Presses Universitaires de France, 2006) examines the contents of the series from a socio-political viewpoint.
42. Although it should be noted that the 2003 *Astérix et la rentrée gauloise* is essentially a compilation of previously published short strips.
43. This anecdote is given in the form of a quotation from Goscinny on p. 100 of Olivier Andrieu's *Astérix* (Paris: Éditions Albert René, 1999). The volume, whose cover title (as opposed to its title-page title) is *Le Livre d'Astérix le Gaulois*, is an entertaining and colourfully illustrated source of trivia on the *Astérix* series; unfortunately, sources of quotations are not given. In a similar vein, but in English, see Peter Kessler, *The Complete Guide to Asterix* (London: Hodder, 1995). This work includes a chapter on the art of translating the *Astérix* series into English.
44. Anthea Bell and Derek Hockridge's English versions provide the following names: 'Abraracourcix' is 'Vitalstatistix'; 'Numérobis' is 'Edifis'; 'Ipipourax' is 'Hipiphurrax'; 'Zebigbos' is 'Mykingdomforanos'; 'Grossebaf' is 'Timandahaf'; 'Soupalognon y Crouton' is 'Huevos y Bacon'; 'Zérozérosix' is 'Dubbelosix'.
45. The first pun is a play on 'Numide' [Numidian] to whom one must not speak dryly [*sèchement*], and the associated homonym 'humide'. The second is a play on 'Alexandrin' meaning 'Alexandrian', as the character in question comes from Alexandria, and 'Alexandrin' meaning 'Alexandrine', as he presents himself with a twelve-syllable line.
46. Numa Sadoul, 'Entretien avec René Goscinny' [Interview with René Goscinny], *Schtroumpf: Les Cahiers de la Bande Dessinée* 22 (1973), 5–18.
47. Olivier Andrieu's *Astérix* quotes Uderzo (without source) to this effect on p. 127.
48. For a listing and detailed analysis of winners up to and including 2002, see Thierry Groensteen, *[Primé à Angoulême]: 30 ans de bandes dessinées à travers le palmarès du Festival*. Ann Miller also provides a listing of winners up to 2007 on pp. 247–48 of *Reading Bande Dessinée: Critical Approaches to French-Language Comic Strip*.
49. 'Feraille' means 'Scrap Metal'.
50. On these and other works by Blutch, see the dossier dedicated to him on pages 110-63 of issue 14 (2008) of *9e Art*.
51. On *Monsieur Jean* and on *Journal d'un album*, see Ann Miller, *Reading Bande Dessinée: Critical Approaches to French-Language Comic Strip*, pp. 192–95 and 223–27 respectively. More generally on Dupuy and Berberian, see the dossier dedicated to them on pages 72-125 of issue 15 (2009) of *9e Art*.
52. The figures are those of *Livres Hebdo* 673 (19 January 2007). See in particular their 'Dossier BD' on pp. 88–132. Pages 112–32 provide the bibliography of mangas to be released. For a clear introduction to mangas in English, see Paul Gravett, *Manga: Sixty Years of Japanese Comics*

(London: Laurence King, 2004). Gravett contextualises Mizuki, but does not mention *NonNonBâ* specifically.

53. Although a 'donjon' is the keep of a castle, the English title is 'Dungeon' in reference to the Dungeons and Dragons gaming to which the series implicitly refers.
54. Again see above, as well as our Chapter 3 on Formal Specificity in the previous section of this book.
55. The title literally means 'Little Rabbit and the Patagonian Carrots', but the related series uses the English title of *The Spiffy Adventures of McConey*.
56. On Trondheim and autobiography, see Ann Miller, *Reading Bande Dessinée: Critical Approaches to French-Language Comic Strip*, pp. 219–23.
57. On *Persepolis*, see Ann Miller, *Reading Bande Dessinée: Critical Approaches to French-Language Comic Strip*, pp. 238–41.
58. This and the following example have been reproduced in Georges Wolinski, *Dans l'Huma* (Paris: Mazarine, 1980), pp. 228 and 22 respectively.
59. This example is taken from Georges Wolinski, *Les Classiques de Wolinski: Hit-parade* (Paris: Albin Michel, 2003), no pagination.
60. Both of these are available in Manu Larcenet, *La Loi des séries* [Series Law] (Paris: Fluide Glacial, 1997).
61. The albums in questions are *Une Aventure rocambolesque de Sigmund Freud: Le Temps de chien* [An Incredible Sigmund Freud Adventure: Heavy Weather] (Paris: Dargaud, 2002); *Une Aventure rocambolesque de Vincent Van Gogh: La Ligne de front* [An Incredible Vincent Van Gogh Adventure: The Front Line] (Paris: Dargaud, 2004); *Une Aventure rocambolesque d'Attila le Hun: Le Fléau de Dieu* [An Incredible Attila the Hun Adventure: God's Scourge] (Paris: Dargaud, 2006).
62. Many of these themes are also explored in the second volume, *Le Combat ordinaire: Les Quantités négligeables* (Paris: Dargaud, 2004), in which Larcenet attempts to come to terms with his father's death. See also Ann Miller, *Reading Bande Dessinée: Critical Approaches to French-Language Comic Strip*, pp. 168–71.
63. For clear analysis of trends in American comics Roger Sabin's *Comics, Comix & Graphic Novels: A History of Comic Art* (London: Phaidon, 2002 [first published 1996]) remains indispensable. For Chris Ware in particular, see issue 200 (December 1997) of *The Comics Journal*, which includes a long interview with him, and Jean-Christophe Menu, 'Le Prodigieux Projet de Chris Ware' [Chris Ware's Prodigious Project], *9e Art* 2 (1997), 45–57.
64. See *Comics, Comix & Graphic Novels: A History of Comic Art*.
65. All albums were initially published by Dargaud. Volumes I to IV are available together as *L'Integrale: La Quête de l'oiseau du temps* (Paris: Dargaud, 1992). On the creation of the series, see Bertrand Pissavy-Yvernault and Christelle Pissavy-Yvernault, *En Quête de l'oiseau du temps* (Paris: Dargaud, 2004). This work consists mainly of interviews with the artists and their associates.
66. See Michel Jans, *Loisel: Une Monographie* (St Egrève: Mosquito, 1998), p.43. Most of the work consists of a lengthy interview with Loisel.
67. See *Livres Hebdo* 497 (17 January 2003), p. 75.
68. Groensteen puts forward and elaborates this theory in *Système de la bande dessinée* (Paris: Presses Universitaires de France, 1999).
69. The same technique will be explored by Marc-Antoine Mathieu's *L'Épaisseur du miroir* [The Depth of the Mirror] (Paris: Delcourt, 1995). His work will be discussed in the 'Cultural Studies and Beyond' chapter of this book.
70. On the multi-media aspect of the BD's development with specific reference to work of Schuiten, see Laurence Grove, 'Multi-Media Emblems and their Modern Day Counterparts', *Emblematic Tendencies in the Art and Literature of the Twentieth Century*, ed. Anthony Harper, Ingrid Höpel and Susan Sirc (Glasgow: GES, 2005), pp. 171–87. The question will also be discussed in

our chapter 'Cultural Studies and Beyond'. On Schuiten's work with Benoît Peeters, see Elizabeth McQuillan, 'Texte, Image, Récit: The Textual Worlds of Benoît Peeters', *The Graphic Novel*, ed. Jan Baetens (Leuven: Leuven University Press, 2001), pp. 157–66. See also the dossier dedicated to Schuiten (pp. 7–48) in *Les Cahiers de la Bande Dessinée* 69 (1986).

71. The 1982 title is in reference to the literary affairs programme, *Apostrophes!* The title can roughly translate as 'Apostrophes!'s Missing Persons'.
72. The title is a play on the notion of complete works, whilst referring to Lermite's habitual suit ('complet').
73. The title is a pun on 'amour propre' meaning self-respect, or, literally, 'clean love', which 'does not stay like that for long'.
74. Another pun, on the wine appellation and the literal meaning, 'crude bourgeois'.
75. This view presents itself in the interviews and articles dedicated to Veyron that form the dossier on him (pp. 5–34) in *Les Cahiers de la Bande Dessinée* 62 (1985).
76. Trondheim's explanation for the title is that, like the BD, shampoo uses lots of bubbles and freshens up one's head.
77. Again, the exception to this general rule has become Art Spiegelman's *Maus*, which although a product of Spiegelman's associations with the Underground, has become a best-seller and Pulitzer Prize winner.

PART III

THE CULTURAL PHENOMENON

CHAPTER 8

POP ART OR BUSINESS PARK?: BARTHES-ERING FOR THE MARKET

Bande Dessinée and Popular Culture

It may seem peculiar to open a section of a book with a subtitle as bland as 'Bande Dessinée and Popular Culture', but an awareness of the implications is essential to our grasp of the BD's place in the wider scheme of things: this may be in terms of its direct relation to popular culture, but also to the high-cultural appropriation of popular culture, as well as to those strands within the medium that are self-reflexive. Up to now I have taken it for granted that the reader is interested in the bande dessinée per se, not a startling assumption given that what you have in front of you, dear reader, is a book on bande dessinée. The previous two parts of this book have attempted therefore to define the form, to look at its technical structure (thereby providing approaches to its analysis), and then to situate it in terms of its historical development.

Were this a book primarily for a French or Belgian audience – in fact its originality lies in the fact that it is precisely not that – there would be less need to justify, or maybe even situate, the form's place as a valid cultural entity.[1] Bande dessinée is the Ninth Art, and we can move straight on to seeing how it can help us deepen our understanding of a variety of further fields, from cooking to colonialism.

Such is not automatically the case for the English-language reader, who, armed with a broad knowledge of *Snoopy* and *Spiderman*, will not necessarily take the BD's Ninth Art status for granted, nor be fully aware of the extent of the medium's importance as an art form. The aim of this initial chapter, therefore, is to outline the place of the BD with relation to relevant artistic currents of the latter part of the twentieth century – principally Pop Art – and to situate it in terms of the critical discourse that exists as regards popular culture and, more generally, the notion of Cultural Studies. Much of what will be said will be applicable to comics culture as a whole, irrespective of national traditions, but the BD is particularly apt for encapsulating theoretical ideas and movements for which French thinking often occupies a central place. Furthermore, works in French on the BD that entertain such an approach are far outnumbered by those that do not.

It is a fitting coincidence that this framework should be visual and then textual, although both subsections will of course consider the bande dessinée as a hybrid whole. One might wonder why this chapter, one that examines the fundamental question of the bande dessinée's critical standing, is not to be found at the very beginning of the book. The short answer is that our first section, 'What is a Bande Dessinée?', was intended as an introduction to BD's *formal* status rather than to the wider debate on its *cultural* status. Again, I felt it was important to concentrate initially on the BD per se, to provide the tools that will allow for this wider application. Now that you, dear reader, have an overview of what the BD is, it is time to give it its place in the broader cultural scheme of things and to apply that knowledge so as to deepen our understanding of francophone civilisation in more general terms.

Popular Culture as Cultural Artefact

Bande dessinée and comics can be related to Pop Art on two levels: firstly as an example of popular culture attaining the status of art, but also as a direct subject for pop artists, specifically Roy Lichtenstein and Andy Warhol in America, but also Bernard Rancillac, and others, in France.

The starting date for Pop Art is open to conjecture, although most accounts give the movement as lasting from the mid 1950s to the mid 1960s.[2] As with the specific case of bande dessinée, the history of popular culture in general can be taken back to the earliest of times, from the broadsheets of early printing, through the fashion for the emblem book to the 'dime novels' of the nineteenth century.[3] It was not before the early stages of the twentieth century, however, that we find the notion of popular culture existing as a self-aware art form.

In 1917, in the context of a series of 'readymades' including the 1913 *Bicycle Wheel*, Marcel Duchamp exhibited his *Fountain* at the Society of Independent Artists in New York. The fountain in question is an upturned urinal inscribed with the name 'R. Mutt'. This is part reference to the Mott sanitary equipment works, but adapted so as to bring to mind the fat, fun-loving, comic strip character of Bud Fisher's *Mutt and Jeff* duo, that had appeared in the *San Francisco Chronicle* in 1907 before being syndicated to New York in 1909, and of which Duchamp was a fan.[4] The importance of Duchamp's *Fountain* is that it champions the everyday object in context. What matters is not so much whether Duchamp (or Richard Mutt!) constructed the work, but that he chose it and gave artistic significance to a domestic item through its title and new placement. Indeed, often in the work of Fisher, it was precisely the displacement of household items that facilitated the zany humour. That a Frenchman should include a reference to comics as an intrinsic part of the process reinforces the notion of bande dessinée as closely connected to the key precepts of popular art.

The central figures of 1960s Pop Art, Roy Lichtenstein and Andy Warhol, perhaps unwittingly, continued the tradition.[5] From the late 1950s Lichtenstein started including iconic cartoon figures such as Mickey Mouse, Donald Duck or Bugs Bunny as main subjects for his studies. Although his work involved several intricate steps from initial drawing to the careful hand painting of the final process, the aim was to give the impression of a mass-produced product of consumer society. Lichtenstein thus blurs the boundaries between artefact and consumable. Ironically, the blurring draws upon a finely defined style of clear-cut lines and colours, one that brings to mind another bande dessinée reference, the *ligne claire* style that Hergé had popularised.

His best-known comic strip pieces date from the early to mid-1960s and include such works as *The Kiss* (1962),[6] *Takka Takka* (1962, a gun barrel scene), *Eddie Diptych* (1962, with text on one panel and image on the next, telling of the girl's pining for Eddie), *Hopeless* (1963, a crying blonde with speech bubble), *In the Car* (1963, a couple exchanging glances with movement lines indicating speed), *Whaam* (1963, an air-fight scene), *Good Morning Darling* (1964, a blonde waking to a picture frame) and *M-Maybe* (1965, an anxious blonde with thought bubble). In *Masterpiece* (1962, Fig. 35) we see a couple looking at the edge of a canvas as the woman's speech bubble enounces, 'Why, Brad darling, this painting is a Masterpiece! My, soon you'll have all of New York clamoring for your work!'

The work has been taken directly from a comic book source, as is the case for many of his iconic pieces of the 1960s.[7] Here, as in almost all of his works, it is the scene in its adapted context that creates the work's resonances. The painting becomes playfully self-referential,

Figure 35. 'Self-Referential Pop Art'. Roy Lichtenstein. *Masterpiece*. 1962. Private collection.

especially as we notice that what we suppose is the New York artist is admiring his painting, whilst the woman is in fact looking flirtatiously at him, and then out to the viewer. What might appear to be a simple reference to the world of romance comics in fact evokes a tradition of European art that includes Jan Van Eyke's *Arnolphini Mariage*, Diego Velasquez's *Las Meñinas* [The Maids of Honour] and his *Rokeby Venus*.

This is a tradition that in turn has become the linchpin of a current vogue for self-reflexive bandes dessinées, one that took its roots in the late 1960s. Marcel Gotlib's work for the *Écho des Savanes* immediately comes to mind, but more recently André Juillard's *Cahier bleu* (more on this in two chapters' time) is a bande dessinée that explores the possibilities of expression in BD form, as do the various publications of L'Association, and in particular the OuBaPo productions.[8] One of the clearest, and most self-conscious examples of the self-reflexive BD is the work of Marc-Antoine Mathieu, also to be explored in the chapter 'Cultural Studies and Beyond'. As with a Lichtenstein painting, it is for the reader to construct (or choose to ignore) the bulk of the 'story' – who is Acquefacques, Mathieu's central character, from where does he come, what are his objectives, or indeed who are Lichenstein's New York characters – but what we do have is a de facto treatise on the techniques and constraints that govern art.

Andy Warhol's references to comic book literature are less frequent, but still present as the 'fifteen minutes of fame' artist comments on the volatile nature of art, like all things in consumer society. He presents objects of mass attention, be they film stars, as in the *Marilyn* or *Elvis* series, everyday objects such as Coke bottles, soup cans or dollar banknotes, or attention-grabbing events including plane crashes and car wrecks. The extent to which Warhol echoes Duchamp's playful encomium of the everyday often goes un-noted, but it is when this is coupled with the eye-candy effect of his bright colour silkscreen prints – a similar effect to that of Lichtenstein's creations – that the powerful contradiction comes to light. Warhol's works, like Lichtenstein's, were carefully prepared: he often spent hours creating the correct effect of a smudged print, or hand painting parts of the final Marilyn of fifty. But the effect is to see the notion of art as contradictory and indefinable, finally no more that that which grabs our attention and pleases us aesthetically. In such a context bande dessinée is clearly art.

Warhol's hybrid output is also on a par with the direction taken by the developing bande dessinée – not just the central mixture of text and image that underpins many of his and Lichtenstein's creations, but the move in his latter career to sculpture, music and, above all, film. Although only resuscitating the Renaissance ideal of the all-encompassing creator, Warhol was instrumental in a twentieth-century de-compartmentalisation of the arts. Grasping this mentality is essential to an understanding of the modern bande dessinée, which although generally accepted as a hybrid text/image form, is often overlooked in its broader interdisciplinary sense. Artists such as

Moebius or Peeters and Schuiten have shown us the importance of exploring film creation – Moebius was heavily involved in the concept design for *Alien*, *Le Cinquième Élément* [The Fifth Element] and *Star Wars V* – or three-dimensionality, as in the case of Peeters and Schuiten or indeed Marc-Antoine Mathieu.[9] It is becoming increasingly rare for a bande dessinée to be no more than a book, as we see from spin-off figurines, theme parks or blockbuster films.

It may seem peculiar that a book so specifically concerned with the Ninth Art as a francophone cultural phenomenon should rely heavily on two American artists. The notion of cultural cross-pollination is important, and it is not a one-way process, as our references to Duchamp and Hergé indicate. Furthermore, as with rap or blockbuster movies, the French were and are quite capable of taking an American phenomenon and leading it in their own direction. Hervé Télémaque in his *Pastorale* (Private collection, 1963) intersperses an idyllic, albeit caricatured, landscape with Goofy, Sylvester the Cat and Tweety Pie. Bernard Rancillac also draws upon icons of comic art, as in his *Sans parole VI: Où es-tu, que fais-tu?* [Without Words VI: Where are You, What are You Doing?] (Private collection, 1965): we see the fun-loving figure of Goofy in a pose of zany movement, but Rancillac warps expectations through threatening elements such as the gun and the axe Goofy holds and the aggressive distortion of the Disney character's features. More generally, Rancillac uses the canvas to express possibilities of narrative. His *Suite américaine* (Paris, Musée National d'Art Moderne, Centre Pompidou, 1970), for example, is divided into three segments, each showing what appear to be figures from American political and gangster life, and thus effectively creating *cases*, although it is again very much for the viewer to construct the storyline. In similar fashion, Gérard Fromanger's *La France est-elle coupée de deux?* [Is France Cut in Two?] (Paris, Musée d'Art Moderne de la Ville de Paris, 1974, Fig. 36) includes a notional division into segmented *case*-like elements, an oblique reference to the hero figure, and an intriguing mixture of text and image. The work, like Rancillac's, would seem to have the characteristics of a bande dessinée, yet the 'easy readability' we might associate with the popular form is undermined by the paintings' startling ambiguity.

Closely linked to the general themes of Pop Art was the *Nouveau Réalisme* or New Realism movement to which we can assign these artists,[10] and that resulted from two manifestos (1960 and 1961) by Pierre Restany.[11] Once again we can see Duchamp as the base inspiration for a group that took everyday objects, such as the compressed cars that became César's leitmotif, and presented them in a new and challenging context. But whereas Duchamp's displacement of the everyday was largely intended to shock, for the *Nouveau Réalistes* it was more a matter of challenging reality in a consumer world. Familiar objects may surround us, but if we remove them from the context to which we are accustomed do they then have any intrinsic meaning beyond that of aesthetic pleasure?

Figure 36. 'Cases and Narrative Heroes?' Gérard Fromanger. *La France est-elle coupée de deux?* 1974. Paris, Musée d'Art Moderne de la Ville de Paris.

As Bruno Lecigne pointed out in one of the earliest of theoretical monographs on BD, *Avanies et mascarades* [Affronts and Mascarades],[12] the cutting-edge trends in the bande dessinée of the 1960s and 1970s were equally founded upon *bricolage* and perpetual re-creation. Referring to the works of Moebius, Lecigne summarises:

> Chaque récit ne pretend pas (à la façon des cycles romanesques, par exemple) brosser le vaste tableau d'un univers complet mais semble au contraire engagé dans un processus d'éternel recommencement. Ainsi, chaque nouveau récit, par rapport aux précédents, n'est pas à saisir dans une perspective cumulative (ou d'emboîtement) mais plutôt à la façon de strates, de couloirs, de ramifications. (107)

> [The individual récit does not claim (in the manner of the Romance Cycles, for example) to paint the vast picture of a complete universe but seems on the other hand to be engaged in a process of perpetual new beginning. In this way each new récit, when considered in respect to previous ones, is not to be understood from a cumulative viewpoint (or from one of encasing), but rather in terms of strata, of passage ways and of ramification.]

Artists such as Moebius, Fred and Chantal Montellier were challenging the figurative realism of traditional strips by presenting us with familiar characters and situations, but then questioning the nature of 'reality' through a disjunctive or non-existent narrative. In the case of Moebius's *Garage hermétique*, as discussed in Chapter 3, it is for the reader to interpret (and reinterpret) as he or she sees fit. Two years after *Avanies et mascarades*, Lecigne and Jean-Pierre Tamine were to make the comparison explicit with *Fac-Similé: Essai paratactique sur le Nouveau Réalisme de la bande dessinée* [Facsimile: A Paratactic Essay on the Bande Dessinée's Nouveau Réalisme].[13]

It is equally non-coincidental that one of the main exhibitions accompanying the rise of *Nouveau Réalisme* represented a key stage in bande dessinée history. *Bande dessinée et figuration narrative* was held from 7 April until 5 June 1967 at the Musée des Arts Décoratifs in Paris and was, to a certain extent, a natural follow-on from previous exhibitions on narrative art, as well as being in keeping with other events, such as a 1967 Paris conference on *Art et littérature d'expression graphique*. Whilst these works laid the emphasis on bande dessinée as a form of sequential expression, they did challenge traditional precepts of linear narrative.[14] The move to promote bande dessinée as a cultural phenomenon was going hand in hand with the artistic movements whose primary subject was the place of the popular image in postwar culture. Bande dessinée was art and art was bande dessinée.

When we examine some of the defining factors in postwar figurative art – the art of the time that also saw the rise of the modern bande dessinée and which for these purposes I have shorthanded under the label of Pop Art – the link between the two appears intrinsic and natural.[15] In terms of context, Pop Art, like many of the postwar trends, was based in the metropolis, specifically New York, London or Paris. The bandes dessinées that took the form into adulthood, like the underground commix of the USA, were similarly the product of an urban milieu – almost exclusively Paris – with a subject matter to match.

Above all, Pop Art was both of interest for its technical qualities in representing the everyday world around us, but also for what, implicitly, it had to say about that everyday world. Lichtenstein, Warhol, Rancillac or Yves Klein produced icons that appeal because they refer to instantly recognisable elements of our lives, but also through the way they are presented, such as the use of distorted primary colours. But by choosing these everyday objects as the very subject for their art, they were giving them a status beyond that of simple motif. With the advent of paintings of soup cans, glossy film star images or even comic strips, they were updating Duchamp's notion of some forty-five years previously, namely that art is all around us; there is no longer a hierarchy of subject matter prejudicing the Bible or Antiquity, since these have been replaced by the gods of the consumer society to which we must now bow.

As a key product of and mirror to that consumer society, the bande dessinée was and is both a valid subject of the new artistic trends, but an equally strong vehicle for such expression. If a silkscreen of a comic was art, so that comic itself could be – art in that the everyday is now art, but also art as a technically adept method of raising questions central to artistic expression, such as the role of narrative or the intrinsic nature of represented reality. Like Pop Art, the adult bande dessinée of the post-*Pilote* era (and underground commix) has become both realist in the subject matter it portrays and figurative in the ideas it implies.

Popular Culture as an Object of Intellectualisation

Pop Art and *Nouveau Réalisme* effectively render directly visual, or put into practice, certain theoretical currents that had started to gain prominence from the late 1950s, including the broad notion of Cultural Studies. Again, we can take the concept of Cultural Studies back to the mid nineteenth century (and beyond) via figures such as Matthew Arnold or F.R. Leavis, but its existence as a self-conscious field of enquiry became apparent by the early years of the 1960s. Cultural Studies in its broadest sense can refer quite simply to culture that is popular (but not necessarily without aesthetic value), culture that is manipulated for the masses or, in a broader sense, to an approach to culture that removes traditional subject divisions and encompasses the written word, sounds, the visual, the past and the present, in short all that makes up the cultural environment that surrounds us. Cultural Studies can concentrate on specific artefacts (a given book, piece of music, film etc.) or it can investigate elements of daily life at a given time or place (leisure activities, spending patterns, linguistic developments and so on). In all of these cases bande dessinée fits the bill.

A quick browse through the shelves of any major library is enough to see that there is a minor industry in Cultural Studies, which, fittingly enough, defies single-location classification and thus can be found under literature, history, sociology, fine arts, and so on, as well as being sub-classified under English, French, German ….[16] This present book cannot, and should not, aspire to giving a full account of the intricacies of Cultural Studies (any more than of Pop Art and related visual movements), but rather aims to outline some of the main concerns and the works of those who have broached them, whilst pointing to aspects that are particularly relevant to the study of bande dessinée.

The work of Roland Barthes is as good a starting place as any: his *oeuvre* is eclectic and vast (the three volumes of his complete works come to over 4,700 pages),[17] but throughout we find a constant preoccupation with the status of the image and its place in the culture of our times. *Le Problème de la signification au cinéma* [The Problem of Signifying in Cinema] (1960) looks at visual codes in cinema fiction; *Le Message photographique* (1961) explores how the picture-taker manipulates bias; *L'Information visuelle* (1961) and *La Civilisation de l'image* (1964) are on how to approach the reading of everyday images; *Rhétorique de l'image* (1964) famously puts this into practice through the example of advertising for pasta; and *Cette vieille chose, l'art …* [Art, that Golden Oldie …] (1980) discusses Pop Art. And these are but a few examples …[18]

It is in *Mythologies* that Barthes gave prominence to the notion of the 'everyday' as a valid subject for intellectual examination.[19] Through a series of essays published between 1954 and 1956, largely in the critical review *Les Lettres Nouvelles* [New Letters], and then brought together in book form (1957), Barthes 'deconstructs' what he calls 'quelques mythes de la vie quotidienne française' [a few myths of French everyday life] (9):[20] the play-acting of the wrestling world, the connotations of a *Paris Match* cover, the tourist clichés eulogised by the *Guide bleu*, medieval epic terminology and the Tour de France, the bourgeois protocols of the striptease ...

'Saponides et détergents' [Soaps and Detergents] (38–40) points to a phenomenon now taken for granted but which 1950s France had not necessarily noticed: advertising uses sex to sell, even if the object, in this case soap powder, would appear entirely non-erotic. Referring to the adverts for Omo, Barthes stresses the importance of 'le profond et le mousseux' [depth and bubbly-ness] (39). With respect to the 'mousse', Barthes emphasises its connotations of luxury as a 'germe vigoureux, une essence saine et puissante' [a vigorous seed, a healthy and powerful essence] (39). As for the soap powder's depth,

> Dire qu'*Omo* nettoie en profondeur (voir la saynète du Cinéma-Publicité), c'est supposer que le linge est profond, ce qu'on n'avait jamais pensé, et ce qui est incontestablement le magnifier, l'établir comme un objet flatteur à ces obscures poussées d'envelopement et de caresse qui sont dans tout corps humain. (39)

> [To say that *Omo* cleans in depth (see the cinema advertising company's ad) is to suppose that linen is deep, something that had never been imagined, and which without doubt exalts it, and establishes it as an object that flatters those obscure desires to envelop and to caress, desires that are in all physical humans.]

Barthes is both underlining the everyday – there is not much more everyday than soap powder – as subject for semiotic codes, but also the way in which the object denoted, the seemingly direct object of discussion (the bland world of soap powders), can be a far cry from that of the connotations, here the depth and frothiness of sexual fantasy.

Barthes opens 'La Nouvelle Citroën' [The New Citroën] (150–52) by comparing the style of the new automobile with the grandeur of by-gone cathedrals:

> Je crois que l'automobile est aujourd'hui l'équivalent assez exact des grandes cathédrales gothiques: je veux dire une grande création d'époque, conçue passionément par des artistes inconnus, consommée dans son image, sinon dans son usage, par un peuple entier qui s'approprie en elle un objet parfaitement magique. (150)

> [I believe that the automobile is today's precise equivalent of the great gothic cathedrals: I mean that it is a great creation of its time, conceived with passion by unknown artists, and consumed via its image, if not by direct use, by an entire people that makes of it an object of pure magic.]

In the text that follows he goes on to analyse the aesthetic qualities of the new car, the effect of its curves and seamless joins. Not only was Barthes stating what is obvious now but was less so then – that a car is not just for getting from A to B – but once again that the beauty of the product can be expressed in terms of human attraction. The comparators Barthes uses opens our attention to the semiotic complexities that underpin the modern world, but he also breaks down the traditional barriers whereby a medieval masterpiece was worthy of intellectual analysis unlike the mundane practicalities of twentieth-century design.

Mythologies (and Barthes's wider opus) has influenced the bande dessinée on a direct level: we saw in our analysis of page 38 of *Astérix gladiateur* (see Chapter 2 on 'Definitions and Component Parts', and Fig. 4) that Goscinny and Uderzo evoke 'Saponides et détergents' by reference to a powder that washers togas 'plus pourpre que pourpre' [more purple than purple]. Along the same lines, in *Astérix et les Normands* (1966) one of the leading characters flaunts a 'sports chariot' in the way that the 'Déesse' (i.e., the new Citroën) received adulation. It is interesting to note in this context the way in which *Mythologies* had effectively become part of the popular culture that it was in itself dissecting. But the chief importance of Barthes's work to our study lies in the fact that icons of everyday life, of which comics are a leading example, could be attributed cultural value worthy of critical attention. It is no coincidence that it is around the late 1950s that the first tentative studies of the bande dessinée were coming to light, as we shall see in the next chapter.

To attribute the bande dessinée critical value per se beyond that of a sociological object is to question a traditional hierarchy of values whereby Poussin and Proust represent 'high culture' and TV and BD are only acceptable as 'low culture'. The status of 'high culture' is conferred via the elitist inaccessibility that comes with time and monetary worth, which means that issues become blurred when we place the bande dessinée in a tradition going back to the Bayeux Tapestry or when certain Tintin albums are valued at 35,000.[21] The high/low culture debate is at the core of Pierre Bourdieu's *La Distinction* (1979),[22] which appeared some years after Umberto Eco had presented a series of studies on comics, as well as on other popular icons such as James Bond. A French version of Eco's study on Superman, 'Le Mythe de Superman et la dissolution du temps' [The Myth of Superman and the Dissolution of Time] was published in an early issue of *Giff-Wiff* (number 11 of September 1964, pp. 10–13), one of the first critical journals – more like a fanzine – dedicated to BD.[23]

The common point thus far has been a tendency towards (or an implicit reaction to) a semiotic investigation of modern culture and, more specifically, a semiotic reading of the image today. Already this is important as it extends Fernand de Saussure's base work on linguistics to the visual:[24] just as we can 'deconstruct' a literary text and demonstrate that the 'real' meaning is not just that of the words' denotative sense but rather the connotations that they conjure up – this is exactly what Barthes does in *S/Z* (1970), where he provides a word-by-word explanation of the various layers of Balzac's *Sarrasine* – the same process can be applied to the image, or in the case of the bande dessinée, to the mixture of text and image.

The possibilities of applying semiotic readings to bandes dessinées have been amply demonstrated by the mini-industry of such studies, which at times enlighten our understanding of key texts, but which can also become repetitive once we have grasped the base concept. Semiotic deconstruction, be it in reference to text, image, or text and image can become a mechanical process, comparable possibly to the way in which one Jackson Pollock canvas might make us think about the possibilities of non-referential expressionism, but a whole room full of them could possibly lead to overkill. Nonetheless we should be aware that any reading of a bande dessinée must involve some deciphering of connotations, and thus, knowingly or not, applies the theories of Barthes, Bourdieu and Eco.

One of the most popular subjects is *Tintin au Tibet*, as explored, for example, by Didier Quella-Guyot and Jean-Marie Floch.[25] Quella-Guyot points to the red lettering on the cover as an indication of emotion and love, but also of blood, thus evoking death when coupled with the cover's other colour, black. He goes on to analyse the composition of the cover with its mixture of lettering, the group of main characters, Milou in isolation, and the footprints that lead out of the image, 'invitant ainsi le lecteur à poursuivre cette presence inquiétante à l'intérieur du volume' [thereby inviting the reader to follow that disturbing presence to within the volume] (23). Floch, whose background is the semiotics of advertising, concentrates specifically on the Barthes-que connotations of the image. In the case of the famous crashed plane *planche* he points to the connotation of Tibet as the domain of death for Tintin. He notes that the vignette is devoid of all movement, as is emphasised by the absence of clouds. The image's composition depends on the scattering of irregular-shaped forms and as such recalls the mayhem strewn by Tintin when he calls out Tchang's name and thereby disturbs the peace in the Hôtel de Vargèse earlier on in the album. Although the two *planches* have very different *signifiés*, their compositional similarities have semiotic affinities thus leading to the association of Tchang with the airline catastrophe. Our understand of the text is therefore dependent not so much on what is said directly, but on the associations Hergé creates through a much more subtle process of semantic implication.

These are good examples that have already drawn upon the work of an artist whose clarity of style and composition are noted, as is the dense layering of signification that results. Nonetheless it should be obvious that a good many modern works of some intricacy, from Claire Bretécher's *Les Frustrés* to Fabrice Neaud's *Journal*, could easily withstand similar close analysis.

A further stage of such reading is to acknowledge the potentially unique position of the bande dessinée as a specific form whose meaning cannot remain fixed. The initial approach to each *case* is largely dependent on the individual reader, whether he or she starts with the text – *bulles* or *récitatif* – or with the image, and if so which part of the image? Is there a 'suggested' direction, as in the footprints on the cover of *Tintin au Tibet* that lead us diagonally from bottom left to top right, or is it a 'global' image as in the central arena scene from page 38 of *Astérix gladiateur* analysed above (Fig. 4, Chapter 2)? In clearer-cut cases such as these the variation from reader to reader is probably minimal, but with more experimental works, for example those of Fred (Fig. 6, Chapter 2) or Druillet, the effect of the BD will vary according to each reader's text/image stratagem.

Equally specific to the bande dessinée are the ambiguities of the *blancs intericoniques*, some of the effects of which we discussed in Chapter 2 on Definitions and Component Parts. The gap between the *cases* allows a sequential visual narrative to be formed from images that are independent and static and so distinguishes the BD from the illusion of constant movement that celluloid (and its digital descendents) produces. Again in the majority of cases there is little leeway for individual construction of this *non dit*; however, that is not always so. In Moebius's *Le Garage hérmetique*,[26] for example, the individual *cases* can often be read in a number of directions and can have little apparent connection from one to the next, with the result that the plot will very much depend on how the reader connects each frame. Moebius says as much in his introduction to the 2000 edition when he states 'Le "Garage hermétique" n'est pas une oeuvre fermée' (5).

Moebius may well have been aware that through reference to the 'oeuvre fermée' he was raising questions central to the work of Jacques Derrida, as well as providing wordplay in keeping with his tone. Specifically in *De La Grammatologie* [Of Grammatology] (1967) and *L'Écriture et la différence* [Writing and Difference] (1967) Derrida questions the role of writing as traditionally subordinated to speech, with writing characterised by absence and artifice. Using the neologism *différance* Derrida considers writing as an act of differing, not just in the sense of enacting difference, but also in the sense of postponement: as linguistic signs (e.g., the word 'garage') are purely arbitrary and can only be defined by other arbitrary signs (e.g., the words 'car shelter'), 'real' meaning never arrives; it is constantly pushed back. By suggesting that a (hermetic) bande dessinée is not an 'oeuvre fermée' we are similarly implying that final meaning is elusive and effectively dependent on each reader's interpretation. Furthermore, as a traditionally marginalised form bande dessinée might seem particularly suitable for Derridean deconstruction, which lays the emphasis on the decentralisation of cultural hegemony.

An extra layer is added by the concept of the author as *bricoleur*, one which Derrida explores in the penultimate chapter of *L'Écriture et la différence*, having appropriated the term from Claude Lévi-Strauss. The *bricoleur* takes whatever he finds around him and adapts it to his current purpose, regardless of original intention. Just as 'tout discours est bricoleur' [all discourse functions as *bricoleur*] (418), in that we inevitably construct our current output from the multifarious strands that our cultural baggage gives us, so the creation of a bande dessinée can be seen as a specific microcosm of the process with the creator/creators bringing together text and image, colour, publishing format and so on, the final effect depending on the individual reader who amalgamates the various pieces.[27]

Individual reactions to the bande dessinée, as with any cultural experience, must depend on personal associations in a manner comparable to the type of response Marcel Proust encapsulates with the madeleine scene in *À La Recherche du temps perdu*. On a wider level, however, all cultural reactions are dependent on place and time, and each individual 'snapshot' is like a postcard that gives us a glance, but no more, at certain clichéd aspects of locations and circumstances that are 'Other'.

Such ideas, formulated by Derrida in *La Carte postale de Socrate à Freud et au delà* [The Postcard: From Socrates to Freud and Beyond] (1980), could, for example, enhance a twenty-first-century reading of Hergé's *Tintin au Congo* (1931 for the album publication), whose apology for Belgian colonialism may appear offensively alien. The historical bande dessinée differs from more self-aware and clearly defined cultural forms in that it is very much a *carte postale*, a mixture of iconic image and (brief) explanatory text that represents the attitudes of a certain moment without necessarily having recourse to the technical artifice of 'high' art. *Tintin au Congo* is an enactment of *différance* in that it presents the alien Other (thus difference) but through the eyes of a time that is no longer our own (thus it has been pushed back, deferred). The album also gives a perfect example of postcolonial creation, perhaps an African version of the orientalism that Edward Said analysed in his book of that title (1978),[28] whereby the exotic is not so much the customs and lifestyles of far-off peoples, but the creation that comes of the mythological portrayal of such lifestyles. *Tintin au Congo* provides an outstanding example of such issues, but so could Bécassine, early American imports, Cold War copies of the communist *Vaillant*, *Ah Nana!*'s 1970s feminism, and so on …

The point of this section is not to go through every exponent of recent critical theory and find an aspect of BD that fits (as if to please a caricature of the 'trendy' intellectual that might influence an academic funding body), nor is it to provide a critical reading of bande dessinée that strongly favours a particular approach. What it hopefully does do is demonstrate that the intrinsic nature of BD leads to the same questions as those raised in the intellectual debate of the latter part of the twentieth century onwards.

We have seen that in some cases, specifically the publications by Quella-Guyot, Floch, or even Eco, different strands of critical approaches have already been applied to the BD. Further examples and analysis of precise critical readings are provided by Ann Miller in her excellent *Reading Bande Dessinée: Critical Approaches to French-Language Comic Strip* (2007),[29] and for this reason I have limited my own examination of currently available critical studies. But my aim has been to indicate that these do already exist, whilst, moreover, pointing to other areas where bande dessinée might be particularly apt for such investigation. Bande dessinée, by its form and through its history, is a prime example of the issues underpinning the worldwide Cultural Studies debate. Bourdieu could not have found a better example of the ambiguous overlap between 'high' and 'low' culture and Stuart Hall would be hard pressed to beat BD for a case of popular mass culture with clear aesthetic value. Above all, the bande dessinée is hybrid and interdisciplinary, and as such is a perfect representative of twenty-first-century expression.[30]

The Alternative: BD as Business

It is important to see the bande dessinée as an intrinsic element of popular culture and, by placing it alongside related intellectual movements such as Pop Art and the semiotics of the everyday image, examine the status of the BD in its wider context. But we should not forget that there is an alternative viewpoint: bande dessinée is big business.

As we have seen in the chapter on contemporary BD, sales of bandes dessinées occupy a place in the French book market that is far beyond any imaginable equivalent in the English-language world. This is not just in terms of overall volume – 2008 saw approximately 4,318 new BD publications,[31] with almost 160 different publishers regularly promising new titles, and, recently, a general sales pattern far better than that of books in general – but also with respect to blockbuster household-name titles. Long before it was released (and even before its title was announced), it was known that the thirty-third *Astérix* volume, *Le Ciel lui tombe sur la tête* (2005), with a print run of 3,075,000, would be the best-seller of 2005. Although Astérix is an unrivalled phenomenon, it is by no means an aberration, in that 2005 saw thirty-two other albums with print runs of over 100,000. These included Van Hamme and Vance's *XIII 17*, Philippe Francq and Van Hamme's *Largo Winch 14*, Binet's *Les Bidochon ont 25 ans* [The Bidochons are 25 Years Old], Jacques Martin and Rafaël Moralès's *Alix 24* and Tome and Janry's *Le Petit Spirou tome 12*.[32]

The business potential of the bande dessinée is not just limited to the books and journals themselves. During the economic recession of the 1980s the vast majority of the main postwar journal titles folded, including *Pif* (*Vaillant*'s successor), *Coeurs Vaillants, Tintin, Pilote* and *Métal Hurlant*. Notable exceptions were *Le Journal de Mickey* and *Fluide Glacial*, which are still going, and *Écho des Savanes*, relaunched under a new format (although with production suspended in December 2006), as well as a few titles (e.g., *Pilote, Métal Hurlant* and *Pif*) that have seen a nostalgia-based rebirth in the twenty-first century. As bande dessinée underwent the transformation from journal publications to album format, from ephemeral throwaway to bookish object, so the transformation to fetishist collectable, and thus higher guaranteed individual sales income, was accompanied by an increasing market for associated paraphernalia.

Figurines and spin-off products were by no means invented in the 1980s. Prior to the First World War *La Semaine de Suzette* carried advertisements for Bécassine-related products including dolls, board games and costumes, and the market was to continue from *Zig et Puce* through to *Astérix*. But it was in the 1980s that spin-off products came to occupy a sizeable part of the BD market, with a number of companies – Pixi, Leblon-Delienne, Aroutcheff – specialising in collectable figurines. A glance in the window of any specialist BD shop will confirm that this market continues, with often as much space given to statuettes as to the albums themselves. Similarly, a quick hunt on eBay for *Tintin* or *Blake et Mortimer* is likely to produce as many references to by-products as to the actual comics.

Nor are such products cheap. A 30 cm statuette of Bécassine retails at 460, an Aroutcheff scene of Tintin and Milou with the whisky train wagon from *L'Île noire* is valued at 1,600, whereas a signed *Astérix* chess set, albeit with sixteen Gaul pieces and sixteen Roman pieces, board and box, costs 2,200. As with any collectables it is important to have the numbered certificate of authenticity and the container.

These valuations are those given in the 2007–2008 edition of the *BDM*, which includes six chapters of some forty-five pages on figurines. The importance of the collectors' market for bandes dessinées can be seen in the success of this encyclopaedic valuation guide, *BDM* being the generally accepted shorthand based on the initials of the authors, Michel Bera, Michel Denis and Philippe Mella. It is to this label that later editions give increasing prominence, although the work retains its initial title of *Trésors de la bande dessinée*. Published bi-annually since 1979 by Éditions de l'Amateur of Paris, the *BDM* serves as the definitive *argus* of bande dessinée collecting, with the main sections arranged by journal publications and by albums. A separate work, the *CEJ*, exists for valuations of artists' signatures, for example given on special editions, bookmarks or promotional covers. The authors are Jean Charvy, Hergé Eschasseriau and Marc Jallon (thus *CEJ*), and the full title is *CEJ: Catalogue encyclopédique: La Signature dans la bande dessinée* (first ed. 1998).

According to the 2009–2010 edition of the *BDM*, for example, one could expect to pay 150 for the first *Journal de Mickey* (21 October 1934) or 1,200 for number 296, the final 1940 issue before the wartime break. A bound copy of 1930s issues of *Coeurs Vaillants* (the journal started in December 1929) is valued at 1,000 and a single copy of *Le Téméraire*'s first issue 120. Modern publications are of course more accessible, but the first number of *L'Écho des Savanes* (May 1972) is nonetheless 27 and that of *Pilote* (October 1959) 60. For albums the 35,000 given to the first issue of the 1930 *Tintin au pays des Soviets* is exceptional, but a 1961 first edition of *Astérix le Gaulois* nonetheless fetches 1,800.

The fact that bande dessinée is now big business goes far beyond the collectable value of individual rarities or even the strength of current sales, representing as they do a considerable slice of the overall publishing industry. Such potential brings the associated marketing strategies, with BD-related advertising being applied to products as diverse as Chanel, Air France and Elf, not only via direct publications, but also using related strategies, such as promotional games.[33]

Television and cinema spin-offs are also considerable. *Les Stroumpfs, Lucky Luke* and *Titeuf* have had – and continue to have – successful television adaptations, as have many other BDs, although this particular market is largely children-based. Not so for the cinema, as one of the earliest blockbuster steps from Ninth Art to Seventh Art was made by Roger Vadim's 1968 *Barbarella*, with the eponymous heroine played by a clearly not-for-children Jane Fonda. Not only have subsequent BD adaptations been plentiful,[34] but peripheral association, such as Moebius's heavy involvement in the concept design for blockbuster movies, has also been important.

Two old favourites deserve specific mention for different reasons. As well as spawning TV versions of the albums, an animated film of *Tintin et le Temple du Soleil* (1969, directed by Eddie Lateste) and a 2002 stage musical of the same name, two earlier productions, *Tintin et le mystère de la Toison d'Or* (1960, André Barret and Jean-Jacques Vierne) and *Tintin et les oranges bleues* (1964, Philippe Condroyer), are interesting in their choice of 'real-life' actors and of original scripts not based on albums. The boyish looks of Tintin actor Jean-Pierre Talbot are almost a throwback to the carefully staged Tintin appearances of the 1930s, as in a triumphal return to Brussels that saw the boy scout greeted by thousands. Long before the current vogue for spin-off fandom via such creations as *Harry Potter* or *Star Wars, Tintin* was an all-encompassing marketing phenomenon that used careful media placement to obtain optimal success for a product, a tradition that is likely to continue with Steven Spielberg's forthcoming adaptation of the adventures of Hergé's hero.[35]

There have been ten *Astérix* animation films, starting with the 1967 *Astérix le Gaulois* (directed by Ray Goossens), followed by seven other full-length animations up to and including the 2006 *Astérix et les Vikings* (directed by Stefan Fjeldmark and Jesper Møller). But it is the 'live action' films that have made the big money. Claude Zidi's 1999 *Astérix et Obélix contre César*, starring Christian Clavier and Gérard Depardieu as the eponymous duo, was a moderate success for what, at the time was one of France's highest-costing films. It was overshadowed by Alain Chabat's 2002 *Astérix et Obélix: Mission Cléopâtre*, starring Clavier and Depardieu once again, but very much updating the album upon which it was based. Its entry figures in excess of 14,000,000 made it the second-placed French film of all time after *La Grande Vadrouille* (1966), but assured it financial success far in excess of that of the latter. A third 'live action' production, *Astérix aux Jeux Olympiques* (directed by Frédéric Forestier and Thomas Langmann), featuring cameos from such personalities as Tony Parker and Zinedine Zidane, was released early in 2008. It is likely to be confirmed as the most expensive European film made to date, although its success both critically and in box-office terms has been limited.[36]

BD-based entertainment also comes in the form of theme parks, of which Parc Astérix is the second most popular in France. The Astérix extravaganza, which opened in 1989 approximately 30 km north of Paris, operates very much along the lines of American parks, offering a mixture of themed entertainment, such as a reconstruction of the Gallic village complete with costumed characters, and thrill rides, including the *Tonnerre de Zeus* [Zeus's Thunder], one of the fastest wooden roller-coasters in Europe. According to the parent company Grévin's 2002 information document,[37] in 2001 Parc Astérix received approximately 1.8 million visitors, with a turnover of 61,600,000, thereby representing 60.9 per cent of the Grévin group as a whole.

One of Parc Astérix's main fears, that it would be hit by the 1992 opening of what was then EuroDisney, did not materialise, since the two attractions tend to complement each other by appealing to different markets. Indeed initially Parc Astérix cashed in on Disney's poor integration strategies. Despite the economic context appearing to play in the new park's favour – it provided much needed employment and thus had received considerable government subsidies – the anti-Disney backlash, figure-headed by Ariane Mnouchkine's highly mediacised description of the venture as a 'Chernobyl culturel', was based largely on reasons of perceived cultural disdain. The company had installed an American managing director, Robert Fitzpatrick, with a view to creating a slice of authentic America in Europe. Basic lifestyle clashes, such as the non-availability of alcohol with meals or the requirement that workers conform to draconic appearance dictates (no beards [dwarfs excepted], no ostensible jewellery …), led to ethical protests and dampened the park's allure.

Disneyland Paris's 1995 directional rethink (including the new name) unwittingly renewed the formula by which Paul Winckler had first introduced Mickey to France. The eye-catching American razzamatazz was still the initial attraction, but in a context that would entice the indigenous population, as well as visitors from further afield.

Restaurants were overhauled, going as far as to receive Gault Millau awards, working regulations were relaxed (officially at least), but above all a new emphasis was laid upon Disney within a European context. The reworking of parades underlined the cultural heritage of Charles Perrault and the Brothers Grimm, the urban architecture of the new Disney Studios park provides a constant reminder of European landmarks in the development of the moving image, and new shows trace the influence of European literature, bande dessinée and cinema. It appears to be working, since at the end of 2004 Disneyland Paris announced its intention to realise a capital increase of 250,000,000 with a view to a Val-de-France expansion that will include four new hotels, an IMAX complex and a sporting Golf Disney. As France's number one tourist attraction, Disneyland Paris parallels the 1934 *Journal de Mickey* that changed the face of the country's youth culture.[38]

All of these associated areas, and others such as the blurring of boundaries between bande dessinée and *dessin animé*, could easily sustain in-depth individual research. They are an intrinsic part of the current BD world, and indeed of the broader make-up of French-language culture, but the place of this study is not to give a full overview of cartoon-based advertising or a history of the Astérix theme park.[39]

Nor should we forget that even when taking a commercial viewpoint on BD there are nuances and differences of opinion as to the optimum strategy, a debate that can very generally be summarised as sales-driven corporate business versus independent art-house production. As of January 2008 75.6 per cent of the French bande dessinée market, in terms of numbers of copies sold, is divided between five major publishing houses:[40]

Groupe Média Participations
(includes Dargaud and Dupuis as well as Lombard, Lucky Comics, Blake et Mortimer and Kana)
34.6 per cent of the market in terms of copies sold
Approximate annual sales for 2007 of 147,300,000

Groupe Glénat
(includes Vents d'Ouest)
15.8 per cent of the market in terms of copies sold
Approximate annual sales for 2007 of 71,000,000

Delcourt
(includes Tonkam)
9.4 per cent of the market in terms of copies sold
Approximate annual sales for 2007 of 47,600,000

Groupe Flammarion
(includes Casterman, Sakka, Jungle, Fluide Glacial and J'ai Lu)
8.3 per cent of the market in terms of copies sold
Approximate annual sales for 2007 of 88,000,000

Groupe MC Productions
(includes Soleil)
7.5 per cent of the market in terms of copies sold
Approximate annual sales for 2007 of 37,200,000

The remaining 24.4 per cent of sales is generally distributed between smaller independent publishers such as Frémok, Cornélius, Ego Comme X or Les Requins Marteaux, many of whom have blossomed since the 1990s.

The most militant of these is L'Association, whose credo and practical effects have been discussed in Chapters 3 and 7. In short, Jean-Christophe Menu, the driving force behind L'Association, advocates a publishing policy that provides an alternative to the standard format and subject matter, encourages stylistic experimentation and new-name authors, whilst providing a viable financial structure – as demonstrated by the success of Marjane Satrapi – without this being the be all and end all.[41] However, as was pointed out at a 2005 French National Library (BnF) conference in response to an attack from Menu on bland big-business publishing strategies, without 'mainstream' BD publishing, 'alternatives' could not exist. This is not just a case of pragmatic logic, but also economic infrastructure. It is the mainstream publishing houses that promote the bande dessinée as a whole, be it as an art form or as a consumable commodity, and in so doing encourage a level of interest that leaves room for the purchase of lesser-known creations. As we have seen in our previous chapter, in recent years a further twist has been added through the development of 'alternative' series out of mainstream companies, as in Dargaud's 'Poisson Pilote'. These give further credence to the viability of Menu's strategies, whilst expanding the range of products that can be included in the BD market.

If we thus revisit the conclusion to our last chapter but from a potentially wider viewpoint, we can see that the debate as to whether the bande dessinée is an art form or a business enterprise is too clear-cut – some would even say Manichean – to produce a satisfactory final answer. It is of course both, in the same way that literature, music and cinema all operate within the framework of money-driven consumer society that creates and promotes them. As with the above section on bande dessinée and critical theory, this book does not claim to be exhaustive. It is hoped, however, that the reader will now be aware of the issues and debates, and understand that the study of bande dessinée involves not just literature, art, history, philosophy and sociology, but also economics and business management. It is also hoped that if – or rather when – a particular angle proves inspiring, he or she will follow up the footnotes and maybe even the footnotes in the footnoted works.

Notes

1. That said, there is an element of contradiction, in France at least, in the bande dessinée's high-profile media but low-profile academic status. This question is explored further in our next chapter, and, more generally, in Thierry Groensteen's *Un Objet culturel non identifié* [An Unidentified Cultural Object] ([Angoulême]: Éditions de l'An 2, 2006).
2. See, for example, Simon Wilson, *Pop* (London: Thames and Hudson, 1974) and Marco Livingstone, *Pop Art: A Continuing History* (London: Thames and Hudson, 1990). A concise guide is also available as a spin-off of the Centre Pompidou exhibition, *Les Années Pop* [The Pop Years]: Christophe Domino, *Les Années Pop* (Paris: Centre Pompidou, 2001). On the specific overlap between BD and Pop Art, see Jean-Paul Gabilliet, 'De L'Art pop au Pop Art: Les Comics et l'art contemporain: Quelques Repères' [From Popular Art to Pop Art: Comics and Contemporary Art: A Guide], *Le Collectionneur de Bandes Dessinées* 94 (2001), 14–23.
3. See, for example, Norman F. Cantor and Michael S. Werthman, eds, *The History of Popular Culture* (New York: Macmillan, 1968). Despite being somewhat dated, this work still gives a good general overview from the Ancient Greeks to the Hippies.
4. See Arturo Schwarz, *The Complete Works of Marcel Duchamp*, 2 vols. (New York: Delano Greenidge, 1997 [first ed., London: Thames and Hudson, 1969]), volume 2, pp. 648–50.
5. On Lichtenstein, see, for example, Diane Waldman, *Roy Lichtenstein* (New York: Abrams, 1971). On Warhol, see, for example, Victor Bockris, *The Life and Death of Andy Warhol* (London: Fourth Estate, 1998 [first ed., New York: Bantam, 1989]).
6. Here and elsewhere I do not reference the holding gallery or collector as many of the Pop Art works mentioned exist in numerous versions and copies, sometimes as prints. In the bibliography I have included such works under the generic medium of 'Painting' and have indicated one of the holders.
7. For a comprehensive coverage of Lichtenstein's comic book sources, see the 'Deconstructing Roy Lichtenstein' website (http://davidbarsalou.homestead.com/LICHTENSTEINPROJECT.html). See also Bradford R. Collins, 'Modern Romance: Lichtenstein's Comic Book Paintings', *American Art* 17.2 (2003), 60–85.
8. The work of L'Association and of OuBaPo have been discussed in the previous chapter.
9. Bande dessinée and three-dimensionality will be explored further in our chapter 'Cultural Studies and Beyond'.
10. Rancillac, Fromanger and Télémaque can also be classed under the wide label of *Figuration Narrative*, as was the case for the Paris, Grand Palais, 2008 exhibition, *Figuration Narrative: Paris, 1960–1972*. Although rich in interesting examples, the exhibition made little attempt to contextualise *Figuration Narrative* as a potential movement, or in terms of other more clearly defined movements such as *Nouveau Réalisme*, or, more generally, Pop Art. The exhibition catalogue, *Figuration Narrative: Paris, 1960–1972* (Paris: Réunion des Musées Nationaux, 2008; no given author) is also available.
11. On the subject see Pierre Restany's later *60/90: Trente ans de Nouveau Réalisme* [60/90: Thirty Years of *Nouveau Réalisme*] (Paris: La Différence, 1990).
12. *Avanies et mascarades: L'Évolution de la bande dessinée en France dans les années 70* [Affronts and Mascarades: The Evolution of the Bande Dessinée in France in the 1970s] (Paris: Futuropolis, 1981).

13. (Paris: Futuropolis, 1983).
14. The catalogue to *Bande dessinée et figuration narrative*, bearing the same title, was produced by Pierre Couperie, Destefanis Proto and Claude Moliterni (Paris: Musée des Arts Décoratifs, [1967]).
15. That is not to say that Pop Art is the only movement in postwar art, but rather to pinpoint Pop Art as indicative of a visual culture that was breaking down the distinction between high art and low art, and which in many ways followed a parallel path to that of the modern bande dessinée.
16. On the notion of Cultural Studies, see, for example, Jill Forbes and Mike Kelly, eds, *French Cultural Studies: An Introduction* (Oxford: Oxford University Press, 1995).
17. Roland Barthes, *Œuvres complètes*, ed. Éric Marty, 3 vols. (Paris: Seuil, 1993–1995).
18. All of these, and other pieces on the status of the image (e.g., via painting or advertising) and its place in modern culture, are available, as the title would suggest, in the *Œuvres complètes*. The original places of publication are diverse. The discussion of Barthes and bande dessinée that follows draws upon much material included in my '*Bande Dessinée*: The Missing *Mythologie*', *Mythologies at 50: Barthes and Popular Culture* (*Nottingham French Studies* Special Number 47.2), ed. Douglas Smith (Nottingham: University of Nottingham, 2008), pp. 29-40.
19. Barthes gave prominence to a notion that was by no means new. On this see John Storey, *Cultural Consumption and Everyday Life* (London: Arnold, 1999).
20. The edition followed is that of 1970 (Paris: Seuil).
21. This pricing is for the first issue of the 1930 *Tintin au pays des Soviets* as given by Michel Béra, Michel Denni and Philippe Melot in *Trésors de la bande dessinée 2009–2010* (Paris: Éditions de l'Amateur, 2008).
22. Ann Miller discusses Bourdieu's work at some length in *Reading Bande Dessinée: Critical Approaches to French-Language Comic Strip* (Bristol: Intellect, 2007). See in particular her chapter 10, 'Social Class and Masculinity' (pp. 179–96).
23. The article was later published as the leading chapter in *Il Superuomo di massia: Studi sul romenzo popolare* [The Superman of the Masses: Studies on the Popular Novel] (Milan: Cooperativa Scrittori, 1978). *Giff-Wiff* will be discussed further in our next chapter in the context of the consecration of the bande dessinée. Eco's studies of popular culture, in particular that of James Bond, will be discussed further in our chapter 'Cultural Studies and Beyond'.
24. Ferdinand de Saussure, in his posthumously published *Cours de linguistique générale* [Course in General Linguistics] (1915), suggests that language is an arbitrary system of signs (e.g., the word 'table' has no intrinsic link to a four-legged piece of furniture). Using the terms *signifiant* [signifier] and *signifié* [signified] he explores the way in which our view of the objects around us is moulded by the connotations of the terms we use to describe them.
25. Jean-Marie Floch, *Une Lecture de Tintin au Tibet* [A Reading of Tintin in Tibet] (Paris: Presses Universitaires de France, 1997); Didier Quella-Guyot, *Lire Tintin au Tibet de Hergé: Lecture Méthodique et documentaire* [Reading Hergé's *Tintin in Tibet*: A Methodological and Documentary Approach] (Poitiers: Le Torii, 1990).
26. This is a retrospective album edition uniting the various episodes that originally appeared in *Métal Hurlant* from 1976 onwards. For further analysis of this work, including illustrations, see my *Text/Image Mosaics in French Culture: Emblems and Comic Strips* (Aldershot: Ashgate, 2005). See also Chapter 3 on Formal Specificity.

27. On the notion of 'bricolage' within the context of Early Modern text/image forms, see Daniel Russell, 'The Emblem and Authority', *Word & Image* 4.1 (1988), 81–87.
28. Edward Said, *Orientalism* (London: Routledge, 1978).
29. This is an update of her doctoral thesis, 'Contemporary *Bande Dessinée*: Contexts, Critical Approaches and Case Studies' (University of Newcastle, 2003).
30. For an in-depth exploration of this last question that draws upon specific BD-based case studies, see my *Text/Image Mosaics in French Culture: Emblems and Comic Strips.*
31. This statistic is taken from page 72 of *Livres Hebdo* 761 (23 January 2009). *Livres Hebdo* remains the clearest way of obtaining statistics concerning BD sales: it provides an overview of new bande dessinée releases as they occur, as well as reviewing the market in regular features in August and January.
32. See *Livres Hebdo* 610 (26 August 2005), in particular the 'Dossier BD' on pp. 132–63.
33. See Alain Lachartre, *Objectif pub: La Bande dessinée et la publicité, hier et aujourd'hui* [Destination Ads: Bande Dessinée and Advertising Yesterday and Today] (Paris: Rober Laffont, 1986). See also the section on 'La BD publicitaire' [BD in Advertising] in recent editions of the *BDM*.
34. Again, for a listing of cinema productions based closely on comics of all national traditions, see 'Bande dessinée et cinéma', pp. 1585–695 of Claude Moliterni, Philippe Mellot, Laurent Turpin, Michel Denni and Nathalie Michel-Szelechowska, *BDGuide 2005: Encyclopédie de la bande dessinée internationale* (Paris: Omnibus, 2004).
35. On the subject of the recent marketing strategy of Hergé's estate, see Mark McKinney, 'Georges Remi's Legacy: Between Half-Hidden History, Modern Myth, and Mass Marketing', *International Journal of Comic Art* 9.2 (2007), 68–80. See also Hugues Dayez, *Tintin et les héritiers: Chronique de l'après-Hergé* [Tintin and the Heirs: A Post-Hergé Chronical] (Paris: Félin, 1999).
36. This brief section is intended to do little more than remind the reader of the position of the BD-based film as an important business phenomenon. The more general question of the overlap between BD and cinema has been discussed in Chapter 3 on Formal Specificity.
37. Grévin et Cie., *Document de référence 2001* [Reference Document 2001] (Plailly: Grévin et Cie, 2002). This is the most recent of such documents available in the Bibliothèque nationale de France.
38. For these and further financial updates, as well as a reliable overview of the park's history and current status, see: www.dlp-guidebook.de.
39. That said, the phenomenon of BD-related theme parks and 3D exhibitions will be discussed briefly in the chapter 'Cultural Studies and Beyond'.
40. The figures that follow are taken from the 'Dossier BD' on pp. 76–108 of *Livres Hebdo* 717 (18 January 2008), in particular p. 78. I refer to the statistics for 2007 as those for 2008 given in *Livres Hebdo* 761 (23 January 2009) do not include sales figures. As might be expected, sales remain largely divided between the five major groups, with slight percentage variations.
41. Menu presents and discusses his editorial policy in *Plates-bandes* (Paris: L'Association, 2005). This work is briefly analysed in the previous chapter.

Chapter 9

Consecration of the Ninth Art: Meaningful Ecos or *Circus* Clones?

The History of the History

To consider the bande dessinée as a cultural phenomenon implies what may be obvious from this book's original subtitle – 'The Ninth Art' – namely that in French-speaking countries (principally, but not exclusively, France and Belgium) the form has received critical attention that in itself is now part of the phenomenon.[1] As one of the first general accounts of the bande dessinée in English, an important aim of this current book is to provide suggestions as to possible readings that the form might sustain, as well as compiling a detached (as far as such is possible) overview of the canonisation that has already occurred in its home countries.

This may be one of the clearest ways into the tricky question of national specificity. Why is it that Hergé features prominently in the Belgian pantheon and Astérix provides the metaphor for national heroes such as Zinedine Zidane, whereas in Scotland, for example, the long life of *The Dandy* is equated with generations of train spotters? This is a problem that is unlikely to produce definitive answers, but an overview of critical developments up to the setting up of the Centre National de la Bande Dessinée et de l'Image, and a glance at circumstances surrounding the dubious debate that saw Rodolphe Töpffer crowned as inventor of the BD, go some of the way to presenting certain central issues.[2]

Although there is relatively little secondary criticism in English on the bande dessinée,[3] this particular area is an exception, but unfortunately not all the key works in question are yet easily available. Ann Miller's 2003 doctoral thesis has, however, been updated to her *Reading Bande Dessinée: Critical Approaches to French-Language Comic Strip* (2007) and, as the title suggests, demonstrates the critical possibilities offered by the bande dessinée, whilst contextualising this via a thorough outline of previous approaches to the form from the nineteenth to the twenty-first centuries. Elizabeth

McQuillan's 2001 University of Glasgow doctoral thesis, 'The Reception and Creation of Post-1960 Franco-Belgian BD', is important not only as the first UK PhD on the bande dessinée, but as one of the only works to examine the current success of the bande dessinée from an angle of detachment and as a subject per se.

This present section will draw heavily on McQuillan's work on the basis that a series of footnotes merely referring to an unpublished dissertation may well have left the reader frustrated. In particular I have relied upon the third section of her Introduction, 'The Institutionalisation of the BD as National Asset' (pp. 35–50) and Chapter I, 'The Intellectualisation of the BD: Critical Responses from 1960 to the Present' (pp. 51–92). This chapter contains three main sections: '*Giff-Wiff*, Metalanguage and Fandom', 'BD à l'université' and 'BD et bédéité'. It is nonetheless hoped that sections of the thesis, if not all of it, will become more widely available in the future.[4]

The Time-line Method

By presenting the reception of the bande dessinée in chronological 'time-line' fashion I hope to provide a concise overview of main events that have taken the BD into the twenty-first century with a status on a possible par with cinema and literature. This method also allows me to synthesise McQuillan and Miller's findings in a 'reader friendly' way, whilst tipping my hat to a landmark of the history under examination: in 1975 Luc Boltanski published one of the first attempts to outline constructively the social phenomenon that was the bande dessinée. Botanski's article, 'La Constitution du champ de la bande dessinée' [The Constitution of the Bande Dessinée's Field of Study], which appeared on pages 37–59 of the first volume (January 1975) of *Actes de la Recherche en Science Sociales*, founded by Pierre Bourdieu, included a time-line section (pp. 55–59), the 'Chronologie de l'entreprise de canonisation de la B D' [A Chronology of the Undertaking to Canonise the BD].

There are drawbacks to a time-line history of the consecration of the BD. A time-line implies a series of monumental events that led to overnight change, which is rarely the case. The consecration of the bande dessinée involves a gradual modification of public attitude and a shift in mentality towards an acceptance of new visual culture. A time-line also baits the trap of retrospective historicism, allowing us to accord importance to events that at the time may have been perceived in an entirely different fashion.

These caveats notwithstanding, the time-line does provide an idea of some of the key events, people, documents and attitudes that have contributed to the BD's growth in status. In an ideal world the reader will consult this time-line, following up its references, seeking out copies of *Giff-Wiff* or *Phénix*, reading some of the early monographs from the 1970s and 1980s, or even, quite simply, chatting with those who have grown up with French comics.

Pre-1920s

In line with the vociferous crowning of Rodolphe Töpffer as inventor of the bande dessinée – see my chapters on the early history of the form – French-language criticism overlooks, underplays or distorts the fact that prior to the 1920s the bande dessinée did not exist as a critical entity.[5]

That is not to say that Töpffer did not comment on his own work or on the nature of text/image narrative: quite the contrary – something we have seen in the previous part of this book – as not only did he publish on photography and on the role of the image in general, his 'Annonce de l'histoire de M. Jabot' of 1837 famously points to the interdependence of text and image in *M. Jabot*. But as such he is just one in a long line of theoreticians of the image. To take but one example, in the 1577 preface to his edition of Andrea Alciato's *Emblemata*, Claude Mignault similarly analyses the relative roles of text and image in the work:

> ... commodè incidit in manus meas Alciati liber Emblematum, quem recèns nobis Lugduno advectum, & aliquot annis antè, Pariisiis excusum, noveram à philologis omnibus non minimùm commendari. [...] Nemo nescit picturam esse poëma tacens, poësim verò picturam loquentem: illa quidem refert animum, hæc corpus. Quo fit ut earum rerum tam multiplicium novitas ... (19–20)

> [...Alciato's book of Emblems conveniently fell into my hands. It has recently arrived from Lyon and had a few years previously been composed in Paris. I had known of it as highly recommended by everyone of learning. [...] Everyone knows that the picture is a silent poem, and the poetry is indeed a talking picture: whereas the latter provides the soul, the former provides the body. Which makes for the novelty of these multifaceted things ...]

Works on Töpffer published in or around his lifetime are relatively scarce, the only book-length studies being Auguste Blondel's *Rodolphe Töpffer: L'Écrivain, l'artiste et l'homme* [Rodolphe Töpffer: The Writer, the Artist and the Man] (1886),[6] and l'Abbé Pierre-Maxime Relave's *Rodolphe Töpffer: Biographie et extraits* (1899). In both these cases emphasis is very much on Töpffer's life, his work as a journalist, as a teacher and as a tourist. When his BDs, as we now know them, are mentioned, as for example on page vii of the 'Préface des éditeurs' of an early edition of the *Voyages en zigzag*,[7] they are viewed not in terms of the originality of the text/image form, but rather with reference to the characterisation. In this example the 'BDs' are merely labelled 'histoires comiques' [comic stories] and the editors concentrate on the personalities and actions of M. Jabot, M. Vieux Bois and M. Crépin.

More generally, the *Dictionnaire historique & bibliographique de la Suisse* has no entry for Töpffer,[8] nor does the *Grande Encyclopédie* of circa 1890.[9] The *Grand Dictionnaire universel du XIX siècle* [The Great

Universal Dictionary of the Nineteenth Century] does dedicate three columns to him,[10] but once again these are largely biographical, underlining Töpffer's role as an artist. There is no mention of the notion of text/image interaction or of narration through pictures.

In short, the view that modern bande dessinée studies present of Rodolphe Töpffer is very much a retrospective one, certainly not a reflection of the analysis of the time. Thierry Groensteen's summary of the beginnings of the BD, 'Töpffer en est bel et bien l'inventeur' [Töpffer is well and truly the inventor],[11] might be contrasted with the 1886 view of things as presented by Blondel:

> En résumé, il ne faut pas chercher dans les albums de caricature de Töpffer autre chose que ce qu'ils étaient pour leur auteur, un passe-temps. (118)
>
> [In short, we should not look for anything more in Töpffer's caricature albums than what they were for their author, a pastime.]

1920s to 1940s

The first self-aware commentaries on the bande dessinée, even if the form was not yet named as such, date from the second quarter of the twentieth century. And although this is considered to be the Golden Age of comics and is also the period that saw the switch to a new level of mass popularity due to the success of *Le Journal de Mickey*, BD criticism, or even acknowledgement of the value of the form in an artistic context, was still relatively rare. When analysts did pass comment on what they described as *histoires en images, histoires illustrés* or *récits imagés* it was generally to criticise or warn of moral consequences. As we have seen in Chapter 6 on the Twentieth Century, Marie-Thérèse Latzarus's *La Littérature enfantine en France dans la seconde moitié du XIX siècle* of 1924 typifies this stance.

Towards the end of the war D. Parker and C. Renaudy prefigured Fredric Wertham's *Seduction of the Innocent: The Influence of 'Horror Comics' on Today's Youth* (1954) by a decade with their *La Démoralisation de la jeunesse par les publications périodiques* (Cartel d'Action Morale, 1944), a pamphlet outlining the moral ills of society that classed the *illustrés* alongside pornography. The Cartel d'Action Morale, like the Ligue de l'Enseignement [Teaching League] and the Union des Oeuvres Catholiques [Union of Catholic Works], was one of a number of groups concerned with public morality in the immediate postwar period. Although their initial approaches would differ depending on the founding base of the group (Catholic, pedagogical…), in general they were conservative and as such opposed to the changes that the new wave of *illustrés* could be perceived as bringing.

A decade later Jean de Trignon, in his *Histoire de la littérature enfantine de Ma Mère l'Oye au Roi Babar* (1950), was continuing the condemnation:

> La Presse enfantine connut à partir de 1880 un double courant. D'une part, croissance en nombre, mais d'autre part, avilissement de qualité. (166)
>
> [The press for children underwent a two-pronged development as from 1880: on one hand the number of publications increased, on the other the quality became more and more degrading.]

As late as 1957 Jacqueline and Raoul Dubois in *La Presse enfantine française* were clear in their disapproval:

> Car rien n'est plus affligeant que la bêtise générale des histoires racontées en images par les illustrés; aucune ne supporte une analyse un peu sérieuse. (6)
>
> [For nothing is more distressing than the general stupidity of the stories that the illustrated publications tell through pictures; none of them could withstand analysis of even the slightest depth.]

As we saw in our outline of the twentieth-century history of the BD, this undercurrent is not overly surprising viewed in the context of the period that saw the 1949 law and then the knock-on effect of Fredric Wertham's *Seduction of the Innocent*, sections of which had appeared in translation in France. The bande dessinée lacked definition, and attempts to analyse the phenomenon as it was perceived were generally limited to the resulting harm, rather than possible positive effects or any intrinsic value.[12]

1950s

The 1950s saw the first studies to consider the BD as an object of value per se rather than as part of a wider – by implication damaging – social trend. Barthélemy Amengual's *Le Petit Monde de Pif le chien: Essai sur un 'comic' français* [The Little World of Pif the Dog: An Essay on a French 'Comic'] (1955) was essentially a study of the theme of childhood in the popular *Vaillant* series, although it does include a section on the technical specificity of expression through BD. Interestingly, this piece has largely been overlooked. This may be because its non-metropolitan publication (Algiers) makes it harder to access, or perhaps because *Pif le chien* has not received the cult status enjoyed by other series.

More attention has been given to Edgar Morin's considerably shorter 'Tintin héros d'une génération' [Tintin Hero of a Generation] that appeared in the monthly social science journal *La Nef* [The Vessel] in January 1958.[13] Here, and in his later monograph *L'Esprit du temps* [The Spirit of the Time] (1962), which includes a piece on BD under the section on the press, Morin analyses the BD for its role as a cultural phenomenon, drawing, in the 1958 piece, upon the specific case of *Tintin*. The retrospective success of this work may be due to Morin's credible status as a leading sociologist, his use of references, such as to the work of Roland Barthes, that now ennoble the form, or the choice of a figure, the Belgian boy scout, now recognised as worthy of nostalgic, academic and pleasure-based adulation. Tellingly, Pol Vandromme's full-length literary analysis, *Le Monde de Tintin* [The World of Tintin] (1959), was to appear the following year. What is interesting is that it is at the same time as critical theory is starting to (re)examine the everyday, specifically through *Mythologies* (as we have seen in the previous chapter), that bande dessinée is taking its first steps as a possible subject of positive intellectual attention.

1962–1975

The notion of BD criticism as a self-conscious body of scholarly activity, rather than a set of isolated works, came into being in the 1960s. The sci-fi magazine *Fiction*, which at first glance might appear to have little link with BD beyond the cover art by Jean-Claude Forest of *Barbarella* fame, was the initial forum for discussions on the founding of a 'Club des Bandes Dessinées', whose stated aim would largely be to reprint favourites from the Golden Age of comics. Following a questionnaire and various articles on science fiction and bandes dessinées, an unsigned announcement in issue number 98 of January 1962 noted, on page 143, that 'ce club est prêt à se former' [this club is ready to be formed].[14]

In hindsight the early days of the Club des Bandes Dessinées, or CBD, was very much a gathering of enthusiastic friends around what was effectively a nostalgic pastime. Early numbers of the Club's journal, *Giff-Wiff*,[15] founded in July 1962, appear amateurish: essentially they are stapled-together photocopies, with hand-drawn graphics where relevant, as in the presentation in number 3 that outlines the geographic whereabouts of the club's members.[16] On the other hand, these numbered approximately 300, a satisfactory figure for any fledgling association, so it is entirely reasonable to attribute the 'home-made' look to the limits of the available publishing technology in the pre-desktop-publishing era.

Early articles tended to be 'antiquarian' in tone, giving the publishing history of comics classics, or through themes, as in Guy-Claude Bonnemaison's review piece on the history of speech bubbles that appeared in number 8,[17] and the Umberto Eco article on Superman of number 11.[18] The account of the AGM in number 7 indicates the presence of Paul Winckler and Edgar Morin, in addition to the main instigators: Francis Lacassin, the University of Paris semiologist, Alain Resnais, the New Wave film director, Pierre Couperie of the École des Hautes Études Historiques, and Jean-Claude Forest.[19] Even if these names were generally not as renowned in 1962 as they are now, they still represent an important cross-section of French avant-garde intelligentsia. This is in keeping with the Club's general membership, as outlined in issue 3,[20] whereby the vast majority were found to be Paris-based professionals, including approximately 15 per cent with journalistic or cinema-related careers.

A closer look at this apparent contradiction – a 'fan club' of enthusiasts with a photocopied fanzine, yet a well-supported gathering of some of the most respected creators and critics of the time – can give us some clues about the reasons for the very specific nature of the bande dessinée. Firstly, what the library documents cannot tell us is the undercurrent prior to the initial postings in *Fiction*. There must presumably have been discussions amongst friends, exchanges in the *marchés de vieux papiers*, nostalgic research requests made to the sellers on the banks of the Seine. Those who enjoyed the fantasy of science fiction presumably remembered and valued *Guy L'Éclair* and *Les Pionniers de l'Espérance*. But similar conditions prevail for other hobbies, such as stamp collecting and train spotting, and these are by no means national art forms.

It is circumstance that makes the difference, and in the case of the BD three specific conditions moulded its development:

- the centralisation of all forms of cultural pursuits upon Paris;
- the propagation of intellectual activity outwith a university environment;
- the specific attraction of a form of visual culture in 1962.

The centralisation of Paris meant that those interested in the bande dessinée, or any other cultural form in France, could meet on a regular basis for informal discussion and exchange. The 'hobby' was perhaps not reason enough to instigate meetings, but geographical circumstance meant the meetings could and presumably did take place. Contacts could be made, a casual circle of friends established and widened, until the informal discussions were frequent and tight-knit enough to warrant further developments via the pages of *Fiction*. Still today much of France's intellectual innovation has its embryonic stages in the corridors of the Bibliothèque nationale de France (BnF); those working in the 'provinces' live nonetheless in Paris, and discussions on even the most non-Parisian of subjects are held in the capital.[21]

The CBD grew essentially from what was a shared nostalgic hobby, with the result that it was not defined from a university standpoint, even if two of its leading members, Lacassin and Couperie, were academics. The fond memories of childhood readings led to description and analysis with popularist appeal, whilst intellectualising elements, such as the contributions of the young Umberto Eco, or, later, Raymond Queneau, were to lend a different sort of credibility. The tradition has continued to this day, with much of the most solid BD scholarship, such as that of the *Collectionneur de Bandes Dessinées* team or the bi-annual *Trésors de la bande dessinée* (otherwise known as *BDM*) remaining the work of dedicated amateurs or specialised publishers or booksellers. As we have seen in our

Introduction, there are very few BD specialists in post as such within French universities, and the national research body, the CNRS (Centre National de la Recherche Scientifique), does not recognise BD as an area for appointment, under the apparent claim that its interdisciplinarity defies their categorisation.[22] On the other hand, much research is carried out via the CNBDI, whose publication, *9e Art*, receives aid from the Centre National du Livre or National Centre for the Book, as do many BDs and BD-related publications. Similarly the BnF mounted a major exhibition, *Maîtres de la bande dessinée européenne* [Masters of the European Bande Dessinée], in 2000–2001 and members of the Académie Française, such as Michel Serres, are known to take an interest in and publish on the subject.

Finally, the fact that BD criticism should leave the starting blocks in 1962 has much to do with the particular circumstances of that era. Technical reasons such as further advances in professional mass printing and the wider availability of cinematographic equipment were giving greater prominence to new visual culture, and to a certain extent allowed BD to ride on the crest of the New Wave. A widespread interest in popular culture through Barthes's *Mythologies* and the worldwide influence of Marshall McLuhan's notions of the new visual Gutenberg galaxy made comic strips, a named 'cool' medium, attractive to cinema-based intellectuals as well as to the general public.

But let us return to our time-line, and the fan-based culture of the 1960s that was, in the wake of *Giff-Wiff* and the CBD, starting to establish the bande dessinée as an object of critical attention in France. A first step was the transformation of the CBD into the much more grandiose CELEG or Centre d'Étude des Littératures d'Expression Graphique [Centre for the Study of Literatures of Graphic Expression]. Two years after *Giff-Wiff*'s initial issue a splinter group wishing further to emphasise the literary attributes of the BD in deference to its nostalgic value, formed SOCERLID, or the Société Civile d'Études et de Recherches des Littératures Dessinées [Civil Society for the Study of and for Research into Drawn Literatures]. October 1966 saw the first issue of SOCERLID's associated journal *Phénix*, the title presumably being a reference to post-1949 rebirth of interest in the BD. *Phénix* was to mix scholarly analysis (for example an article on Töpffer by François Caradec in number 43, thus as early as 1975),[23] interviews with creators, accounts of festivals worldwide and an overview of the latest publications, thereby in many ways providing the format that was to be followed by the *Collectionneur de Bandes Dessinées*. It is interesting, however, to note that even by the mid-1970s the list of fifteen foreign correspondents did not include any representatives from the British Isles.

A further by-product of SOCERLID's activities was the 1967 exhibition at the Musée des Arts Décoratifs in Paris, *Bande dessinée et figuration narrative*.[24] In hindsight this may not appear to be a particularly forward-looking display,[25] one whose BD content was based largely on reproductions of chosen *planches* (see Fig. 37), but it did put out certain important pointers in terms of the BD's evolving consecration. Firstly, and most obviously, bande dessinée had been deemed worthy of a Parisian national institution, an accolade that was to be mirrored by the 2000–2001 BnF exhibition. Perhaps more significantly, the Ninth Art, as it had been labelled since 1964,[26] was being examined in the context of other arts, as the exhibition looked at the links between BD and *Nouveau Réalisme* and Pop Art, including display of some Lichtenstein works.

The first self-conscious analysis of the workings of the bande dessinée in terms of its text/image interaction appears to have been by Elisabeth Gerin in *Tout sur la presse enfantine* (1958). Here, Gerin gives examples of cases in which the text explains the image or, conversely, of the 'triomphe de l'image', as well as analysing the different uses and presentations of text (e.g., 'ballons') in terms of the narration. The first self-conscious historical analysis of the 'BD' as a genre per se seems to have been a Remo Forlani *histoire en images* series that appeared from 1961 at regular intervals in *Pilote*. In the first episode of the series, *Le Roman vrai des bandes dessinées*, the project is described as 'une histoire qui n'avait jamais encore été écrite' [a story that thus far had never been written], an epithet that to all intents and purposes appears accurate. We should note, however, that for the author of the series, the 'inventor' of the modern bande dessinée is R.F. Outcault, the creator of *Yellow Kid* (1895), with Rodolphe Töpffer receiving no mention.

The latter part of the 1960s and the early 1970s saw a number of BD-dedicated works successfully applying a breadth of critical approaches. The outlets in which they appeared, academic journals and university presses, also suggest an emphasis far different from the popular appeal of a series in *Pilote*, however great its erudition. McQuillan refers to the 1970s as the 'university' stage of BD's critical progress, the one after fandom but before journalism.[27] This would appear to be an accurate summary of the development in question, although we should be aware that there is always overlap and exceptions to neat classifications.

As early as 1966 Evelyne Sullerot explored the bande dessinée as a sociological phenomenon in *Bande dessinée et culture*, whilst Gérard Blanchard's 1969 *La Bande dessinée: Histoire des histoires en images de la préhistoire à nos jours* was, as the title implies, one of the first historical studies, one that took the BD back to cave paintings, thereby giving it credibility on a par with other ancient forms of expression. Francis Lacassin drew upon the material of his Sorbonne seminars – in themselves a landmark in BD history, one that was scarcely followed up – for his *Pour un 9ème Art: La Bande dessinée* (1971), a socio-historic study that included an important section on the comparison between BD and cinema. In 1972 Pierre Fresnault-Deruelle's *La Bande dessinée: L'Univers et les techniques de quelques comics d'expression française: Essai d'analyse sémiotique* [The Bande Dessinée: The Universe and the Techniques of a Selection of Comics in French: An Essay of Semiotic Analysis] opened a new approach, aiming to do to BD images what Barthes and others had done to text,[28] although in practice, here and in his other works, the use of the term 'semiotic' could be rather loose.[29]

Maurice Horn, Milton Caniff et Gérald Gassiot-Talabot dans les salles réservées à la Figuration narrative. Au fond, Pierre Couperie.

Salle consacrée à l'image narrative.

1re salle: étude du ballon sous ses divers aspects.

Figure 37. '1967 BD Exhibition, Paris, Musée des Arts Décoratifs'. *Phénix*. No. 4 (1967). p. 90. © C. Moliterni.

Furthermore, non BD-specific publications were showing an interest, in particular *Communications*, the high-profile social sciences journal, whose issue 24 (1976) was on 'La Bande Dessinée et son discours'. Previous issues had hinted at an interest in the field, as in number 15 (1970) on 'L'Analyse des images', including articles on advertising, as well as a piece by Violette Morin on 'Le Dessin humoristique' [Humoristic Drawings] (pp. 110–31), largely based on *Paris Match* cartoons, and a further semiotic introduction to BD in general, and speech bubbles in particular, by Pierre Fresnault-Deruelle, 'Le Verbal dans les bandes dessinées' (pp. 145–61). The 1976 special number was also largely semiotic in tone, with an additional article by Fresnault-Deruelle, as well as another version by Umberto Eco of his work on the myth of Superman.[30] Above all, retrospectively at least, the journal was openly proclaiming BD as a valid subject for academic investigation.[31] For many, however, the ultimate accolade had already been bestowed through René Clair's 1974 address on the subject of bande dessinée and cinema with which he had graced the Académie Française.

The BD's split personality, divided between popular pastime and fledgling object of intellectualisation, which had marked the early *Giff-Wiff* analysis, was not to be lost. The form's popular status grew in step with the success of *Pilote*, and the 1960s saw (or rather heard) broadcasts related to the journal's sponsorship by Radio Luxembourg. These were to prefigure a number of successful television programmes, in particular *La Bande à bédé* [The BD Gang] on Antenne 2 from 1981. Popular conventions were also growing, spearheaded by the initial 1974 gathering in Angoulême (which in turn took much inspiration from an Italian meeting in Lucca), but the 1970s also saw embryonic festivals in Paris and elsewhere, even if these were largely marts for fans to complete their collections and meet the artists at book signings.

When in 1975 Luc Botanski published his survey of the BD's canonisation, his account was, maybe unwittingly, the seal to confirm that the form had indeed been canonised. It was fitting that the final blurring of the distinctions between bande dessinée's status of 'low art' or 'high art' should occur in the opening pages of a journal launched by Pierre Bourdieu. Not only was BD the object of critical books, exhibitions and journals, a subject for television comment and a valid focus for some of the most intellectual minds of France, it was now a semantic entity boasting its own dictionary definition.

As obvious as it may seem, the fact that the BD had its own definition in 1975 need not be taken for granted. The subject catalogue of the Bibliothèque nationale de France does not include 'bande dessinée' before the 1960s. Alain Rey, in his *Dictionnaire historique de la langue française* [Historic Dictionary of the French Language],[32] does give the term 'bande dessinée' as existing from 1940 in Paul Winkler's contracts, and *The Trésor de la langue française* strangely presents it as being synonymous with 'dessin animé'.[33] The *Nouveau Petit Robert* gives the initial date of 1929.[34] However, as I have suggested at the outset of my chapter 'Definitions and Component Parts', the instances Rey and Robert have picked are of the noun 'bande' being qualified by the adjective 'dessinée'. 'Bande dessinée' as a semantic unit does not appear to have existed until the end of the 1950s. Indeed, the *Robert* of as late as 1969 gives no mention of the term despite providing more than a full column on the word 'bande' and associated phrases ('bande de fer', 'bandes de billard', 'plate-bande', 'bande d'idiots' ...).[35] By the mid-1970s the BD was a self-aware critical phenomenon, but we should not overlook the newness of this position.

Consecrating the consecrated

In hindsight and from a non-French viewpoint, the status of bande dessinée as we know it had largely been reached by 1975. Progress was to continue, but there is an important difference between building upon a recognised tradition and creating a new one, and it is in this context that we must view consecration landmarks from the 1980s onwards.

A further sign of consecration was the fact that the BD was now the subject of intellectual fisticuffs. In 1985 Bruno Lecigne, whose *Avanies et mascarades* (1981) had marked a new phase in analytical monographs on the BD,[36] entered into an exchange with Thierry Groensteen over the desired content of the *Cahiers de la Bande Dessinée*, the editorial duties of which had been under Groensteen's charge from 1984. Launched by Glénat in 1969, during the early years *Les Cahiers* had operated essentially as a journalistic fanzine, as implied by the less cerebrally appealing initial title of *Schtroumpf*, with *Les Cahiers de la Bande Dessinée* as subtitle. Lecigne's comments were instrumental in changing the publication's direction to a more critically aware style of content, one that had entirely broken with the fandom of *Giff-Wiff*. The journal's initial subtitle had paid homage to the critical insight that the *Les Cahiers du Cinéma* had applied to the Seventh Art from 1951 onwards, but the content change put such aspirations into practice.

In keeping with the change in direction taken by *Les Cahiers*, Groensteen was also to initiate a prestigious 1987 conference at the château de Cerisy-la-Salle in Normandy, this being the event at which Jean-Christophe Menu was to meet Lewis Trondheim and float the initial ideas that eventually led to the creation of L'Association and of OuBaPo. Cerisy has built up a reputation for high-powered intellectual gatherings, with previous meetings, for example, on Marcel Proust (1962), the *Nouveau Roman* (1971) and Roland Barthes (1977) and subsequent ones on Norman architecture (1994), Jacques Derrida (1997) and Hélène Cixous (1998). The 1987 conference had 'BD récit et modernité' as its topic, which, as is often the case for the topoi of academic gatherings, could easily lend itself to discussions of all manner whilst giving the impression of addressing a specific problematic.[37]

In terms of a general culture of BD criticism, this was created not only by the numerous monographs that feature throughout the footnotes of this book – works by Baetens and Lefèvre, Moliterni, Gaumer, Peeters and Groensteen, for example – but also through a host of further journals. Some of these would be dedicated entirely to criticism, as in *Les Cahiers de la Bande Dessinée* (1969–1990), whilst others mixed creation and criticism. New publications such as *Circus* (1975–1989) did this, but existing works also realised the importance of intellectualising the BD, for example later issues of *Pilote*, which had important review and analysis sections.

By Contrast: BD Criticism in English

Here it will be useful to move away from our time-line and consider, by way of comparison, the way BD scholarship has developed, much more recently, in English-speaking countries. As with the French tradition of scholarship there had been some 'precursor' articles, such as Hugh Starkey's 1990 'Is the BD "à bout de souffle"?' on the relative positions of bande dessinée and cinema,[38] or Ann Miller's 1998 entry on 'Comic Strips/Cartoonists' in the *Encyclopaedia of Contemporary French Culture*,[39] but there was no coherent group of Anglophone bande dessinée scholars before the 1999 International Bande Dessinée Conference held at the University of Glasgow.[40]

The University of Glasgow can be seen as a logical site for developments in text/image scholarship given its strong library collections in the tradition of image culture,[41] partly as a result of which a course on BD had been running for Honours students of French since 1996; nonetheless the 1999 conference was largely the outcome of happy circumstances resulting from a mixture of BD-interested staff and students. Furthermore the 1999 conference showed that potential BD scholars in the English-speaking countries of Europe had no firm geographical base, with representatives arriving from Brighton, Bristol, Cardiff, Dublin, Leicester, London, Manchester, Nottingham and Southampton.

Further bi-annual conferences in Glasgow (2001), Leicester (2003), Manchester (2005) and London (2007 and 2009), together with the founding of the International BD Society (IBDS) in 2001, have strengthened BD scholarship this side of the Channel. This has been helped by cooperation between IBDS and the American BD Society (ABDS, founded in 2004), a website (www.arts.gla.ac.uk/ibds), a growing number of publications and PhD theses – for full references see the bibliography elements of our Introduction – and an associated journal, *European Comic Art*, whose first issue was published by Liverpool University Press in June 2008.

In many ways the developments of BD studies in French-speaking countries in the 1960s and in on-looking nations in the late 1990s have much in common. The push has come from individuals working together in a field that is not generally their primary preoccupation, but tends to be a sideline, albeit pleasurable, interest. The field is one that was not generally associated with scholarly activity – articles in *The Scotsman* in 1999 bear witness to this – but which forward-looking intellectuals are prepared to accept given the importance of other visual fields, in particular cinema studies. But such similarities could perhaps be found in most fledgling fields of inquiry. What is interesting with relation to the bande dessinée and its consecration is precisely the differences between approaches within and outwith France.

Firstly, the lack of a geographic base can perhaps account for English-language approaches to the BD being more eclectic than their early French counterparts, and, moreover, with progress being considerably slower. There has tended to be a flurry of activity around the IBDS conferences, patched by lulls in the intervening months. The casual exchanges that must have nourished the 1962 Paris-based bédéphiles can be compared to the ad hoc e-mail correspondence of the twenty-first century, including via the 'BDFIL' listing (see: BDFIL@listserv.liv.ac.uk), but although these make the exchange of information accessible, they cannot replace the informal zeal nurtured by a café culture.

The main peculiarity of English-language BD scholarship has been its base within academia. This may be from necessity, since the nostalgic longing for the publications of childhood that spurred on the CBD would not have gripped the general public overseas, even if some of the IBDS members do have French backgrounds. More cynically, one could point to research assessment exercises creating a need for new dynamic areas of investigation, and BD, in the wake of cinema studies, fits the bill.

The resulting approaches to bande dessinée scholarship reflect their origins. Historical studies, whether nostalgia-based or otherwise, are rare, although some studies have fallen prey to the need to introduce a foreign audience to the pillars of the modern BD, thereby resulting in overly descriptive works. Above all, as one might expect from a university context, English-language studies have tended to engage with literary critical theory, aspects of Cultural Studies, and applied sociology, in a way that French works often did and do not. Examples of such studies will be given in the next chapter, and a specific case study in point will be seen with respective analyses of André Juillard's *Le Cahier bleu*.

This latter tendency can further be linked to the time scales in question. Just as the 1960s saw the beginnings of interest in everyday phenomena as worthy objects of cultural analysis, so 'Anglo-Saxon' academia of the 1990s had provided analysts with a full armoury of critical apparatus from Barthes to Derrida, much of which has fitted the BD admirably, as we have seen in the previous chapter. Leading French-language critics such as Groensteen, Morgan and Peeters have engaged fruitfully with Deleuze, Foucault and Lacan, but as a general rule academia in France tends to apply greater caution to such critical approaches. This above all holds true for the considerable analytical body that operates outwith academic circles, and, of course, in respect to a corpus capable of attracting household attention. The fact that French writers on the BD can earn themselves considerable royalties with best-selling coffee-table books, whereas the few BD books from English presses, including this very offering, tend to be limited in financial scope with an academic market in mind, makes for a French content that is more accessible, although often critically and historically repetitive.

Where Now?

The aim of this chapter is not to give a blow-by-blow account of all events and publications that have contributed, in the last quarter of the twentieth century onwards, to the accomplishment of the BD's current status. It is at this point that the consecration of the BD and history of the form become intertwined, a notion I have reflected in the shared subtitle given here as well as to the final section of my chapter on Contemporary BD. Jack Lang's 'Quinze Mesures' have led to greater visibility and freer experimentation, whereas the CNBDI in Angoulême (Fig. 30, Chapter 6) and its associated high-profile festival have, to a certain extent, laid the (often disputed) standards for BD production. These landmarks, as well as the CBBD and new movements in critical thought, such as those related to OuBaPo and L'Association, have been discussed in the later parts of my chapters on the BD's history.

But to return to the beginning, one event is worth considering, not so much for the event itself, but for the attitudes it revealed: the commemorations in 1996 of the 150th anniversary of Rodolphe Töpffer's death. Yves Fremion, a prominent journalist and novelist with about sixty books to his name, a regular contributor to *Fluide Glacial*, a onetime ecologist Member of the European Parliament and Conseiller Régional for Île de France (political representative for the Paris region), opened the Angoulême conference on the origins of the bande dessinée as follows:[42]

> C'est bien connu, les Américains ont tout inventé: l'aviation (qui est germano-française), la fusée (qui est russo-allemande), l'homme dans l'espace (ce fut un russe [*sic*]), le cinéma (qui est français), le sida (qui est zaïrois), la science-fiction (qui est anglaise), les Jeux Olympiques (qui sont grecs), le blue-jean (qui vient de Nîmes) et les Grottes de Lascaux. Quelques-uns tentent également de fêter cette année le centenaire de la BD, qui en a bientôt deux. Pour des Américains incultes ne sachant même pas où placer l'Europe sur la carte entre le Japon et la Russie, rien d'étonnant à ce qu'ils prennent pour base ce qu'ils ont choisi: l'anniversaire du *Yellow Kid* de Outcault, puisque c'est une BD américaine comme eux. Plus ennuyeux est de savoir qu'ils ont entraîné dans cette galère certains officiels belges et même Morris, ordinairement plus avisé. [...]

Il me revient l'honneur, en commençant ce colloque, d'orienter le débat clairement pour éviter qu'il ne dévie vers un résultat mitigé, et pour que cette imposture soit démasquée sans ambiguïté. En réalité, tout ce que nous pouvons fêter cette année, c'est le cent-cinquantenaire de la mort de l'inventeur de la BD, Rodolphe Töpffer. (6)

[Everyone knows it, the Americans invented everything: aviation (which is Franco-German), the rocket (which is Germano-Russian), man in space (that was a Russian), cinema (which is French), AIDS (that is from Zaire), science fiction (which is English), the Olympic Games (which are Greek), blue jeans (which come from Nimes) and the Lascaux caves. Some are even trying to celebrate this year as the centenary of the BD, although it is almost two hundred years old. For cultureless Americans, who cannot even find Europe's place on the map between Japan and Russia, it is not surprising that they should base their views on the choice that suits them: the anniversary of *Yellow Kid* by Outcault, since it is a BD that is American like them. What is more annoying is to learn that they have roped in a few Belgian dignitaries, and even Morris, who should know better. [...]

In opening this conference I have the honour of setting the debate clearly in the right direction so as to avoid it going off on a dubious tangent, and in order for such impostures to be well and truly outed. In truth, all that is to be celebrated this year is the 150th anniversary of the death of the inventor of the BD, Rodolphe Töpffer.]

Frémion's address was doubtless tongue-in-check, but it did underline the perceived importance of not only giving the BD a history, but moreover a European and indeed French-language history. As we have seen, the naming of Rodolphe Töpffer as 'inventeur de la bande dessinée' is dubious at best, but the act of such naming was an important landmark in the history of the form's consecration.

One might be tempted to suggest that with consecration has come stagnation, as the form now battles for supermarket space rather than for recognition, with the emphasis increasingly on marketable paraphernalia and coffee-table productions that provide little more than variations upon a set of themes. A cynical view of this type is the easy way to end a chapter on consecration, but it is over-simplistic. Expansion of the bande dessinée phenomenon has led to stratification, and although the new market allows for conveyer-belt criticism that comments on the stereotype sex strips and the formulaic thrillers, it also means there is room for iconoclasts such as Jean-Christophe Menu, whose L'Association productions constantly challenge, not only in the realm of production (see my chapter on the Contemporary BD) but also in terms of critical reaction through works such as *Plates-bandes* (2005), and the recent *L'Éprouvette* (three issues from 2006 to 2007).

Whereas in France cutting-edge BD criticism often operates from financially marginal bases, the expansion of the general market has, one must assume, been a factor in the increased attention now being paid from non-francophone sources, of which the publication by the University Press of Mississippi of the translation of Thierry Groensteen's *Système de la bande dessinée,*[43] and the launch from Liverpool University Press of the journal *European Comic Art*, are two examples. Such criticism also comes from sources that are not mainstream, since academic productions are unlikely to be headline grabbers, but it does represent a solid base from which BD can expand now to become an object of international critical attention. And it is precisely at this point that this very book comes in ...

Notes

1. The subtitle was dropped for the sake of concision.
2. An alternative viewpoint is that despite current media attention and general market-related approbation, the bande dessinée has still not attained the cultural kudos it deserves. Such is the presumption that underpins Thierry Groensteen's *Un Objet culturel non identifié* ([Angoulême]: Éditions de l'An 2, 2006). Groensteen's work is of particular relevance to this chapter: in accounting for the bande dessinée's ambiguous status he provides, specifically in chapters 5 to 9 (pp. 98–181), an overview of the development of its critical reception from the early 1960s onwards.
3. See my Introduction for a brief survey, as well as the following chapter, which indicates some examples of BD study in the broader context of 'Cultural Studies and Beyond'.
4. In the meantime elements of this thesis have been synthesised in McQuillan's Introduction (pp. 7–13) of *The Francophone Bande Dessinée* edited by McQuillan, Charles Forsdick and myself (Amsterdam: Rodopi, 2005).
5. On this subject see Laurence Grove, 'BD Theory before the Term "BD" Existed', in *The Francophone Bande Dessinée*, pp. 39–49. Parts of this section have been taken from that article.
6. A facsimile reproduction of the work was produced by Slatkine of Geneva in 1976 and 1998.
7. Rodolphe Töpffer, *Voyages en zigzag* (Paris: Jacques-Julien Dubochet, 1846). This work was reprinted by Statkine of Geneva in 1996.
8. (Neuchatel: Administration du Dictionnaire Historique & Bibliographique de la Suisse, 1932).
9. (Paris: Société Anonyme de la Grande Encyclopédie, [c.1890]).
10. (Paris: Administration du Grand Dictionnaire Universel, 1876).
11. This quote is taken from p. 13 of the introduction to the catalogue that accompanied the 1996 Geneva exhibition in honour of Töpffer, *Rodolphe Töpffer: Aventures graphiques* ([Geneva]: [Musées d'Art et d'Histoire], 1996). No author's or editor's name is given.
12. Again, for a fuller overview of critical approaches in this period, see my 'BD Theory before the Term "BD" Existed', cited above.
13. The article appeared in number 13, pp. 56–61.
14. 'Le Club des Bandes Dessinées va-t-il prendre naissance?', *Fiction* 98 (1962), 143–44.
15. The title is a reference to a mythological hybrid animal character that featured in *Le Journal de Mickey* and took nourishment from precious pearls.
16. Pierre Couperie, 'Sociologie du Club des Bandes Dessinées', *Giff-Wiff* 3 (1962), 9–13.

17. Guy Claude Bonnemaison, 'À Propos du ballon dans les bandes dessinées' [Regarding the Speech Bubble in Bandes Dessinées], *Giff-Wiff* 8 (1963), 39–41.
18. Umberto Eco, 'Le Mythe de Superman et la dissolution du temps' [The Myth of Superman and the Dissolution of Time], *Giff-Wiff* 11 (1964), 10–13. This was in fact a translation of a previously published work.
19. Francis Lacassin, 'Notre Assemblée Générale' [Our AGM], *Giff-Wiff* 7 (1963), 5–8.
20. Pierre Couperie, 'Sociologie du Club des Bandes Dessinées'.
21. A point in case is the meetings of the 'Amis de Tristan L'Hermite'. Although the poet (1601–1650) was distinctly Limousin (i.e., from central France), annual gatherings take place in various Parisian venues.
22. It should be noted that the same is not true of Belgium where university studies in the BD, particularly at Leuven, thrive. For the sake of concision this chapter has deliberately concentrated on the question of the consecration of BD in France, although many of the key developments (e.g. the CBD, CELEG and SOCERLID) involved Belgian scholars and were instrumental to the form's development in Belgium. An in-depth study of the comparative consecration of the BD in France and in Belgium remains to be written.
23. François Caradec, 'Rodolphe Töpffer', *Phénix* 43 (1975), 7-11.
24. The artistic context of this exhibition has been discussed briefly in the previous chapter.
25. My analysis of the exhibition is based on the unsigned account of it given in *Phénix*: 'Bande dessinée et figuration narrative', *Phénix* 4 (1967), 90–94. This includes a number of photographic illustrations.
26. On the history of this appellation, see the penultimate section of our chapter on the Twentieth Century.
27. As stated above, these divisions are reflected in the sections that compose chapter I (pp. 51–92) of her doctoral thesis, 'The Reception and Creation of Post-1960 Franco-Belgian BD'.
28. See, for example, Barthes's *S/Z* (Paris: Seuil, 1970) in which he provides a near word-by-word analysis of the possible connotations of a Balzac short story.
29. These are of course just a selection of key texts from this fledgling period of BD criticism. For further details of these, and of other works, see the studies by McQuillan and by Miller quoted above, as well as Harry Morgan and Manuel Hirtz's bibliography of secondary sources on the BD, *Le Petit Critique illustré* (Paris: PLG, 2005 [first ed. 1997]).
30. Pierre Fresnault-Deruelle, 'Du Linéaire au tabulaire', *Communications* 24 (1976), 7-23; Umberto Eco, 'Le Mythe de Superman', *Communications* 24 (1976), 24-40.
31. McQuillan analyses this special number of *Communications* in some detail on pp. 66–70 of 'The Reception and Creation of Post-1960 Franco-Belgian BD'.
32. (Paris: Robert, 1998). Rey is also the author of a work on the theory of the bande dessinée, *Les Spectres de la bande* (Paris: Minuit, 1978).
33. Imbs, Paul, ed., *Trésor de la langue française: Dictionnaire de la langue du XIXe et du XXe siècle (1789–1960)* [Treasure of the French Language: Dictionary of the Language of the Nineteenth and Twentieth Centuries], 16 vols (Paris: CNRS, 1975).
34. The edition consulted is that of 1994 (Paris: Robert).
35. *Le Robert: Dictionnaire alphabétique et analogique de la langue française* [The Robert: Alphabetic and Analogical Dictionary of the French Language] (Paris: Société du Nouveau Littré, 1969), pp. 403–04. The terms cited mean 'iron band', 'billiard cushion', 'flower bed' and 'gang of idiots' respectively. These conclusions on the history of the term 'bande dessinée' are largely confirmed in a note by Jean-Claude Glasser in the 'rubrique courrier' of *Les Cahiers de la Bande Dessinée* 80 (March 1988).

36. *Avanies et mascarades: L'Évolution de la bande dessinée en France dans les années 70* (Paris: Futuropolis, 1981).
37. The acts of the conference are available as Thierry Groensteen, ed., *BD récit et modernité* (Poitiers: Futuropolis, 1988).
38. *French Cultural Studies* 1 (1990), 95–110.
39. *Encyclopedia of Contemporary French Culture*, ed. Alex Hughes and Keith Reader (London: Routledge, 1998). The article is on pp. 116–19.
40. The emphasis here is on a body of *bande dessinée* scholarship. In North America scholars working on the world tradition of comics, albeit with an Anglophone bias, have met since 1997 at the annual International Comic Arts Festival (ICAF) conference in Georgetown, and since 1999 the *International Journal of Comic Art* (*IJOCA*) has provided a publishing outlet for such activities. On the early days of *comics* scholarship, see issues 1.1 (1999), 4.1 (2002), 5.1 (2003), 5.2 (2003) and 7.2 (2005) of the *International Journal of Comic Art*, which have major sections on the subject.
41. Glasgow University Library is home to the Stirling Maxwell collection of emblem books, a form, as we have seen in Chapter 4, that integrated text and image from the early sixteenth century onwards. Glasgow thus has a strong tradition of scholarship in this field.
42. Frémion's paper has been published as 'Inventions, inventeurs et inventards: Un Inventaire, une aventure' [Inventions, Inventors and Inventing Types: An Inventory, an Adventure], in *Les Origines de la bande dessinée*, ed. Thierry Groensteen, *Le Collectionneur de Bandes Dessinées* hors série (no. 79, 1996), 6–10.
43. Thierry Groensteen, *The System of Comics*, trans. Bart Beaty (Jackson, MS, University Press of Mississippi, 2007). The University Press of Mississippi has a series specifically dedicated to Comics and Popular Culture.

CHAPTER 10

CULTURAL STUDIES AND BEYOND: CASES IN POINT AND FURTHER READING

Theory into Practice

When, at the end of the last century, this book saw its first embryonic stages, the aim was to provide a substantial section of case studies. These would draw upon a variety of methodologies under the broad aegis of Cultural Studies,[1] not only to put into practice ideas and approaches mooted throughout this book, but also to underline the notion of BD as playing an integral role in the current cultural make-up of French-speaking life. The bande dessinée is of interest per se, but also as a key to understanding broader elements of the world around us.

Towards the end of the first decade of the current century these goals are still as valid, but their context has evolved. When this project was started studies in English on the bande dessinée were rare, often inaccessible, and, perhaps as a result of audience ignorance, tended to generalise.[2] As we have seen, in 1999 a hesitant gathering of scholars in Glasgow explored the idea of BD as a discipline within the academia of English-speaking Europeans. Further bi-annual conferences ensued, the IBDS (International Bande Dessinée Society) was founded and links were forged with like-minded scholars in North America. The same period saw the successful defence of three UK doctoral dissertations and some initial BD-centred book publications, as well as a number of articles and conference papers.[3] As this book goes into publication, a subject-specific journal, *European Comic Art*, produced by Liverpool University Press, has seen its first issues.

These developments have underlined the validity of the initial premise of this chapter, whilst, in practical terms, meaning that a large number of in-depth case studies can now readily be found in many major libraries, studies that I would actively encourage the reader to consult. Nonetheless it is still useful to have, easily to hand, a couple of elaborated examples of what can be done, as well as the indications and suggestions of areas that have now been explored, or could be explored further. These examples will draw upon the wide umbrella that is Cultural Studies, but will also dip into other areas that could feasibly enrich any broad programme of learning in an English-speaking context.

The Specificity of English?

The particularity of this book lies in the fact that it is one of the first general works on bande dessinée (i.e., comic strips in French) in English. And although there are a number of highly reliable and informative works on this very subject in French, many of which I have drawn upon, this is not a translation of their findings. This current work is specifically an examination of a quintessentially French, or French-language, subject from a cross-Channel viewpoint. As such it should provide a slightly different approach, fostered by a different cultural baggage and relying upon a different set of methodological givens. It makes sense for the case studies of this chapter to continue this trajectory.

It would nonetheless be folly to pretend that French scholarship on the subject does not exist or to reinvent the wheel (e.g., Michel Vaillant's) by overlooking or discarding what are often examples of top-quality research. In some cases these studies may not be easily accessible to the English-language reader, but he or she should be aware of them and be encouraged to use them as a possible starting point if practical circumstances permit.

To that end it is important to preface this chapter with reference to three major bibliographies that are erudite, reliable and reasonably accessible. All provide listings of studies that analyse bande dessinée in its wider cultural context and which should therefore be consulted before embarking on an in-depth study of any particular area.

- Harry Morgan and Manuel Hirtz, *Le Petit Critique illustré: Guide des ouvrages consacrés à la bande dessinée*. Montrouge: PLG, 1997 and 2005.

  An annotated bibliography divided into the following sections: 'Ouvrages généraux' [General Works], 'Monographies', 'Théorie', 'Pédagogie', 'Catalogues', 'Miscellanea' and 'Principaux Ouvrages de langue anglaise' [Principal Works in English] as well as indexes.

  The bibliography is exhaustive and generally accurate. Its chronological listings include all major milestones of BD criticism (thus is also a useful appendix to my previous chapter), sometimes flexing the definition of such so as to include key texts from the 1920s onwards. Morgan and Hirtz do not, however, generally include articles or chapters in non-BD based books.

  The authors' comments make for amusing reading, although their dismissive tone (in reference to the subtitle of Annie Baron-Carvais' work, 'Que-sais-je?' [What Do I Know?]

they reply 'Rien' [Nothing]) can be outspoken and unreasonably anti-academic.

The seventh chapter, 'Principaux Ouvrages de langue anglaise' is new to the second edition (2005), but very little is given that does not relate to English or USA traditions.

Morgan's website (http://www.sdv.fr/pages/adamantine/) includes regular updates to *Le Petit Critique illustré*.

- Michel Béra, Michel Denis and Philippe Mellot, *Trésors de la bande dessinée*. Paris: Éditions de l'Amateur. Published every two years staring from 1979.

  The *argus* of bande dessinée giving suggested prices for albums and journals, as well as supplements on associated products (e.g., figurines, adverts, key rings, phonecards etc.) depending on the edition. Each edition gives and updates a bibliography of secondary sources with works cited generally listed in chronological order of publication.

  The following bibliographical sections appear in the 2009–2010 edition: 'Catalogues, guides, argus, répertoires et annuaires' [Catalogues, Guides, Price Listings, Indices and Year Books], 'Encyclopédies et dictionnaires', 'Anthologies', 'Études historiques et panoramas synoptiques' [Historical Studies and Synoptic Overviews], 'Pédagogie, éducation, censure et législation', 'Signification et langage', 'Sociologie, économie et politique', 'Technique', 'Variations thématiques', 'Monographies' and 'Ouvrages étrangers essentiels' [Essential Foreign Works].

  'Monographies' is the largest section, with listings by BD author's name, character's name and BD journals. Most entries are in fact articles rather than monographs in the English sense of the word.

  Of the 'Ouvrages étrangers essentiels', only one, on Astérix, is an English-language work on bande dessinée. As with Morgan and Hirtz this is partly due to over-zealous bibliographic streamlining, but remains nonetheless an indication of the extent to which the field is unexplored.

- John A. Lent, *Comic Art of Europe: An International Comprehensive Bibliography*. Bibliographies and Indexes in Popular Culture 5. Westport, CT: Greenwood, 1994.

  The work comprises over 600 pages and nearly 9,000 entries, with an opening comparative chapter followed by seven further chapters on various countries or regions. Chapter 3, in itself some 184 pages, is dedicated to France, with sections on general works, historical questions, artists, characters and different formats, including animation, comic strips, comic books and political cartoons. Other chapters cover Belgium and Switzerland.

Although the work can appear haphazard at times, it contains much USA-based information not to be found elsewhere. A glance through the section on France again confirms the lack of work available on the BD in English, although Lent does point to numerous short pieces of interest. These include various entries in *The Comics Journal* (the Seattle-based glossy monthly founded in 1976) on French authors, as well as articles in high-profile publications such as *Newsweek*, *Time* and *Ms*. Lent's entries are not, however, annotated, and we should remember that the work stops in 1994.

Cultural Studies

In the opening chapter of this broader section I explored the place of bande dessinée within the broad intellectual movement known as Cultural Studies, one that displaced the emphasis from the lives and texts of canonic dead white males to encompass broader elements of the surrounding culture. This previous chapter dipped into, or at least evoked, related writings by Barthes, Bourdieu, Derrida, Said (ironically all canonic dead white males) and others, suggesting that if examples were needed that put their theory into practice, then BD would fit the bill. The idea of this current section is to provide such examples, or at least to suggest where further examples might be found.

To that end, the first of this chapter's longer case studies, 'Bond Dessinée', will examine the BD in its relationship with the outside cultural world. The topic of James Bond allows us to consider the broad theme of the relationship between bande dessinée and postwar popular fiction, whilst evoking more specific questions of national and gender-based identities.

The selection following this main study, one that is intended to provide a wide spread as well as picking up on some of the themes explored in the Bond section, is based on published studies that already exist, studies that I would like to see explored, and studies carried out by students in my University of Glasgow Honours French option on bande dessinée, and to whom I would like to express my gratitude. These surveys can be broadly categorised under Representations of History, Intellectual Context, Social Structures, Sexuality and Gender, Nationality and Otherness, and Multi-media Expression.

Case study: Bond dessinée[4]

When the Bibliothèque nationale de France organised a 2007 conference on the theme of James Bond, an event that fortuitously fell in line with the release of the film version of *Casino Royale*, the event grabbed the attention of international media from England to India. The attraction seemed to be that an august national institution was lending credibility to the most popular of popular fiction, and, perhaps above all, that a bastion of France's intelligentsia was to hail a hero seen to encapsulate Englishness.

In many ways the conference stood as a role model in the field of Cultural Studies: the Bond saga was explored as literature, musical creation and as visual culture, in terms of evolving gender roles and national stereotypes, as an insight into the world of consumer fashion and as an icon of the economics of the leisure industry. It became clear that Bond's success could be attributed to his ability to represent the many facets of postwar international culture in the broadest of senses. I was delighted that the organisers should see the bande dessinée as an integral element, although one might ask if this would have been the case for a non French-organised event.

James Bond has existed in comic form since 1958 when the original adaptation of *Casino Royale*, scripted by Anthony Hern and drawn by John McLusky, appeared in the pages of England's *Daily Express*. The strip is a starting point for considering the way in which comics, and in particular the bande dessinée, as a hybrid text/image form, encapsulate much of the 'Spirit of 007'. This in turn leads to certain wider questions, such as how the essential text/image mix works in James Bond fiction – both the books and the films – why it should indeed occupy such a central position in the hybrid culture of today's world, and how a knowledge of bande dessinée can help us understand this.

James Bond comics

From McLusky's initial version that first appeared on 7 July 1958 up until 1983, fifty-two Bond adventures appeared in newspapers in England and elsewhere.[5] Eighteen were based directly on Ian Fleming's work, although other versions were by Kingsley Amis or even Jim Lawrence. The artwork was mainly by McLusky, but with later versions by Yaroslav Horak. It was the norm for a single strip of between two and five frames to appear each day, the adaptations made for short independent units, often with an initial text summary to situate the plot, and if possible, a cliffhanger ending. Fleming's lengthy visual descriptions were often lost, as in the case of the history of the town of Royale-les-Eaux, which was replaced by a single elongated frame giving a general panorama of the seaside resort. Other elements were toned down for the *Daily Express*'s readership: in the comic-strip version of the torture scene in *Casino Royale*, Le Chiffre, the evil mastermind, repeatedly hits Bond's head, rather than his nether regions, with a carpet beater, and the force of the novel's final words, 'the bitch is dead', becomes no more than 'yes, she's dead!'

There are also several James Bond comic-book albums, either based on original scripting or taken from whatever film was on release at the time. These often use attention-grabbing bright colours, thus understandably aimed at a popular audience, as in the case of

Mike Grell's *James Bond 007: Licence to Kill* (1989).[6] In general such publications, including album versions of the early serialised strips, would be rapidly translated into French editions.[7] James Bond also makes cameo or pastiche appearances in several French productions, of which the best known is probably the character Zérozérosix (Dubbelosix in English), a central spy figure in *L'Odyssée d'Astérix* (1981),[8] through whom Uderzo caricatures Sean Connery.

Spirit of 007

The real interest in studying James Bond in the context of bande dessinée (and vice versa) lies in the notion of a 'Spirit of 007'. We can give this name to a strand in popular culture that is to be found in the characterisation of certain BD heroes, in the intrinsic action/exposition/ideology mixture, and in key elements of the BD's narrative structure.

From the 1930s Golden Age onwards examples of Bond-like comic strip heroes are readily available. The Superheroes alone could be worthy of an entire study in this context, although there are plenty of suitable mortal protagonists, as in Tailspin Tommy (Jean Bolide in French), Hal Forrest's 1930s fearless flyer and saviour of damsels in distress, or even Chester Gould's Dick Tracy, whose French version appeared in *Le Journal de Toto* from 1937 and *Spirou* from 1938. For French-language creations one could mention *Le Chrysanthème de Jade*, a spy adventure that took the front cover of *Coeurs Vaillants* throughout much of the 1950s, Jean-Michel Charlier and Raymond Poïvet's *Allo! D/M/A*, a leading feature of the 1960s *Pilote* in which Guy Lebleu embarks on various detective/spy missions, or of course *Blake et Mortimer* with their typical English reserve, even if Blake is Welsh and Mortimer Scottish. These are but a few of the characters in postwar BD publications who share personality traits with James Bond, many in English, but above all, and with remarkable regularity, in French.

Of all of these intrepid heroes who give themselves fearlessly to the greater good, one lesser-known example deserves a little more attention: Josse's Marc le Téméraire [Marc the Bold], a daring young agent who featured on page 5 of the collaborationist *Le Téméraire* throughout its existence between January 1943 and August 1944 (see Fig. 28, Chapter 6).[9] In the course of his work for the French Secret Services Marc le Téméraire would take on both the communists and the English. His attributes were exactly those that would grace James Bond, namely boldness, patriotism, physical beauty and intelligence, the very qualities that Umberto Eco outlines in 'Les Structures narratives chez Fleming' [Fleming's Narrative Structures]:[10]

> Bond oppose sa réponse à chaque attribut spécifique du Méchant: la Loyauté au Service de la Mesure anglo-saxonne contre la Nature Exceptionnelle du sang-mêlé, le choix de la Privation et l'acceptation du Sacrifice contre le Faste affiché par l'ennemi, le coup de génie (Aléa)

> opposé à la froide Programmation pour triompher d'elle, le sens de l'Idéal opposé à la Cupidité. (176)
>
> [Bond offers his own reply to each of the Baddy's specific attributes: Loyalty in the Service of Anglo-Saxon Restraint as opposed to the Exceptional Nature of mixed blood, the choice of Deprivation and the acceptance of Sacrifice as opposed to the Splendour that the enemy displays, the stroke of genius (Luck) as opposed to cold Calculating in order to overcome it, the sense of an Ideal as opposed to Cupidity.]
>
> Devoir et Sacrifice sont les éléments d'un débat intérieur chaque fois que Bond sait qu'il lui faudra dévoiler le plan du Méchant au risque de sa propre vie, c'est l'idéal patriotique (Grande-Bretagne, Monde Libre) qui l'emporte, sans oublier l'exigence raciste de démontrer la supériorité de l'homme britannique. (177)
>
> [Duty and Sacrifice are the elements of an internal debate each time Bond knows that he will have to thwart the Baddy's plot at the risk of his own life, and it is the ideals of patriotism (Great Britain, the Free World) that win the day, without forgetting the racist requirement that the superiority of the Briton must be shown.]

All we need to do is to replace 'Anglo-Saxon', 'Great Britain' and 'Briton' with 'Nazi', 'Germany' and 'Aryan' and the description fits Marc le Téméraire perfectly. Needless to say, the influence is not a direct one – it is hard to imagine that Fleming could have read *Le Téméraire* – it is more a question of noting that during and after the Second World War popular fiction, and above all comics and bandes dessinées, revelled in a stereotypical *pro patria* action hero. The works of Fleming thrive on accounts of wartime derring-do, and James Bond is an exact example of such a hero.

If a single comic-strip character is to be pinpointed as sharing Bond's attributes it is surely Tintin, Hergé's boy scout whose missions ran from 1929 to 1986. In both cases – Bond and Tintin – the adventures follow a three-point schema, that of action/exposition/ideology. The action is encompassed in high-speed chases, fist fights and the frequent endangering of life. The exposition, or narration, revolves around a well-constructed plot, with numerous cliffhanger moments (again often involving the endangering of life) and sudden twists. Thumbing through any *Tintin* album will provide numerous specific examples of such elements, but *L'Affaire Tournesol* [The Calculus Affair] (1956) probably encapsulates them best, all the more so because it was created at the height of the Cold War and features an East–West spying plot involving fictional countries – Syldavie and Bordurie (Syldavia and Borduria in English) – that are nonetheless instantly recognisable as caricatures of communist states.

The third element, ideology, is one that evolves both for Tintin and for Bond, in the case of whom, for example, we see the anti-communism of the novel of *Casino Royale* (1953) become the war on terrorism in the 2006 film. Eco summarises the mechanism that allows for such a change in ideology:

> Fleming cherche des oppositions élémentaires; afin de donner un visage aux forces premières et universelles, il recourt à des clichés. Pour identifier ces clichés, il se réfère à l'opinion publique. En période de tension internationale, ce sera le méchant communiste ou le criminel nazi impuni – cliché désormais historiquement acquis. Fleming les emploie tous deux avec la plus grande indifférence. (190)
>
> [Fleming looks for elementary oppositions: in order to give a face to forces that are basic and universal, he resorts to clichés. In order to identify these clichés, he turns to public opinion. In a period of international tension, it will be the communist baddy or the unpunished Nazi criminal, a cliché that has since become a historic given. Fleming uses both indiscriminately.]

Thus Tintin goes from the anti-communism of *Tintin au pays de Soviets* (1930 for the album publication) and the colonialism of *Tintin au Congo* (1931) to the Cold War politics of *L'Affaire Tournesol* and beyond, towards a quest for an ideal of shared human exchanges that marks the later albums.

Our three-point schema – action/exposition/ideology – is paralleled by a three-point entertainment strategy based upon gadgets, travel and humour. Gadgets, for example the umbrella whose secret compartment hides a microfilm, tend to be the domain of Professeur Tournesol – on a par with Bond's 'M' – and exotic travels lead both of our heroes to Eastern Europe, to the Moon, and even to Scotland. The humour can be visual, as in a champagne cork that hits a baddy in the nose (*L'Affaire Tournesol*, p. 55), or indeed verbal, often in the form of Bond/Tintin's famous puns.

Like Bond, Tintin has his baddies, his allies, and his secondary characters, without whom the saga could not exist – but what he does not have, and nor does Marc le Téméraire, are the women. To a certain extent this is to be expected given the inherent differences between a serialised children's publication and Bond's double context of best-seller fiction and Hollywood movies. Since Tintin started life in the pages of the highly Catholic *Petit Vingtième*, he could hardly be seen throwing himself into the arms of sexy young temptresses! Bianca Castafiore, the diva who features in ten albums from 1939 onwards, with her imposing physical stature and stony face, and whose name indicates a white and chaste flower, is the only woman to feature prominently in Tintin's sexless world, where men live amongst men. That said, an interesting alternative study would be a mapping of the evolution of the Bond Girl as compared to that of the role of women as sex objects (or otherwise) in the bande dessinée of the 1960s and 1970s.

A final example of the 'Spirit of 007' in comics and bandes dessinées brings us to the question of overall narrative structure as pinpointed by Eco:[11]

> [Les livres de Fleming sont dominés par certaines situations clés que nous appellerons 'situations de jeu'. On a d'abord quelques situations archétypes comme le Repas ou le Voyage. (180)
>
> [Fleming's books are dominated by certain key situations that we shall call 'game situations'. First of all there are a few archetypal situations such as the Meal or the Journey.]
>
> Parallèlement à la séquence de coups directs, on a de nombreux coups périphériques, qui enrichissent de choix imprévus l'aventure, sans pour autant altérer le schéma de base. (182)
>
> [In tandem with the sequence of main events, we also find a number of peripheral events that enrich the adventure with unexpected choices, without in any way changing the basic schema of things.]
>
> [C]e qui caractérise le roman policier, fût-il d'investigation ou d'action, ce n'est pas tant la variation des faits que le retour d'un schéma habituel dans lequel le lecteur reconnaîtra quelque chose de déjà vu auquel il s'est attaché. (187)
>
> [What characterises the detective novel, be it based on investigation or on action, is not so much plot variation as the return to a habitual schema of things in which the reader can recognise something he or she has already seen and to which he or she has become attached.]
>
> Les noms mêmes des protagonistes participent de cette nature mythologique; par une image ou un calembour, ils révèlent dès le début le caractère du personnage [.] (191)
>
> [Even the names of the protagonists play their part in this mythological set-up: through an image or a play on words they reveal the personality of the character from the very beginning.]

Just as the structures described fit the Bond narratives, so they also encapsulate a good number of bandes dessinées (including *Tintin*), a key example being the *Astérix* series. As we have seen in the chapter on Contemporary BD, much of Goscinny and Uderzo's humour is in the wordplay on the protagonists' names; the themes of the meal and of the journey are fundamental (the return and the final banquet scene is essentially the leitmotif of the series); and the reader's pleasure lies not in knowing whether all will finish well, but how.

Icons of the text/image age

It would be entirely possible to provide a lengthy and descriptive comparison between the James Bond books and films and certain leading BDs. We should not, however, overlook the wider question of the specific cultural circumstances that make for the creation and success of our two phenomena, Bond and BD. In short, both are largely products of a postwar visual age, but one in which visual culture goes hand in hand with the culture of the text, the latter being inherent since the great novels of the nineteenth century.

Marshall McLuhan broaches such questions in his *Gutenberg Galaxy*,[12] a work that is one of the starting points for my own *Text/Image Mosaics*.[13] Umberto Eco had also noted that Fleming plays upon a mixture of plot-based *récit* – textual elements – and descriptive and therefore visual passages, with the amalgam creating the overall global impression:[14]

> Il est en effet surprenant de constater la minutie acharnée et oiseuse de ses [i.e., Fleming] interminables descriptions d'objets, de paysages ou de gestes en apparence non essentielles à l'aventure; et inversement, l'extrême style télégraphique avec lequel il liquide en quelques lignes les actions les plus inopinées et les plus improbables. (195–96)

> [It is in effect surprising to note the obstinate and superfluous attention to detail we find in his [Fleming's] never-ending descriptions of objects, of scenery or of acts that do not appear to be essential to the adventure: and, conversely, the extreme concision, telegram-style, with which he dispatches in a few lines the most unexpected and improbable events.]

Such a method transfers admirably to the visual splendour of the big screen, which is not the case for all novels. Similarly, hybrid construction is what makes the bande dessinée what it is, with its mixture of text-based linear progression (the plots in *Tintin*, with the necessary explanations provided by speech bubbles, *récitatifs*, or even close-ups on newspaper cuttings) and visual ambience (as in single-*case* pages, such as the famous plane crash scene on page 28 of *Tintin au Tibet*).

In more general terms, this hybridity, this mixture of textual *récit* and visual *éclat*, is at the very base of our current Western culture, one that is founded upon the written word, but which, since the advent of photography, cinema and television is becoming increasingly, if not predominantly, visual. It is a mixed text/image culture now to be found in the dominant elements of daily life, be they advertising, newspaper composition or the internet. Our heroes are perfect enactments of this hybrid culture, to the extent that the true icons of our current text/image era have become James Bond and Tintin.

This brief excursion into the world of thrill-a-minute intrigue will, I hope, highlight the wider role comics play in international Western culture. Just as James Bond has evolved to reflect a fantasy version of everyday values, for better or for worse, on questions such as national identity, the nature of Evil, the prerequisites of a consumer world and the representation of gender roles, in similar manner much the same can be said of high-profile comics. James Bond in the novels remains quintessentially English (even if it can be argued that he is in fact Scottish through his father) and the Hollywood Bond increasingly flies the flag for a range of American ideals, yet it would appear that the comic strip's opposite numbers are most suitable when drawn from the French-speaking tradition. Perhaps it is too sweeping a statement to suggest that the modern iconic adventure novel is English, film is American, whilst the Franco-Belgian contribution to international popular culture is the bande dessinée. But what this analysis does point to is the cultural paradox that the narrative strategies and ideological underpinnings associated with the quintessentially English Bond should be found to be so prevalent in the francophone BD.

Resistance and collaboration

BDs that explore history, such as André Juillard's *Les 7 Vies de l'épervier* series set in pre-Revolution France and its colonies,[15] are not the same thing as using BD to explore history. As my chapter on the pre-history of the BD has, hopefully, shown, if we extend the notion of bande dessinée so as to fall beneath the broad aegis of France's rich history of text/image narratives, the placing of the form in its broader cultural context can help us to consider such issues as the development of image-based propaganda, or the move towards or away from a society of visual communication. These broad concepts are the subject of many sections of my *Text/Image Mosaics*.

More recently, one of the historical periods most worthy of attention from non-Gallic eyes is that of the Occupation during the Second World War. It is easy to understand that the question of collaboration has often been a taboo subject, although recent works have started to bring it into the open. These have been spearheaded by Pascal Ory's 1976 work *Les Collaborateurs*, which has since seen further reprints and editions. In English, works on wartime collaboration have delved into the popular arts: Gerhard Hirschfeld and Partick Marsh's edited volume *Collaboration in France* includes chapters on popular literature and wartime cinema production,[16] as does Christopher Lloyd's *Collaboration and Resistance in Occupied France*.[17] In this respect Thierry Crépin's *'Haro sur le gangster!': La Moralisation de la presse enfantine 1934–1954* (2001) is groundbreaking in that it includes lengthy analysis of collaborationist press for children, in particular *Le Téméraire*.

Perhaps the distance of time, but also the geographical distance of a cross-Channel viewpoint, allow for a more balanced view on a touchy subject and its aftermath. Is the question of Vichy and of collaboration in the occupied zone still in any way taboo today, albeit in the aftermath of a certain amount of cinematic and literary attention? Just as France has a tradition of the image, is it reasonable to talk in terms of a French anti-Semitic tradition, one that often expresses itself through image-based propaganda, and that goes back to Dreyfus and beyond? Was the influence of *Le Téméraire* upon the youth of the 1940s so indelible that it could go some way to accounting for the Front National's standing at around 15 per cent and the almost unthinkable situation of the 2002 Presidential election whereby a far-right candidate made it to the final run-off?

The bande dessinée is a useful tool with which to approach such questions because it represents the 'everyday', in other words the nearest we have to a keyhole to the thoughts and values of the masses. In particular *Le Téméraire*, with its fortnightly sales of up to 200,000 copies, allows us to see what the youth of Paris enjoyed, or at least what it was willing to accept. Further to Crépin's work, Pascal Ory's *Le Petit Nazi illustré: Vie et survie du Téméraire (1943–1944)* (2002) presents, describes and contextualises the journal,[18] as do, to a lesser extent, the Introduction and 'Twentieth Century' chapter of this present book, as well as further analysis provided in my *Text/Image Mosaics*.

The last decades have therefore seen a certain amount of BD-related work on the question of collaborationist propaganda, and as such this provides a base for further potential research. There are no studies in English on other Pétainist BD publications such as *Fanfan la Tulipe*, *Benjamin* or, in Brittany, *O Lo Lê*. Not only would descriptive analysis of these be helpful so as to provide an overview, but a more precise study could examine the functioning role of the image in the strips. Were the *histoires en images* associated with traditionalism and, by implication, Pétain, whereas the speech bubbles of *Le Téméraire* were more forward-looking, despite the American influence? To what extent did the tone of the strips – humoristic, adventure, fantasy – bear on the content? Is there a potential comparison with the expression of similar ideology (e.g., via Oswald Mosley) in England?

Nor should potential studies overlook the aftermath of such publications. In *Text/Image Mosaics* I have given some account of the successful careers led by the ex-*Téméraire* team, but my findings are far from exhaustive. Further study could document the postwar reception of artists such as Raymond Poïvet and Erik, with a possible comparison with Hergé, some of whose wartime albums appear to have far-right leanings. Why, in short, did these figures meet with little or no opposition on their paths to bande dessinée stardom?

Finally, it would be interesting to look at BD portrayals of the Resistant or the Collaborator in postwar publications such as *Vaillant*, *Coq Hardi* or even *Coeurs Vaillants*. Laurent Marie has provided an admirable example, drawing upon the character of Resistance hero Le Grêlé 7/13, who appeared in *Vaillant* and then *Pif-Gadget* from 1966 to 1973.[19] Marie points to the ironic prolonged Manichean portrayal of 'baddies' through Semitic or Romany traits, a continuation of the *délit de sale gueule* that had functioned so well for *Le Téméraire*. Nonetheless *Le Grêlé 7/13* was far more objective than accounts propagated in the immediate postwar period. Further research could trace such evolution, whilst asking whether in more recent BDs the caricatural visual racism has been transferred to the 'outsiders' of today's world.

Underground or métropolitain?

The bande dessinée can be an incisive historical witness, part of whose testimony will also broach sociological issues: the way culture is manufactured, where its origins lie and the reception it receives. Bande dessinée, as we have seen, can be studied for what it tells us about specific time periods, but it can also be studied in terms of the broader intellectual context in which we achieve expression, and, more specifically, expression of dissidence.

Like many cultural forms, the bande dessinée is often at its strongest when challenging established values. And just as comic art perhaps came of age in the era of Pop Art, so that same broad time span also saw a reign of political and social dissidence, be it via the '68 movement and its aftermath in Europe, or the hippy generation and the anti-Vietnam cause in America.

In the USA it was the 1960s that saw the birth and development of the Underground comics movement, with figures such as Robert Crumb, Harvey Kurtzman and Art Spiegelman at the helm. Breaking with the tradition that for many placed comics as a children's preoccupation, 'comix' or 'commix', as underground works were (and are) known in deference to conventional creations, were deliberately 'adult'. This meant broaching subjects such as anti-war propaganda, drug culture, rock music and, most graphically, sex, in a quasi-deliberate attempt to contradict the requirements of the Comics Code and as part of a wider anti-mainstream counter-culture. The Underground thrived, initially at least, through home-produced fanzines such as *Air Pirates* (known for its parody of Disney) and *Zap* (led by Robert Crumb) and had no geographical base, although San Francisco, New York and Austin were leading centres. A glance at any of the bibliographies above will provide a number of works in English (although virtually none in French) on the Underground, but Roger Sabin's *Comics, Comix & Graphic Novels: A History of Comic Art* (1996) can be singled out as providing an accessible and reliable overview of the subject.[20]

Sabin also provides a chapter on European and Japanese comics that includes a succinct survey of French dissidence from the 1970s onwards,[21] and Bart Beaty's *Unpopular Culture* has important sections on French non-mainstream production and on L'Association in particular.[22] The breakaway from *Pilote*, the French counter-culture of the late twentieth century, and, more recently, the rise of independent 'art-house' publishing has been chronicled in my chapters 'The Twentieth Century' and 'Contemporary BD'. What can be noted throughout this alternative history of French comics is that although the content can be as challenging and shocking as anything the Underground produced, the provenance is entirely predictable. With the exception of the wartime years and a few dissident presses,[23] the history of bande dessinée production, be it mainstream or even alternative, is largely based on Paris, with a few quick excursions to Angoulême and Brussels.

Although, as stated previously, L'Association has done much to push the boundaries of the BD form and to raise its status as a vehicle that can be *engagé* and *contestataire*, an art form and not just a business, if we look closer does it not in fact function through the established channels? At a one-day conference on 10 May 2005 Jean-Christophe Menu vociferously attacked Philippe Osterman, Dargaud's editorial director, but the attack nonetheless took place amidst Parisian acquaintances and at the Bibliothèque nationale de France. The polemic between Gilles Ratier and Didier Pasamonik, two BD critics, and Menu, for which some of the correspondence appears in the first issue of *L'Éprouvette* ('Correspondance', pp. 278–82), revolves around reactions to reviews that appeared in Parisian journals of books that had been published in Paris.

From an outside viewpoint, therefore, it could be argued that French comics can never be truly subversive since sooner or later even the most avant-garde publications must pass through the centralised Parisian system and enter the clique that is the BD intelligentsia, albeit superficially to denounce such circles. Could such a homogenising environment be responsible for a possible lull in BD production?

The history of the background to BD production is one that is still very much to be written, and which could benefit from an external viewpoint: not only might it be possible to produce a more distanced and maybe cynical viewpoint, but it would also make for easier comparison with other traditions such as the Underground. Building on current studies, including this present volume, that concentrate on the final BD product, an alternative history could delve specifically into the backgrounds of the main artists and distributors, examine questions of readership – who exactly is reading what and where – as well as considering the type of associated marketing and media usage. We may find that the bande dessinée is very similar to French literary criticism and philosophy in that its 'makers and shakers' are in fact a clique of old friends gravitating around the Boulevard St Michel. If such is the case, the study of the bande dessinée could well be the next stage if we are to understand the *exception française* and full context of French intellectual history.

BD and banlieue

To draw upon the bande dessinée as a portrayal of modern French society, and thus as a source of related insight, is perhaps one of the more obvious applications of the form in terms of Cultural Studies.[24] As such it follows on from similarly directed analysis and application of cinema, detective novels, posters and clothing fashions to similar ends. The figure of Charles de Gaulle stands as an obvious case within such a schema, not least because he famously reported Tintin to be his main rival.[25] Despite denials of intention from the authors, it is easy to read the *Astérix* series as a mirror to Fifth Republic society, with the indomitable Gauls holding out against the Roman/USA/NATO invader. More recently, the French World Cup winning side of 1998, and in particular Zinedine Zidane, can be seen to encapsulate the intelligence and bravado of Goscinny and Uderzo's feisty Gauls, as James Steel has pointed out.[26]

The problem with proclaiming the BD as a 'mirror to modern society' is that such statements can become bland, or purely descriptive rather than analytical. But with such caveats in mind, the current theme of the *banlieue* presents an aspect of French society that is central to its political direction and to its difference from countries such as England or the USA, where the inner cities provide the nearest comparison with the French outskirts. The *banlieue*'s role in French politics is far from peripheral, as the importance of Nicolas Sarkozy's 2006 'racaille' [scum] comments and their aftermath have shown, events that have already been represented in BD form, such as Philippe Cohen and Richard Malka's album *La Face karchée de Sarkozy* [Sarkozy's Hidden Side] (2006). The bande dessinée can be useful on a primary level in terms of portrayal of *banlieue*, but perhaps more importantly as a mouthpiece for *banlieue* attitudes.

It is surprising that the work of Frank Margerin has received relatively little attention from Anglophone scholars.[27] Margerin's humoristic portrayal, from the 1980s onwards, of Lucien and his *banlieue* gang can serve as a catalogue of life at the end of the twentieth century, providing a written record of speech patterns, a narrative of daily lifestyle exploits, albeit exaggerated, and a visual portrayal, via background details of posters, architecture and objects, of the trappings of routine existence and of its development.

A study of the evolution of Margerin's work, in terms of both content and reception, could, in addition, benefit from the hindsight of time and from the distance of an outsider's viewpoint. A *fait divers* in *Y'a plus de jeunesse* [There's No Youth Any More] (1990; p. 43) showing wasteland bullies raping a young boy as a prank was, at the time, generally seen as part of Margerin's light-hearted over-the-top humour. By the late 1990s Margerin had received stern criticism for the gag, and a debate followed on the question of the taboo and/or the politically correct in France. In the twenty-first century Margerin's main hero has become Momo, the *beur* delivery-boy from the *banlieue*.[28] For a character of North African origin to be the comical hero of a mainstream series may have been unthinkable in the 1980s.[29] To what extent does Margerin represent real evolution in French attitudes, or is it a question of naïve tokenism in the build-up to and aftermath of the 2006 racial tension?

The BD can also raise serious social questions through non-caricatural publications, of which Tito's *Tendre banlieue* series is a popular example. First published by Okapi in 1983 and then by Casterman from the fifth volume in 1991 onwards, and with eighteen titles as of 2009, Tito uses a *ligne claire* near-realist style to present his adolescent audience with issues of relevance: racism, sexual discovery, AIDS, reactions to disabilities, parental relationships, anorexia, bullying and so on. The setting is generally life in a non-specific *banlieue* lycée, and the albums take their charm from a strong mixture of narrative, characterisation and descriptive visual details. It is hoped that future studies would avoid a descriptive presentation of subjects discussed and their outcomes, but rather might analyse what the approaches taken tell us. Does the simplistic artwork suggest a simplification of complex issues? Do the albums rely on image for scene-setting but on text for raising key points? Is there a certain naïveté in the use of an essentially bourgeois medium to address questions unlikely to affect its de facto readers? Or does the success of the series suggest that the bande dessinée has a youth credibility that could not be attained in Anglo-Saxon cultures?

Isabelle Papieau in *La Banlieue de Paris dans la bande dessinée* [The Paris Suburbs in Bande Dessinée] (2001), apparently the only monograph on the *banlieue* and BD, does raise the issue from a sociological viewpoint whilst suggesting that the *banlieue*, like the BD, functions as an amalgam of different constituent factors. A final approach, linking in with that of our previous suggestion on the intellectual context of dissidence, might be to investigate BD creation from a *banlieue* standpoint, such as examples of fanzines, *banlieue* artists who have (or have not) become mainstream, or via communications with *banlieusards* as to how they see the specificity and usefulness of the bande dessinée in representing their situation.

Sex and sexuality

The wide theme of sex and sexuality could be explored in at least three different ways: representations of the relative roles of men and women in bandes dessinées from the earliest of times onwards; the role of bande dessinée (or not) in the feminist movement; and the use of bande dessinée to express questions pertaining to sexuality.

Analysis of BD journals from the early part of the twentieth century would most likely point to a reinforcing of set gender roles. *La Semaine de Suzette* and *Âmes Vaillantes*, both aimed at bourgeois Catholic girls, are likely to show women as supports to the menfolk, fulfilling domestic tasks and advancing the cause of motherhood. As with 'BD and *banlieue*', a study that merely catalogues and describes such portrayal might form a useful base for further research, but would not achieve full potential per se. Such observations could, however, be applied further: to what extent does the role of women evolve over time? Are there any exceptions? To what extent are 'women's tasks' portrayed as background visual details, thereby suggesting them to be the insignificant norm? Does the portrayal of women in BDs differ from that to be found in cinema or novels of the same time? Do BDs in France conform to visual portrayals in other countries, such as the famous 'ideal home' presentations of the 1950s?

As an outlet for feminist expression, or even expression by women, bande dessinée is conspicuous by its absence. The reasons for male domination of the medium could be explored, although it is hard to imagine explanations going beyond the purely conjectural. It is interesting to note, however, that the few female BD artists that are active have received a considerable amount of attention from English-language critics.

Claire Bretécher is undoubtedly the *grande dame* of the BD world, having worked on *Pilote* during its formative years before breaking away to help form the *Écho des Savanes*. As stated in my chapter on the Contemporary BD, Bretécher's lead characters, such as Monique, Agrippine, Cellulite or the women of *Les Frustrés* (see Fig 3, Chapter 2), often deal with issues that would suggest feminist leanings, although Bretécher herself has always avoided such a label. Elizabeth McQuillan discusses the subject in her 2001 University of Glasgow doctoral thesis, 'The Reception and Creation of Post-1960 Franco-Belgian BD',[30] as well as in a 2000 book chapter, '"I Live my Body I am my Body": The Comic Bodies of Claire Bretécher'.[31] A further case study already available is that of Nhu-Hoa Nguyen, 'The Rhetoric of Parody in Claire Bretécher's *Le Destin de Monique*',[32] in which she examines the visual references (e.g., to Manet or Botticelli) used by Bretécher in her humorous portrayal of the self-centred Monique's (anti)feminist world, gags that undermine any potential seriousness the subject matter (embryo refrigeration and in vitro insemination) might have.

The work of Chantal Montellier is equally ambiguous, but for different reasons.[33] As we saw in my chapter on the Twentieth Century, Montellier was a leading figure in the short-lived 1970s feminist BD journal *Ah! Nana*, one whose explicit content led to its downfall when it received an 'adults only' classification. In her *Julie Bristol* series Montellier parallels the life of her detective-heroine with that of other victimised women, including Artemisia Gentileschi, the seventeenth-century artist raped by her mentor Agostino Tassi.[34] Whereas Bretécher's 'feminism' is ambiguous on account of its detached irony, with Montellier the explicit nature of many of the images leaves us wondering how a work that fetishises the female form can effectively undermine the destructive male gaze. These are the very questions that Ann Miller explores in her 2001 *French Studies* article, 'Chantal Montellier's *Faux Sanglant*: Sex, Death, Lies and Videotape'.[35]

As with BDs by women, openly gay bandes dessinées with goals other than pornographic pleasure have, until recently, been rare,[36] but what is now available has received relatively copious and incisive analysis in English. Fabrice Neaud remains the groundbreaker in this field, his multi-volume *Journal* (published by Ego Comme X, see Fig. 10,

Chapter 2) expressing the tribulations of gay life in small-town France. In the final chapter of *Gay and Lesbian Cultures in France*, Murray Pratt gives a critical overview of Neaud's techniques and themes, with specific attention to the question of potential gay attitudes when faced with heterosexual hegemony.[37] The first stages of this research had been presented at the 2001 Australian Society for French Studies conference in Canberra, and Pratt explored the subject further, examining in particular the *Journal*'s autobiographical techniques, for the 2003 Leicester IBDS conference, at which Neaud was a guest of honour. The tradition continued at the 2007 London IBDS conference when, in a session dedicated to Neaud, Michael Johnson studied his pictorial representation of the face in terms of its explicit link with gay identity, Lawrence Schehr considered the *Journal* as a mock-religious 'devotion' that plays upon specific aspects of the BD form, and Philippe Chavasse compared the work of Neaud with the literature and philosophy of right-wing gay essayist Renaud Camus (born 1946).

It would be interesting to examine the general differences of approach between these studies and those that have appeared in French, for example in issue 9 (2003) of *9e Art*. This sixteen-page section (pp. 84–99) of the CNBDI-sponsored journal concentrates on linguistic effects and constructions of style in Neaud's work.[38] The dossier is unusual in that its authors are all based in French universities, and the emphasis on structure and mechanics may be due to their background in linguistics and communication, but it is still interesting to note that such studies put the social and sexual content to second place. Again, even if the approach is specific to the orientation of the Lyon symposium at which the work was first presented,[39] it remains a general rule that anglophone BD studies differ in their attraction to fields such as feminism and queer studies, where a solid critical apparatus is in place.

Ils sont fous ces Caledoniens

Just as anglophone academia of recent decades has explored and expanded the disciplines of women's studies and queer studies, so works on colonialism and postcolonialism have flourished. Obvious BD-related studies in this respect would be on *Tintin* and colonialism, or, more recently, on works such as Jacques Ferrandez's *Carnets d'Orient* [Oriental Notebooks], an eight-volume series published in album form by Casterman (1994 onwards) that tells a family story set against the backcloth of the French presence in Algeria between 1830 and 1954. Mark McKinney in particular has fruitfully applied postcolonial theory to the bande dessinée, firstly in a number of articles, more generally in a 2008 edited volume, *History and Politics in French-Language Comics and Graphic Novels*,[40] and above all in a forthcoming monograph, *Redrawing Empire: Imperialism, Colonialism and Immigration in French and Belgian Comic Books.*

As stated in my Foreword, it is for reasons of concision and unity that this current study concentrates on the French and Belgian BD traditions. Nonetheless I am aware that much work remains to be done on bande dessinée production outwith metropolitan France, be it in relation to French-speaking African or Asian countries, the DOM TOMs, Switzerland or Quebec, or indeed on BD creation by ethnic minorities from within France.[41] Definitions of nationality and *appartenance* could also be explored via non-colonial minority cultures within France, such as Breton or Occitan, and their expression through bande dessinée. In all of these cases it would be useful to look at the culture of non-Paris-based BD production in the context of work that has already been applied to other forms, such as cinema or crime fiction.

The core cultural question of national identity could also be examined in terms of bande dessinée portrayal of France's European partners. Images of Scotland, for example, could be a case study, starting with the be-kilted Tintin in *L'Île noire*, and the passing portrayal of the 'caledoniens' as parsimonious in *Astérix chez les Bretons*. Less well known would be portrayals of Scotland in nineteenth-century *histoires en images*, or even in early twentieth-century strips, as in Bécassine's view of Scottish soldiers in the First World War. More recently, Jean-Claude Forest's Hypocrite, a brunette sex symbol of the 1970s (cf. Barberella, the blonde of the '60s), battles against bagpipe-playing ghosts in *Hypocrite et le monster du Loch Ness* (reissued in album form by L'Association in 2001), whereas the top-selling opening volume of the *Décalogue* series, *Le Manuscrit*, and its follow-up *Le Rendez-Vous de Glasgow*, the opening volume of the *Légataire* series,[42] set the murderous intrigue against the backcloth of modern post-industrial Glasgow.

Such a catalogue of Scottish references, or indeed a similar work based on other nations, could initially provide a historical and aesthetic overview of the BD via a thematic précis of specific interest to non-French readers. Perhaps more importantly, such an overview could raise questions as to the nature of the development of stereotypes, for example whether the portrait passes principally through the image or the text, or whether this in turn depends on the nature of the stereotype. More broadly, from the viewpoint of Scottish or Celtic studies it could be useful to investigate the vision that others have and how it has evolved through an image-based cultural form that is in many ways specific to France. Finally, it goes without saying that such portrayals often tell us more about the artist than the subject, and as such could stand as a case study of the French view of the outside, and by implication 'exotic' Other, albeit one of isolation and tentative superiority.

3D BD

Although the notion of Cultural Studies is most generally associated with approaches to content-related issues, as we have seen in our section on 'Underground or *métropolitain*', the way that society expresses itself can tell us much about that society's values. In terms of exploring the bande dessinée's format – how it says what it says – and its relationship to wider developments in the expression of cultural concepts, the final progression is the move beyond the BD as we know it, a two-dimensional mixture of text and image largely distributed on paper and possibly discarded after reading, to what in recent years has often become a large-scale multi-format phenomenon involving all of the senses, an all-encompassing experience.

In the next section I will consider approaches to the output of Marc-Antoine Mathieu, an artist who delves into the three-dimensional via his creations with the production group Lucie Lom. As we shall see, one of his main influences is the work of Benoît Peeters and François Schuiten, whose trademark series, the *Cités obscures*, can be explored not only through the books, but also via the website (www.urbicande.be) and the stage production, *L'Affaire Augustin Desombres*. This played in Paris in April 2000 having been on a limited tour of other French cities, and included film clips, animation clips, stills of bandes dessinées, musical performance and the presentation of various objects and artefacts. Taking a step further, Peeters and Schuiten were to allow the audience to become part of the *cités obscures* via walk-through exhibitions such as the 1992 *Opéra bulles* at the Grande Halle de la Villette in Paris (for which a section was also the work of Lucie Lom), or even the remodelled Paris Arts et Métiers underground station.[43] Similarly, be it *Astérix* or *Barbarella*, with the advent of figurines, spin-off films and theme parks, the bande dessinée now goes beyond the storybook: it is a phenomenon rather than a narrative.

Although many works in French will mention the vast number of films that are related to the bande dessinée, be they as cartoon or 'real life' versions, often such studies can be little more than descriptive lists. Alternatively, as we have seen briefly in Chapter 3, 'Formal Specificity', there has been a tendency in post-1970s BD criticism to analyse the formal qualities of the bande dessinée in terms of their possible affinity with those of cinema.[44] This may have been due to a lack of known apparatus for visual criticism, or an implicit desire to associate the success of the Seventh Art with the Ninth. In English, one of the earliest scholarly articles on bande dessinée was Hugh Starkey's 'Is the BD "à bout de souffle"?' in which he outlined the history and possible future directions of the BD, whilst comparing these with those of cinema.[45]

Much could be done to update and build upon Starkey's findings, be it on the level of the thematic social analysis of a cinema/BD topos, as in the case of our James Bond study above, or in terms of the way in which BD now goes beyond the page and, often, into the international market. The New Wave career of director Alain Resnais, his association with the early Club des Bandes Dessinées and the frequent references to comics and to French/Anglo-Saxon interaction, as in *I Want to Go Home* (1989) and *Smoking/No Smoking* (1993), could provide the material for such a study. Drawing upon individual films one could explore the 'Frenchness' of the 2007 Cannes success of *Persepolis*, the Vincent Paronnaud and Marjane Satrapi film based on Satrapi's albums, or, in terms of market, the leap made by *Astérix* into box-office hits.[46]

The *Astérix* prodigy also encapsulates the 3D phenomenon of the BD-based theme park, as we have seen in the business section of my chapter 'Pop Art or Business Park?'. Parc Astérix, just north of Paris, is France's second most popular theme park, but is several million visitors per year behind Disneyland Paris, currently Europe's number one tourist destination. A comparative study of the two parks remains to be done, perhaps analysing their respective relationships with the bandes dessinées on which they are based, and tracing the development towards the three-dimensional. Alternatively, it would be possible to consider the way in which a BD theme park draws upon the same strategies of enticement as previous text/image forms. Louis Marin has famously analysed the way in which Disneyland draws visitors to the central axis of its park and creates a linear narrative of the American Utopian Dream from past ('Frontierland') to future ('Tomorrowland', or 'Discoveryland' in the French park).[47] I have applied Marin's findings to demonstrate how this functions in a similar way to the Versailles of Louis XIV, whereby the narrative of the Sun King is created by reference to Early Modern text/image forms such as emblems and devices.[48]

As the bande dessinée moves forward it seems inevitable that its direction will bring in new technology and further expansion towards multi-media. Multi-mediatisation may imply globalisation; or the BD, like cinema, may keep its own very French specificity. Such speculation, which could be expanded to further analyses, is a fitting line to draw under our Cultural Studies case studies, allowing us to leave them whilst looking to the possible future of the form.

Beyond ...

We have seen from our surveys of contemporary BD and of its move towards artistic consecration that the BD's position within the cultural field is changing. With self-awareness the form has gone beyond being a simple piece in the wider cultural jigsaw to being a self-dependent entity, one that merits consideration on its own terms. Pragmatically, work of this kind can be fulfilling per se, but it can also demonstrate that the study of BD will complement a variety of sometimes unexpected spheres within programmes of research and teaching.

Our principal case study will consider approaches to narratology by looking at BD and formal experimentation. André Juillard's *Le Cahier bleu* (1994) allows us to investigate such questions through external viewpoints, and examine how a series of events can be depicted from different perspectives, and how the bande dessinée is particularly suited to such expression. The work of Marc-Antoine Mathieu, and in particular *La 2,333e dimension* (2004), raises questions from a self-reflexive stance, exploring the bande dessinée's potential role as flagship for experimental literature and playful explorer of the intrinsic nature of representational art forms.

The shorter studies will do no more than refer to existing pieces or evoke possible future directions, but will allow the reader to consider exploring the wider categories of Aesthetics, Psychoanalysis, Semiotics and Pedagogy.

Case study: formal experimentation

Just as formal experimentation has allowed both avant-garde cinema and the novel to explore different levels and methods of interactive communication, so the same is possible for bande dessinée. In our chapter on Contemporary BD we considered broad movements that challenge the norms of formal expression: L'Association with its promotion of *BD d'auteur* encouraging artists to break with the restrictions of traditional publishing, and, more specifically, the works of OuBaPo that rise to the challenge of self-imposed constraints so as to demonstrate the variety of methods, and ambiguities, of expression that can be produced.

The same sort of investigation can also be carried out on the level of the individual album, and to that end two works of recent decades exemplify distinct approaches to formal experimentation. André Juillard's *Le Cahier bleu* (1994; second edition 2003) is a break from the author's historical epic cycles generally produced in partnership with a scriptwriter such as Patrick Cothias,[49] whilst Marc-Antoine Mathieu's *La 2,333e dimension* (2004) forms part of a formally experimental series with the main character, Julius Corentin Acquefacques, as linchpin.

Le Cahier bleu: experiments with narratology

Le Cahier bleu is divided into three equal sections of which the first two tell the main sequence of events from two different viewpoints: firstly that of the main character, Louise, and then that of her lover, Victor Sanchez, as related in his diary, the eponymous *cahier bleu*. The third section relates the episode's conclusion from a retrospective viewpoint of a police enquiry. The action as a whole takes place in Paris, with key scenes situated on line 6 of the metro (Nation-Charles de Gaulle Étoile) at the Dupleix station. Juillard's depiction of recognisable Parisian cityscapes is an important element of the album. Just as Louise is exotic – frequent references are made to her Québecois accent – and seemingly unattainable (just like an accent in a bande dessinée), so the setting, in contrast, is the recognisable world of Juillard's everyday existence. In a previous volume, *Nation/Étoile*,[50] Juillard had published sketches of the metro line that serves his home.

Le Cahier bleu draws upon the specific qualities of the BD medium so as to engage with the subjectivity of any portrayal of external events, a theme dear to the exponents of the *Nouveau Roman*, and indeed Juillard points to Alain Robbe-Grillet's *La Maison de rendez-vous* (1965) as a possible influence.[51] What appears, from the first chapter, to be a straightforward linear narrative of a woman's involvement with two lovers, and in particular the first, Armand Laborie, takes on new twists through the alternative viewpoint of the second chapter, wherein we see events from Sanchez's perspective.

Juillard's narrative layering operates on several levels. Firstly it can be a straightforward double-take on events, such as the initial scene when we see Louise undressed in her flat and glancing at the passing overhead metro whilst commenting to herself that she should install curtains (p. 9) compared with Victor's same view of the scene from the metro in question, where he indeed glimpses Louise's nakedness (p. 31).[52] Further on, when the couple part after a visit to a photography exhibition, we initially see the scene from the top of the stairs (p. 23), Louise's viewpoint, and then again from Victor's angle (p. 49) as he looks longingly up at her.

One step further, the double-take can modify events on the level of characterisation: on page 15 (Fig. 38) we see a rushed Louise (she is about to leave for her date with Armand) taking Victor's initial phone call in which he poses as a financial services salesman, 'un raseur' [pest] as she later describes him. The corresponding visual account of Victor's viewpoint (pp. 39–40) provides a contrast that paints his character whilst avoiding direct statement. He (and thus the reader) initially visualises Louise answering the phone naked but for a towel, as he had seen her from the metro, but as he realises his request for a meeting is to be refused we switch to a graveside scene, what we might assume to be Victor's father, child in arms, mourning his mother. The conversation continues and as Victor comments on Louise's Canadian accent we jump to a frame of her in the foreground of a snowy scene with rural North American architecture. A banal unwanted call – from Louise's viewpoint – allows us to see the Freudian effect of a lost mother on a psyche that equates eroticism with exoticism.

The third level of double-take produces new significance for the reader. Once we have read Victor's account of how he initially tailed Louise (pp. 35–37), a re-reading of page 15 (Fig. 38), Louise's view of things, reveals additional details that would at first have passed unnoticed. A shadow in the courtyard as Louise leaves her building is now known to be Victor, as indeed is the unnoticed, and accordingly semi out of frame, figure on the opposite metro platform. What appears to be simply a new paragraph as we first see and read the journal itself (p. 29, repeated on p. 31) is later revealed to be the space left by Armand's eventual Tippex-ing out of his own name, an element that provides a further twist to the initial event as the pre-doctored text adds the knowledge that Louise's two future lovers were friends together in the metro carriage. The astute reader may have noticed the Tippex-ed change when a *mise-en-abyme* technique presents us with Victor writing the beginning of the journal we are reading (p. 34), but the missing statement is 'J'étais avec Bobo' [I was with Bobo], 'Bobo' being Armand's nickname, which we have not heard at that stage. In terms of critical theory, this is a prime example of a shifting text (cf. Derrida's *différance*), one whose meaning depends on the individual reader, although the process is circular as the reader's standpoint evolves as he or she explores the album.

Whereas sections 1 and 2 are largely contemporaneous, section 3 advances the time sequence whilst providing elements of flashback. It is through this section in particular that Juillard plays with differing levels of reader knowledge, creating alternatively what one might term an omniscient reader, a 'partially-scient' reader or a 'non-scient' reader. The omniscient reader is aware of elements unknown to the characters, such as when Victor wonders why Armand should have wanted to give Louise the *cahier bleu*, as compared with the reader, who is fully aware that the two are rivals for her attentions (p. 59). Despite having seen the story from both Louise/Armand's viewpoint and Victor/Louise's viewpoint, until part 3 the 'partially-scient' reader does not know that the two men are friends and were in the initial metro carriage together, notwithstanding the double portrayal of the scene.

Such levels of knowledge are finally undermined by a conclusion that leaves the reader 'non-scient', a fitting ending for a book that plays upon the subjectivity of our knowledge of the external world. Victor is released from prison as a result of the alibi given by Elena, a conquest of Armand who then befriends Victor, but we never know if events were as depicted or if the new couple colluded, and, either way, the question of who did kill Armand remains unresolved. The same is true of the nature of the central relationship of Louise and Victor. We see Louise rushing to meet Victor as he leaves prison, unbeknown to him as he walks off with Elena. The final text, 'mais la vie continue' [but life continues], is a cliché offering no certainty, and the ambiguities are compounded when in Juillard's 1998 sequel, *Après la pluie* [After the Rain],[53] the opening *planches* show Victor and Louise together again although no explanation is given.

Once we become aware that Juillard's art depends on a careful game of narrative viewpoints we can see, retrospectively at least, that the text is intricately constructed, or indeed falsely constructed in the same way that the many parallels in *Mme Bovary* create an artifice that undermines the initial illusion of realism. On a textual level, for example, Armand's statement to Louise, 'et donc je vous ai vue "dans le plus simple appareil"' [and so I saw you in the 'simplest of states'] (p. 11) is taken from Act II Scene 2 of Jean Racine's *Britannicus* (1669).

Figure 38. 'Louise's Viewpoint'. André Juillard. *Le Cahier bleu.* [Paris]: Casterman, 2003. First published 1994. p. 15. © Casterman.

Here Néron describes his love for Junie upon seeing her, a love that will lead to a struggle between desire and morality, and thus a fitting premonition of Armand's behaviour. A further artifice throughout the album is the constant interplay between the direct speech of the *bulles*, the external narration of the *récitatifs*, and the internal narration of the *cahier*'s handwritten text.

Visual parallels can often appear in the secondary details not necessarily essential to the central plot. On a simple level, symmetry is created by three *cases* in which each of Louise's admirers glances at her legs in keeping with his character: Armand boldly as she stands in the doorway (p. 10), M. Carpi, her boss, cautiously as she is up a ladder at work (p. 18) and Victor, with subtlety, at a concert (p. 47). Similarly, as Victor talks to Louise by phone he views an erotic print of a woman's backside (p. 50),[54] whereas at the same moment Louise's body is the subject of an analogous gaze from Armand (p. 25).

More discreet is the reference to an exhibition photo by Robert Doisneau (p. 23) that appears to catch the moment by chance but is in fact carefully orchestrated, and thus provides a *mise en abyme* of Victor's pursuing of Louise. Similarly, certain references to carefully constructed works of art – a Piet Mondrian print (p. 11) or the symmetry of the Palais de Tokyo (p. 37) – reflect the balanced construction of Juillard's creation. More generally, in the interview that precedes the 2003 edition of *Le Cahier bleu* Juillard refers briefly to his fascination with Edward Hopper, a detail that clarifies the haunting presence created in certain *cases* depicting freeze-frame slices of life.

At times it is the interaction of text and image that creates the effect. The text on page 14, Louise's thoughts, tells us that 'pas un instant, cher Monsieur, je n'ai pensé à vous' [not for a moment, Dear Sir, did I think of you], but the image shows her looking onto the metro line as if in search of Armand, ironically, we will later learn (p. 32), at the very moment that Victor is in the train.

Finally, on an overall level the predominance of the blue on the album's front and back covers, including the title lettering (in the 2003 edition), creates a layering whereby the album becomes the *cahier bleu* of the title, a further *mise en abyme* with the textual diary as the key to the visual album of which it is the linchpin. Ironically, as Juillard points out in the interview for the monograph dedicated to him,[55] when the work was initially serialised in *[À Suivre]* (1993) the whole process was undermined by the omission due to a printer's error of page 29, the arrival of the *cahier bleu*!

Juillard's *Le Cahier bleu* shows us how the bande dessinée can use formal techniques to engage explicitly with questions of perception and representation. It is of course possible to create similar effects using other media, as for example in the film series *Trois couleurs: Bleu, blanc, rouge* [Three Colours: Blue, White Red] (directed by Krzysztof Kieslowski, 1993–1994) whereby details of the three films' narratives sporadically overlap.[56] However, the BD, and in particular this BD, is specific in that it facilitates the essential element of re-reading. Whereas it is possible to replay DVDs to recheck precise details, that is not the norm. By contrast we can reasonably expect the reader of *Le Cahier bleu*, once he or she reaches the second part and becomes aware of the double narrative, to flip back and forth to compare analogous scenes, such as the initial view of Louise (pp. 9

and 31) or the visit to the exhibition (pp. 22–23 and 49). As more of the complexities become apparent a secondary retrospective reading will produce an experience that is very different from the initial linear approach, but it is one that is no less valid.

Le Cahier bleu is a complex multi-layered construction that withstands highly theoretical critical analysis, but it is also a high-selling mainstream publication. The album can be read as an attractive narrative of the everyday or purely for its *ligne claire* graphic qualities, the visual pleasure of the Parisian cityscapes or the mild eroticism that accompanies the characterisation. In these aspects the work has much the same qualities as Juillard's previous work, for example the historical cycle *Les 7 Vies de l'épervier*, and to which it is often compared. Indeed it is interesting to note that in the various French interviews and articles, of which there are a fair number,[57] it is the graphic qualities, the non-use of a scriptwriter or the relationship between the cityscapes and the author's own world that tend to dominate. On the other hand, in general French criticism shows little or no concern for the formal intricacies of the album and the theory-related questions that it raises.[58] The account of *Le Cahier bleu* in *[Primé à Angoulême]*,[59] is typical:

> Tout commence par une rame de métro aérien immobilisée et par un coup de foudre provoqué par la vision d'une jeune femme nue, derrière les fenêtres d'un immeuble situé face à la ligne.
>
> À partir de la trame élémentaire (*boy meets girl*) utilisée pour (presque) toutes les histoires d'amour, André Juillard recourt à une habile construction qui lui permet de raconter plusieurs fois la même histoire selon des points de vue différents, sans que cette petite méchanique ne relègue au second plan les personages. Ce sont bien eux qui occupent le devant de la scène et nous touchent au-delà du raisonnable. Peut-on sans ridicule avouer être tombé amoureux d'un personnage de papier, avoir été séduit par sa ligne de rein, conquis par sa grâce? Et qui plus est succomber à chaque fois?
>
> Car en dépit de la perte de toute surprise quant à l'intrigue, les relectures successives n'émoussent jamais notre plaisir.
>
> Si cet auteur est un maître en matière de clarté, ce n'est pas seulement par la totale lisibilité de son récit mais par son travail sur les formes, son emploi de teintes chaudes, avec des jaunes pâles dominants qui adoucissent les blessures de l'âme de ses personages, sa minutie à determiner la place exacte de chaque objet.
>
> Outre le prix du meilleur album, André Juillard en aurait mérité un second: celui de l'élégance. (75)

> [Everything starts with an overhead metro train that has stopped and by the love at first sight brought about by the vision of a naked young woman behind the windows of a building that is opposite the metro line. Starting with this basic boy-meets-girl framework that is used for (almost) all love stories, André Juillard draws upon skilful construction to allow him to tell the same story several times according to different

> viewpoints, without this mechanism putting the characters into the background. They are well and truly front of stage and affect us beyond the expectations of reason. Is it possible to admit, without appearing ridiculous, to having fallen in love with a fictional character, to have been seduced by the curve of her backside, conquered by her grace? And, furthermore, to have succumbed each time?
>
> For in spite of the loss of all element of surprise with respect to the plot, further re-readings never diminish our pleasure.
>
> If the author is a master of clarity, it is not only on account of the complete readability of his *récit*, but through his expression of form, his use of warm shades, with pale yellows that dominate and soften the hurt his characters feel in their soul, and the meticulous way in which he finds the perfect place for each object.
>
> As well as the prize for best album, André Juillard would have deserved a second one: a prize for elegance.]

By contrast, the two main studies that have appeared in English, by Teresa Bridgeman and Ann Miller,[60] are less concerned with the use of colours and the shape of Louise's backside, engaging instead with techniques of figuration, systems of modality and codes of representation. Why should this be so?

The answer may not be to do with an English obsession with theory or a French obsession with backsides, but quite simply because in France Juillard is a mainstream author and the critical attention he receives has developed accordingly. His popularity and recognition in everyday circles stems firstly from his work on *Les 7 Vies de l'épervier*, and, perhaps even more emphatically, from his work with Yves Sante on the resurrection of Edgar-Pierre Jacobs's cult detectives Francis Blake and Philip Mortimer (see my chapter on the Contemporary BD). Both creations received and continue to receive considerable attention in the mainstream BD and general press, as well as a limited amount of more specialised analysis.[61] The emphasis overwhelmingly lies with Juillard's fine-line style, his role as the modern-day continuation of Hergé, and his place in the crossover between bande dessinée and graphic realism in the style of Edward Hopper and others. To ignore this trademark style when discussing *Le Cahier bleu* might seem out of place, especially given that the album is the first to transpose his style to a modern context.

Anglo-Saxon criticism does not have that baggage to bear and as a result can almost broach *Le Cahier bleu* ex nihilo. Indeed if an apology is needed for a little-known author whose chosen format sometimes requires justification beyond its home boundaries, what better way than to point to the work as exemplifying the theories of Derrida and Barthes? Perhaps a middle ground is best, one that acknowledges the graphic qualities and universal appeal of *Le Cahier bleu*, whilst underlining its importance as an object of reflection that raises and challenges questions associated with the base precepts of visual and textual representation.

La 2,333e dimension: self-reflexive experimentation

In the case of Marc-Antoine Mathieu's series featuring Julius Corentin Acquefacques, such questions of critical emphasis are less marked, as it is difficult to avoid discussing his work in terms of theories of representation and formal experimentation. For Mathieu there are virtually no external referents, the subject of these bandes dessinées is the bandes dessinées themselves. And the exclusivity of male characters in his monochrome Acquefacques albums in general makes it impossible for us to be distracted by the colours or by the aesthetics of the female backside.[62]

Mathieu is slightly unusual in that, despite his immense success, his work as a bande dessinée artist is not really his 'day job'. His background and continued career is with Lucie Lom, a production company specialising in the production of posters, publicity and interactive exhibitions. Examples of work from Lucie Lom include a recreation of a campsite for the 'Holidays' section of *Opéra bulles*, the 1992 scenic walk-through exhibition on BD at Paris's Grande Halle de la Villette, numerous installations (e.g., fossil cars breaking through the pavement) for the 1999 Accroche-Coeurs festival in Angers, 3-D BD displays on the Spanish, Italian and USA Underground traditions (1989, 1995 and 2008) for the Angoulême festival, and an interactive children's exhibition on the theme of shadows for the Villette science centre in Paris. The link is not without logic, however, as a company that specialises in creating spaces that grab the attention shares one of the key factors of the Acquefacques albums, the element of surprise.

The character's surname is a phonetic reversal of Kafka, as befits one caught up in a nightmarish universe of dark tunnels or, as the series' subtitle puts it, a 'prisonnier des rêves' [Prisoner of Dreams].[63] Verticality dominates the graphics and there are no skies and few horizons, all of which contributes to the claustrophobic effect. Acquefacques has few distinguishing physical characteristics – his round face, hidden by hat and glasses, make him a stereotypical cartoon non-entity (see Fig. 39) – nor can we perceive any specific personality traits. The absence of female characters removes love interest – Acquefacques tells us that women would only take up space – and the lack of outside locations removes any possibility of local colour. In short, Mathieu reduces 'reality' to a minimum thereby eliminating all subject matter other than the work itself. In his own words,[64]

> ... dans les albums de *Julius Corentin Acquefacques*, c'est l'histoire qui prime, en même temps qu'un discours sur le médium. Le dessin est secondaire: je n'ai pas besoin d'être un grand dessinateur pour raconter ces histoires. (63–64)

> [... In the Julius Corentin Acquefacques albums the story is first and foremost, together with my reflection on the medium. The drawing takes second place: I do not need to be a great artist to tell these stories.]

Each of the five Acquefacques albums that have appeared between 1990 and 2004 explores a different area of formal experimentation, be it the *mise en abyme* of a book within a book, distorted reading through a single *case* physical hole in a page or a paper spiral glued to a later page, the intermingling of finished design, preliminary sketch and photos of the artist at work, or the use of 3-D glasses to take the *cases* beyond the page.[65] The effect is always playful and even gimmick-like, but it allows us to reflect upon the nature of artistic representation with specific reference to the bande dessinée. It is for the reader to construct (or choose to ignore) the bulk of the 'story' – who is Acquefacques, from where does he come, what are his objectives – but what we do have is a de facto treatise on the techniques and constraints that govern the BD.

In brief, *L'Origine* (1990) introduces us to Julius Corentin Acquefacques, who occupies a bedsit not far from the 'Ministère de l'Humour' [Ministry of Humour] where he works. A mysterious envelope that arrives on page 15 contains page 4 of the album that we are in the process of reading and with it the first of many *mise-en-abyme* flashbacks and flash-forwards.[66] Acquefacques explores a bi-dimensional world in which he is just a character, and which depends on the outer three-dimensional world that created it, before ending with the realisation, at the bottom of *planche* 42, that 'nous sommes en fin de page 42' [we are at the end of page 42]. The main 'gimmick' is the 'trou de matière' [matter hole] between *planches* 37 and 38 thereby allowing *cases* from the previous and subsequent *planches* to receive a double reading.

La Qu … (1991) introduces further meta-realism via photographs of the author burning *planche* 42 of the previous album (as had been suggested would happen in that very *planche*) with the characters falling into his coffee (p. 7, Fig. 39).[67] As the album ends, Acquefacques opens the roof of the strip, a porthole onto the outside world, thereby allowing an influx of the 'qu … qu … quadrichromie' to which the title refers. These are the only splashes of colour in the series, and they are quickly dismissed as a dream.

In the third album, *Le Processus* [The Process] (1993), Mathieu piles on the artifices so as to highlight the problems of temporal narration within spatial distribution. Acquefacques goes from BD *planches* to a world of photographs and unfinished sketches – his own past world in the process of his creation – via a paper spiral, the gimmick that physically links the pages. Much reference is made to the clock motif: time does not advance despite the progress of the narrative, indeed the final *mise en abyme* of the initial pages creates the paper illusion of time going backwards.

L'Épaisseur du miroir (1995) is two albums in one, each with their own cover and with a central meeting point at which Acquefacques climbs through the mirror to meet his double. In *Le Début de la fin* [The Beginning of the End] Acquefacques's day advances in reverse chronological order – he shaves and then becomes stubble-ridden – whereas in *La Fin du début* [The End of the Beginning] the reverse

Figure 39. 'Mixed Media'. Marc-Antoine Mathieu. *La Qu* .... Paris: Delcourt, 1991. p. 7. © Delcourt.

occurs. The mirror is the album's central gimmick, not only via the subject matter, such as the proper name palindromes – 'le Professeur Evariste Etsirave', 'Avenue Euneva' – but moreover on the level of the object itself, the double-faced book. A further layer is added through the implicit reference to François and Luc Schuiten's *NegegoN* (1991), an earlier album that created the same reversal effect from an artist whose *Cités obscures* series is a key influence on Mathieu.

It is worth looking at the fifth album in the series, *La 2,333e dimension* (2004), slightly more closely as it unites the main themes of the previous works while adding a new and overriding gimmick, that of three-dimensionality. The fact that the album ends on the inside leaf of the back cover with the long-awaited catching of the elusive dream seems to imply that this is the final volume in the series, but one never knows …

As a bande dessinée that, as stated, provides a wry look at the formal qualities of the medium itself, it is not surprising that the theme of the narrative should be prominent. The narrative we are reading can be one of many: that of Acquefacques as he continues in his cloistered world; that of the dream-catchers who break into his flat; that of the dream, the physical sheet that escapes them and that we have in our hands; or indeed that of the events lived by Acquefacques during the dream, including the subworlds of the 'Inframonde' [Infraworld] and of the three-dimensional 'Trou Gris' [Grey Hole]. And although in all of these cases the narrative viewpoint would appear to be that of an omniscient third person, Mathieu makes sure to create levels of ambiguity. As Acquefacques enters the three-dimensional section, Dilbert Dugommier, the 'Directeur de Distribution des Décors Divers' [Distribution Director for Diverse Décors] hands him a pair of 3-D glasses, with the words, 'je vous conseille de mettre ça … le filter bleu sur votre oeil droit. Sinon c'est le mal de crane assuré!' (47) [I'd advise you to put these on … with the blue filter on the right eye. Elsewise you're guaranteed a headache!]. The reader becomes Acquefacques as he or she takes said glasses, which are glued on at that point in the album, but which need to be reverse folded so as to get the blue filter on the right eye! A page later the *cases* themselves start to break down as physical self-referentiality surpasses conventional narrative schemes.

Indeed the album becomes an *exercise de style* with Mathieu throwing in constant references to his art. The title page of chapter 2, 'Le Rêve à ne pas faire' [The Dream to Avoid] (p. 11) provides a flash-forward *mise en abyme* as the dream-catchers chase it from page 8 onwards. Much of the 'plot' involves a lost vanishing point, contextualised via diagrams that explain this key concept of graphic representation. Here, as in *Le Processus*, a great deal is made of different media: not just the 3-D section (to which we will return below), but also the pencilled sketches of the world of 'ébauches', characters waiting for their time to come, and the photos of the crumpled-up sketches when Acquefacques and his neighbour Hilarion abandon them to step into a galaxy of parallel universes.

The parallel universes allow Mathieu to acknowledge the medium of which *La 2,333e dimension* is a self-reflexive example. Acquefacques leaves the two-dimensional verticality of his present album to observe other spherical worlds from a distance, although the act of taking off into the 'Inframonde' transforms the current pages into the first of the 'planets' (p. 33). The next of these is in fact his own *L'Origine*, with specific reference to 'La page 27', a *planche* which also arrives in an envelope and so first appears four pages before its 'true' place, thereby evoking the series's album-within-an-album theme. The next world we pass is that of Benoît Peeters and François Schuiten's *La Fièvre d'Urbicande* [The Fever of Urbicande] (1985), a reference to the extra-textual worlds of the *Cités obscures* and the pioneering work, much admired by Mathieu, that stretches the boundaries of the BD form. Mathieu shows his esteem through the characters, who, when next to Peeters and Schuiten's world, state that 'l'imagination n'a décidément aucune limite' [the imagination decidedly knows no limits] (42).

The final 'planet', also on page 42, takes us to today's world of the self-aware experimental bande dessinée by reference to Lewis Trondheim's *La Mouche* (1995). As we have seen, Trondheim uses caricature figures to provoke deeper reflection on the status of the form, as befits productions from L'Association, and indeed his 2005 work *Désoeuvré* specifically examines the world of BD production from the viewpoint of an artist about to turn forty.[68] Mathieu, therefore, is temporarily removing us from the introspective flatness of the current work so as to suggest that there is potentially a whole galaxy of bandes dessinées, including his own, that provide formal experimentation.

Although Acquefacques will eventually return to the closed-in world of his bedsit accommodation, this will not be before the album breaks down a further barrier, that of two-dimensionality. The fact that pages 45 to 59 jump out at the reader (either wholly or just for certain *cases*) when viewed through the glasses provided is, on a primary level, the latest physical production gimmick in the series that started with the hole in *planches* 37/38 of *L'Origine*. On a wider level, Mathieu is evoking another aspect of the bande dessinée's evolution, and indeed of the evolution of visual culture in general, namely the move beyond the printed page towards an interactive format that is increasingly multi-media.[69]

Not all the gags of *La 2,333e dimension* are visual, however, thereby underlining the dual text and image nature of our medium. Puns abound, as in a play upon the loss of a vanishing point ('ce sont des ennuis … en perspective' [there are problems … in perspective], p. 15) or characters transformed into two-dimensional cut-outs now needing someone upon whom they can depend ('il nous faut quelqu'un de solide' [we need a solid type], p. 22). In the case of Dilbert Dugommier, the Décor Distribution Director, his initials-based nickname D.D. or Dédé is also enacted visually in that he is seen playing with two dice or 'dé dé' (p. 47), a gag that taps into the reference to the philosophical commonplace of God as dice-thrower.

The work of Marc-Antoine Mathieu is a twenty-first-century *deffence et illustration* of the bande dessinée's formal potential. The

Acquefacques albums playfully present age-old philosophical questions – as well as God as a dice-thrower, also God as a clockmaker, our existence as pre-written – whilst exploring different formal techniques that can be applied. Visuality is at the core, thereby underlining the specificity of the medium, but it is a *deffence et illustration* that is highly palatable, never pedantic, and constantly laced with humour. This is perhaps the final microcosm, that of the form itself: the bande dessinée is an enjoyable medium, often a 'comic' one, but it has much to say using devices that are frequently unique.

There are many other albums or works that could sustain analysis in terms of formal experimentation. A particularly fruitful period might be the 1960s and 1970s, the era of Fred (see Fig. 6, Chapter 2), Moebius and Druillet, when the three-by-four *case* system was challenged and the disintegration of the narrative became more frequent. But self-aware bandes dessinées had existed for some time previously, one such example being Gire's *Pension Radicale* [The Radical Household], a favourite in 1950s *Vaillant*, in which one episode sees an insubordinate goat that eats the journal we are in the midst of reading (number 462 of 21 March 1954) and later the artist's own hand features, disseminating confusion amongst the characters (number 465 of 11 April 1954). Such references are forerunners of the self-referential play made famous by Marcel Gotlib in the *Rubrique-à-brac*, a regular feature of *Pilote* from January 1968 until December 1972.[70]

It may seem unusual that I have chosen to concentrate the longest of my case studies on works that, unlike most, have already received thorough and incisive analysis in English. The reason for this choice is that I would hope to inspire further (and of course different) reflection upon BDs that are deceptively complex yet little known beyond France and Belgium, whilst also allowing you, dear reader, to analyse the analysis. The works of Juillard and of Mathieu exemplify the BD's capacity to engage with formal experimentation – a capacity that we take for granted in the case of novels or films – but the writings of Bridgeman and Miller on this very subject, as compared to those of counterparts in France, also exemplify the differences in cross-Channel viewpoints. The transition might be compared to that of a popular film such as *La Grande Vadrouille*, which in its country of origin is generally seen as household culture free of intellectual clutter, but which, when subtitled in a cinema on this side of the Channel, can rightly be admired for certain art-house qualities.

More generally, a quick glance at the history of formal experimentation could tell us much about the BD form per se. Just as in the United States the boom period of the turn of the twentieth-century supplements saw Winsor McCay experiment with the dream world of *Little Nemo in Slumberland*, so the periods of experimentation in France outlined briefly above – the 1950s, the 1970s, and, with our specific examples, the 1990s into the twenty-first century – correspond to the boom periods of the bande dessinée. In hindsight this is perfectly comprehensible since a form that promotes experimentation and self-reflection on a formal level, must, almost by definition, be an established one with flourishing canonical norms.

International aesthetics

Applied Art History is one of the major disciplines contributing to Cultural Studies, but just as we might consider the bande dessinée's intrinsic value in terms of potential for formal experimentation, it would also be entirely fitting to evaluate it per se in terms of visual aesthetics. At the 2007 London IBDS conference two papers did precisely that: Karl Kegler explored futuristic cityscapes for their role in recent bandes dessinées, and in particular the way in which futuristic architecture of the past (i.e., 1920s) can be reappropriated in a form of visual nostalgia; Catherine Labio looked specifically at BD artists' interest in Art Nouveau, considering the work of Winsor McCay and of Peeters and Schuiten in terms of the challenge to high art, order and conservative forces that they, and Art Nouveau, offer.[71]

The possibilities that the bande dessinée offers to the student of Art History are endless. Some artists, such as Honoré Daumier or Hergé, blur the distinction between high art and low art, and their BD work can be analysed as fruitfully as can museum pieces of the same style. More generally, it would be interesting to see how the aesthetics of BD fit the trends of the time. For example, do the caricatures of the nineteenth century adhere to representational realism in a way that Academy art might have done? Or can traces of the avant-garde, such as impressionism or, later, cubism, ever be found? What would such findings tell us about the status of the proto-BD as a (non-)conformist medium? Does political ideology and BD overlap in the same way that ideology and architecture might do, for instance in the case of the well-defined lines of Art Deco favoured by the right in the 1930s and 1940s?

Post-1945 aesthetics might seem to fit more naturally with BD studies, if only because it is the period that saw a shift in attitudes towards popular culture, with comic art central to such evolution. As we saw two chapters ago, the overlap between BD and Pop Art has already been the object of scholarly attention, but much remains to be done. In particular it would be interesting to explore the different national traditions in Pop Art and their relationship with corresponding traditions in the BD/graphic novel. Later movements, such as *Nouveau Réalisme*, are also known to have influenced BD and indeed been influenced by BD, as Bruno LeCigne and Jean-Pierre Tamine demonstrated in their seminal *Fac-Similé: Essai paratactique sur le Nouveau Réalisme de la bande dessinée*,[72] a work whose themes have since been re-explored in English by Matthew Screech.[73] The basic notion of *Nouveau Réalisme*, that everyday objects can become unfamiliar and challenging in estranged contexts, was evidently in keeping with the iconoclastic strips of *Pilote* and *Métal Hurlant*, but it is interesting to note that they received no mention whatsoever in the 2007 Paris Grand Palais exhibition on *Nouveau Réalisme*.

Once again such an omission may be indicative of the difference between cultural analysis in France and in the more theory-laden and interdisciplinary academes of the English-speaking world.[74] Other current art trends, such as Hyperrealism, have received little attention in terms of their relationship to the bande dessinée, as is also true of the more general phenomenon of artistic works that include text as an integral part. In all of these cases analysis of specific visual aesthetics through reference to the BD would be of interest per se as well as in terms of the broader questions it raises.

For instance, the nature of 'high art' as compared to 'low art' (and the blurring of the two) might be revisited, with a view to tracing changes since Pierre Bourdieu's *La Distinction* of 1979. Such discussions could be linked in with analysis of the current direction of art in France and elsewhere, which in turn brings us back to the question of the nature and (non-)existence of national boundaries in a post-digital artistic world. Technology itself is a key issue in the world of international aesthetics, and issues could fruitfully be compared with those in current BD production, where computer graphics and web-based publication are increasingly common. On the broadest of levels we can ask whether bande dessinée can any longer be distinguished from 'Art', and, if not, when did the two merge?

Psychoanalysis

In common with other artefacts and works of literature and art, the BD can stand as a gateway to the author, or indeed mankind's psychological constructs. Best known in this domain are the works of Serge Tisseron, himself a practising psychiatrist and psychoanalyst. Tisseron's readings of the *Tintin* series in *Tintin chez le psychanalyste* (1985) and then *Tintin et les secrets de famille* [Tintin and the Family Secrets] (1990) relate elements of Hergé's life to the characters he has created, and in particular Capitaine Haddock and the ancestral father figure/Hergé's own 'lost' grandfather. Tisseron applies Freudian analysis to BD in general in *Psychanalyse de la bande dessinée* (1987).

In English, Ann Miller's *Reading Bande Dessinée: Critical Approaches to French-Language Comic Strip* places psychoanalytical evaluation of the BD within the broader context of the expression of subjectivity. Her eleventh chapter, 'Psychoanalytic Approaches to Tintin' (pp. 201–14) assimilates the works of Tisseron, whilst also applying further, and generally later, studies by Benoît Peeters, Michael David and Tom McCarthy. Above all, Miller's overview allows us to see how the theories of Sigmund Freud and Jacques Lacan might be applied to bande dessinée (and vice versa), and how as an inroad to our unconscious processes it can, arguably, increase our understanding both of its readers and of its writers.

Signs and symbols

BD can be viewed in terms of narrative experimentation, visual aesthetics and psychoanalytical theories, but it is also a vehicle for linguistic textual, and para-textual, constructs. The ways in which the bande dessinée conveys meaning, textually and visually, and through the interaction of the two, and the ambiguities of such meaning, have been at the core of a number of semiotic orientated studies. As we have seen in the two previous chapters, and in Chapter 3 on Formal Specificity, these works, such as Didier Quella-Guyot's close analysis of the visual connotations of *Tintin au Tibet*,[75] exemplify a certain thrust in French academic BD studies.

The bande dessinée, like any other written (or indeed visual) enunciation, can be viewed as a system of signs that needs to be decrypted. To take a simple example, one used by Pierre Masson in *Lire la bande dessinée* [Reading the Bande Dessinée] (1985), Tintin's car in *Les Sept boules de cristal* [The Seven Crystal Balls] signifies luxury and order, as compared to the disorder and darkness connoted by the vehicle fished out of the docks. In many ways any semiotic approach will be indebted to Roland Barthes's work on the concepts of denotation and connotation, as well as his more specific *Mythologies* (1957; see my Introduction, and Chapter 8), and the readings it offers of everyday phenomena, including the car.

Four milestones in the theory and practice of the semiotic approach are Pierre Fresnault-Deruelle's *La Bande dessinée: L'Univers et les techniques de quelques comics d'expression française: Essai d'analyse sémiotique* (1972), the special number of *Communications* (number 24, 1976) on 'La Bande dessinée et son discours', Thierry Groensteen's *Système de la bande dessinée* (1999) and Harry Morgan, *Principes des littératures dessinées* (2003). As might be expected, all have already been discussed at various stages in this book. In English, once again Ann Miller's applied analysis of bande dessinée is outstanding. In particular, in chapter 5, 'The Codes and Formal Resources of Bande Dessinée' (pp. 75–102), of *Reading Bande Dessinée: Critical Approaches to French-Language Comic Strip* she contextualises concepts such as semiotics, Saussurian linguistics and codes of articulation through the example of Baru's 1995 album *L'Autoroute du soleil.*

On the level of textual linguistics, however, much could still be done. Henry Tyne gave a glimpse of the possibilities at the 2007 London IBDS conference when he used the example of *Titeuf* to promote sociolinguistic awareness via BD. Starting from the central linguistic question of representing the spoken language in the written medium and the inevitable loss of authenticity such a transition implies, Tyne went on to explore the perceived characteristics of colloquial French in terms of how we classify Zep's characters socially. Expressions such as 'i croient' for 'ils croient' [they believe] and 'chais pó' for 'je ne sais pas' [I do not know] convey a linguistic subculture entailing a high level of reader assimilation on a corresponding social level.

Papers such as this suggest that bande dessinée could usefully be applied to synchronic linguistics, but the specifics of the form would also lend it to diachronic studies. From Bécassine onwards, and possibly before, the language of the everyday has been represented in the text of BDs. Bande dessinée, as a popular medium, may provide an authentic key to the type of speech patterns that would not have been noted in 'higher' literature, and for which, in some cases, there are few available sound recordings. A study of a long-lasting character such as Tintin, or later even Astérix, could provide unexpected insight into the evolution of language over time.

Learning from BD

Bande dessinée might also be applied to comparative linguistics or to the broader field of language acquisition. Here the *Astérix* series provides an outstanding example, as the ingenious translations into English by Anthea Bell and Derek Hockridge (approved by Goscinny) allow us to compare the natural functioning of the two languages in terms of verb/noun transfer, overall sentence structure and, of course, punning. On an initial level of pedagogy, *Astérix* can be an excellent tool for language learning, whereby students can follow with the aid of the images (supported even by cartoon versions of the albums), enjoy the numerous visual gags, and work towards the textual linguistic jokes, checking as need be (and dependent on the language-learning methodology) against their native language version.

Indeed the bande dessinée can be applied to pedagogy of all sorts, as has increasingly become the case. BDs now guide us through the problems of mathematics, enliven classics by Racine and Molière, recount the social development of music, and teach us history and geography. In the latter category a series of related books published by Casterman, *Les Carnets de route de Tintin* [Tintin's Travel Diaries] provides older children with background dossiers on the exotic locations Tintin visits. In the case of Scotland,[76] for example, a reproduction of Milou licking up the drips from a 'Loch Lomond Whisky' barrel are accompanied by an illustrated explanation of the whisky-making process (pp. 32–33). Unfortunately, despite the volume's pedagogical goal, the information given is often far from reliable; for example, it attributes the Scots' reputation for meanness to the harshness of the Highland Clearances (p. 43) and characterises postindustrial Glasgow by its 'trop célèbres hooligans' [only too famous hooligans] (p. 49)!

Why, and to what extent, bande dessinée should be an effective pedagogical tool is open to conjecture: it may be the accessibility of popular culture ('comics are fun'), or the inherent attraction of an image that retains the learner's global attention while the text pinpoints the specific message to be retained. But is the implication that fun visual learning need not worry about factual accuracy? A few studies in French have analysed the type of pedagogical uses to which the BD can be put, and more specifically how they function in educational terms. As early as 1970 Antoine Roux had outlined possibilities in *La Bande dessinée peut être educative* [Bande Dessinée Can Be Educational], and more recently Didier Quella-Guyot is editing a series, *La BD de case en classe* [BD from Frame to Class], whose various volumes help adapt aspects of the BD for school curricula.[77] Relatively little exists in English, at least with respect to French-language comics, which suggests that bande dessinée study at university need not be limited to the Faculty of Arts, but could yet be applied by comparative language and culture specialists within a Faculty of Education.

A final comment on the educational possibilities of the bande dessinée concerns the use of related products. Animation in particular has a potential role to play in the broader learning curriculum, although whereas English-language productions such as *Dora the Explorer* or *The Numberjacks* are increasingly popular, there appear to be few BD-based French equivalents. Computerised animation has also picked up on the formula that mixes fun with technology to produce learning. One could consider to what extent and how international companies such as VTech or Atari market pedagogical games based on bandes dessinées. In short, there is scope for analysis of the broader workings of a learning process that mixes media to reinforce the age-old hybrid formula of *plaire et instruire*.

Further Further Reading

To reiterate, these case studies represent only a selection of possibilities. Hopefully the footnotes and in-text references will allow you, dear reader, to explore further. Alternatively, the fourteen chapters of *The Francophone Bande Dessinée* can be consulted as examples that explore a wide range of possible approaches, a notion outlined in the words of the back-cover summary:

> Theoretical issues – including the reception of the early proto-BD prior to its modern definition, approaches to the construction of a BD (presented here in BD form by leading artist Tanitoc), semiology and the reading of the current form, or the specificity of the French/US (non) overlap – complement historical approaches, such as Bécassine read in the light of postcolonialism, Le Corbusier and BD techniques in architecture, post-war BD and nostalgia for the resistance, or *Pilote* and the 60s revolution. And whilst broaching issues such as feminism or masculinity, social class, AIDS, exoticism or futurism, the volume presents chapters on some of the cutting-edge artists of the field today: Baru, Moebius, Juillard, Binet, Bilal ...

Conference abstracts on popular culture are often available on-line or in printed form, and I am delighted that *European Comic Art*, Liverpool University Press's journal dedicated, as its title implies, to the bande dessinée and its European neighbours, is now available as you read this. Most importantly, this chapter and other sources such as those mentioned will, hopefully, allow you to think of your own examples, and to see how BD connects to your life. The bande dessinée can be capable of moving great emotion, as can cinema, painting or poetry, and this is most likely to happen in context.

Notes

1. For a brief discussion of the possible definitions of the concept of Cultural Studies, see the opening chapter of Part III.
2. See my Introduction for a critical overview of early BD studies in English.
3. These works are also outlined with full bibliographical details in the Introduction. Chapter 9, 'Consecration of the Ninth Art', includes a more substantial outline of the history and progress of BD studies in English-speaking countries.
4. As stated below, the section that follows is based upon a paper originally given at the BnF in 2007. The French written version, also entitled 'Bond Dessiné(e)', has appeared on pp. 269–74 of the volume resulting from the conference: Françoise Hache-Bissette, Fabien Boully and Vincent Chenille, eds, *James Bond (2)007: Anatomie d'un mythe populaire* (Paris: Belin, 2007).
5. For a full listing see Paul Simpson, 'The Complete James Bond Syndicated Newspaper Checklist', *James Bond 007: Casino Royale*, by Ian Fleming, Anthony Hern, Henry Gammidge and John McLusky, ed. Paul Simpson (London: Titan, 2005), final page of an unnumbered sequence.
6. (Sonoma County CA: Eclipse).
7. In this case *James Bond 007: Permis de tuer*, trans. Jean-Loup Leuriaux ([np]: Himalaya, 1989). For the list of French James Bond albums, see the 'James Bond 007' entry in Michel Béra, Michel Denni and Philippe Mellot, *Trésors de la bande dessinée*.
8. (Paris: Éditions Albert-René).
9. On *Le Téméraire*, see below, as well as my chapter on the Twentieth Century. The main secondary work on the subject is Pascal Ory's *Le Petit Nazi illustré: Vie et survie du Téméraire (1943–1944)* (Paris: Nautilus, 2002).
10. This text originally appeared in Italian as part of a collective work, *Il Caso Bond* [The Bond Case] (Milan: Fabbri & Bompiani Sonzoguo, 1965), edited by Umberto Eco and Oreste del Bueno, wherein the article was entitled 'Le Strutture narrative in Fleming'. Eco also provided a French version, under the title of 'James Bond: Une Combinatoire narrative' [James Bond: A Combinative Narrative], for issue 8 of *Communications* (1966, pp. 77–93), whose topic was 'L'Analyse structurale du récit', and which included contributions from Roland Barthes, A. J. Greimas, Violette Morin, Christian Metz, Tzvetan Todorov and Gérard Genette. An expanded and updated version of the *Communications* article appeared, with Eco's collaboration, as 'Les Structures narratives chez Fleming', in *De Superman au Surhomme* [From Superman to Super Man], trans. Myriem Bouzaher (Paris: Grasset, 1993), pp. 163–207. It is from this edition that my quotations are taken. An English version of *Il Caso Bond* is available as *The Bond Affair*, trans. R.A. Dowie (London, Macdonald, 1966); however, Eco reputedly did not approve the translation. The current translation is my own.
11. Again, in 'Les Structures narratives chez Fleming'.
12. *The Gutenberg Galaxy: The Making of Typographic Man* (Toronto: Toronto University Press, 1962).

13. *Text/Image Mosaics in French Culture: Emblems and Comic Strips* (Aldershot: Ashgate, 2005).
14. Again, in 'Les Structures narratives chez Fleming'.
15. For a brief analysis of this series, see my 'Graphic classics' section in the 'Contemporary BD' chapter.
16. *Collaboration in France: Politics and Culture during the Nazi Occupation, 1940–1944* (Oxford: Berg, 1989). This work also includes a useful bibliography of further secondary sources.
17. *Collaboration and Resistance in Occupied France: Representing Treason and Sacrifice* (Basingstoke: Palgrave Macmillan, 2003).
18. This is an update of the original 1979 edition (Paris: Albatros). Further bibliography relating to *Le Téméraire* is given in my chapter on the Twentieth Century.
19. Laurent Marie, '*Le Grêlé 7/13*: A (Communist) Children's Guide to the Resistance', *The Francophone Bande Dessinée*, ed. Charles Forsdick, Laurence Grove and Libbie [Elizabeth] McQuillan (Amsterdam: Rodopi, 2005), pp. 73–82. The character's name refers to the seven and thirteen freckles on the two sides of his face.
20. In particular, chapter 5, 'Going Underground' (pp. 92–129), should be consulted.
21. Chapter 9, 'International Influences', on pp. 217–35.
22. Bart Beaty, *Unpopular Culture: Transforming the European Comic Book in the 1990s* (Toronto: University of Toronto Press, 2007).
23. E.g., Les Requins Marteaux in Albi, Six Pieds sous Terre [Six Feet Under] in Montpellier and L'Œil Électrique [The Electric Eye] in Rennes.
24. Indeed I have already touched upon such possibilities as part of my survey of current production in the 'Contemporary BD' chapter of this book.
25. As we stated in our Introduction, Charles de Gaulle is reported to have told André Malraux, 'Au fond, vous savez, mon seul rival international, c'est Tintin!'
26. James Steel, '*Let's Party!*: Astérix and the World Cup (France 1998)', *The Francophone Bande Dessinée*, pp. 201–18.
27. In French, see *Les Cahiers de la Bande Dessinée* 77 (1987), with its dossier on Margerin (pp. 7–36). See also Michel Jans, Jean-François Douvry, Gilles Ratier and Serge Tisseron, eds, *Margerin: Une Monographie* (Saint-Egrève: Mosquito, 1995). Both works are based extensively on interviews with the artist. In English Ann Miller has provided incisive analysis of Margerin's social portrayal on pp. 186–90 of her *Reading Bande Dessinée: Critical Approaches to French-Language Comic Strip* (Bristol: Intellect, 2007). Here she compares portrayal of the working classes in the *Lucien* albums with scrutiny offered by Pierre Bourdieu.
28. See, for example, Frank Margerin, *Momo le coursier* [Momo the Delivery-Boy] (Paris: Albin Michel, 2002).
29. Here the work of Mourad Boudjellal can be seen as an exception, although his main outlet, Futuropolis, was arguably not mainstream.
30. See, in particular, pp. 139–40.
31. On pp. 91–103 of *Corporeal Practices*, ed. Hannah Thompson and Julia Prest (Bern: Peter Lang, 2000).
32. *International Journal of Comic Art* 3.2 (2001), 162–74.
33. Montellier's work in the context of its left-wing political engagement has been discussed briefly in my chapter on 'Contemporary BD'.
34. See Chantal Montellier, *Faux sanglant* [False Blood] (Paris: Dargaud, 1992).
35. *French Studies* 55.2 (2001), 207–20.
36. Of the pornographically orientated production, the work of French-Canadian artist Patrick Fillion is nonetheless worthy of mention for the cult following that his larger-than-life depictions now enjoy.

37. Murray Pratt, 'The Diary of Neaud's Body: Approaching the Subject of Heterocentricity', *Gay and Lesbian Cultures in France*, ed. Lucille Cairns (Bern: Peter Lang, 2002), pp. 257–73. See also Ann Miller and Murray Pratt, 'Transgressive Bodies in the Work of Julie Doucet, Fabrice Neaud and Jean-Christophe Menu: Towards a Theory of "AutobioBD"', *Belphégor* 4.1 (2004). Pratt also broaches the subject of institutionalised homophobia, with reference to Neaud, in 'The Dance of the Visible and the Invisible: AIDS and the Bande Dessinée', *The Francophone Bande Dessinée*, pp. 189–200.
38. The dossier consists of the following articles: Sylvianne Rémi-Giraud, 'Métaphore et métonymie dans le *Journal* de Fabrice Neaud', pp. 85–89; Hugues de Chanay, 'Temps partagés, temps retrouvés: Lectures sous influence' [Time Shared, Time Rediscovered: Readings under the Influence], pp. 90–94; Marie Poix-Tétu, 'Du Journal à l'ajour' [From the Journal to Openwork], pp. 95–99.
39. The papers were presented as part of the Université Lumière Lyon II research project on 'Langues, Textes, Images' [Languages, Texts, Images] led by Pierre-Yves Carlot.
40. On Ferrandez, for example, see Mark McKinney, '"Tout cela, je ne voulais pas le laisser perdre": Colonial *lieux de mémoire* in Ferrandez's Comic Books', *Modern and Contemporary France* 9.1 (2001), 43–53. *History and Politics in French-Language Comics and Graphic Novels*, published by the University Press of Mississippi, includes chapters on European colonialism and immigrant culture, as well as on collaboration, anti-Semitism and on the feminist movement. As such it is relevant to several of the possible subject areas outlined in this current chapter.
41. Again on this subject see Mark McKinney, 'Histoire et critique sociale dans les bandes dessinées africaines-américaines et franco-africaines' [History and Social Criticism in Afro-American and Franco-African Bandes Dessinées], *Minorités postcoloniales anglophones et francophones: Études culturelles comparées* [Anglophone and Francophone Postcolonial Minorities: Comparative Cultural Studies], ed. Alec G. Hargreaves (Paris: L'Harmattan, 2004), pp. 199–218; '*Métissage* in Post-Colonial Comics', *Post-Colonial Cultures in France*, ed. Alec G. Hargreaves and Mark McKinney (London: Routledge, 1997), pp. 169–99. More generally, Catriona MacLeod is preparing a University of Glasgow PhD on the subject of post-colonial female representations in BD. See also the special Bande Dessinée issue, number 145 (2001), of *Notre Librairie: Revue des Littératures du Sud* [Our Book Shop: The Journal of Literature South of Europe], which pays particular attention to the styles, content and influences of BD in Africa, and number 32 (2000) of *Africultures*, whose topic is 'BD d'Afrique'. On Québecois BD, see Mira Falardeau, *La Bande dessinée au Québec* ([Montreal]: Boréal, 1994). This monograph provides four chapters on the history of the form in Quebec starting from the eighteenth century, before outlining more recent production through the general set-up of the BD profession, analysis of a selection of artists and fanzines active at the time of writing, and finally a chapter on the economics of the market.
42. *Le Manuscrit* (Grenoble: Glénat, 2001) is by Frank Giroud and Joseph Béhé. *Le Rendez-Vous de Glasgow* (Grenoble: Glénat, 2006) is by Giroud, Béhé and Camille Meyer.
43. A printed account of these and other similar projects (including some that have not been taken beyond planning stages) is also available: Benoît Peeters and François Schuiten, *Voyages en utopie* [Travels in Utopia] (Tournai: Casterman, 2000). For more on Peeters and Schuiten, see also my chapter on Contemporary BD.
44. Again, see, for example, Jean-Pierre Tibéri, *La Bande dessinée et le cinéma* (Izy: Regards, 1981), as well as the special issues of *Cinéma 71* (159,

September 1971), *Cinématographe* (21, October 1976) and *Cinémaction* (no number, summer 1990) dedicated to the subject of cinema and BD.

45. Hugh Starkey, 'Is the BD "à bout de souffle"?', *French Cultural Studies* 1.2 (1990), 95–110.
46. On the subject of *Astérix* films see my chapter on 'Formal Specificity'. The general economic aspects of the bande dessinée is another area for which there have been few studies in English.
47. Louis Marin, *Utopiques: Jeux d'espaces* (Paris: Minuit, 1973), pp. 297–324. The work is available in English as *Utopics: Spacial Play* (London: Macmillan, 1984).
48. Laurence Grove, 'Multi-Media Emblems and Their Modern-Day Counterparts', *Emblematic Tendencies in the Art and Literature of the Twentieth Century*, ed. Anthony J. Harper, Ingrid Höpel and Susan Sirc (Glasgow: Glasgow Emblem Studies, 2005), pp. 171–87. As the title suggests, this article goes on to discuss other three-dimensional text/image forms, and in particular the creations of Peeters and Schuiten.
49. *Le Cahier bleu* is also available in English as *The Blue Notebook*, translated by Jacinthe Leclerc (New York: NBM, 1997).
50. (Chatenay-Malabry: Alain Beaulet, 2000).
51. Michel Jans, Jean-François Douvry and Nadine Douvry, eds, *Juillard: Une Monographie* (Saint-Egrève: Mosquito, 1996), p. 52. Much of the volume is taken by an extensive interview with Juillard, in which he points to the influence in question.
52. These *planches* and five others from *Le Cahier bleu* are reproduced in Ann Miller's *Reading Bande Dessinée: Critical Approaches to French-Language Comic Strip*. Miller's analysis of *Le Cahier bleu* will be discussed below.
53. ([Paris]: Casterman). The album is available in English as *After the Rain*, translated by Joe Johnson (New York: NBM, 1999).
54. In the interview for *Juillard: Une Monographie* the artist tells us that the prints are those of Bettina Rheims, a collection depicting transvestites. The sexual ambiguity of the prints thus underlines the ambiguities of Victor's characterisation (p. 56).
55. *Juillard: Une Monographie*, p. 60.
56. Indeed Juillard acknowledges his admiration for this work in the interview for *Juillard: Une Monographie* (p. 56).
57. For a full listing see the bibliography of the *BDM*. Several studies and interviews are brought together in the Mosquito volume, *Juillard: Une Monographie*, noted above. See also the following footnotes for further bibliography, in French and in English, on Juillard and on *Le Cahier bleu*.
58. This is true even of the dossier on André Juillard and *Le Cahier bleu* that features on pp. 22–35 of *9e Art* 2 (1997). Following an interview with Juillard (pp. 22–31), Jacques Samson's 'Un Souffle romanesque' [Storybook Inspiration] (pp. 32–35) alludes to some of the narrative ploys at work in *Le Cahier bleu*, but little in-depth analysis is given, and Samson continues to underline the characterisation and the stylistic sensuality. Similarly, Pierre-Yves Lador in 'André Juillard: *Le Cahier bleu*' on pp. 106–21 of *Juillard: Une Monographie* is clearly aware of the technical complexities, but provides a catalogue of important moments (again with emphasis on the sensual aspects) rather than theoretical analysis. More recently, however, a Belgian academic press has provided Éric Lavanchy's *Étude du Cahier bleu d'André Juillard: Une Approche narratologique de la bande dessinée* (Louvain-la-Neuve: Academia-Bruylant, 2007), which, as the title suggests, offers a narratological study of the album.
59. Thierry Groensteen, ed., *[Primé à Angoulême]: 30 ans de bandes dessinées à travers les palmarès du Festival* (Angoulême: Éditions de l'An 2, 2003). As the title implies, this work gives an overview of the major prize-winners

at the Angoulême festival up to and including 2002. The text cited is by Évariste Blanchet.

60. Teresa Bridgeman, 'Figuration and Configuration: Mapping Imaginary Worlds in BD', *The Francophone Bande Dessinée*, pp. 115–36. In *Reading Bande Dessinée: Critical Approaches to French-Language Comic Strip*, Ann Miller explores *Le Cahier bleu* as an example of enunciation techniques, drawing upon it as the main example for her sixth chapter, 'Narrative Theory and Bande Dessinée' (pp. 103–24).
61. Descriptive articles on Juillard's work have appeared in BD publications such as *Canal BD, La Lettre de Dargaud* [The Dargaud Newsletter], *Bo Doï* and *Bandes Dessinées Magazine*, all of which target a popular audience, and more general articles have frequently featured in the mainstream press such as *Libération*. More surprisingly, in the third volume (2004) of the new series of *Les Cahiers de la Bande Dessinée* published by Glénat, in this case authored by Henri Filippini under the title *Les Cahiers de la Bande Dessinée présentent Les 7 Vies de l'épervier*, we find little more than publication bibliography, plot summary and interviews with authors. More analytical is number 56 (1984) of *Les Cahiers de la Bande Dessinée* (old series), with its dossier on Juillard on pp. 4–36, and indeed issue 2 (1997) of *9e Art* and *Juillard: Une Monographie* noted above, although, as stated, even these are extremely limited in theoretical scope.
62. As we shall see below, a fleeting exception is to be found at the end of *La Qu ...* (Paris: Delcourt, 1991). The title, *La Qu ...* , is an elliptic reference to the four-colour printing system or 'quadrichromie'.
63. The subtitle did not, however, appear on the first edition of the first album, *L'Origine* (Paris: Delcourt, 1990). All five albums are published by Delcourt.
64. Extract from an interview with Thierry Groensteen, 'Julius Corentin et moi: Entretien avec Marc-Antoine Mathieu' [Julius Corentin and I: An Interview with Marc-Antoine Mathieu], *9e Art* 4 (1999), 62–70. On Marc-Antoine Mathieu, see also Laurent Gerbier, 'Les Pièges de l'analogie' ['The Traps of Analogy'], *9e Art* 4 (1999), 71–77. Above all, see chapter 7 (pp. 125–46) of Ann Miller's *Reading Bande Dessinée: Critical Approaches to French-Language Comic Strip*, in which she provides a thorough analysis of the work of Mathieu as an example of postmodernist narrative. Miller's chapter also includes seven illustrations taken from the Acquefacques albums.
65. Two additional works not featuring Acquefacques but still evoking his labyrinthine world have been published by L'Association in their 'Patte de Mouche' series: *Le Coeur des ombres* [The Heart of Shadows] (1999) and *La Mutation* (2001). Further albums take place in a more recognisable contemporary setting, but continue to explore abstract notions such as the status of art – *Le Dessin* [The Drawing] (Paris: Delcourt, 2001), *Les Sous-sols du révolu* [The Basements of Bygone Days] (Paris: Futuropolis/ Gallimard, 2006) – or even the social effects of information technology – *Mémoire morte* [Dead Memory] (Paris: Delcourt, 2000).
66. It should be noted that in *L'Origine* page numbers do not correspond to *planche* numbers, which are four behind in sequence (thus p. 5 is *planche* 1, p. 15 is *planche* 11, and *planche* 42 is in fact p. 46).
67. In *La Qu ...* page numbers are two ahead of *planche* numbers, thus p. 7 is *planche* 5.
68. The works of Peeters and Schuiten and of Lewis Trondheim are discussed in my chapter on 'Contemporary BD'.
69. The question of the move towards multi-media forms has been evoked as the final discussion in the 'Cultural Studies' section above.
70. I present these examples in my 'Autobiography and Early Bande Dessinée', *Belphégor* 4.1 (2004). The article, part of *Belphégor*'s special number on bande dessinée, alludes to the potential overlap between self-

referential expression and autobiography.

71. Catherine Labio's contribution was part of a wider study currently under preparation on the subject of comics and architecture.
72. (Paris: Futuropolis, 1983).
73. Matthew Screech, 'Jean Giraud/Moebius: *Nouveau Réalisme* and Science Fiction', *The Francophone Bande Dessinée*, pp. 97–113.
74. Indeed Didier Eribon, in his keynote speech to the 2007 Society for French Studies conference in Birmingham, underlined such a gap between French- and English-speaking worlds in terms of willingness to engage with theory (Postcolonialism, Queer Studies) and interdisciplinarity.
75. Didier Quella-Guyot, *Lire Tintin au Tibet de Hergé: Lecture Méthodique et documentaire* (Poitiers: Le Torii, 1990).
76. J.-L. Mathon and M. Dauber, *Les Carnets de route de Tintin: L'Écosse* (Paris: Casterman, 1999).
77. The series, whose first volume appeared in 1999, is produced by the Regional Centre for Pedagogical Documentation ('Centre Régional de Documentation Pédagogique') in Poitiers.

CHAPTER 11

CONCLUSION: DICK TURPIN RIDES AGAIN

> The latest boffin wheeze arrived this week: an honours degree module in comic books, offered by Glasgow University. And, later this month, the alma mater will host a two-day conference for 60 cartoon professionals and scholars from around the globe, all of them no doubt muttering: 'You mean the government gives you money to study this dreck?!'
>
> Of course, the usual academic Dick Turpin has been drafted in to explain that comic books/old picture postcards/sweetie wrappers are treasure troves of sociological fascination. In this instance it's Dr Lawrence [*sic*] Grove of the French Department, under whose auspices will Oor Wullie be probed for valuable insights into teenage delinquency during the inter-war years.
>
> 'In France,' he says, 'comic books are regarded as a valid art form and it is widely acknowledged they act as a political, cultural and historical mirror on society.'
>
> Surely everything is a mirror of the culture from which it hailed. But this is to miss the pertinent phrase in Grove's claim: 'in France'. Of course, the French consider comic books to be golden repositories of meaning. The French are funny that way[.]
>
> 'Degree's a Funny Business', *Sunday Times* (Scottish edition), 13 May 2001, p. Ecosse 12.

A few years ago, in the wake of publicity surrounding the 2001 IBDS conference in Glasgow, media attention focused briefly on the fact that the University was offering an Honours option on the bande dessinée. One article, in the *Sunday Times* (Scottish edition) of 13 May 2001 (see Fig. 40), took a humorously critical stance, suggesting that the study of cartoons was a waste of public money and that the 'boffin' responsible was no more than an 'academic Dick Turpin'.

I presented the article to students for the final session of the bande dessinée course in question and was delighted by the level of support voiced in reaction against the newspaper's claims. Without coaxing or bribery students pointed to the pleasure of appreciating the 'hidden' complexities of a form they had always taken for granted, the subtlety and intricacy they had found in certain strips (Montellier

Degree's a funny business

THOSE with a grain of common sense never fail to be appalled by the nonsense with which many of our academics fill their time — the scholastic equivalent of digging ditches and filling them in again, like convicts on a Carolina chain gang.

In the past year alone, Scotland's universities have trousered awesome sums of public subsidy to investigate whether smoking more leads to more smoking, whether weather affects moods, and other such nonsenses that fall into the Bleeding Obvious category.

The latest boffin wheeze arrived this week: an honours degree module in comic books, offered by Glasgow University. And, later this month, the alma mater will host a two-day conference for 60 cartoon professionals and scholars from around the globe, all of them no doubt muttering: "You mean the government gives you money to study this dreck?!"

Of course, the usual academic Dick Turpin has been drafted in to explain that comic books/old picture postcards/sweetie wrappers are treasure troves of sociological fascination. In this instance it's Dr Lawrence Grove of the French department, under whose auspices will Oor Wullie be probed for valuable insights into teenage delinquency during the inter-war years.

"In France," he says, "comic books are regarded as a valid art form and it is widely acknowledged they act as a political, cultural and historical mirror on society."

Surely everything is a mirror of the culture from which it hailed. But this is to miss the pertinent phrase in Grove's claim: "in France". Of course, the French consider comic books to be golden repositories of meaning. The French are funny that way, never happier than when prodding lumps of brie for insights into the revolutionary condition. The French regard Jerry Lewis and Mickey Rourke as living gods. Are we to expect an MPhil on The Nutty Professor?

That's funny: young Beano fan cribbing for his PhD viva

Figure 40. 'Degree's a Funny Business'. *Sunday Times* (Scottish edition). 13 May 2001. Page Ecosse 12. © Times Newspapers.

and Juillard were particularly popular), but above all the way in which it had inspired connections not previously imagined: not just a question of sweetie wrappers and sociological fascination, but the wider links between visual cultures, in terms of cinema, photography and Pop Art, and also the broader historical contextualisation and the relevance to current theories of cultural reception.

The main criticism of the course (yes, I did accept them) was that it was not the expected 'easy option'; that it was impossible in the time given to broach all the possible angles of approach or to get anything more than a taster of the vast world of French-language text/image culture, the context from which bande dessinée cannot be separated. Such 'criticism' was in fact a compliment, one that bears witness to the dimensions of the project – the project which is now that of this book. A few years further on, the 'criticism' would perhaps not have had to be made, as an increased awareness of comic art in general, through the works to which I have referred in the preceding pages, but also through high-profile festivals, television and radio programmes (often the work of Paul Gravett), has also meant that the English-speaking world is slightly more knowledgeable with respect to our cross-Channel art form. And awareness of the richness of the form is also awareness that it cannot be covered in a single course, or indeed in the pages of a monograph.

Notwithstanding, now is perhaps the moment to try and summarise potential answers to the base question: why is the bande dessinée adulated in the French-speaking world (they're funny that way), and what can a cross-Channel viewpoint bring to the subject?

My answers can only be tentative, and are, moreover, largely limited to the culture of France, in the hope that others will some day provide comparators with other countries of French-language culture. Whilst aiming to give an overview of the status of the bande dessinée today, and of the ways in which it can be related to the wider contemporary world, this study is nonetheless unashamedly historical in its foundation, and it is through the optic of history that some of the 'why' questions can be broached. If the bande dessinée has a status that equivalent forms in, say, England, are only starting to enjoy, it is perhaps because for at least a quarter of a century the BD has benefited from government patronage, via festivals, book subsidies, exhibitions in national institutions, and, above all, the creation of its own national institutions. These came as a result of a de facto following, one that had built up in the years of postwar rebuilding.

Historical expediency can account for the importance of the bande dessinée (even if it was not officially labelled as such) in France of the 1950s. The two main pressure groups, the communists and the Catholics, both expressed their ideals through top-selling BD journals, *Vaillant* and *Coeurs Vaillants*, and as a result generations of youngsters literally grew up with *Pif le Chien* or even *Tintin*, for the most part without an inkling of their political bias. If the groups concerned chose to promote their beliefs through the medium of these journals it was surely in deference to the 'excellent' job *Le Téméraire* had done in the previous years, as any comparative analysis of the format of these journals will show. *Le Téméraire* in turn had taken its success from the imitation of Paul Winckler's *Le Journal de Mickey*, a publication whose essential Frenchness is understandably overlooked and underplayed. I would hope that after a couple of hundred pages of historical analysis such a summary bears no surprise, but it is hardly astonishing that the inevitable précis, that the Ninth Art with which France challenges the world should owe its pedigree to American enterprise and Nazi sympathisers, should come from outwith France.

But just as anti-Semitism did not start with Second World War collaboration, so the culture of the image did not arrive with *Le Journal de Mickey* and *Le Téméraire*. To take the question back a lot further, as I have indeed done, is to point to French productions as occupying a central position in the visual revolution that followed the advent of printing. And again at a time of experimentation with respect to new techniques, France, a country for which the ideological split of the Wars of Religion was still latent, was quick to draw upon the power of the image for promoting textual 'truths'. Georgette de

Montenay's Protestant *Emblemes ou devises chrestiennes* (1571) was the first religious emblem book,[1] but moreover a trailblazer in a genre that would use the text/image form to promote faiths of all types, as well as establishment and anti-establishment politics, and indeed general musings on love, death and the universe.

It is here that I should remind the reader that France has had an exceptional history of devotion to visual culture, not just through emblem books and early image narratives, through the 'high art' stories that now adorn the walls of another world-beater, the Louvre, and in the prints through which the propaganda of the Revolution was fought, but also, in the modern industrial era, through the invention and wide-scale propagation of photography, the illustrated press, the moving image and, more recently, the internet, of which Minitel was the original forerunner.

One of the main obsessions of BD criticism in French has been with the need to define the bande dessinée. Of course any book (including this one) can be expected to draw upon a working set of givens for practical purposes, but an overview of post-1970 criticism, including the works of Moliterni, Gaumer, Lacassin, Baron-Carvais, Peeters, Morgan and Groensteen, can strike us with the vehemence with which critics defend their own defining factor, be it the starting date, the use of speech bubbles, the primacy of the narrative, or the essential visual, as opposed to textual, status of the form. The definition obsession continues in round-table debates at festivals, columns of journals, be they specialised or *grand public*, and on the walls of exhibition halls.

In the context of a study whose base is in a wide historical overview, I would suggest that post-Forest definitions suffer from not seeing the trees for the wood. The bande dessinée is a product of, an integral part of, and indeed a continuation of a depth of text-based visual culture that has come to the fore in French-language expression. Rather than trying to shoehorn Töpffer, Cham, *Bécassine*, *Tintin*, *Barbarella*, Peeters and Schuiten, Satrapi and OuBaPo into a single definition, let us think outwards rather than inwards; let us read and view them in the context of medieval illuminations, narrative woodblocks, and the tales of early cinema. The *Sunday Times* is in fact right to suggest that a course on BD lacks substance. Perhaps it is time to replace the option on bande dessinée with what it is really about: French texts through the culture of the image. *À suivre …*

Notes

1. The work was first published in 1567. I have discussed it in some detail in my *Text/Image Mosaics in French Culture: Emblems and Comic Strips* (Aldershot: Ashgate, 2005).

Bibliography

The fact that this book aims to consider the broader context of the bande dessinée, and as such takes care to analyse key works about bandes dessinées as well as the bandes dessinées themselves, means that it is difficult, and sometimes meaningless, to differentiate between 'Primary' and 'Secondary' sources. This is therefore an integrated bibliography.

Bandes dessinées (and their precursors) originally published as single strips in journals are not listed individually; the reader should refer to the index in order to locate the sections in which these journals are discussed.

When a series is discussed (e.g., *Blake et Mortimer*, *Astérix*), bibliographical references are given only for those albums specifically mentioned.

I have limited myself to providing details only of the editions of works to which I have referred in the text and which are relevant to this study. When several editions of a single work have been consulted but the variations between publications are not discussed, for the sake of concision I have indicated only the existence of previous and/or subsequent editions.

Printed Works

9e Art 2 (1997), 22–35. Special dossier on André Juillard.

9e Art 9 (2003), 84–99. Special dossier on Fabrice Neaud.

9e Art 10 (2004), 72–99. Special dossier on OuBaPo.

9e Art 14 (2008), 110–63. Special dossier on Blutch.

9e Art 15 (2009), 72–125. Special dossier on Dupuy and Berberian.

Adams, Alison. 'The *Cent Nouvelles Nouvelles* in MS Hunter 252: The Impact of the Miniatures', *French Studies* 46.4 (1992), 385–94.

Adams, Alison, ed. *L'Hecatongraphie (1544)* [One Hundred Pictures (1544)], by Gilles Corrozet. Geneva: Droz, 1997.

Adams, Alison, Stephen Rawles and Alison Saunders. *A Bibliography of French Emblem Books*. 2 vols. Geneva: Droz, 1999–2002.

Africultures 32 (2000). Number on 'BD d'Afrique'.

Alciato, Andrea. *Emblematum liber* [Book of Emblems]. Augsburg: Heinrich Steiner, 1531. Several subsequent editions.

Amengual, Barthélemy. *Le Petit Monde de Pif le chien: Essai sur un 'comic' français* [The Little World of Pif the Dog: An Essay on a French 'Comic']. Algiers: Travail et Culture d'Algérie, 1955.

Andrews, Lew. *Story and Space in Renaissance Art: The Rebirth of Continuous Narrative*. Cambridge: Cambridge University Press, 1995.
Andrieu, Olivier. *Astérix*. Paris: Éditions Albert René, 1999.
Armstrong, Carol. *Scenes in a Library: Reading the Photograph in the Book, 1843–1875*. Cambridge, MA: MIT, 1998.
Arnold, H.J.P. *William Henry Fox Talbot: Pioneer of Photography and Man of Science*. London: Hutchinson Benham, 1977.
['Assassination of Henri IV']. *Série Qb1: Histoire de France en Estampes*. [Bibliothèque nationale de France, Département des Estampes]. Single print. 1610.
Baecque, Antoine de. *La Caricature révolutionnaire*. Paris: CNRS, 1988.
Baetens, Jan, ed. *The Graphic Novel*. Leuven: Leuven University Press, 2001.
Baetens, Jan and Pascal Lefèvre. *Pour une lecture moderne de la bande dessinée* [For a Modern Reading of the Bande Dessinée]. Brussels: CBBD, 1993.
'Bande dessinée et figuration narrative', *Phénix* 4 (1967), 90–94.
Barbier, Frédéric. 'L'Industrialisation des techniques' [The Industrialisation of Printing Techniques]. *Histoire de l'édition française: Tome III: Le Temps des éditeurs: Du Romantisme à la Belle Époque* [The History of Publishing in France: Volume III: The Age of the Publishers: From Romanticism to the Belle Epoque], ed. Henri-Jean Martin and Roger Chartier. Paris: Promodis, 1985, pp. 57–67.
Baron-Carvais, Annie. *La Bande dessinée*. Paris: Presses Universitaires de France [Que Sais-je?], 1985. Several re-editions.
Barrie, J.M. *Peter Pan*. London: Collins, 1988. First published 1911.
Barthes, Roland. *Mythologies*. Paris: Pierres Vives, 1957. Second edition, 1970 (Paris: Seuil). In English as *Mythologies*, trans. Annette Lavers. London: Vintage, 1993. First published 1972.
———. *Œuvres complètes* [Complete Works], ed. Éric Marty. 3 vols. Paris: Seuil, 1993–1995.
———. *S/Z*. Paris: Seuil, 1970. In English as *S-Z*, trans. Richard Miller. London: Cape, 1975. First published 1974.
Baru. *L'Autoroute du soleil*. Tournai: Casterman, 1995.
Bataille des Pyramides [The Battle of the Pyramids]. Single print. 1830.
Bataille de Waterloo. Single print. 1821–1822.
Beaty, Bart. *Fredric Wertham and the Critique of Mass Culture*. Jackson, MS: University Press of Mississippi, 2005.
———. *Unpopular Culture: Transforming the European Comic Book in the 1990s*. Toronto: University of Toronto Press, 2007.
Beerbohm, Robert and Doug Wheeler. 'Töpffer en Amérique', *9e Art* 6 (2001), 10–21.
Béra, Michel, Michel Denis and Philippe Mellot. *Trésors de la bande dessinée*. Paris: Éditions de l'Amateur, 1979. Further editions have appeared every two years.
Biblia pauperum [Bible of the Poor]. [Netherlands]: n.p., [Mid fifteenth century].
Bilal, Enki. *La Femme piège*. Paris: Dargaud, 1986. In English as *The Woman Trap* [part of *The Nikopol Trilogy*], trans. Taras Otus. Hollywood, CA: Humanoids Publishing, 1999.
Binet, Christian. *Les Bidochon ont 25 ans* [The Bidochons Are 25 Years Old]. Paris: Fluide Glacial/Audié, 2005.
———. *Roman d'amour* [Love Story]. Paris: Fluide Glacial/Audié, 1980. Several subsequent re-editions.
Blain, Christophe. *Isaac le pirate: Les Amériques*. Paris: Dargaud, 2001. Reissued in black and white 2003. In English as *Isaac the Pirate: 1 To Exotic Lands*, trans. Joe Johnson. New York: NBM, 2003.
———. *Isaac le pirate: La Capitale*. Paris: Dargaud, 2004. In English as *Isaac the Pirate: 2 The Capital*, trans. Joe Johnson. New York: NBM, 2004.

———. *Isaac le pirate: Les Glaces*. Paris: Dargaud, 2002. Reissued in black and white 2003. In English as *Isaac the Pirate: 1 To Exotic Lands*, trans. Joe Johnson. New York: NBM, 2003.
———. *Isaac le pirate: Olga*. Paris: Dargaud, 2002. Reissued in black and white 2003. In English as *Isaac the Pirate: 2 The Capital*, trans. Joe Johnson. New York: NBM, 2004.
Blanchard, Gérard. *La Bande dessinée: Histoire des histoires en images de la préhistoire à nos jours* [The Bande Dessinée: The Story of Stories in Pictures from Prehistory to Today]. Verviers: Marabout, 1969.
Blanchet, Évariste. *'Le Cahier bleu'* [The Blue Notebook]. In *[Primé à Angoulême]: 30 ans de bandes dessinées à travers le palmarès du Festival* ['[Prize winners at Angoulême]: 30 Years of Bandes Dessinées through the Festival Awards], ed. Thierry Groensteen. [Angoulême]: Éditions de l'An 2, 2003, pp. 74–75.
Blondel, Auguste. *Rodolphe Töpffer: L'Écrivain, l'artiste et l'homme* [Rodolphe Töpffer: The Writer, the Artist and the Man]. Paris: Hachette, 1886. Facsimile edition 1976 and 1998 (Geneva: Slatkine).
Blutch. *La Beauté*. Paris: Futuropolis, 2008.
———. *Blotch: Face à son destin* [Blotch: Facing his Destiny]. Paris: Audie, 2000.
———. *Blotch: Œuvres complètes* [Blotch: The Complete Works]. Paris: Audie, 2009.
———. *Blotch: Le Roi de Paris* [Blotch: The King of Paris]. Paris: Audie, 1999.
———. *C'était le bonheur* [Those Were Happy Days]. Paris: Futuropolis, 2005.
———. *Péplum*. Paris: Cornélius, 1998.
———. *Le Petit Christian*. Paris: L'Association 1998.
———. *Le Petit Christian 2*. Paris: L'Association 2008.
———. *Vitesse moderne* [Today's Pace]. Brussels: Dupuis, 2002.
———. *La Volupté*. Paris: Futuropolis, 2006.
———. *Waldo's Bar*. Paris: Audie, 1992.
Bockris, Victor. *The Life and Death of Andy Warhol*. London: Fourth Estate, 1998. First published 1989 (New York: Bantam).
Bonnemaison, Guy-Claude. 'À Propos du ballon dans les bandes dessinées' [Regarding the Speech Bubble in Bandes Dessinées], *Giff-Wiff* 8 (1963), 39–41.
Bory, Jean-François, ed. *Nadar: Tome 2: Dessins et écrits* [Nadar: Volume 2: Drawings and Writings]. Paris: Arthur Hubschmid, 1979.
Botanski, Luc. 'La Constitution du champ de la bande dessinée' [The Constitution of the Bande Dessinée's Field of Study], *Actes de la Recherche en Science Sociales* 1 (1975), 37–59.
Bouhours, Dominique. *Les Entretiens d'Ariste et d'Eugene* [The Discussions between Ariste and Eugene]. Paris: Sebastien Mabre-Cramoisy, 1671. Several subsequent editions.
Bourdieu, Pierre. *La Distinction: Critique sociale du jugement*. Paris: Minuit, 1979. Several subsequent editions. In English as *Distinction: A Social Critique of the Judgement of Taste*, trans. Richard Nice. London: Routledge, 1984.
Bradley, Noelle P. 'Masks That Reveal: Social Inequality in J.-J. Grandville's *Les Métamorphoses du Jour* (1828–1829)', *International Journal of Comic Art* 8.1 (2006), 1–16.
Brandt, Sebastian. *Stultifera navis* [Ship of Fools]. Basle: Johann Bergmann von Olpe, 1494. Several subsequent editions.
Breeze, David. *Hadrian's Wall*. London: Penguin, 2000. First published 1976. Several further editions, including a number published by English Heritage (London).
Bretécher, Claire. *Les Angoisses de Cellulite* [Cellulite's Anguishes]. Neuilly-sur-Seine: Dargaud, 1974. Several subsequent editions.

———. *Les Frustrés*. Paris: Claire Bretécher, 1975. Several subsequent re-editions.
———. *Les Frustrés 2*. Paris: Claire Bretécher, 1977. First published 1976. Several subsequent re-editions.
———. *Les Frustrés 5*. Paris: Hyphen, 2001. Several subsequent re-editions.
Bridgeman, Teresa. 'Figuration and Configuration: Mapping Imaginary Worlds in BD'. In *The Francophone Bande Dessinée*, ed. Charles Forsdick, Laurence Grove and Libbie [Elizabeth] McQuillan. Amsterdam: Rodopi, 2005, pp. 115–36.
Brown, Dan. *Da Vinci Code*, trans. Daniel Roche. Paris: JC Lattès, 2004. Paris: Pocket, 2005.
Buyssens, Danielle, Jean-Daniel Candaux, Jacques Droin and Daniel Maggetti, eds. *Propos töpffériens* [Remarks about Töpffer]. Geneva: Société d'Etudes Töpffériennes, 1998.
Les Cahiers de la Bande Dessinée 56 (1984). Number on André Juillard.
Les Cahiers de la Bande Dessinée 62 (1985). Number on Martin Veyron.
Les Cahiers de la Bande Dessinée 69 (1986). Number on François Schuiten.
Les Cahiers de la Bande Dessinée 77 (1987). Number on Frank Margerin.
Calvaire de Jérusalem [Jerusalem Calvary]. Single print. 1827.
Cambier, Jean-Luc and Éric Verhoest. *Blake et Mortimer: [Histoire d'un retour]* [Blake et Mortimer: [The Story of a Comeback]]. Paris: Dargaud, 1996.
Cantor, Norman F. and Michael S. Werthman, eds. *The History of Popular Culture*. New York: Macmillan, 1968.
Caradec, François. 'Christophe', *Le Collectionneur de Bandes Dessinées* 100 (2003), 14–19.
———. 'Rodolphe Töpffer', *Phénix* 43 (1975), 7–11.
Caran d'Ache. *Carnet de chèques* [Cheque Book]. Paris: E. Plon, Nourrit et cie, 1892. Facsimile edition 2000 (Orleans: Corsaire).
Carlebach, Michael L. *The Origins of Photojournalism in America*. Washington: Smithsonian Institute Press, 1992.
Castelli, Alfredo. 'Monsieur Lajaunisse: Première bande dessinée française' [M. Lajaunisse: The First French Bande Dessinée], *Le Collectionneur de Bandes Dessinées* 108 (2006), 22–28.
Centre de l'amour [Centre of Love]. N.p.: 'chez Cupidon', [*c.*1680].
Champfleury. *Histoire de la caricature moderne* [The History of Modern Caricature]. Paris, E. Dentu, [1865].
———. *Histoire de l'imagerie populaire* [The History of Popular Imagery]. Paris: E. Dentu, 1869.
Chanay, Hugues de. 'Temps partagés, temps retrouvés: Lectures sous influence' [Time Shared, Time Rediscovered: Readings under the Influence], *9e Art* 9 (2003), 90–94.
Chaponnière, Paul. *Caricatures töpffériennes*. Neuchatel: La Baconnière, 1941.
Chartier, Roger. *The Cultural Uses of Print in Early Modern France*. Princeton: Princeton University Press, 1987.
Charvy, Jean, Hergé Eschasseriau and Marc Jallon. *CEJ: Catalogue encyclopédique: La Signature dans la bande dessinée*. Paris: Éditions de l'Amateur, 1998. Further edition in 2000.
Chatenet, Aymar du, ed. *Le Dictionnaire Goscinny*. Paris: JC Lattès, 2003.
Chertablon, M. de. *La Maniere de se bien preparer a la mort* [The Way to Prepare Oneself Well for Death]. Antwerp: George Gallet, 1700.
Chotard, Loïc. *Nadar: Caricatures et photographies*. Paris: Paris-Musées, 1990.
Christophe. *La Famille Fenouillard*. Paris: Armand Colin, [1893].
Cinéma 71 159 (1971). Special number on cinema and BD.
Cinémaction [No number] (1990). Special number on cinema and BD.
Cinématographe 21 (1976). Special number on cinema and BD.
Cizo and Winschluss. *Monsieur Feraille* [Mr Scrap-Metal]. Albi: Les Requins Marteaux, 2001.

[Clermont-Ferrand, Musées de Clermont-Ferrand]. *Greuze et Diderot: Vie familiale et education dans la seconde moitié du XVIIIème siècle* [Greuze and Diderot: Family Life and Education in the Second Half of the Eighteenth Century]. Clermont-Ferrand: Musées de Clermont-Ferrand, 1984.

'Le Club des Bandes Dessinées va-t-il prendre naissance?', *Fiction* 98 (1962), 143–44.

Cohen, Philippe and Richard Malka. *La Face karchée de Sarkozy* [Sarkozy's Hidden Side]. Issy-les-Moulineaux: Vents de l'Ouest, 2006.

Colin, Fabrice and Laurent Cilluffo. *World Trade Angels*. Paris: Denoël Graphic, 2006.

Le Collectionneur de Bandes Dessinées 14 (1978). Number on wartime *illustrés*.

Le Collectionneur de Bandes Dessinées 35 (1982). Number on the Société Parisienne d'Édition (SPE).

Le Collectionneur de Bandes Dessinées 48 (1985). Number on *Zig et Puce*.

Le Collectionneur de Bandes Dessinées 105 (2005). Number on *Le Journal de Mickey* and its European equivalents.

Collins, Bradford R. 'Modern Romance: Lichtenstein's Comic Book Paintings', *American Art* 17.2 (2003), 60–85.

Colonna, Francesco. *Hypnerotomachia Poliphili* [Dream of Poliphile]. [Venice]: [Aldus Manutius], 1499. Several subsequent editions. In English as *Hypnerotomachia Poliphili: The Strife of Love in a Dream*, trans. Joscelyn Godwin. London: Thames & Hudson, 2005.

Combe, William and Thomas Rowlandson. *The English Dance of Death*. 2 vols. London: Rudolph Ackermann, 1816.

———. *The Tour of Doctor Syntax*. 3 vols. London: Nattali and Bond, 1817. First published 1812.

The Comics Journal 200 (1997). Number on Chris Ware.

Comix 2000. Paris: L'Association, 2000.

Communications 8 (1966). Number on 'L'Analyse structurale du récit'.

Communications 15 (1970). Number on 'L'Analyse des images'.

Communications 24 (1976). Number on 'La Bande dessinée et son discours'.

Corrozet, Gilles. *Hecatomgraphie* [One Hundred Pictures]. Paris: Denis Janot, 1540.

Couderc, Marie-Anne. *Bécassine inconnue* [Unknown Bécassine]. Paris: CNRS, 2000.

Couperie, Pierre. 'Sociologie du Club des Bandes Dessinées', *Giff-Wiff* 3 (1962), 9–13.

Couperie, Pierre, Proto Destefanis, Edouard François, Maurice Horn, Claude Moliterni and Gerald Gassiot-Talabot. *Bande dessinée et figuration narrative*. Paris: Musée des Arts Décoratifs, 1967.

Crépin, Thierry. '1950–1954: La Commission de surveillance entre intimidation et répression' [1950–1954: The Surveillance Commission: Between Intimidation and Repression], *9e Art* 4 (1999), 21–27.

———. *'Haro sur le gangster!': La Moralisation de la presse enfantine 1934–1954* ['Shame on the Gangster!': The Moralisation of the Press for Children 1934–1954]. Paris: CNRS, 2001.

Crépin, Thierry and Thierry Groensteen, eds. *'On Tue à chaque page': La loi de 1949 sur les publications destinées à la jeunesse* ['They Kill on Every Page': The 1949 Law on Publications Aimed at Youth]. Paris: Éditions du Temps, 1999.

Daeninckx, Didier. *Le Der des ders*. Paris: Gallimard, 1984. In English as *A Very Profitable War*, trans. Sarah Martin. London: Serpent's Tale, 1994.

Daeninckx, Didier and Jacques Tardi. *Le Der des ders* [A Very Profitable War]. Tournai: Casterman, 1997.

David B. *Le Cheval blême* [The Bleak Horse]. Paris: L'Association, 2000.

Davodeau, Étienne. *Les Mauvaises gens: Une Histoire de militants* [The Wrong Type of People: A Story of Militants]. Paris: Delcourt, 2005.

Dayez, Hugues. *Tintin et les héritiers: Chronique de l'après-Hergé* [Tintin and the Heirs: A Post-Hergé Chronical]. Paris: Félin, 1999.

Degrés des âges [Steps of the Ages]. Single print. [*c*.1820].

Départ du soldat [The Soldier's Departure] and *Retour du soldat* [The Soldier's Return]. Two related prints. [*c*.1810].

Derib. *Jo*. Paris: Fondation pour la Vie, 1991.

Derrida, Jacques. *La Carte postale de Socrate à Freud et au delà*. Paris: Flammarion, 1980. In English as *The Postcard: From Socrates to Freud and Beyond*, trans. Alan Bass. Chicago: University of Chicago Press, 1987.

———. *De La Grammatologie*. Paris: Minuit, 1967. Several subsequent editions. In English as *Of Grammatology*, trans. Gayatri Chakravorty Spivak. Baltimore, MD: Johns Hopkins University Press, 1997. First published 1976.

———. *L'Écriture et la différence*. Paris: Seuil, 1967. Several subsequent editions. In English as *Writing and Difference*, trans. Alan Bass. London: Routledge, 1978.

De Sá, Leonardo. 'Aubert, le "pirate" qui a inventé les albums de bandes dessinées' [Aubert, the 'Pirate' Who Invented the Bande Dessinée Album], *Le Collectionneur de Bandes Dessinées* 108 (2006), 32–33.

Dickens, Charles. *Pickwick Papers*, ed. James Kinsley. Oxford: Clarendon, 1986. Originally published in serial form 1836–1837.

Dictionnaire historique & bibliographique de la Suisse. Neuchatel: Administration du Dictionnaire Historique & Bibliographique de la Suisse, 1932.

Diderot, Denis. *Salons*. 4 vols, ed. Jean Seznec and Jean Adhémar. Oxford: Clarendon, 1957–1967. First published 1759–1781. Partially available in English as *Diderot on Art*, ed. and trans. John Goodman. New Haven, CT: Yale University Press, 1995.

Dierick, Charles, ed. *Le Centre Belge de la Bande Dessinée*. Brussels: Dexia, 2000.

Domino, Christophe. *Les Années Pop* [The Pop Years]. Paris: Centre Pompidou, 2001.

Douglas, Allen and Fedwa Malti-Douglas. 'Tardi and Daeninckx: Comic Strips, Detective Novels and World War I', *International Journal of Comic Art* 5.1 (2003), 134–46.

Douillet, Joseph. *Moscou sans voiles: (Neuf ans de travail au pays des Soviets)* [Moscow without Veils: (Nine Years of Work in the Land of the Soviets)]. Paris: Spes, 1928.

Dubois, Jacqueline and Raoul Dubois. *La Presse enfantine française*. Paris: Éditions de Francs et Franches-Camarades, 1957.

Dubourg, Maurice. 'Louis Forton et Les Pieds Nickelés: Essai de chronologie' [Louis Forton and the Pieds Nickelés: A Chronological Essay], *Le Collectionneur de Bandes Dessinées* 35 (1982), 17–23.

Dupuy, Philippe and Charles Berberian. *Le Journal d'Henriette* [Henriette's Diary]. Paris: Audie/Fluide Glacial, 1988.

———. *Journal d'un album* [Diary of an Album]. Paris: L'Association, 1994.

———. *Monsieur Jean, l'amour et la concierge* [Monsieur Jean, Love, and the Concierge]. Geneva: Les Humanoïdes Associés, 1991.

———. *Monsieur Jean: Les Femmes et les enfants d'abord* [Monsieur Jean: Women and Children First]. Geneva: Les Humanoïdes Associés, 1994.

Eco, Umberto. 'Entretien avec Umberto Eco' [Interview with Umberto Eco]. In *Le Mouvement Pop*, by Henri Tissot. Lausanne: Éditions Grammont, 1975, pp. 8–33.

———. 'James Bond: Une Combinatoire narrative' [James Bond: A Combinative Narrative], *Communications* 8 (1966), 77–93.

———. 'Le Mythe de Superman', *Communications* 24 (1976), 24–40.

———. 'Le Mythe de Superman et la dissolution du temps' [The Myth of Superman and the Dissolution of Time], *Giff-Wiff* 11 (1964), 10–13.

———. *Il Superuomo di massia: Studi sul romenzo popolare* [The Superman of the Masses: Studies on the Popular Novel]. Milan: Cooperativa Scrittori, 1978. In French as *De Superman au Surhomme* [From Superman to Super Man], trans. Myriem Bouzaher. Paris: Grasset, 1993.

Eco, Umberto and Oreste del Bueno, eds. *Il Caso Bond* [The Bond Case]. Milan: Fabbri & Bompiani Sonzoguo, 1965. In English as *The Bond Affair*, trans. R.A. Dowie. London, Macdonald, 1966.

Falardeau, Mira. *La Bande dessinée au Québec*. [Montreal]: Boréal, 1994.

Farwell, Beatrice. *The Charged Image: French Lithographic Caricature 1816–1848*. Santa Barbara: Santa Barbara Museum of Art, 1989.

Fiction 98 (1961). Number that announced the founding of the Club des Bandes Dessinées.

Figuration Narrative: Paris, 1960–1972. Paris: Réunion des Musées Nationaux, 2008.

Filippini, Henri. *Les Cahiers de la Bande Dessinée présentent Les 7 Vies de l'épervier* [The Cahiers de la Bande Dessinée Present the 7 Lives of the Sparrowhawk]. Grenoble: Glénat, 2004.

———. *Dictionnaire encyclopédique des héros et auteurs de BD*. 3 vols. Grenoble: Glénat, 1998–2000.

———. *Histoire du journal et des éditions Vaillant* [The History of *Vaillant* the Journal and its Publications]. Grenoble: Glénat, 1978.

Filippini, Henri, Jacques Glénat, Numa Sadoul and Yves Varende. *Histoire de la bande dessinée en France et en Belgique des origins à nos jours* [The History of the Bande Dessinée in France and in Belgium from its Beginnings to Today]. Grenoble: Glénat, 1979.

Flaubert, Gustave. *Mme Bovary*, ed. Pierre-Marc de Biasi. Paris: Seuil, 1992. First published 1857. In English as *Mme Bovary*, trans. Geoffrey Wall. London: Penguin, 2002.

Fleming, Ian. *Casino Royale*. London, Penguin, 2004. First published 1953.

Fleming, Ian, Anthony Hern, Henry Gammidge and John McLusky. *James Bond 007: Casino Royale*, ed. Paul Simpson. London: Titan, 2005.

Floch, Jean-Marie. *Une Lecture de Tintin au Tibet* [A Reading of Tintin in Tibet]. Paris: Presses Universitaires de France, 1997.

Forbes, Jill and Mike Kelly, eds. *French Cultural Studies: An Introduction*. Oxford: Oxford University Press, 1995.

Forest, Jean-Claude. *Hypocrite et le monster du Loch Ness*. Paris: L'Association, 2001.

Forsdick, Charles. 'Exoticising the *Domestique*: Bécassine, Brittany and the Beauty of the Dead'. In *The Francophone Bande Dessinée*, ed. Charles Forsdick, Laurence Grove and Libbie [Elizabeth] McQuillan. Amsterdam: Rodopi, 2005, pp. 23–37.

Forsdick, Charles, Laurence Grove and Libbie [Elizabeth] McQuillan, eds. *The Francophone Bande Dessinée*. Amsterdam: Rodopi, 2005.

Foulet, Alain and Olivier Maltret. *Presque tout Tardi* [Almost All of Tardi]. Dieppe: Sapristi, 1996.

Fourment, Alain. *Histoire de la presse des jeunes et des journaux d'enfants (1768–1988)* [History of Youth Press and Children's Journals (1768–1988)]. Paris: Eole, 1987.

François, Edouard and Pierre Couperie, eds. *Benjamin Rabier*. Paris: Pierre Horay, 1982.

Francq, Philippe and Jean Van Hamme. *Largo Winch 14: La Loi du Dollar* [Largo Winch 14: the Law of the Dollar]. Brussels: Dupuis, 2005.

Frémion, Yves. *Le Guide de la bédé francophone* [Guide to French-language BD]. Paris: Syros, 1990.

———. 'Inventions, inventeurs et inventards: Un Inventaire, une aventure' [Inventions, Inventors and Inventing Types: An Inventory, an

Adventure]. In *Les Origines de la bande dessinée* [The Origins of the Bande Dessinée], ed. Thierry Groensteen. *Le Collectionneur de Bandes Dessinées* special number ['hors série'] 79 (1996), 6–10.

Fresnault-Deruelle, Pierre. *La Bande dessinée: L'Univers et les techniques de quelques comics d'expression française: Essai d'analyse sémiotique* [The Bande Dessinée: The Universe and the Techniques of a Selection of Comics in French: An Essay of Semiotic Analysis]. Paris: Hachette, 1972.

———. 'Du Linéaire au tabulaire', *Communications* 24 (1976), 7–23.

———. 'Le Verbal dans les bandes dessinées', *Communications* 15 (1970), 145–61.

Frise des douze apotres [Frieze of the Twelve Apostles]. Single print. 1760.

Gabilliet, Jean-Paul. 'De L'Art pop au Pop Art: Les Comics et l'art contemporain: Quelques Repères' [From Popular Art to Pop Art: Comics and Contemporary Art: A Guide], *Le Collectionneur de Bandes Dessinées* 94 (2001), 14–23.

Gabut, Jean-Jacques. *L'Âge d'or de la BD: Les Journaux illustrés 1934–1944* [The Golden Age of BD: Illustrated Journals 1934-1944]. Paris: Catleya, 2001.

Gandais, M. *Le Don Quichotte romantique, ou voyage du Docteur Syntaxe à la recherché du pittoresque et du romantique; poëme en XX chants, traduit librement de l'anglais et orné de 26 gravures* [The Romantic Don Quioxote, or the Journey of Doctor Syntax in Search of the Picturesque and Romantic: A Poem in XX Verses, Translated Freely from the English and Decorated with 26 Engravings]. Paris: chez L'Auteur et Pélicier, 1821.

Garnier-Pelle, Nicole. *L'Imagerie populaire française II: Images d'Épinal gravées sur bois* [French Popular Imagery II: Woodcut Images d'Épinal]. Paris: Réunion des Musées Nationaux, 1996.

Gaumer, Patrick. *Les Années Pilote: 1959–1989* [The *Pilote* Years: 1959–1989]. Paris: Dargaud, 1996.

Gaumer, Patrick and Claude Moliterni. *Dictionnaire mondial de la bande dessinée* [World Dictionary of the Bande Dessinée]. Paris: Larousse, 2000. First published 1994.

[Geneva, Musées d'Art et d'Histoire]. *Rodolphe Töpffer: Aventures graphiques* [Rodolphe Töpffer: Graphic Adventures]. [Geneva]: [Musées d'Art et d'Histoire], 1996.

Gerbier, Laurent. 'Les Pièges de l'analogie' [The Traps of Analogy], *9e Art* 4 (1999), 71–77.

Gerin, Elisabeth. *Tout sur la presse enfantine* [Everything About the Press for Children]. Paris: Centre de Recherches de la Bonne Presse, 1958.

Gipi. *Notes pour une histoire de guerre* [Notes for a War Story], trad. Hélène Dauniol-Remaud. Arles: Actes Sud, 2006. First published 2004. In English as *Notes for a War Story*. No named translator. New York: First Second, 2007. Originally in Italian as *Apunti per una storia di guerra*. Bologna: Coconino, 2004.

Giraud, Jean. See Moebius.

Giroud, Frank and Joseph Béhé. *Le Manuscrit*. Grenoble: Glénat, 2001.

Giroud, Frank, Joseph Béhé and Camille Meyer. *Le Rendez-Vous de Glasgow*. Grenoble: Glénat, 2006.

Glasser, Jean-Claude. 'Note' for the 'Rubrique Courrier' [Readers' Letters], *Cahiers de la Bande Dessinée* 80 (1988). No pagination.

Goscinny, René and Albert Uderzo. *Astérix aux Jeux Olympiques*. Neuilly-sur Seine: Dargaud, 1968. Several subsequent editions. In English as *Asterix at the Olympic Games*, trans. Anthea Bell and Derek Hockridge. Leicester: Brockhampton, 1972. Several subsequent editions.

———. *Astérix chez les Belges*. Neuilly-sur-Seine: Dargaud, 1979. In English as *Asterix in Belgium*. Several subsequent editions. Trans. Anthea Bell and Derek Hockridge. London: Hodder Dargaud, 1980. Several subsequent editions.

———. *Astérix chez les Bretons*. Neuilly-sur-Seine: Dargaud, 1966. Several subsequent editions. In English as *Asterix in Britain*, trans. Anthea Bell and Derek Hockridge. Leicester: Brockhampton, 1970. Several subsequent editions.

———. *Astérix chez les Goths*. Neuilly-sur-Seine: Dargaud, 1963. Several subsequent editions. In English as *Asterix and the Goths*, trans. Anthea Bell and Derek Hockridge. Leicester: Brockhampton, 1974. Several subsequent editions.

———. *Astérix chez les Helvètes*. Neuilly-sur-Seine: Dargaud, 1970. Several subsequent editions. In English as *Asterix in Switzerland*, trans. Anthea Bell and Derek Hockridge. Leicester: Brockhampton, 1973. Several subsequent editions.

———. *Astérix en Corse*. Neuilly-sur-Seine: Dargaud, 1973. Several subsequent editions. In English as *Asterix in Corsica*, trans. Anthea Bell and Derek Hockridge. London: Hodder Dargaud, 1980. Several subsequent editions.

———. *Astérix et Cléopâtre*. Neuilly-sur-Seine: Dargaud, 1965. Several subsequent editions. In English as *Asterix and Cleopatra*, trans. Anthea Bell and Derek Hockridge. Leicester: Brockhampton, 1969. Several subsequent editions.

———. *Astérix et la rentrée gauloise*. Paris: Éditions Albert René, 2003. In English as *Asterix and the Class Act*, trans. Anthea Bell and Derek Hockridge. London: Orion, 2003.

———. *Astérix et les Normands*. Neuilly-sur-Seine: Dargaud, 1966. Several subsequent editions. In English as *Asterix and the Normans*, trans. Anthea Bell and Derek Hockridge. London: Hodder and Stoughton, 1978. Several subsequent editions.

———. *Astérix gladiateur*. Neuilly-sur-Seine: Dargaud, 1977. First published 1964. Several subsequent editions. In English as *Asterix the Gladiator*, trans. Anthea Bell and Derek Hockridge. Leicester: Brockhampton, 1969. Several subsequent editions.

———. *Astérix le Gaulois*. Neuilly-sur-Seine: Dargaud, 1961. Several subsequent editions. In English as *Asterix the Gaul*, trans. Anthea Bell and Derek Hockridge. Leicester: Brockhampton, 1969. Several subsequent editions.

———. *Le Combat des chefs*. Neuilly-sur-Seine: Dargaud, 1966. Several subsequent editions. In English as *Asterix and the Big Fight*, trans. Anthea Bell and Derek Hockridge. Leicester: Brockhampton, 1971. Several subsequent editions.

———. *Le Devin*. Neuilly-sur-Seine: Dargaud, 1972. Several subsequent editions. In English as *Asterix and the Soothsayer*, trans. Anthea Bell and Derek Hockridge. Leicester: Brockhampton, 1975. Several subsequent editions.

———. *Le Domaine des Dieux*. Neuilly-sur-Seine: Dargaud, 1971. Several subsequent editions. In English as *The Mansions of the Gods*, trans. Anthea Bell and Derek Hockridge. Leicester: Brockhampton, 1973. Several subsequent editions.

———. *La Grande Traversée*. Neuilly-sur-Seine: Dargaud, 1975. Several subsequent editions. In English as *Asterix and the Great Crossing*, trans. Anthea Bell and Derek Hockridge. London: Hodder and Stoughton, 1975. Several subsequent editions.

———. *La Serpe d'or*. Neuilly-sur-Seine: Dargaud, 1962. Several subsequent editions. In English as *Asterix and the Golden Sickle*, trans. Anthea Bell and Derek Hockridge. London: Hodder and Stoughton, 1975. Several subsequent editions.

Goscinny, René and Albert Uderzo. See also Uderzo, Albert.

Goulet, Alain. *Le Parcours moebien de l'écriture: Le Voyeur* [Writing's Moebian Path: The Voyeur]. Paris: Lettres Modernes, 1982.

Le Gourmand. Single print. 1791.

Grand-Carteret, John. 'En Manière de Préface' [By Way of a Preface]. *Le Livre et l'Image* [The Book and the Image] 1 (1893), 1–2.

Grand Dictionnaire universel du XIX siècle [The Great Universal Dictionary of the Nineteenth Century]. Paris: Administration du Grand Dictionnaire Universel, 1876.

Grande Encyclopédie. Paris: Société Anonyme de la Grande Encyclopédie, [*c*.1890].

Gravett, Paul. 'The Cartoonist's Progress: The Inventors of Comics in Great Britain'. In *Forging a New Medium: The Comic Strip in the Nineteenth Century*, ed. Pascal Lefèvre and Charles Dierick. Brussels: VUP University Press, 2000, pp. 79–103. First published 1998.

———. *Graphic Novels: Stories to Change Your Life*. London: Aurum, 2005.

———. *Manga: Sixty Years of Japanese Comics*. London: Laurence King, 2004.

Grell, Mike. *James Bond 007: Licence to Kill*. Sonoma County, CA: Eclipse, 1989. In French as *James Bond 007: Permis de tuer*, trans. Jean-Loup Leuriaux. [Np]: Himalaya, 1989.

Grévin et Cie. *Document de référence 2001* [Reference Document 2001]. Plailly: Grévin et Cie, 2002.

Groensteen, Thierry. *Les Années Caran d'Ache* [The Caran d'Ache Years]. Angoulême: CNBDI. 1998.

———. *La Bande Dessinée*. Paris: Milan, 1996.

———. 'C'était le temps où la bande dessinée corrompait l'âme enfantine ...,' [It Was the Time When the Bande Dessinée Corrupted the Souls of Childrenn...], *9e Art* 4 (1999), 14–19.

———. 'Entretien avec Frank Margerin' [Interview with Frank Margerin], *Les Cahiers de la Bande Dessinée* 77 (1987), 8–17.

———. 'Histoire de la bande dessinée muette' [History of Silent Bande Dessinée], *9e Art* 2 (1997), 60–75; *9e Art* 3 (1998), 92–105.

———. 'Introduction'. In *Rodolphe Töpffer: Aventures graphiques* [Rodolphe Töpffer: Graphic Adventures], by [Geneva, Musées d'Art et d'Histoire]. [Geneva]: [Musées d'Art et d'Histoire], 1996, p. 13.

———. 'La Mise en cause de Paul Winckler' [Paul Winckler Under Fire]. In *'On Tue à chaque page': La loi de 1949 sur les publications destinées à la jeunesse* ['They Kill on Every Page': The 1949 Law on Publications Aimed at Youth], ed. Thierry Crépin and Thierry Groensteen. Paris: Éditions du Temps, 1999, pp. 53–60.

———. *Un Objet culturel non identifié* [An Unidentified Cultural Object]. [Angoulême]: Éditions de l'An 2, 2006.

———. 'Un Premier bouquet de contraintes' [A First Bouquet of Constraints]. In *OuPus 1*. Paris: L'Association, 1997, pp. 13–59.

———. *Système de la bande dessinée*. Paris: Presses Universitaires de France, 1999. In English as *The System of Comics*, trans. Bart Beaty. Jackson, MS: University Press of Mississippi, 2007.

———. 'Töpffer, the Originator of the Modern Comic Strip'. In *Forging a New Medium: The Comic Strip in the Nineteenth Century*, ed. Pascal Lefèvre and Charles Dierick. Brussels: VUP University Press, 2000, pp. 105–14. First published 1998.

———. 'Gustave Doré's Comics', *International Journal of Comic Art* 2.2 (2000), 111–20.

Groensteen, Thierry, ed. *BD récit et modernité*. Poitiers: Futuropolis, 1988.

———. *Le Docteur Festus: Histoire de monsieur Cryptogame: Deux odyssées* [Doctor Festus: The Story of Mr Cryptogame: Two Odysseys], by Rodolphe Töpffer. Paris: Seuil, 1996.

———. *Essai de physiognomonie*, by Rodolphe Töpffer. [Paris]: Kargo, 2003.

———. 'Julius Corentin et moi: Entretien avec Marc-Antoine Mathieu' [Julius Corentin and I: An Interview with Marc-Antoine Mathieu], *9e Art* 4 (1999), 62–70.

———. *Monsieur Crépin: Monsieur Pencil: Deux égarements de la science* [M. Crépin: M. Pencil: Two Scientific Distractions], by Rodolphe Töpffer. Paris: Seuil, 1996.

———. *Monsieur Jabot: Monsieur Vieux Bois: Deux histoires d'amour* [M. Jabot: M. Vieux Bois: Two Love Stories], by Rodolphe Töpffer. Paris: Seuil, 1996.

———. *Les Origines de la bande dessinée* [The Origins of the Bande Dessinée]. *Le Collectionneur de Bandes Dessinées.* Special number ['hors série'] 79 (1996).

———. *[Primé à Angoulême]: 30 ans de bandes dessinées à travers le palmarès du Festival* [[Prize winners at Angoulême]: 30 Years of Bandes Dessinées through the Festival Awards]. Angoulême: Éditions de l'An 2, 2003.

Groensteen, Thierry and Benoît Peeters. *Töpffer: L'Invention de la bande dessinée* [Töpffer: The Invention of the Bande Dessinée]. Paris: Hermann, 1994.

Groensteen, Thierry and Gaby Scaon, eds. *Les Musées imaginaires de la bande dessinée* [The Bande Dessinée's Imaginary Museums]. Angoulême: Éditions de l'An 2, 2004.

Grojnowski, Daniel, ed. *De la plaque Daguerre: À propos des Excursions daguerriennes,* by Rodolphe Töpffer. Cognac: Le Temps qu'Il Fait, 2002.

Grove, Laurence. 'Autobiography and Early Bande Dessinée', *Belphégor* 4.1 (2004). No pagination.

———. '*Bande Dessinée*: The Missing *Mythologie*'. In *Mythologies at 50: Barthes and Popular Culture* (*Nottingham French Studies* Special Number 47.2), ed. Douglas Smith. Nottingham: University of Nottingham, 2008, pp. 29-40.

———. 'BD Theory before the Term "BD" Existed'. In *The Francophone Bande Dessinée*, ed. Charles Forsdick, Laurence Grove and Libbie [Elizabeth] McQuillan. Amsterdam: Rodopi: 2005, pp. 39–49.

———. 'Bond Dessiné(e)'. In *James Bond (2)007: Anatomie d'un mythe populaire*, ed. Françoise Hache-Bissette, Fabien Boully and Vincent Chenille. Paris: Belin, 2007, pp. 269-74.

———. 'Emblems with Speech Bubbles'. In *Visual Words and Verbal Pictures: Essays in Honour of Michael Bath*, ed. Alison Saunders and Peter Davidson. Glasgow: GES, 2005, pp. 89–103.

———. 'Mickey, *Le Journal de Mickey* and the Birth of the Popular BD', *Belphégor* 1.1 (2001). No pagination.

———. 'Multi-Media Emblems and Their Modern Day Counterparts'. In *Emblematic Tendencies in the Art and Literature of the Twentieth Century*, ed. Anthony Harper, Ingrid Höpel and Susan Sirc. Glasgow: Glasgow Emblem Studies, 2005, pp. 171–87.

———. *Text/Image Mosaics in French Culture: Emblems and Comic Strips.* Aldershot: Ashgate, 2005.

Grove, Laurence and Daniel Russell. *The French Emblem: A Bibliography of Secondary Sources.* Geneva: Droz, 2000.

Guerard, Roland and Nicolas Prevost. ['Assassination of Henri III']. *Série Qb1: Histoire de France en Estampes.* [Bibliothèque nationale de France, Département des Estampes]. Single print. 1589.

Gueroult, Guillaume. *Premier Livre des emblemes* [The First Book of Emblems]. Lyon: Balthazar Arnoullet, 1550.

Guibert, Emmanuel, Didier Lefèvre and Frédéric Lemercier. *Le Photographe* [The Photographer]. 3 vols. Marcinelle: Dupuis, 2003–06.

Guller, Angèle. *Le 9e Art: Pour une connaissance de la chanson française contemporaine (de 1945 à nos jours)* [The 9th Art: Towards an Understanding of French Contemporary Song (from 1945 to the Current Day]. Brussels: Vokaer, 1978.

Gundersheimer, Werner L., ed. and trans. *The Dance of Death*, by Hans Holbein. New York: Dover, 1971.

Heins, Daniel. *Emblemata amatoria* [Emblems of Love]. Amsterdam: Dirck Pietersz, 1608.

———. *Quaeris quid sit amor* [You May Ask What Love Is]. Amsterdam: Dirck Pietersz, [1607].

Henry, Avril. *Biblia pauperum* [Bible of the Poor]. Aldershot: Scolar, 1987.

Hergé. *L'Affaire Tournesol*. Tournai: Casterman, 1956. Several subsequent editions. In English as *The Calculus Affair*, trans. Leslie Lonsdale-Cooper and Michael Turner. London: Methuen, 1960. Several subsequent editions.

———. *Les Bijoux de la Castafiore*. Tournai: Casterman, 1963. Several subsequent editions. In English as *The Castafiore Emerald*, trans. Leslie Lonsdale-Cooper and Michael Turner. London: Methuen, 1963. Several subsequent editions.

———. *L'Étoile mystérieuse*. Tournai: Casterman, 1942. Several subsequent editions. In English as *The Shooting Star*, trans. Leslie Lonsdale-Cooper and Michael Turner. London: Methuen, 1961. Several subsequent editions.

———. *L'Île noire*. Tournai: Casterman, 1938. Several subsequent editions. In English as *The Black Island*, trans. Leslie Lonsdale-Cooper and Michael Turner. London: Methuen, 1966. Several subsequent editions.

———. *Le Lotus bleu*. Tournai: Casterman, 1936. Several subsequent editions. In English as *The Blue Lotus*, trans. Leslie Lonsdale-Cooper and Michael Turner. London: Methuen, 1983. Several subsequent editions.

———. *Objectif Lune*. Tournai: Casterman, 1953. Several subsequent editions. In English as *Destination Moon*, trans. Leslie Lonsdale-Cooper and Michael Turner. London: Methuen, 1959. Several subsequent editions.

———. *On a marché sur la Lune*. Tournai: Casterman, 1954. Several subsequent editions. In English as *Explorers on the Moon*, trans. Leslie Lonsdale-Cooper and Michael Turner. London: Methuen, 1959. Several subsequent editions.

———. *Les Sept boules de cristal*. Tournai: Casterman, 1948. Several subsequent editions. In English as *The Seven Crystal Balls*, trans. Leslie Lonsdale-Cooper and Michael Turner. London: Methuen, 1962. Several subsequent editions.

———. *Tintin au Congo*. [Brussels]: Éditions du Petit Vingtième, 1931. Several subsequent editions. In English as *Tintin in the Congo*, trans. Leslie Lonsdale-Cooper and Michael Turner. London: Sundancer, 1991.

———. *Tintin au pays des Soviets*. [Brussels]: Éditions du Petit Vingtième, 1930. Several subsequent editions. In English as *Tintin in the Land of the Soviets*, trans. Leslie Lonsdale-Cooper and Michael Turner. London: Sundancer, 1989. Several subsequent editions.

———. *Tintin au Tibet*. Tournai: Casterman, 1960. Several subsequent editions. In English as *Tintin in Tibet*, trans. Leslie Lonsdale-Cooper and Michael Turner. London: Methuen, 1962. Several subsequent editions.

———. *Tintin et l'Alph'Art*. Tournai: Casterman, 1986. Several subsequent editions. In English as *Tintin and Alph-Art: Tintin's Last Adventure*, trans. Leslie Lonsdale-Cooper and Michael Turner. London: Sundancer, 1990.

Heuet, Stéphane and Marcel Proust. *À La Recherche du temps perdu: Combray*. Paris: Delcourt, 1998. In English as *Remembrance of Things Past: Combray*, trans. Stanislas Brezet. New York: NBM, 2001.

Hirschfeld, Gerhard and Partick Marsh, eds. *Collaboration in France: Politics and Culture during the Nazi Occupation, 1940–1944*. Oxford: Berg, 1989.

Hogarth, William. *Before* and *After*. Two related prints. 1736.

———. *The Rake's Progress*. Series of eight prints. 1735, with reworkings up to 1763.

Holbein, Hans. *Les Simulachres et historiées faces de la mort* [Images and Illustrated Facets of Death]. Lyon: Melchior and Gaspar Trechsel, 1538. Several subsequent editions.

Horn, Maurice, ed. *The World Encyclopedia of Comics*. Philadelphia: Chelsea House, 1999. First published 1976.
Horn, Pierre L. 'American Graffiti – French Style: Three Comic Strip Artists Look at Pre-War America', *International Journal of Comic Art* 3.1 (2001), 86–92.
Hugo, Herman. *Pia desideria* [Pious Desires]. Antwerp: Hendrick Aertssens, 1624. Several subsequent editions.
Imago primi saeculi Societatis Iesu [The Image of the First Century of the Society of Jesus]. Antwerp, Balthasar Moretus, 1640.
Imbs, Paul, ed. *Trésor de la langue française: Dictionnaire de la langue du XIXe et du XXe siècle (1789–1960)* [Treasure of the French Language: Dictionary of the Language of the Nineteenth and Twentieth Centuries]. 16 vols. Paris: CNRS, 1975.
Innis, Harold. *The Bias of Communication*. Toronto: University of Toronto Press, 1964. First published 1951.
International Journal of Comic Art 1.1 (1999), 1–16. Special dossier on the history of USA comics scholarship.
International Journal of Comic Art 4.1 (2002), 5–96. Special dossier on early comics scholarship.
International Journal of Comic Art 5.1 (2003), 3–73. Special dossier on pioneers of comics scholarship.
International Journal of Comic Art 5.2 (2003), 205–60. Special dossier on pioneers of comics scholarship.
International Journal of Comic Art 7.2 (2005), 3–88. Special dossier on pioneers of comics scholarship.
Jans, Michel. *Loisel: Une Monographie*. St Egrève: Mosquito, 1998.
Jans, Michel, Jean-François Douvry and Nadine Douvry, eds. *Juillard: Une Monographie*. Saint-Egrève: Mosquito, 1996.
Jans, Michel, Jean-François Douvry, Gilles Ratier and Serge Tisseron, eds. *Margerin: Une Monographie*. Saint-Egrève: Mosquito, 1995.
Jardin, Alexandre. *Le Petit Sauvage* [The Little Savage]. Paris: Gallimard, 1992.
Juillard, André. *Après la pluie*. [Paris]: Casterman, 1998. In English as *After the Rain*, trans. Joe Johnson. New York: NBM, 1999.
———. *Le Cahier bleu*. [Paris]: Casterman, 1994. Second edition 2003. In English as *The Blue Notebook*, trans. Jacinthe Leclerc. New York: NBM, 1997.
———. *Nation/Étoile*. Chatenay-Malabry: Alain Beaulet, 2000.
Juillard, André and Yves Sante. *La Machination Voronov* [The Voronov Plot]. Brussels: Éditions Blake et Mortimer, 2000.
———. *Les Sarcophages du sixième continent* [The Sarcophagi of the Sixth Continent]. 2 vols. Brussels: Éditions Blake et Mortimer, 2003–2004.
Kaenel, Philippe. *Le Métier d'illustrateur 1830–1880: Rodolphe Töpffer, J.-J. Grandville, Gustave Doré* [The Illustrator's Profession 1830–1880: Rodolphe Töpffer, J.-J. Grandville, Gustave Doré]. Paris: Messene, 1996.
Kaenel, Philippe, ed. *M. Trictrac*, by Rodolphe Töpffer. Paris: Favre, 1988.
Kempeneers, Michel. 'Cham: Un Pionnier oublié' [Cham, A Forgotten Pioneer], *Le Collectionneur de Bandes Dessinées* 108 (2006), 29–31.
Kerr, David S. *Caricature and French Political Culture 1830–1848: Charles Philipon and the Illustrated Press*. Oxford: Oxford University Press, 2000.
Kessler, Peter. *The Complete Guide to Asterix*. London: Hodder, 1995.
Kunzle, David. *The Early Comic Strip: Narrative Strips and Picture Stories in the European Broadsheet from c. 1450 to 1825: History of the Comic Strip Volume 1*. Berkeley: University of California Press, 1973.
———. *The Early Comic Strip: The Nineteenth Century: History of the Comic Strip Volume 2*. Berkeley: University of California Press, 1990.
———. *Father of the Comic Strip: Rodolphe Töpffer*. Jackson, MS: University Press of Mississippi, 2007.

———. 'Goethe and Caricature: From Hogarth to Töpffer', *Journal of the Warburg and Courtauld Institutes* 48 (1985), 164–88.
———. '*L'Illustration*, journal universel 1843–1853', *Nouvelles de l'Estampe* [News on Engravings] 43 (1979), 8–19.
Kunzle, David, ed. and trans. *Rodolphe Töpffer: The Complete Comic Strips*. Jackson, MS: University Press of Mississippi, 2007.
Lacassin, Francis. 'Notre Assemblée Générale' [Our AGM], *Giff-Wiff* 7 (1963), 5–8.
———. *Pour un 9ème Art: La Bande dessinée* [For a Ninth Art: The Bande Dessinée]. Paris: 10/18, 1971.
Lachartre, Alain. *Objectif pub: La Bande dessinée et la publicité, hier et aujourd'hui* [Destination Ads: Bande Dessinée and Advertising Yesterday and Today]. Paris: Rober Laffont, 1986.
Lador, Pierre-Yves. 'André Juillard: *Le Cahier bleu*', in *Juillard: Une Monographie*, ed. Michel Jans, Jean-François Douvry and Nadine Douvry. Saint-Egrève: Mosquito, 1996, pp. 106–21.
Langlois, Claude. *La Caricature contre-révolutionnaire*. Paris: CNRS, 1988.
La Perrière, Guillaume de. *La Morosophie* [Foolish Wisdom]. Lyon: Macé Bonhomme, 1553.
———. *Le Théâtre des bons engins* [Theatre of Good Devices]. Lyon: Denis Janot, [1540].
Larcenet, Manu. *Une Aventure rocambolesque d'Attila le Hun: Le Fléau de Dieu* [An Incredible Attila the Hun Adventure: God's Scourge]. Paris: Dargaud, 2006.
———. *Une Aventure rocambolesque de Sigmund Freud: Le Temps de chien* [An Incredible Sigmund Freud Adventure: Heavy Weather]. Paris: Dargaud, 2002.
———. *Une Aventure rocambolesque de Vincent Van Gogh: La Ligne de front* [An Incredible Vincent Van Gogh Adventure: The Front Line]. Paris: Dargaud, 2004.
———. *Le Combat ordinaire*. Paris: Dargaud, 2003. In English as *Ordinary Victories*, trans. Joe Johnson. New York: NBM, 2005.
———. *Le Combat ordinaire: 2 Les Quantités négligeables*. Paris: Dargaud, 2004. In English as *Ordinary Victories*, trans. Joe Johnson. New York: NBM, 2005.
———. *La Loi des séries* [Series Law]. Paris: Fluide Glacial, 1997.
Latzarus, Marie-Thérèse. *La Littérature enfantine en France dans la seconde moitié du XIX siècle* [Children's Literature in France in the Second Half of the Nineteenth Century]. Paris: Presses Universitaires de France, 1924.
Laughton, Bruce. *Honoré Daumier*. New Haven, CT: Yale University Press, 1996.
Lavanchy, Éric. *Étude du Cahier bleu d'André Juillard: Une Approche narratologique de la bande dessinée*. Louvain-la-Neuve: Academia-Bruylant, 2007.
Lax. *Chiens de fusils* [Gun Dogs]. Issy-les-Moulineaux: Vents d'Ouest, 1996.
Le Brun, Charles. *Méthode pour apprendre à dessiner les passions* [Method for Learning to Draw the Passions]. Amsterdam: François Van der Plaats, 1702. Facsimile edition 1982 (Hildesheim: Georg Olms Verlag).
Lecigne, Bruno. *Avanies et mascarades: L'Évolution de la bande dessinée en France dans les années 70* [Affronts and Mascarades: The Evolution of the Bande Dessinée in France in the 1970s]. Paris: Futuropolis, 1981.
Lecigne, Bruno and Jean-Pierre Tamine. *Fac-Similé: Essai paratactique sur le Nouveau Réalisme de la bande dessinée* [Facsimile: A Paratactic Essay on the Bande Dessinée's Nouveau Réalisme]. Paris: Futuropolis, 1983.
Lécroart, Étienne. 'Strips-Acrostiches'. In *OuPus 1*. Paris: L'Association, 1997, p. 8.
Lefèvre, Pascal. 'Recovering Sensuality in Comic Theory', *International Journal of Comic Art* 1.1 (1999), 140–49.

———. 'La Bande dessinée belge au XXe siècle' [Belgian Bande Dessinée in the Twentieth Century]. *Le Centre Belge de la Bande Dessinée*, ed. Charles Dierick. Brussels: Dexia, 2000, pp. 168–207.

Lefèvre, Pascal and Charles Dierick, eds. *Forging a New Medium: The Comic Strip in the Nineteenth Century*. Brussels: VUP University Press, 2000. First published 1998.

Lent, John A. *Comic Art of Europe: An International Comprehensive Bibliography*. Westport, CT: Greenwood, 1994.

['Life of Turenne']. *Série Qb1: Histoire de France en Estampes*. [Bibliothèque nationale de France, Département des Estampes]. Single print. 1675.

Livingstone, Marco. *Pop Art: A Continuing History*. London: Thames and Hudson, 1990.

Le Livre d'or du journal Pilote [The Golden Book of the Journal *Pilote*]. Neuilly-sur-Seine: Dargaud, 1980.

Livres Hebdo [Books Weekly] 4 (1985), 79–104. Special dossier on BD.

Livres Hebdo [Books Weekly] 610 (2005), 132–63. Special dossier on BD.

Livres Hebdo [Books Weekly] 629 (2006), 80–121. Special dossier on BD.

Livres Hebdo [Books Weekly] 673 (2007), 88–132. Special dossier on BD.

Livres Hebdo [Books Weekly] 717 (2008), 76–108. Special dossier on BD.

Livres Hebdo [Books Weekly] 761 (2009), 64-91. Special dossier on BD.

Lloyd, Christopher. *Collaboration and Resistance in Occupied France: Representing Treason and Sacrifice*. Basingstoke: Palgrave Macmillan, 2003.

Loisel, Régis. *Peter Pan: 1 Londres*. Issy-les-Moulineaux: Vents de l'Ouest, 1990. In English as *Peter Pan: 1 London*, trans. Mary Irwin. [London]: Heavy Metal Magazine, 1992.

———. *Peter Pan: 2 Opikanoba*. Issy-les-Moulineaux: Vents de l'Ouest, 1992. In English as *Peter Pan: 2 Neverland*, trans. Mary Irwin. [London]: Heavy Metal Magazine, 1992.

———. *Peter Pan: 5 Crochet* [Hook: Peter Pan 5]. Issy-les-Moulineaux: Vents de l'Ouest, 2002.

Loisel, Régis and Serge Le Tendre. *L'Integrale: La Quête de l'oiseau du temps* [The Complete Series: The Quest for the Time Bird]. Paris: Dargaud, 1992.

———. *La Quête de l'oiseau du temps 1: La Coque de Ramor* [The Quest for the Time Bird 1: Ramor's Hull]. Paris: Dargaud, 1983.

———. *La Quête de l'oiseau du temps 5: L'Ami Javin* [The Quest for the Time Bird 5: Our Friend Javin]. Paris: Dargaud, 1998.

McCloud, Scott. *Making Comics: Storytelling Secrets of Comics, Manga and Graphic Novels*. New York: Harper, 2006.

———. *Reinventing Comics: How Imagination and Technology Are Revolutionizing an Art Form*. New York: Paradox, 2000. In French as *Réinventer la bande dessinée*, trans. Jean-Paul Jennequin. Paris: Vertige Graphic, 2002.

———. *Understanding Comics: The Invisible Art*. Northampton, MA: Tundra, 1993. Several subsequent re-editions. In French as *L'Art invisible: Comprendre la bande dessinée*, trans. Dominique Petitfaux. Paris: Vertige Graphic, 1999.

McKinney, Mark. 'Georges Remi's Legacy: Between Half-Hidden History, Modern Myth, and Mass Marketing', *International Journal of Comic Art* 9.2 (2007), 68–80.

———. 'Histoire et critique sociale dans les bandes dessinées africaines-américaines et franco-africaines' [History and Social Criticism in Afro-American and Franco-African Bandes Dessinées]. In *Minorités postcoloniales anglophones et francophones: Études culturelles comparées* [Anglophone and Francophone Postcolonial Minorities: Comparative Cultural Studies], ed. Alec G. Hargreaves. Paris: L'Harmattan, 2004, pp. 199–218.

———. '*Métissage* in Post-Colonial Comics'. In *Post-Colonial Cultures in France*, ed. Alec G. Hargreaves and Mark McKinney. London: Routledge, 1997, pp. 169–99.

———. '"Tout cela, je ne voulais pas le laisser perdre": Colonial *lieux de mémoire* in Ferrandez's Comic Books', *Modern and Contemporary France* 9.1 (2001), 43–53.

McKinney, Mark, ed. *History and Politics in French-Language Comics and Graphic Novels*. Jackson, MS: University Press of Mississippi, 2007.

McLuhan, Marshall. *The Gutenberg Galaxy: The Making of Typographic Man*. Toronto: Toronto University Press, 1962. Several subsequent editions.

———. *Understanding Media: The Extensions of Man*. London: Routledge, 1964. Several subsequent editions.

McQuillan, Elizabeth [Libbie]. 'Between the Sheets at *Pilote*: 1968–1973', *International Journal of Comic Art* 2.1 (2000), 159–77.

———. 'Les Bidochon assujettis académiques'. In *The Francophone Bande Dessinée*, ed. Charles Forsdick, Laurence Grove and Libbie [Elizabeth] McQuillan. Amsterdam: Rodopi, 2005, pp. 159–74.

———. '"I Live my Body I am my Body": The Comic Bodies of Claire Bretécher'. In *Corporeal Practices*, ed. Hannah Thompson and Julia Prest. Bern: Peter Lang, 2000, pp. 91–103.

———. 'Introduction'. In *The Francophone Bande Dessinée*, ed. Charles Forsdick, Laurence Grove and Libbie [Elizabeth] McQuillan. Amsterdam: Rodopi: 2005, pp. 7–13.

———. 'The Reception and Creation of Post-1960 Franco-Belgian BD'. PhD dissertation, University of Glasgow, 2001.

———. 'Texte, Image, Récit: The Textual Worlds of Benoît Peeters'. In *The Graphic Novel*, ed. Jan Baetens. Leuven: Leuven University Press, 2001, pp. 157–66.

Maggetti, Daniel, ed. *Töpffer*. Geneva: Albert Skira, 1996.

Marchant, Guy. *Danse macabre*. Paris: Guy Marchant, 1485.

Margerin, Frank. *Lucien 4: Chez Lucien*. Paris: Les Humanoïdes Associés, 1998. Several subsequent re-editions.

———. *Momo le coursier* [Momo the Delivery Boy]. Paris: Albin Michel, 2002.

———. *Tranches de brie*. Paris: Les Humanoïdes Associés, 1998. Several subsequent re-editions.

———. *Y'a plus de jeunesse* [There's No Youth Any More]. Paris: Écho des Savanes/Albin Michel, 1990. Several subsequent re-editions.

Marie, Laurent. '*Le Grêlé 7/13*: A (Communist) Children's Guide to the Resistance'. In *The Francophone Bande Dessinée*, ed. Charles Forsdick, Laurence Grove and Libbie [Elizabeth] McQuillan. Amsterdam: Rodopi, 2005, pp. 73–82.

Marin, Louis. *Utopiques: Jeux d'espaces*. Paris: Minuit, 1973. In English as *Utopics: Spacial Play*, trans. Robert A. Vollrath. London: Macmillan, 1984.

Martin, Denis. *Images d'Épinal*. Quebec: Musée du Québec, 1995.

Martin, Henri-Jean and Roger Chartier, eds. *Histoire de l'édition française: Tome III: Le Temps des éditeurs: Du Romantisme à la Belle Époque* [The History of Publishing in France: Volume III: The Age of the Publishers: From Romanticism to the Belle Époque]. Paris: Promodis, 1985.

Martin, Jacques and Rafaël Moralès. *Alix 24: Roma Roma....* Paris: Casterman, 2005.

Martinet, [le Sieur]. *Emblemes royales a Louis le Grand* [Royal Emblems for Louis the Great]. Paris: Claude Barbin, 1673.

Masson, Pierre. *Lire la bande dessinée* [Reading the Bande Dessinée]. Lyon: Presses Universitaires de Lyon, 1985.

Mathieu, Marc-Antoine. *La 2,333e dimension*. Paris: Delcourt, 2004.

———. *Le Coeur des ombres* [The Heart of Shadows]. Paris: L'Association, 1999.

———. *Le Dessin* [The Drawing]. Paris: Delcourt, 2001.

———. *L'Épaisseur du miroir* [The Depth of the Mirror]. Paris: Delcourt, 1995.

———. *Mémoire morte*. Paris: Delcourt, 2000. In English as *Dead Memory*, trans. Helge Dascher. Milwaukie, OR: Dark Horse, 2003.

———. *La Mutation*. Paris: L'Association, 2001.
———. *L'Origine*. Paris: Delcourt, 1990.
———. *Le Processus* [The Process]. Paris: Delcourt, 1993.
———. *La Qu ...* Paris: Delcourt, 1991.
———. *Les Sous-sols du révolu: Extraits du journal d'un expert* [The Basements of Bygone Days: Extracts from the Journal of an Expert]. Paris: Futuropolis/Gallimard, 2006.
Mathon, J.-L. and M. Dauber. *Les Carnets de route de Tintin: L'Écosse* [Tintin's Travel Diaries: Scotland]. Paris: Casterman, 1999.
Maupassant, Guy de. *Bel-Ami*, ed. Daniel Leuwers. Paris: Garnier, 1988. First published 1885. In English as *Bel-Ami*, trans. Douglas Parmee. London: Penguin, 1975.
Melot, Michel. 'Le Texte et l'image'. In *Histoire de l'édition française: Tome III: Le Temps des éditeurs: Du Romantisme à la Belle Epoque* [The History of Publishing in France: Volume III: The Age of the Publishers: From Romanticism to the belle Epoque], ed. Henri-Jean Martin and Roger Chartier. Paris: Promodis, 1985, pp. 286–312.
Menestrier, Claude-François. *L'Art des emblemes*. Lyon: Benoist Coral, 1662.
———. *Histoire du Roy Louis le Grand* [History of King Louis the Great]. Paris: J.B. Nolin, 1689.
Menu, Jean-Christophe. 'Le Prodigieux Projet de Chris Ware' [Chris Ware's Prodigious Project], *9e Art* 2 (1997), 45–57.
———. 'Ouvre-Boîte-Po'. In *OuPus 1*. Paris: L'Association, 1997, pp. 9–12.
———. *Plates-bandes* [Flat Strips/Flowerbeds]. Paris: L'Association, 2005.
Menu, Jean-Christophe, ed. 'Correspondance', *L'Éprouvette* [The Test Tube] 1 (2006), 278–82.
Michallat, Wendy. '*Pilote* Magazine and the Evolution of French Bande Dessinée between 1959 and 1974'. PhD dissertation, University of Nottingham, 2002.
———. '*Pilote*: Pedagogy, Puberty and Parents'. In *The Francophone Bande Dessinée*, ed. Charles Forsdick, Laurence Grove and Libbie [Elizabeth] McQuillan. Amsterdam: Rodopi, 2005, pp. 83–95.
Mignault, Claude, ed. [Preface]. *Emblemata*, by Andrea Alciato. Antwerp: Christopher Plantin, 1577.
Miller, Ann. 'Chantal Montellier's *Faux Sanglant*: Sex, Death, Lies and Videotape', *French Studies* 55.2 (2001), 207–20.
———. 'Comic Strips/Cartoonists'. In *Encyclopaedia of Contemporary French Culture*, ed. Alex Hughes and Keith Reader. London: Routledge, 1998, pp. 116–19.
———. 'Contemporary *Bande Dessinée*: Contexts, Critical Approaches and Case Studies'. PhD dissertation, University of Newcastle, 2003.
———. 'Oubapo: A Verbal/Visual Medium Is Subjected to Constraints', *Word & Image* 23.2 (2007), 117–37.
———. *Reading Bande Dessinée: Critical Approaches to French-Language Comic Strip*. Bristol: Intellect, 2007.
Miller, Ann and Murray Pratt. 'Transgressive Bodies in the Work of Julie Doucet, Fabrice Neaud and Jean-Christophe Menu: Towards a Theory of the "AutobioBD"', *Belphégor* 4.1 (2004). No pagination.
Miller, Jeffrey A. 'Comics Narrative as Striptease', *International Journal of Comic Art* 4.1 (2002), 143–50.
Mister, Jean, François Blaudez and André Jacquemin. *Épinal et l'imagerie populaire*. Paris: Hachette, 1961.
Mizuki, Shigeru. *NonNonBâ*, trans. Patrick Honnoré and Yukari Maeda. Paris: Cornélius, 2006.
Moebius/Giraud, Jean. *Arzach*. Paris: Les Humanoïdes Associés, 2006. First published in album form 1976. In English as *Arzach*, trans. Randy Lofficier and Jean-Marc Lofficier. Milwaukie, OR: Dark Horse, 1996.

———. *Le Garage hermétique*. Paris: Les Humanoïdes Associés, 2000.

———. *Moebius Giraud: Histoire de mon double* [Moebius Giraud: The Story of my Two Sides]. Paris: Éditions 1, 1999.

Moliterni, Claude, Philippe Mellot, Laurent Turpin, Michel Denni and Nathalie Michel-Szelechowska. *BDGuide 2005: Encyclopédie de la bande dessinée internationale*. Paris: Omnibus, 2004.

Moliterni, Claude, Philippe Mellot and Laurent Turpin. *L'ABCdaire de la bande dessinée* [The ABC of Bande Dessinée]. Paris: Flammarion, 2002.

Montellier, Chantal. *Les Damnés de Nanterre*. Paris: Denoël, 2005.

———. *Faux sanglant: Une Aventure de Julie Bristol* [False Blood: A Julie Bristol Adventure]. Paris: Dargaud, 1992.

———. *Shelter*. Paris: Les Humanoïdes Associés, 1979.

Montellier, Chantal and Pierre Charras. *Le Sang de la Commune* [The Blood of the Commune]. Paris: Futuropolis, 1982.

Montenay, Georgette de. *Emblemes ou devises chrestiennes*. Lyon: Jean Marcorelle, 1571. First published 1567.

Morgan, Harry. *Principes des littératures dessinées* [Principles of Drawn Literatures]. Angoulême: Editions de l'An 2, 2003.

Morgan, Harry and Manuel Hirtz. *Le Petit Critique illustré: Guide des ouvrages consacrés à la bande dessinée* [The Illustrated Pocket Critic: A Guide to Secondary Studies on the Bande Dessinée]. Montrouge: PLG, 2005. First edition 1997.

Morin, Edgar. *L'Esprit du temps* [The Spirit of the Time]. Paris: Grasset, 1962.

———. 'Tintin héros d'une génération' [Tintin Hero of a Generation], *La Nef* [The Vessel] 13 (1958), 56–61.

Morin, Violette. 'Le Dessin humoristique' [Humoristic Drawings], *Communications* 15 (1970), 110–31.

Mouchart, Benoît. *La Bande dessinée*. Paris: Le Cavalier Bleu [Idées Reçues], 2003.

Mougin, Jean-Paul. [Editorial], *[À Suivre]* [[To Be Continued]] 1 (1978). No pagination.

Muñoz, José and Carlos Sampayo. *Alack Sinner*. No named translator. [Paris]: Éditions du Square, 1977.

———. *Le Bar à Joe* [Joe's Bar], trans. Christine Vernière. Tournai: Casterman, 2002. First published in album form 1981.

———. *Flic ou privé* [Cop or PI], trans. Dominique Grange. Tournai: Casterman, 1983.

Nadar. *Nadar: Tome 1: Photographies*, ed. Philippe Néagu. *Nadar: Tome 2: Dessins et écrits* [Nadar: Volume 2: Drawings and Writings], ed. Jean-François Bory. Paris: Arthur Hubschmid, 1979.

Néagu, Philippe, ed. *Nadar: Tome 1: Photographies*. Paris: Arthur Hubschmid, 1979.

Neaud, Fabrice. *Journal 1: Février 1992–septembre 1993*. Angoulême: Ego Comme X, 1996.

———. *Journal 2: Septembre 1993–décembre 1993*. Angoulême: Ego Comme X, 1998.

———. *Journal 3: Décembre 1993–août 1995*. Angoulême: Ego Comme X, 1999.

———. *Journal 4: Août 1995–juillet 1996: Les Riches heures*. Angoulême: Ego Comme X, 2002.

Nguyen, Nhu-Hoa. 'The Rhetoric of Parody in Claire Bretécher's *Le Destin de Monique*', *International Journal of Comic Art* 3.2 (2001), 162–74.

Notre Librairie: Revue des Littératures du Sud [Our Book Shop: The Journal of Literature South of Europe] 145 (2001). Special number on BD.

Le Nouveau Petit Robert. Paris: Robert, 1994. Several prior and subsequent editions.

Nye, Russel B. 'Death of a Gaulois: René Goscinny and Astérix', *Journal of Popular Culture* 14.2 (1980), 181–95.

Ory, Pascal. *Les Collaborateurs*. Paris: Seuil, 1976. Several subsequent editions.

———. *Le Petit Nazi illustré: Vie et survie du Téméraire (1943–1944)* [The Little Nazi Illustrated: The Life and Afterlife of Le Téméraire (1943–1944)]. Paris: Nautilus, 2002. First published 1979.

[OuBaPo]. *OuPus 1*. Paris: L'Association, 1997.

———. *OuPus 2*. Paris: L'Association, 2003.

———. *OuPus 3: Les Vacances de l'OuBaPo* [OuPus 3: OuBaPo on Holiday]. Paris: L'Association, 2000.

———. *OuPus 4*. Paris: L'Association, 2005.

Papieau, Isabelle. *La Banlieue de Paris dans la bande dessinée* [The Paris Suburbs in Bande Dessinée]. Paris: L'Harmattan, 2001.

[Paris, Bibliothèque nationale de France, Département des Estampes]. *Série Qb1: Histoire de France en Estampes*. Chronological series of prints.

Parker, D. and C. Renaudy. *La Démoralisation de la jeunesse par les publications périodiques* [The Harming of the Morality of Youth by Periodical Publications]. Paris: Cartel d'Action Morale, 1944.

Parvillez, Alphonse de. *Que Liront nos jeunes*? [What Will Our Youth Read?]. Paris: Les Éditions du Temps Présent, 1943.

Peeters, Benoît. *Case, planche, récit: Comment lire une bande dessinée* [Frame, Plate, Narrative: How to Read a Bande Dessinée]. Tournai: Casterman, 1991. Updated versions in 1998 and 2002.

Peeters, Benoît and François Schuiten. *L'Archiviste*. Tournai: Casterman, 1987. Several subsequent editions.

———. *L'Écho des Cités* [The Journal of the Cities]. Tournai: Casterman, 2001.

———. *La Fièvre d'Urbicande*. Tournai: Casterman, 1985. Several subsequent editions. In English as *Fever in Urbicand*, trans. Elizabeth Bell, Randy Lofficier and Jean-Marc Lofficier. New York: NBM, 2002.

———. *Les Murailles de Samaris*. Tournai: Casterman, 1988. Several subsequent editions. In English as *The Great Walls of Samaris*, trans. Elizabeth Bell, Randy Lofficier and Jean-Marc Lofficier. New York: NBM, 2001.

———. *Voyages en utopie* [Travels in Utopia]. Tournai: Casterman, 2000.

Perec, Georges. *La Disparition*. Paris: Denoël, 1969. Several subsequent editions. In English as *A Void*, trans. Gilbert Adair. London: Harvill, 1994.

Pétillon, René. *Les Disparus d'Apostophes!* [*Apostrophes!'s* Missing Persons]. Paris: Dargaud, 1982.

———. *L'Enquête corse* [The Corsican Investigation]. Paris: Albin Michel, 2000.

———. *Jack Palmer et le top model*. Paris: L'Écho des Savanes/Albin Michel, 1995.

Pissavy-Yvernault, Bertrand and Christelle Pissavy-Yvernault. *En Quête de l'oiseau du temps* [On a Quest for the Time Bird]. Paris: Dargaud, 2004.

Poix-Tétu, Marie. 'Du Journal à l'ajour' [From the Journal to Openwork], *9e Art* 9 (2003), 95–99.

Pratt, Murray. 'The Dance of the Visible and the Invisible: AIDS and the Bande Dessinée'. In *The Francophone Bande Dessinée*, ed. Charles Forsdick, Laurence Grove and Libbie [Elizabeth] McQuillan. Amsterdam: Rodopi, 2005, pp. 189–200.

———. 'The Diary of Neaud's Body: Approaching the Subject of Heterocentricity'. In *Gay and Lesbian Cultures in France*, ed. Lucille Cairns. Bern: Peter Lang, 2002, pp. 257–73.

Praz, Mario. *Studies in Seventeenth-Century Imagery*. Rome: Edizioni di Storia e Letteratura, 1964. First published 1939–1947.

Prévost, M., Roman d'Amat and H. Tribout de Morembert, eds. *Dictionnaire de biographie française* [Dictionary of French Biography]. 18 vols. Paris: Letouzey and Ané, 1985.

Quella-Guyot, Didier. *Lire Tintin au Tibet de Hergé: Lecture Méthodique et documentaire* [Reading Hergé's *Tintin in Tibet*: A Methodological and Documentary Approach]. Poitiers: Le Torii, 1990.

Rabier, Benjamin. *Benjamin Rabier*, ed. Edouard François and Pierre Couperie. Paris: Pierre Horay, 1982.

Racine, Jean. *Britannicus*, ed. Georges Forestier. Paris: Gallimard, 1995. First published 1669. In English as *Britannicus*, trans. Robert David MacDonald. London: Oberon, 1998.

Reidelbach, Maria. *Completely Mad: A History of the Comic Book and Magazine*. Boston: Little, Brown and Company, 1991.

Relave, Pierre-Maxime. *Rodolphe Töpffer: Biographie et extraits*. Lyon: Emmanuel Vitte, 1899.

Rémi-Giraud, Sylvianne. 'Métaphore et métonymie dans le *Journal* de Fabrice Neaud', *9e Art* 9 (2003), 85–89

Renard, J.-B. *Clefs pour la bande dessinée* [Keys to the Bande Dessinée]. Paris: Seghers, 1978.

Renou, Krishnâ. *Journal Universel: L'Illustration: Un Siècle de vie française* [The Universal Journal: Illustration: A Century of French Life]. Paris: Paris-Musées, 1987.

Restany, Pierre. *60/90: Trente ans de Nouveau Réalisme* [60/90: Thirty Years of *Nouveau Réalisme*]. Paris: La Différence, 1990.

Le Retour de l'Île d'Elba [The Return from the Island of Elba]. Single print. 1833.

Rey, Alain. *Dictionnaire historique de la langue française* [Historic Dictionary of the French Language]. Paris: Robert, 1998.

———. *Les Spectres de la bande*. Paris: Minuit, 1978.

Richardson, Joanna. *Gustave Doré: A Biography*. London: Cassell, 1980.

Rickman, Lance. '*Bande dessinée* and the Cinematograph: Visual Narrative in 1895', *European Comic* Art 1.1 (2008), 1–19.

Robbe-Grillet, Alain. *La Maison de rendez-vous*. Paris: Minuit, 2003. First published 1965. In English as *La Maison de Rendez-Vous and Djinn: Two Novels*, trans. Richard Howard, Yvonne Lenard and Walter Wells. New York: Grove, 1994.

———. *Le Voyeur*. Paris: Editions de Minuit, 1955. Several subsequent editions. In English as *Le Voyeur*, trans. Richard Howard. New York: Grove, 1994.

Le Robert: Dictionnaire alphabétique et analogique de la langue française [The Robert: Alphabetic and Analogical Dictionary of the French Language]. Paris: Société du Nouveau Littré, 1969.

Robichon, François. *Benjamin Rabier: L'Homme qui fait rire les animaux* [Benjamin Rabier: The Man Who Makes the Animals Laugh]. Paris: Hoëbeke, 1993.

Ronis, Willy. *Belleville-Ménilmontant*. Paris: Arthaud, 1989. Second edition, with additional text by Didier Daeninckx, 1999 (Paris: Hoëbeke).

Rossiter, Caroline. 'Early French Caricature (1795-1830) and English Influence', *European Comic Art* 2.1 (2009), 39-62.

Rouvière, Nicolas. Astérix *ou les lumières de la civilisation* [*Asterix* or the Lights of Civilisation]. Paris: Presses Universitaires de France, 2006.

Roux, Antoine. *La Bande dessinée peut être educative* [Bande Dessinée Can Be Educational]. Paris: L'École, 1970.

Rowlandson, Thomas. *Reform Advised ....* Single print. [*c*.1790].

Rowling, J.K. *Harry Potter et l'Ordre du Phénix*, trans. Jean-François Menard. Paris: Gallimard, 2003.

———. *Harry Potter et le prince du sang-mêlé* [Harry Potter and the Half-Blood Prince], trans. Jean-François Menard. Paris: Gallimard, 2005.

Rubin, James H. *Nadar*. London: Phaidon, 2001.

Russell, Daniel. 'The Emblem and Authority', *Word & Image* 4.1 (1988), 81–87.

———. *The Emblem and Device in France*. Lexington, KY: French Forum, 1985.

———. 'Emblems and the Ages of Life: Defining the Self in Early Modern France', *Emblematica* 14 (2005), 23–53.

Sabin, Roger. *Comics, Comix & Graphic Novels: A History of Comic Art*. London: Phaidon, 2002. First published 1996.

Sadoul, Numa. 'Entretien avec René Goscinny' [Interview with René Goscinny], *Schtroumpf: Les Cahiers de la Bande Dessinée* 22 (1973), 5–18.

Said, Edward. *Orientalism*. London: Routledge, 1978. Several subsequent editions.

Samson, Jacques. 'Un Souffle romanesque' [Storybook Inspiration], *9e Art* 2 (1997), 32–35.

Satrapi, Marjane. *Persepolis*. 4 vols. Paris: L'Association, 2000–2003. In English as *The Complete Persepolis*. No named translator. New York: Pantheon, 2007.

———. *Poulet aux prunes*. Paris: L'Association, 2004. In English as *Chicken with Plums*. No named translator. New York: Pantheon, 2006.

Saussure, Ferdinand de. *Cours de linguistique générale*, ed. Charles Bally, Alber Sechehaye and Albert Reidlinger. Paris: Payot, 1968. First published 1915. In English as *Course in General Linguistics*, trans. Wade Baskin. London: Fontana, 1974. First published 1959.

Schuiten, François and Luc Schuiten. *NogegoN*. Norma: Barcelona, 1991.

Schwarz, Arturo. *The Complete Works of Marcel Duchamp*. 2 vols. New York: Delano Greenidge, 1997. First published 1969 (London: Thames and Hudson).

Schwarz, Heinrich. 'Daumier, Gill and Nadar', *Gazette des Beaux Arts* 19 (1957), 89–106.

Scott, Randell W. *European Comics in English Translation: A Descriptive Sourcebook*. Jefferson, NC: McFarland, 2002.

Screech, Matthew. 'Jean Giraud/Moebius: *Nouveau Réalisme* and Science Fiction'. In *The Francophone Bande Dessinée*, ed. Charles Forsdick, Laurence Grove and Libbie [Elizabeth] McQuillan. Amsterdam: Rodopi, 2005, pp. 97–113.

———. *Masters of the Ninth Art: Bandes Dessinées and Franco-Belgian Identity*. Liverpool: Liverpool University Press, 2005.

Simpson, Paul. 'The Complete James Bond Syndicated Newspaper Checklist'. In *James Bond 007: Casino Royale*. By Ian Fleming, Anthony Hern, Henry Gammidge and John McLusky, ed. Paul Simpson. London: Titan, 2005. Final page of an unnumbered sequence.

Sollers, Philippe and Martin Veyron. *Portrait du joueur* [Portrait of the Gambler]. Paris: Futuropolis, 1991.

Soncini Fratta, Anna, ed. *Tintin, Hergé et la 'Belgité'*. Bologna: CLUEB, 1994.

Spiegelman, Art. *In the Shadow of No Towers*. London: Penguin Viking, 2004.

———. *Maus: A Survivor's Tale*. London: Penguin, 2003. First published in book form 1986–1991.

Starkey, Hugh. 'Is the BD "à bout de souffle"?', *French Cultural Studies* 1.2 (1990), 95–110.

Steel, James. '*Let's Party!*: Astérix and the World Cup (France 1998)'. In *The Francophone Bande Dessinée*, ed. Charles Forsdick, Laurence Grove and Libbie [Elizabeth] McQuillan. Amsterdam: Rodopi, 2005, pp. 201–18.

Storey, John. *Cultural Consumption and Everyday Life*. London: Arnold, 1999.

Sullerot, Evelyne. *Bande dessinée et culture*. Paris: Opéra Mundi, 1966.

Talbot, William Henry Fox. *The Pencil of Nature*. London: Longman, Brown, Green, and Longmans, 1844. Facsimile edition, edited by Larry J. Schaaf, 1989 (New York: Hans P. Kraus Jr.).

Tan, Shaun. *Là où vont nos pères*. Paris: Dargaud, 2007. Originally published as *The Arrival*. South Melbourne: Lothian, 2006.

Tardi, Jacques, ed. *Voyage au bout de la nuit* [Journey to the End of the Night], by Louis-Ferdinand Céline. Paris: Futuropolis, 1988.

Teulé, Jean. *Gens d'ailleurs* [Folk from Elsewhere]. Paris: Casterman, 1990.

Théâtre d'amour [The Theatre of Love]. N.p. [*c*.1620].

Thorp, Nigel. *The Glory of the Page: Medieval & Renaissance Illuminated Manuscripts from Glasgow University Library*. London: Harvey Miller, 1987.

Thronus Cupidinis [Cupid's Throne]. [Utrecht]: [Crispin de Passe], [*c.*1617].
Tibéri, Jean-Pierre. *La Bande dessinée et le cinéma*. Izy: Regards, 1981.
Tilleuil, Jean-Louis, Catherine Vanbraband and Pierre Marlet. *Lectures de la bande dessinée: Théorie, méthode, applications, bibliographie* [Bande Dessinée Readings: Theory, Method, Applications, Bibliography]. Louvain-la Neuve: Academia, 1991.
Tisseron, Serge. *Psychanalyse de la bande dessinée*. Paris: Presses Universitaires de France, 1987.
———. *Tintin chez le psychanalyste*. Paris: Aubier, 1985.
———. *Tintin et les secrets de famille* [Tintin and the Family Secrets]. Paris: Séguier, 1990.
Tissot, Henri. *Le Mouvement Pop*. Lausanne: Éditions Grammont, 1975.
Tombeau de Napoléon [The Tomb of Napoleon]. Single print. 1832.
Tome and Janry. *Le Petit Spirou 12: C'est du joli!* [Petit Spirou 12: That's Nice!]. Brussels: Dupuis, 2005.
Töpffer, Rodolphe. *Rodolphe Töpffer: The Complete Comic Strips*, ed. and trans. David Kunzle. Jackson, MS: University Press of Mississippi, 2007.
———. *Le Docteur Festus: Histoire de Monsieur Cryptogame: Deux odyssées* [Doctor Festus: The Story of Mr Cryptogame: Two Odysseys], ed. Thierry Groensteen. Paris: Seuil, 1996. First published, by Schmidt of Geneva, 1840 (*Le Docteur Festus*) and 1845 (*Histoire de Monsieur Cryptogame*).
———. *Mélanges* [*Varia*]. Paris: Joël Cherbuliez, 1852. Facsimile edition 1999 (Paris: Phénix).
———. *Monsieur Crépin: Monsieur Pencil: Deux égarements de la science* [M. Crépin: M. Pencil: Two Scientific Distractions], ed. Thierry Groensteen. Paris: Seuil, 1996. First published, by Schmidt of Geneva, 1837 (*Monsieur Crépin*) and 1840 (*Monsieur Pencil*).
———. *Monsieur Jabot: Monsieur Vieux Bois: Deux histoires d'amour* [M. Jabot: M. Vieux Bois: Two Love Stories], ed. Thierry Groensteen. Paris: Seuil, 1996. First published, by Schmidt of Geneva, 1833 (*Monsieur Jabot*) and 1837 (*Monsieur Vieux Bois*).
———. *M. Trictrac*, ed. Philippe Kaenel. Paris: Favre, 1988. Facsimile edition of *c.*1830 manuscript.
———. *Nouvelles genevoises* [News from Geneva]. Paris: Garnier, 1876. Facsimile edition 1998 (Paris: Slatkine).
———. *Voyages en zigzag* [Journeys in a Zigzag]. Paris: Jacques-Julien Dubochet, 1832 and 1846. Several subsequent re-editions. Facsimile edition 1996 (Geneva: Statkine).
[Töpffer, Rodolphe as R.T.] *Essai de physiognomonie*. Geneva: Schmidt, 1845. Reprint edition, ed. Thierry Groensteen, 2003 ([Paris]: Kargo).
———. 'Réflexions à propos d'un programme' [Reflections on a Programme], *Bibliothèque Universelle de Genève* [Geneva Universal Library] 1 (1836), 42–61. *Bibliothèque Universelle de Genève* 2 (1836), 314–41.
Trignon, Jean de. *Histoire de la littérature enfantine de Ma Mère l'Oye au Roi Babar* [History of Children's Literature from Mother Goose to Babar]. Paris: Hachette, 1950.
Trondheim, Lewis. *A.L.I.E.E.N.* Rosny-sous-Bois: Bréal, 2004. In English as *A.L.I.E.E.E.N.* No named translator. New York: First Second, 2006.
———. *Approximativement*. Paris: Cornélius, 1995.
———. *Désoeuvré* [Inactive]. Paris: L'Association, 2005.
———. *Lapinot et les carottes de Patagonie* [Little Rabbit and the Patagonian Carrots]. Paris: Le Lézard and L'Association, 1992.
———. *La Mouche* [The Fly]. Paris: L'Association, 1995.
Trondheim, Lewis and Jean-Christophe Menu. *Moins d'un quart de second pour vivre* [Less than a Quarter of a Second to Live]. Paris: L'Association, 1991.

Trondheim, Lewis and Thierry Robin. *Bonjour Petit Père Nöel* [Hello Little Father Christmas]. Brussels: Dupuis, 2000.
Trondheim, Lewis and Joann Sfar. *Coeur de Canard* [Duck Heart]. Paris: Delcourt, 1998.
Tufts, Clare. 'Vincent Krassousky: Nazi Collaborator or Naïve Cartoonist?', *International Journal of Comic Art* 6.1 (2004), 18–36.
Uderzo, Albert. *Astérix et Latraviata*. Paris: Éditions Albert René, 2001. Several subsequent editions. In English as *Asterix and the Actress*, trans. Anthea Bell and Derek Hockridge. London: Orion, 2001.
———. *Astérix et Latraviata: L'Album des crayonnés* [Astérix and the Actress: The Album of the Preparatory Work]. Paris: Éditions Albert René, 2001.
———. *Le Ciel lui tombe sur la tête*. Paris: Éditions Albert René, 2005. In English as *Asterix and the Falling Sky*, trans. Anthea Bell and Derek Hockridge. London: Orion, 2005.
———. *La Galère d'Obélix*. Paris: Éditions Albert René, 1996. Several subsequent editions. In English as *Asterix and Obelix All at Sea*, trans. Anthea Bell and Derek Hockridge. London: Hodder and Stoughton, 1996. Several subsequent editions.
———. *Le Grand Fossé*. Paris: Éditions Albert René, 1980. Several subsequent editions. In English as *Asterix and the Great Divide*, trans. Anthea Bell and Derek Hockridge. London: Hodder and Stoughton, 1981. Several subsequent editions.
———. *L'Odyssée d'Astérix*. Paris: Éditions Albert René, 1981. Several subsequent editions. In English as *Asterix and the Black Gold*, trans. Anthea Bell and Derek Hockridge. London: Hodder and Stoughton, 1982. Several subsequent editions.
Vandromme, Pol. *Le Monde de Tintin* [The World of Tintin]. Paris: Gallimard, 1959.
Van Hamme, Jean and Ted Benoit. *L'Affaire Francis Blake*. Brussels: Éditions Blake et Mortimer, 1996. Several subsequent re-editions.
———. *L'Étrange Rendez-vous* [The Strange Encounter]. Brussels: Éditions Blake et Mortimer, 2001. Several subsequent re-editions.
Van Hamme, Jean and Jean Giraud. *XIII 18: La Version irlandaise* [XIII 18: The Irish Version]. Paris: Dargaud, 2007.
Van Hamme, Jean and William Vance. *XIII 17: L'Or de Maximilien* [XIII 17: Maximilien's Gold]. Paris: Dargaud, 2005.
Van Veen, Otto. *Amoris divini emblemata* [Emblems of Divine Love]. Antwerp: Martin Nutius and Joannes Meursius, 1615.
———. *Amorum emblemata* [Emblems of Love]. Antwerp: Hieronymus Verdussen, 1608. Several subsequent editions.
Veyron, Martin. *L'Amour propre ne le reste jamais très longtemps* [Self-Esteem is Always Short Lived]. Paris: Albin Michel, 2001.
———. *Bernard Lermite en complet* [The Full Bernard Lermite]. 2 vols. Paris: Albin Michel, 2001.
———. *Cru bourgeois*. Paris: Albin Michel, 1998.
———. *Executive Woman*. Paris: Albin Michel, 1986.
———. *Politiquement incorrect*. Paris: Hoëbeke, 1995.
Vovelle, Michel. *La Révolution française: Images et récit: 1789–1799*. 5 vols. Paris: Messidor, 1986.
Vuillemin, Philippe. *Les Sales Blagues de L'Écho 6: Sucré ou salé* [The Echo's Dirty Jokes 6: Sweet or Sour]. Paris: L'Écho des Savanes/Albin Michel, 1996.
———. *Les Sales Blagues de L'Écho 11* [The Echo's Dirty Jokes 11]. Paris: L'Écho des Savanes/Albin Michel, 2003.
Vulson, Marc de. *Les Portraits des hommes illustres* [The Portraits of Illustrious Men]. Paris: Charles de Sercy, 1650. Several subsequent editions.
Waldman, Diane. *Roy Lichtenstein*. New York: Abrams, 1971.

Ware, Chris. *Jimmy Corrigan*, trans. Anne Capuron. Paris: Delcourt, 2002. Originally in English as *Jimmy Corrigan*. New York: Pantheon, 2000.
Weaver, Mike. *Henry Fox Talbot: Selected Texts and Bibliography*. Oxford: Clio, 1992.
Wechsler, Judith. *A Human Comedy: Physiognomy and Caricature in 19th Century Paris*. London: Thames and Hudson, 1982.
Wertham, Fredric. *Seduction of the Innocent: The Influence of 'Horror Comics' on Today's Youth*. New York: Rinehart, [1954].
Wilson, Adrian and Joyce Lancaster Wilson. *A Medieval Mirror: Speculum humanae salvationis, 1324–1500*. Berkeley: University of California Press, 1985.
Wilson, Simon. *Pop*. London: Thames and Hudson, 1974.
Winshluss. *Pinocchio*. Albi: Les Requins Marteaux, 2008.
———. *Welcome to the Death Club*. Montpellier: 6 Pieds Sous Terre, 2002.
Wolinski, Georges. *Les Classiques de Wolinski: Hit-parade*. Paris: Albin Michel, 2003.
———. *Dans l'Huma*. Paris: Mazarine, 1980.
Zep. *Titeuf 9: La Loi du préau* [Titeuf 9: The Law of the Playground]. Grenoble: Glénat, 2002.
———. *Titeuf 10: Nadia se marie* [Titeuf 10: Nadia Gets Married]. Grenoble: Glénat, 2004.
———. *Titeuf 11: Mes meilleurs copains* [Titeuf 11: My Best Friends]. Grenoble: Glénat, 2006.
———. *Titeuf 12: Le Sens de la vie* [Titeuf 12: The Meaning of Life]. Grenoble: Glénat, 2008.
———. *Titeuf: Dieu, le sexe et les bretelles* [Titeuf: God, Sex and Braces]. Grenoble: Glénat, 1993.
Zep and Hélène Bruller. *Le Guide du zizi sexuel* [The Guide to the Sexual Willy]. Grenoble: Glénat, 2001.
Zola, Émile. *La Bête humaine*, ed. Gisèle Séginger. [Paris]: Fasquelle, 1997. First published 1890. In English as *La Bête humaine*, trans. Leonard Tancock. London: Penguin, 1977.

Manuscripts

Anselm. *Treatises*. *c*. Mid twelfth century. Glasgow University Library MS Hunter 244 (U.4.2).
Bible. *c*. Mid thirteenth century. Glasgow University Library MS Hunter 338 (U.8.6).
Boccaccio, Giovanni. *De Casibus virorum illustrium* [The Fall of Princes]. 1457. Glasgow University Library MS Hunter 371–372 (V.1.8–9).
Book of Hours. 1460. Glasgow University Library MS Euing 4.
Cent nouvelles nouvelles [The Hundred New Stories]. Late fifteenth century. Glasgow University Library MS Hunter 252 (U.4.10).
Chroniques de Saint Denis. Late fifteenth century. Glasgow University Library MS Hunter 203 (U.1.7).
Codex medicinalis. Late eighth or early ninth century. Glasgow University Library MS Hunter 96 (T.4.13).
Foix, Gaston de. *Miroir de Phébus* [The Mirror of Phoebus]. Early fifteenth century. Glasgow University Library MS Hunter 385 (V.2.5).
Miroir de l'humaine salvation [The Mirror of Human Salvation]. 1455. Glasgow University Library MS Hunter 60 (T.2.18).
Petrarch. *Visions*, trans. Clément Marot. Early sixteenth century. Glasgow University Library SMM 2.
Vie de Cesar [Life of Caesar]. Late fourteenth century. Glasgow University Library MS Hunter 373 (V.1.10).

Paintings and Sculpture

Cousin, Jean. *Eva Prima Pandora* [Eve the First Pandora]. 1550. Paris, Louvre.
Duchamp, Marcel. *Bicycle Wheel*. 1913. New York, Museum of Modern Art (1951 copy, 'original' destroyed).
———. *Fountain*. 1917. Paris, Musée National d'Art Moderne (Centre Pompidou) (1964 copy, 'original' destroyed).
Fromanger, Gérard. *La France est-elle coupée de deux?* [Is France Cut in Two?]. 1974. Paris, Musée d'Art Moderne de la Ville de Paris.
Greuze, Jean-Baptiste. *Jeune fille qui pleure son oiseau mort* [A Girl with a Dead Canary]. 1765. Edinburgh, National Gallery of Scotland.
———. *La Malédiction paternelle: Le Fils ingrat* [The Father's Curse: The Ungrateful Son]. 1777. Paris, Louvre.
———. *La Malédiction paternelle: Le Fils puni* [The Father's Curse: The Son Punished]. 1778. Paris, Louvre.
Hogarth, William. *The Rake's Progress*. Series of eight paintings. 1732–1733. London, Sir John Soane's Museum.
Lichtenstein, Roy. *Eddie Diptych*. 1962. Private collection.
———. *Good Morning Darling*. 1964. Private collection.
———. *Hopeless*. 1963. Private collection.
———. *In the Car*. 1963. Edinburgh, Scottish National Gallery of Modern Art.
———. *The Kiss*. 1962. Private collection.
———. *Masterpiece*. 1962. Private collection.
———. *M-Maybe*. 1965. Private collection.
———. *Takka Takka*. 1962. Private collection.
———. *Whaam*. 1963. London, Tate Modern.
Manet, Edouard. *Déjeuner sur l'herbe* [Luncheon on the Grass]. 1862–1863. Paris, Musée d'Orsay.
Rancillac, Bernard. *Sans parole VI: Où es-tu, que fais-tu?* [Without Words VI: Where are You, What are You Doing?]. 1965. Private collection.
———. *Suite américaine*. 1970. Paris, Musée National d'Art Moderne (Centre Pompidou).
Rembrandt van Rijn. *The Anatomy Lesson of Dr. Nicolaes Tulp*. 1632. The Hague, Mauritshuis.
Rubens, Peter Paul. *Medici Cycle*. Series of twenty-four paintings. 1622–1625. Paris, Louvre.
Télémaque, Hervé. *Pastorale*. 1963. Private collection.
Van Eyke, Jan. *Arnolphini Mariage*. 1434. London, National Gallery.
Velasquez, Diego. *Las Meñinas* [The Maids of Honour]. 1656. Madrid, Prado.
———. *Rokeby Venus*. c.1649–1651. London, National Gallery.
Vermeer, Johannes. *A Lady Standing at the Virginal*. c.1672–1674. London, National Gallery.
Warhol, Andy. *Elvis*. 1963. Pittsburgh, The Andy Warhol Museum.
———. *Marylyn*. 1964. Pittsburgh, The Andy Warhol Museum.

Films

À Bout de souffle [Breathless]. Dir. Jean-Luc Godard. 1960.
L'Agent a le bras long [The Long-Armed Policeman]. Dir. Romeo Bosetti. 1909.
Alien. Dir. Ridley Scott. 1979.
L'Amour propre ne le reste jamais très longtemps [Self-Esteem Is Always Short Lived]. Dir. Martin Veyron. 1985.
L'Arroseur arrosé [The Waterer Watered]. Dir. Auguste Lumière and Louis Lumière. 1895.

Astérix aux Jeux Olympiques. Dir. Frédéric Forestier and Thomas Langmann. 2008.
Astérix chez les Bretons [Asterix in Britain]. Dir. Pino Van Lamsweerde. 1986.
Astérix et Cléopâtre. Dir. René Goscinny and Lee Payant. 1968.
Astérix et les Vikings. Dir. Stefan Fjeldmark and Jesper Møller. 2006.
Astérix et Obélix contre César [Asterix and Obelix against Caesar]. Dir. Claude Zidi. 1999.
Astérix et Obélix: Mission Cléopâtre. Dir. Alain Chabat. 2002.
Astérix le Gaulois [Asterix the Gaul]. Dir. Ray Goossens. 1967.
Barbarella. Dir. Roger Vadim. 1968.
Les Bidochon. Dir. Serge Korber. 1996.
Casino Royale. Dir. Martin Campbell. 2006.
Le Cinquième Élément [The Fifth Element]. Dir. Luc Besson. 1997.
Circulez y a rien à voir [Keep Moving, There's Nothing to See]. Dir. Patrice Leconte. 1983.
Cleopatra. Dir. Joseph Mankiewicz. 1963.
Diva. Dir. Jean-Jacques Beineix. 1980.
L'Enquête corse [The Corsican Investigation]. Dir. Alain Berberian. 2004.
Le Fabuleux destin d'Amélie Poulain [Amélie]. Dir. Jean-Pierre Jeunet. 2001.
Forrest Gump. Dir. Robert Zemeckis. 1994.
La Grande Vadrouille [Don't Look Now ... We're Being Shot At!]. Dir. Gérard Oury. 1966.
In the Name of the Father. Dir. Jim Sheridan. 1993.
I Want to Go Home. Dir. Alain Resnais. 1989.
Metropolis. Dir. Fritz Lang. 1927.
Le Père Noël est une ordure [Father Christmas Is Pure Filth]. Dir. Jean-Marie Poiré. 1982.
Persepolis. Dir. Vincent Paronnaud and Marjane Satrapi. 2007.
Peter Pan. Dir. Walt Disney. 1953.
Philadelphia. Dir. Jonathan Demme. 1993.
Les Quatre-cents coups [The 400 Blows]. Dir. François Truffaut. 1959.
Smoking/No Smoking. Dir. Alain Resnais. 1993.
Star Wars Episode IV: A New Hope. Dir. George Lucas. 1977.
Star Wars V: The Empire Strikes Back. Dir. Irvin Kershner. 1980.
Steamboat Willie. Dir. Walt Disney. 1928.
Tintin et le mystère de la Toison d'Or [Tintin and the Mystery of the Golden Fleece]. Dir. André Barret and Jean-Jacques Vierne. 1960.
Tintin et les oranges bleues [Tintin and the Blue Oranges]. Dir. Philippe Condroyer. 1964.
Tintin et le Temple du Soleil [Tintin and the Temple of the Sun]. Dir. Eddie Lateste. 1969.
Train Arriving at the Station in La Ciotat. Dir. Auguste Lumière and Louis Lumière. 1895.
Triplettes de Belleville [Belleville Rendezvous]. Dir. Sylvain Chomet. 2003.
Trois couleurs: Bleu, blanc, rouge [Three Colours: Blue, White, Red]. Dir. Krzysztof Kieslowski. 1993–1994.
The Truman Show. Dir. Peter Weir. 1998.
Voyage dans la Lune [Journey to the Moon]. Dir. Georges Méliès. 1902.
Workers Leaving the Factory. Dir. Auguste Lumière and Louis Lumière. 1895.

Websites

The following is a list of websites to which I refer directly in the text. Needless to say, there are endless other BD-related sites, many of which are accessible via the links sections of those listed below, or easily found via a search engine.

www.actuabd.com

Discussion forum providing updates on BD publications and events.

www.arts.gla.ac.uk/ibds

Site of the International Bande Dessinée Society, the English-language society for the study of comics in French. Includes links to the 'BDFIL' e-mail exchange group.

http://chnm.gmu.edu/revolution/imaging/

Imaging the French Revolution site. This is a joint project of George Mason University's Centre for History & New Media and the University of California, Los Angeles's Department of History.

www.culture.gouv.fr/culture/actual/misfred2.htm

Section of the Ministry of Culture's website that outlines the 1997 *New Measures to Promote the BD*, an update of the *Fifteen Measures* originally introduced in 1982.

www.dal.ca/~etc/belphegor

Site of *Belphégor*, the Canadian-based e-journal on popular culture that has dedicated two special issues, volume 4.1 of November 2004 and volume 5.1 of December 2005, to the bande dessinée.

http://davidbarsalou.homestead.com/LICHTENSTEINPROJECT.html

The 'Deconstructing Roy Lichtenstein' website that points to many of the comic book sources of his works.

www.dlp-guidebook.de

A fan-based site on Disneyland Paris that includes financial updates, as well as a reliable overview of the park's history and current status.

www.educnet.education.fr/insee/chomage

The site of the Institut National de la Statistique et des Études Économiques ('L'INSEE') or National Institute for Statistics and Studies of Economics, giving unemployment figures relevant to the period that saw a slump in BD sales and production.

www.foxtalbot.arts.gla.ac.uk

Site of the William Henry Fox Talbot Project, one that includes transcriptions and translations of Talbot's correspondance.

www.ijoca.com

International Journal of Comic Art's site, including a full listing of articles published by the Journal.

www.internationalcomicsartsforum.org

Site of the group known for its annual Georgetown conferences on Comic Art, with full listings of titles of papers presented.

www.lewistrondheim.com/blog

Lewis Trondheim's blog entitled *Les Petits riens* [Little Bits of Nothing].

www.lib.gla.ac.uk

Glasgow University Library's site, via which the Special Collections Department site can be accessed. Includes many virtual exhibitions, often featuring text/image material, as well as scans of documents mentioned in Chapter 4.

www.louvre.fr
Site of the Louvre with numerous reproductions available.
www.nationalgalleries.org
Site of the National Galleries of Scotland with numerous reproductions available.
www.paulgravett.com
Site of leading English-language scholar offering news of comics worldwide.
http://www.sdv.fr/pages/adamantine/
Harry Morgan's website, including articles, analysis and an updating of his *Petit Critique illustré*.
www.tintin.be
Official *Tintin* site, include bibliographical details, interviews, links and general trivia.
www.urbicande.be
Site of Peeters and Schuiten's *Cités obscures*, including full bibliography and references to places explored in the albums. The site also encourages visitors to tell of their experiences of the *cités obscures*.

Index